WITHDRAWN
FROM
STOCK

PLUS ÇA CHANGE

WITHDRAWN
FROM
STOCK

PLUS ÇA CHANGE

~

Jean-Benoît Nadeau

AND

Julie Barlow

ROBSON
BOOKS

An imprint of Anova Books Company Ltd

Published in Canada in 2006 by Alfred A. Knopf Canada

ISBN 1 86105 917 5

A CIP catalogue record for this book is available from
the British Library.

10 9 8 7 6 5 4 3 2 1

Printed and bound by MPG Books Ltd, Bodmin, Cornwall
Colour reprograhics by Spectrum Colour Ltd, Suffolk

This book can be ordered direct from the publisher.
Contact the marketing department, but try your bookshop first.

Contents

Acknowledgments

THIS BOOK WAS A big project, and if we managed to research and write it in less than thirty months, it's because a great number of people and institutions gave us financial, intellectual and moral support.

Among our backers we would like to thank the Canada Council for the Arts for its considerable financial assistance at an early stage of the project. We were thrilled (and a little relieved) that our three original editors, Michael Schellenberg of Knopf Canada, Michael Flamini of St. Martin's Press and Jeremy Robson of Robson Books, signed us on so quickly. As for our principal editor, Michael Schellenberg, his professionalism, flexibility, wise observations and guidance have been a great source of reassurance to us during every stage of the process. We also received support in the form of grants from Jacques Saada, Canada's minister responsible for the Francophonie; Monique Gagnon-Tremblay, Quebec's minister of international affairs and the Francophonie; Line Beauchamp, Quebec's minister of culture and communications; and Nathalie Normandeau, Quebec's minister of tourism and regional affairs. Diane Audet, of the Air France office in Montreal, arranged for special ticket prices for some of our travels.

It would be impossible to thank the couple of hundred people we interviewed for this book, but some individuals made a particularly important intellectual contribution, for which we are especially grateful. Linguist Henriette Walter, who has authored many books, was something of an intellectual godmother to us.

Abdou Diouf, secretary-general of the Organisation internationale de la Francophonie, supported our project wholeheartedly from the start, as did Alain Marquer, vice-president in charge of development for the Fédération des Alliances françaises. Xavier North, then director of cultural cooperation and French language at France's ministry of foreign affairs; Laurent Personne, cabinet director of the French Academy's permanent secretary; and Bernard Cerquiglini, then director of the Délégation générale à la langue française et aux langues de France, provided us with key institutional insight. Françoise Ploquin generously opened the archives of *Le Français dans le monde* for us. Professor Edy Kaufman, of the Hebrew University in Jerusalem and the University of Maryland, gave us information, insights and hospitality in both Israel and the United States.

We also benefited from the help and insight of Guy Dumas, deputy minister in charge of Quebec's Secretariat à la langue française; and of Jean-Louis Roy, president of Rights and Democracy, former Quebec delegate in Paris and former head of the Agence de coopération culturelle et technique. Astou Gueye, liaison officer at the Canadian embassy in Dakar, made our trip to Senegal an invaluable experience. Jayne Abrate and Margot Steinhardt of the American Association of Teachers of French and Chris Pinet of the *French Review* all supported us warmly and opened many doors for us in the world of French teaching in the United States and beyond.

A number of specialists assisted us in the late stage of reviewing. In addition to Guy Dumas and Jean-Louis Roy, we would like to thank Professor Clyde Thogmartin of Iowa State University of Science and Technology; Professor Albert Valdman, director of the Creole Institute; and Philippe Blanchet, director of the Centre de recherche sur la diversité linguistique de la francophonie at the University of Rennes in Brittany.

Finally we would like to thank five people whose contribution had a more personal significance to us. To start with, Jean-Benoît's father, Yvan Nadeau, got us out of a few financial pickles during our costly research. Jean-François Nantel and Valérie Lehmann offered us both friendship and the use of their Paris apartment as a pied-à-terre. Our agent, Ed Knappman, gave early impetus to the project. And finally, Peter Martin, former director of the Institute of Current World Affairs, sent us to study the French in 1999–2000. Without his support and confidence back then, we would never have dreamed of writing this book.

All these people were behind the scenes of *Plus ça Change* and we would like to thank them, as well as all the others who generously offered us their time and insight while we were researching and writing.

This map shows the languages that pre-existed French. The shaded part of the map is present-day France. Over the centuries, the language developed out of a linguistic melting pot. Although French ultimately superseded them, most of these regional languages and dialects are still spoken today in France.

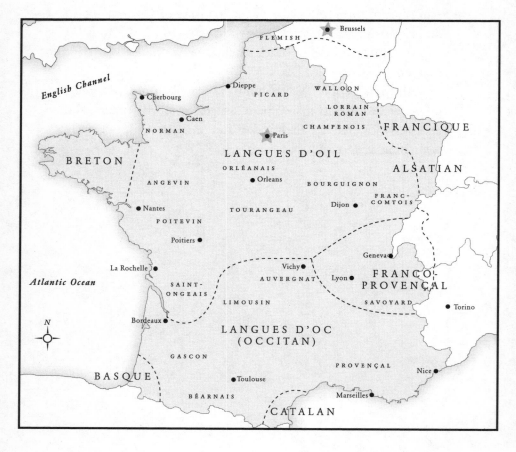

BRETON	:	Linguistic groups
BOURGUINON	:	Dialects spoken
Bordeaux	:	Cities
- - - - - - - - -	:	Language/dialect borders

MAP 2 - MAP OF THE FRENCH-SPEAKING WORLD

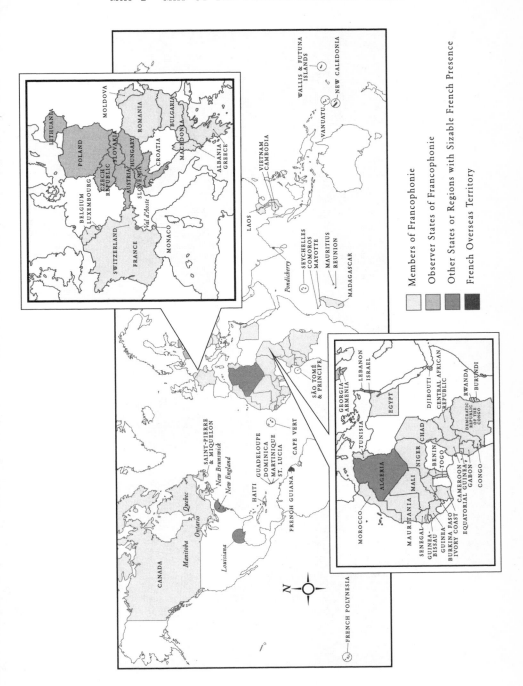

Members of Francophonie

Observer States of Francophonie

Other States or Regions with Sizable French Presence

French Overseas Territory

Introduction

IF THERE WAS ONE place in the world where we never expected to hear French, it was Tel Aviv. Julie had twice travelled extensively in Israel before we started to research this book, and it had simply never occurred to her that there was a significant francophone presence there. Most Israelis speak Hebrew and English, so it's hard to imagine that French has even a fighting chance as a second language among them. Yet the first language we heard when we stepped out of our hotel in Tel Aviv was French—a pair of women chatting at a corner store across the street.

That was a surprise, since we hadn't gone to Israel to meet francophones. Our goal was to visit the Hebrew Language Academy in Jerusalem. We had chosen it almost randomly from among some seventy bodies that regulate language across the world to illustrate the fact that France isn't the only country with a language academy. But when we looked at Israeli society through francophone eyes, we discovered that ten percent of Israelis speak French, including almost all the Moroccan immigrants who live there. In fact, Israel has many more French speakers than Louisiana does.

It turns out there are French-speaking communities not only in the cities of Netanya and Ashdod, but also in urban centres. Tel Aviv has a substantial francophone population; Jerusalem has a vibrant French cultural centre, Le Centre culturel français Romain Gary; a French bookstore, Librairie Vice-Versa; and a large French expatriate community. When we strolled through the Arab quarter of the Old City chatting in French, merchants beckoned us into their shops in French.

When we ran into communication problems with an Israeli taxi driver who didn't speak English, French provided a miracle solution.

Our dip into the Middle East solidified an impression that got stronger throughout our research for this book: that French is more resilient than people generally believe. No matter how people feel about France, they are still interested in the French language. Israel was a case in point. Because of diplomatic tensions over the Palestinian question, very few Israelis hold France in high esteem today. But the reputation of the French language in Israel has suffered very little by association. Jerusalem's Centre culturel français attracts enough students to offer French courses regularly, and Israel still has two French *lycées,* plus a dozen or so French schools run by Catholic religious orders referred to as *les frères.* While the use of French is probably not increasing in Israel, it is holding its own, as both a mother tongue and a second language.

This basic impression was confirmed everywhere we travelled to research this book, including Louisiana, the eastern United States, the Canadian Maritimes, northern Ontario, Senegal, Tunisia, Guadeloupe, Algeria, France, Belgium and Switzerland. In terms of relative numbers of speakers, French may be declining as an international language, but it has an enduring hold on the world, a level of influence that in many ways surpasses—and is even independent of—France's.

When people think of the "French paradox," they are usually thinking about how the French can eat rich foods and drink great quantities of wine yet somehow remain slim. But there is another French paradox, this one about the language: In spite of the ascendancy of English, French has held on to its influence. Where did this influence come from, and how has French retained it? These are the questions we set out to answer in *Plus ça Change.*

As an international language, French is said to be waning. English not so long ago surpassed French as the world's lingua franca and is now the undisputed international language of business, diplomacy and academic exchange. In numbers of speakers, French ranks only ninth in the world, far behind Chinese, Hindi, Spanish and English, and neck-and-neck with Portuguese. It has relatively little economic clout; the combined GDP of the countries where French is spoken places it far behind English, well behind both Japanese and German, and just ahead of Spanish. French speakers seem to be so insecure that they pass laws banning other languages and spend millions of taxpayers' dollars making sure their language gets used in literature, music and film.

From other perspectives, however, French appears to be flourishing. Among international languages, French is in a class of its own. Of the six thousand languages now spoken on Earth, French is one of only fifteen spoken by more than a hundred million people, and one of a dozen used as official languages in more than one country. Among these, only four—English, French, Spanish and Arabic—have official status in more than twenty countries. French, with thirty-three countries, ranks second to English, with forty-five. Two G8 countries (France and Canada) are French-speaking, as are four member countries of the European Union (France, Belgium, Luxembourg and soon-to-be member Romania). French is the number-two second-language choice of students across the planet, attracting learners as far away as Lesotho and Azerbaijan, with two million teachers and a hundred million students worldwide. It is the only language besides English that is taught in every country of the world. Finally, there have never been as many French speakers in the world as there are today: The number has tripled since the Second World War. (For more details on these figures, refer to the Appendix.)

It doesn't seem like an exaggeration to claim that French is another global language, and, as we have seen, perhaps *the* other global language, in an increasingly English-dominated world.

As two Canadians, we have a unique relationship with French that in some ways made us well-suited to explore its paradoxes. Along with Mauritius, the Seychelles, Cameroon and Vanuatu, Canada is one of five countries in the world where French and English are both official languages. Montreal, where we have lived for almost twenty years, is a rare bicultural metropolis, and the only one in the world where English and French co-exist almost equally in day-to-day life.

Jean-Benoît is a native French speaker. He was born and raised in Quebec, a Canadian province that was a French-speaking "Lost World" for two hundred years (it was cut off from contact with France from the end of New France in 1763 until the 1960s). His family is francophone, a term French speakers in Canada commonly use to distinguish themselves from both the European French, and North American English speakers, whom they refer to as anglophones. Jean-Benoît learned English when he was a teenager and decided to continue his studies in English at McGill University in Montreal. That's where he met Julie, who, like him, had just enrolled in the political science program. Julie is an anglophone who was raised in English-speaking Ontario. She moved to Montreal to study (in English), but decided to stay and learn French after she graduated.

When we moved in together in 1991, Julie's French was still pretty shaky, so we started our own system of language exchange, alternating the household language weekly between French and English, starting every Monday morning. The system worked well. Jean-Benoît started publishing magazine articles in English in 1994, and Julie started publishing in French in 1995. We have been writing for national magazines in both of

Canada's official languages ever since. This is unusual, even in Canada, where only a small minority of Canadians are truly bilingual, and fewer yet are bicultural. But working in both media worlds has given us a first-hand understanding of how differently anglophone and francophone Canadians see the world.

In 1999 we added a European twist to our bilingual profile by moving to Paris. Jean-Benoît became a fellow of the Institute of Current World Affairs. His mandate was to explain why the French were resisting globalization, a topic that was on everyone's mind at the time. The problem was that, two weeks after we arrived in France, we realized that the French weren't resisting globalization at all. Luckily Jean-Benoît was allowed to switch his subject, so we both spent the next two years writing about who the French are and explaining why they think and organize themselves the way they do.

That work inspired us to write a book, *Sixty Million Frenchmen Can't Be Wrong*, which we released in the middle of the Iraq crisis in 2003. Our objective was to explain the reality behind perceptions of the French, particularly to the Anglo-American press. The timing for the book turned out to be risky, but we survived the intense French-bashing at the beginning of the Iraq war and the book has been selling well ever since. It was translated into French in 2005, and turned out to be as popular in France as it is in the English-speaking world.

Although *Plus ça Change* was written after *Sixty Million Frenchmen*, we got the idea for both books at the same time. Four months after we arrived in France, Jean-Benoît visited Monaco to attend an international conference of finance ministers of the Francophonie, the organization of French-speaking countries that resembles the Commonwealth. During this conference he realized how much language had become a new political reality on the international scene, with countries aligning themselves on issues on the basis of their native or adopted tongues—many propagandists in favour of invading Iraq in 2003 did so on the basis of "Anglo-Saxon" solidarity. When he saw the Francophonie at work, Jean-Benoît also understood to what extent the French language had become a globalizing force of its own—with or without France.

We decided to write a book to explain how this happened, starting from the very beginning of the story. From the outset we wanted to explore a few large themes—or myths. One was the Académie française, the French Academy. When people think of the French language, this is often the first thing that springs to mind. The Academy has long been a pet peeve of Anglo-American commentators, who hold it up as proof that the French are stuck in the past. In a way, as we learned, critics are right to laugh at the forty "immortals" wearing Napoleonic hats and carrying swords who get together every week to root out unworthy words from the French language. The French Academy is a little obsolete.

At the same time, when they are ridiculing the Academy, commentators almost always miss the point. The Academy in no way "polices" French. Its main job has always been to produce a French dictionary, and that's still mostly what it does. Insofar as it regulates the language at all, it has hardly played more than a symbolic role since the mid-nineteenth century. But that doesn't make the Academy any less important, either historically or today.

The creation of the French Academy in the seventeenth century was actually a breakthrough for European languages, and one of the main factors that enabled French to become the language of Europe's elite. That in turn was one of the reasons why French spread across Europe, and eventually the world. In other words, the Academy was progressive, and it played an important historical role in making French what it is today, not only grammatically but also geopolitically. Today it still functions, if only symbolically, as a kind of museum of French-language *normes,* or standards. While these are often ridiculed, especially in the English-language media, language norms are an important facet of francophone culture, a value that stands on its own.

As for language protection, another francophone society, Quebec, took that on in the twentieth century and did a much more thorough job of it than the French ever have. Along with many other countries in the world, France considers Quebec's standards to be a reference point in the field.

One peculiar and often overlooked feature of French is that, unlike English, it is still very much associated with its European "mother" country. Indeed, of all the international languages, French is the only one of which the majority of native speakers are still in their country of origin. The French never migrated en masse, so all native francophones outside of France and Algeria form a minority in their respective countries. As a result, France and Paris still tend to dominate the world view of French speakers, unlike Britain, Spain or Portugal, which have been surpassed by larger nations that speak their tongues.

But all that is changing. As we discovered during our research, the French language is less and less "controlled" by Paris. While the French Academy continues to play its (largely symbolic) role in defining French, francophones the world over use the language as it suits them. Real French, the language spoken by 175 million people across the planet, is alive and kicking and readily adapting to different political, cultural and religious contexts. Under the influence of local regionalisms, argots, *verlan* (slang) and other languages such as English and Arabic—to name but the most important—French speakers communicate in their own versions of French, not the stiff parlance taught in schools. And, increasingly, francophone societies outside France are speaking with each other, often completely bypassing Paris.

This vitality is one of the reasons why francophones have their own star system in literature, film, music and more, in spite of the global reach of American pop culture. Céline Dion and Gérard Depardieu may be the only names known to non-francophones, but singers such as Garou and Johnny Hallyday, poets such as Luc Plamondon and Amadou Kourouma, authors such as Michel Houellebecq and Tahar Ben Jelloun, and actors such as Gad Elmaleh or Djamel Debbouze are household names among francophones all over the world.

There is no doubt that francophones are borrowing liberally from English. But is it fair to deduce that they are insecure about their language? Given the amount of time and energy francophone societies spend thinking and talking about their language, it's not surprising that Anglo-American commentators have so often jumped to this conclusion. However, these commentators usually overlook an important phenomenon among francophones: their attachment to the *norme,* to language rules and standards. Far from being a defensive reaction to the growing influence of English—as it is often portrayed—attachment to the *norme* is a cultural feature among francophones that has its own history and significance.

While most native English speakers (and many French speakers as well) assume that the progress of English is hurting the prospects of French, we found that, globally, that's just not happening. Language is not a zero-sum game. There definitely appears to be a struggle: Outside France and Algeria, most francophones in the world are a minority in their country and have long had to fight for their language. But with the exception of Quebec, most of these efforts by francophones have been, and continue to be, directed towards other languages, not English. The French themselves are not insecure about their language and are not particularly concerned about English, for a simple reason: So far, they have no need to be.

How did French develop, spread and acquire its own set of values? And why does it remain important? These are the central questions underlying *Plus ça Change*. Throughout this narrative we explain the events that spawned the different features of French: its intense politicization, the rigidity of its rules, the sense of cultural exceptionality that inhabits every French speaker, the centrality of France, the adherence of all francophones to language norms and regulations, and even the influence of French on English—and vice versa. Geographical and political circumstances; decisions by important political figures; French and Belgian colonial policies and practices; the world wars; trade; the export of literature, art, cinema and luxury products, industrial policies and scientific discoveries—all of these, and more, have shaped French. *Plus ça Chnnge* is divided into four parts, representing the main stages in the story of the language: origins, spread, adaptation and change. In each we relate the events, people and places, large and small, that shaped the destiny of the French language, from the temerity of William the Conqueror to the staunchness of Cardinal Richelieu, the charisma of Voltaire and the determination of Red Cross founder Henri Dunant, to Quebec's language laws and Léopold Sédar Senghor's activism in the wake of African independence. As far as we know, this is the first popular history of the language that addresses these issues in a narrative that stretches from Charlemagne to actress Jodie Foster, who appears in French films speaking perfect French—a pure product of France's cultural diplomacy efforts.

Sociolinguists often joke that a language is a dialect with an army. We are not linguists ourselves, but graduates of political science, history and English literature, and we sympathize with this view. Although we do discuss linguistics in four chapters, our general approach is sociolinguistic rather than purely linguistic (readers who are looking for detailed accounts of grammatical or spelling developments can consult the books listed under "The French Language" and "Linguistics and Other Languages" in the Selected Bibliography). *Plus ça Change* approaches French as a dialect with an army, a navy and an economy, strong diplomatic skills, aggressive cultural policies and ideas and, of course, some luck. The spread of French, like that of many international languages, was a by-product of these factors, though the French language persisted in some countries even after these forces had disappeared.

Plus ça Change includes spectacular failures and unexpected successes, and it is not always a nice story. Colonialism, slavery and genocide have all happened in French. It is by no means our intention to endorse these horrors, but, from the perspective of dissemination of European languages, they cannot be overlooked. Monstrous though they were, the Spanish conquest of the Americas, the deportation of the Acadians, the massacre of Australian Aborigines, the Angolan slave trade and the seventh- and eighth-century jihads all played an important role in making English, Spanish, Portuguese and Arabic into international languages. Languages do not become international for nothing.

Of course, war and violence weren't the only ways in which French spread. In the 1950s the French philosopher, author and Nobel Prize–winner Albert Camus said, "*Ma patrie, c'est la langue française*" ("My country is the French language"). Camus was born in Algeria into a family of European settlers, and although he's a French icon, he was a francophone in spirit. His famous comment expressed a reality that few people understood in postwar Europe. Already traditional borders were becoming less important and language was becoming a new frontier. The French had already understood this at the end of the nineteenth century, when they began actively exporting their language in the form of international networks of French schools, Alliances françaises and cultural centres. World leaders in the field of cultural diplomacy, the French–and francophones–are still expanding the frontiers of French with their "soft power."

In writing *Plus ça Change,* we had to confront many prejudices, not only about French, but also about English. Many serious writers are convinced that English is sweeping the planet, because it is better suited than any other language to commerce, trade, logic, popular culture and even democracy. Many also claim that the success of English comes from its special capacity for absorbing new words. In our opinion, this is ethnocentrism applied to language. Saying that English is especially suited to trade is a little like saying that French is especially suited to cuisine; there are good historical reasons why each language came to be associated with these activities (although plenty of business is also carried out in French, and plenty of good cooking is done in English). Writers rarely mention, for instance, how the British *Navigation Act* of 1652 got English off to a good start. The Act banned all non-British ships or crews from landing at British ports, which destroyed Dutch commerce, led to the downfall of Holland's navy and opened the seas to British control, greatly enhancing British trade. The fact that in the twentieth century one English-speaking empire (the United States) replaced another (Great Britain) certainly helped boost the prospects of English, to put it mildly.

But we did not write *Plus ça Change* to compare the fates of French and English–there is no comparison. English has achieved an international presence that is unprecedented in the history of languages. The English language has become so prevalent in world affairs that most educated people in most modern, developed countries no longer consider it a foreign language—including the French. Yet, as we show, English is not the only global language. And, more important, it is not erasing the differences in how language groups think and see the world. The destruction of the World Trade Center showed everyone that religion is still an important mental frontier that defines cultures. Christians have bought millions of books on Islam since September 11, 2001, in an effort to understand the events of that day. And, in our globalized world, language is also a mental frontier.

One of those mental frontiers is French. When we went to Paris in 1999, our neighbour, Thorfinn Johnston, was a Scot from the Orkney Islands. As Thorfinn himself pointed out, he had much more in common with Julie, an English-speaking North American, than he did with his fellow Europeans the French. The same is true of Jean-Benoît and his French, Algerian and Senegalese friends; they share something inaccessible that goes beyond mere words or cultural references. A translated novel by Michel Houellebecq or Michel Tremblay remains inherently French (in the case of Houellebecq) or Québécois (in the case of Tremblay).

Plus ça Change explores what's inside the mental universe of French speakers. French has been an important global language practically from the moment it became distinct from Latin, and throughout its history it has functioned as a vector for a distinct set of values. French carries with it a vision of the State and of political values, a particular set of cultural standards and even a clear idea of its role in the world, though this has changed drastically over the centuries. Francophones are also united in their strong adherence to norms, contrary to English speakers, because French relies on strict written rules to define its grammar, lexicon and syntax.

As many chapters of this book show, the French language has remained influential not only in spite of but also because of the influence of English. English speakers have always reserved a pre-eminent place for French in their culture and, to a certain extent, as it sweeps the planet English is carrying and spreading this vision of French with it. By the same token, some of French's power to promote itself comes from the fact that, more than any other language, it offers a counterbalance to the influence of English.

This last point is crucial. In countries such as Israel, Mexico and Egypt, all clearly outside the French sphere of influence, elites still school their children in French. The U.S. and Mexico have the two biggest networks of Alliances françaises in the world. The Egyptian elite in Alexandria began schooling their children in French *lycées* to counterbalance the influence of British colonialism, and some still do so now to resist American hegemony; the former secretary-general of the Francophonie and of the United Nations, Boutros Boutros-Ghali, is a product of that philosophy. As French linguist Henriette Walter, author of *Honni soit qui mal y pense,* a history of the relationship between the French and English languages, told us, English speakers are not necessarily conscious of it, but "people are still proud to belong to the club of French speakers."

Comparing French-speaking countries did raise some problems for us. For one thing, statistics on the English and French languages are somewhat crude. One reason is that it is difficult to define exactly what is a French speaker or an English speaker. Both are not only native languages but also important languages of choice in many other countries. The various people designing surveys don't always make the same distinctions between different types of speakers (native, partial or occasional, for example). When talking about francophones we use the generally accepted figure of 175 million speakers, but that doesn't count the estimated 100 million occasional speakers or the 100 million French students in the world. (In the case of English, the same categories vary even more widely, from 375 million to 600 million native speakers, plus an additional 500 million occasional speakers and 500 million students.)

We use the terms *anglophone* and *francophone* for people who speak English or French, respectively, in order to emphasize the fact that not all French speakers are French. We also often refer to both the Francophonie and the francophonie. The nuance is important. Francophonie with a capital F is the fifty-three-member Organisation internationale de la Francophonie (International Organization of the Francophonie), whose purpose it is to promote French. The small-f francophonie is the real planet of francophones. Countries such as Israel and Algeria, and the United States—where 1.6 million speakers make French the third language after English and Spanish—are not part of the capital-F Francophonie (see table 6 in Appendix). In 127 countries of the world, mostly outside the (official) Francophonie, there are tens of millions of students, adults and children, learning French in one of the world's roughly 1,500 Alliances françaises and French *lycées* and *collèges*. An additional twenty million students are learning French in national education programs outside the fifty-three member countries (plus ten observers) of the Francophonie.

Not a bad performance for a language that ranks ninth in the world for number of speakers! And education is just one of the ways in which French has held on to its rank as the world's second international language. This is the story of how French became a global language, and why it will likely remain one for many years to come.

Part One ~

ORIGINS

Chapter 1

THE ROMANCE OF FRENCH

VERY FEW PEOPLE KNOW that French has its place in the world not in spite of English, but because of it. We began to think about this when we were at university, back in the days when the Berlin Wall was falling. Jean-Benoît arrived at McGill University speaking a kind of abstract English that was much more formal than the language the anglophones around him were using, especially in casual conversation. Fellow students usually knew what was meant when he mentioned that he was "perturbed" by a sore ankle or had "abandoned" his plan to travel to Africa. But off campus, such stiff language produced blank stares. Julie often served as an interpreter, explaining that Jean-Benoît's ankle was bothering him and that he had given up his travel plans.

Jean-Benoît's sophisticated English was normal for a French speaker. French is the Latin of anglophones. Nearly half of the commonly used words in English—for example, *chase, catch, surf, challenge* and *staunch*—are of French origin. And while their French origins have been largely forgotten by the majority of English speakers (who tend to believe the words come straight from Latin), the influence of French has remained in their linguistic subconscious. For the most part, so-called Latinate words in English are used only in formal speech: People will say "commence" or "inaugurate" instead of "begin" or "start."

English is in fact the most Latin, and the most French, among Germanic languages, while French—for reasons that we will see—is the most Germanic among Latin languages. The French and English languages share a symbiotic relationship, and that should come as no surprise, as their histories have been inextricably linked for the past ten centuries. And that connection resulted from events that took place in the ten centuries before that. Few anglophones realize that by keeping French words in the "upper stratum" of their discourse, they are granting French a lofty position in their language and culture. As they export English all around the world, French and its high status have become part of the package. It's one of the least-known explanations for the resilience of French today.

It is impossible to say exactly when French began. Linguists who study European languages spoken before the second millennium consider themselves lucky to recover sentences, known words or even fragments of written text. In most cases they reconstruct ancient languages by examining how they influenced more recent ones. Historians know more about what happened in France between 400 and 1000 CE than they know about the languages spoken there during that period. The most that can be said is that before French there were many Romance languages; before that there was Gallo-Roman; before that there was Latin, and before that, Gaulish. Three main events pushed the language from one phase to the next: the fall of the Roman Empire, the conquest of England and the rise of Paris as a centre of power.

Before the Romans arrived in what is today the northern half of France, its inhabitants spoke different Celtic languages. They were the descendants of tribes of Indo-Europeans who may have originated in Kazakhstan and who migrated to northern Europe during the third millennium BCE. The tongue of the Celts, like Latin or Gaelic, belongs to the family of Indo-European languages, which also includes Greek and Hindi.

The term was coined in 1787 by William Jones, a British Orientalist. He was puzzled by the fact that basic words such as *papa* and *mama* are remarkably similar in Greek, Latin, German, English, Sanskrit and Celtic, and he came up with the theory that most European languages were derived from a forgotten original tongue, which he called Indo-European.

The first Celts arrived with their Indo-European tongue in what is today northern France sometime during the first millennium BCE. In the south of France, long before the Celts arrived, the Greeks had established a colony in Marseilles among the Ligurian people living there. But it was the Celts, not the Greeks, who spread across what is now France, pushing other inhabitants such as the Basques into remote corners of the territory. (Linguists describe the Basque language, which is still spoken in southern France and Spain, as pre–Indo-European. It is regarded as Europe's oldest language.)

The Celts had barely met up with the Greeks in the south of France when the Romans entered the region in the second century BCE. By then Gaul had somewhere between ten million and fifteen million inhabitants, prosperous and innovative farmers and stockbreeders who had invented the threshing machine, the plow and the barrel. But the Gauls were also good fighters, which explains why it took Rome a century and a half to subdue them; Julius Caesar finally conquered Gaul around 50 BCE.

Curiously, the Celts of Gaul assimilated quickly into the culture of the Romans and started speaking their language. The Celts of Britannia (Britain), which was conquered by the Romans shortly afterwards, never did assimilate. Historians are still trying to understand this difference. Part of the explanation comes from the fact that prior to the Roman conquest, Gaul was already within the Roman economic sphere of influence. Gauls were already using the Roman sesterce as their currency of reference. When the Roman victors showed up with a new system of administration based on cities, a seductive urban culture, unparalleled building techniques and a complete and unified writing system, the Gauls saw the advantages of Roman culture. It didn't take long for the Gaulish elite to start speaking Latin.

The Gaulish language ended up contributing very little to the vocabulary of modern French. Only about a hundred Gaulish words survived the centuries, mostly rural and agricultural terms such as *bouleau* (birch), *sapin* (fir), *lotte* (monkfish), *mouton* (sheep), *charrue* (plow), *sillon* (furrow), *lande* (moor) and *boue* (mud)—that's eight percent of the total. However, Gaulish is still relatively well-known, partly because it left many place and family names in northern France. For example, the name Paris comes from the Parisii, a Gaulish tribe, and the word *bituriges* (which meant "kings of the world") produced the names Bourges and Berry (the difference comes from whether the original name was pronounced with a Latin or a Gaulish accent). Linguists believe that Gaulish also contributed to development of the peculiar sonority of French, and that it was at the root of some important linguistic variations in what would become French. But, contrary to what some people believe, modern French is not Latin pronounced with a Gaulish accent.

The Roman occupation spawned a new language that would play an important role in the formation of modern French. In the Roman province of Gaul only one percent of the population was literate, and those who wrote used Latin. The rest of the population spoke a rustic, popular "street" Latin that would come to be known as Gallo-Roman. By the fourth or fifth century CE, Gaulish had all but disappeared, though a few speakers stuck it out in Normandy until about the ninth century. (The Celtic language spoken in Brittany today was actually imported by Celts who fled to Brittany from Britannia in the fifth and sixth centuries CE, to escape the barbarian invasions.)

Gallo-Roman went on to have more lasting power than the Roman Empire, which crumbled in the fifth century CE. Germanic "barbarians" (a Greek term referring to peoples who don't speak Greek; any other language sounded like "bar-bar" to them) had already been invading Gaul for a century. Tribes including the Vandals, Goths, Saxons and Vikings all settled in different areas of France, where they intermarried with the inhabitants. Curiously, although the invaders left important traces of their language wherever they settled, they all picked up the local Gallo-Roman dialect. This created a galaxy of different dialects across what would become French territory, all of which shared many words and characteristics. The last barbarian invaders, the Vikings, spoke Norse, and were called Norsemen or Normans. At the beginning of the tenth century they settled around the mouth of the Seine, where they established the powerful Duchy of Normandy. Like other invaders, the Norsemen were soon speaking a Gallo-Roman dialect, and Norse donated only a few sea terms to modern French, including *crabe* (crab), *homard* (lobster) and *vague* (wave). But the Normans would have a profound impact on the future of French, thanks to a Norseman who would conquer England.

Of all the invaders, it was the Franks who had the greatest impact on the evolution of French, at least inside France. This tribe from northern Germany filled the power vacuum left by the crumbling Roman Empire. In 430 the Franks created a federation they called Francia, in today's Belgium. After the sack of Rome in 476, they moved into the province of Gaul, establishing themselves around Lutetia (now Paris). Under king Clovis I, the Franks seized large sections of southern

France and Spain, subdued rival tribes and consolidated their control all over Gaul. Clovis founded a dynasty that lasted three centuries. In French political mythology he is considered the first king of France, and many French kings who followed him used a modern variant of his name—Louis. The political influence of the Franks would rise and fall, but even so it lasted seven centuries.

The Franks, like all the other invaders, quickly picked up Gallo-Roman, although the Frankish kings remained bilingual (in German) until at least the tenth century. Because of their political power they contributed more words to modern French than any of the other Germanic invaders. Roughly ten percent of modern French words come from Frankish, including words describing home life, clothing, war and emotions, such as *fauteuil* (armchair), *gant* (glove), *robe* (dress), *champion, guerre* (war), *muraille* (wall), *falaise* (cliff), *émoi* (emotion), *honte* (shame) and *orgueil* (pride). Although eighty percent of the words in modern French have Latin or Gallo-Roman roots, the Frankish influence explains why French went on to become the most Germanic of Latin-based languages. The Franks also created a strong "brand"—until the tenth century the king in Paris was called King of the Franks. Germans to this day call France *Frankreich* (empire of the Franks). Over the centuries the language of the Franks gradually came to be known as Françoys.

All languages have three parts: phonetics (pronunciation), grammar and a lexicon (vocabulary), and each part changes constantly. The lexicon changes the most quickly because of exposure to other languages and because of erosion (words tend to lose sounds or syllables), while pronunciation and grammar evolve more slowly. Because of their relative stability, grammar and phonetics form the skeleton of a language. It was Frankish influence on the Latin spoken in Gaul that gave it a new grammatical and phonetic skeleton, making it distinct from Latin (Italian, Spanish and Romanian became distinct much later). Linguists have found convincing evidence that, by the eighth century, even the Latin-speaking clergy in France were speaking a new language. In that century (the exact date is unknown), some monks in Picardy produced a small glossary, known to posterity as the *Gloses* of Reichenau, which translated some 1,300 Latin words into the vernacular, which had little to do with Latin. The word for ewe appears as *berbice,* a term much closer to the modern French *brebis* than the classic Latin *ovis.* The liver was called *ficato,* a word closer to the French *foie* that had very little resemblance to the Latin *jecur.* By then nobody said *forum* (market), *arena* (sand), *liberi* (children) or *uvas* (grapes), but *mercatum, sabulo, infantes* and *racemos.*

It didn't take long for a new label to be applied to this proto-French. In 813 the Council of Tours encouraged priests to preach in *rusticam romanam linguam* (the rustic Roman language). It was the first clear indication that people outside of the Church spoke not Latin, but *Roman.* In English this language is often referred to as Romanic and more generally as Romance, derived from *romanz,* as it was spelled in Romance. The term actually applied to all the Latin-based languages being spoken in France at the time. They are also called Gallo-Romance languages to distinguish them from the Romance languages of Spain, Italy and Romania (Basque and Breton do not fall into this category).

The first complete text to appear in French Romance was *Les serments de Strasbourg* (the Oaths of Strasbourg), a treaty struck between two grandsons of the Frankish Holy Roman Emperor Charlemagne (742–814), Louis the German and Charles the Bald, in 842. One version of the text is in Romance, the other is in a German vernacular called Francique. According to the treaty, Louis took his oath in Romance in front of his brother's men, who spoke Romance, while Charles made the same pledge to Louis's men in Francique. However, since the document that survives is a transcription of the original document made a century later, no one knows for sure what the Romance version actually looked like. A later Romance text, the *Cantilène de Sainte-Eulalie* (a twenty-nine-verse lyrical poem about the saint's martyrdom, dated 880 or 881), is a more reliable example of Romance.

When we compared the two texts, we were struck by the differences between them. The *Serments de Strasbourg* is written in language that is diplomatic and official, and the Latin influence is clear. It takes a specialist to recognize that the sentence "*In o quid il mi altresi frazet*" ("under the condition that he does the same to me") is not Latin. However, some sentences taken from the *Cantilène* are almost intelligible to modern readers of French:

> *Buona pulcella fut eulalie.*
> *Bel auret corps bellezour anima.*
> *Voldrent la veintre li deo inimi.*
> *Voldrent la faire diaule servir.*
> Eulalie was a virtuous maiden.
> She had a beautiful body and a soul even more
>   beautiful.
> God's enemies wanted to conquer her,
> wanted to have her serve the devil.*

Despite their differences, both texts show clear signs that Romance had grown a new linguistic skeleton and was no longer Latin. The main change was the erosion of the system of inflection. Inflection involves changing the end of a noun to show its

---

* Translated by Brigitte Cazelles

function in the sentence—a feature typical of Latin and Old English that is still used in modern Russian and German. *Rosa* (rose, in Latin) is a subject, but *rosam* is a direct object, and the endings reflect these functions no matter where the words fall in the sentence. In all, Latin nouns have six inflected cases that correspond to the six functions of a word in a sentence (subject, addressee, direct object, possessive, indirect object and adverbial). In ninth-century Romance the inflections were simplified; only two cases survived, one for the subject and the other for the object. The name Romance, for example, was written as *romanz* when it was a subject and *romanans* when it was an object.

This erosion of the inflection system did not end there, and during the ensuing centuries French nouns lost their variety of cases. The position of words in a sentence became the primary way of marking their grammatical functions—the subject usually comes before the verb, and the object after the verb. However, modern French vocabulary has retained some traces of the old case system. For example, the French pronoun *me* was the accusative (object form) of the Latin *ego* (I). Modern English has retained even more features of the old inflection system. The apostrophe *S*—as in "my father's"—is a hangover from the genitive (possessive) case in Latin. And *who, whom, whose* and *whence* come from cases in Old English or Germanic languages and are still used as such today. *Whom* and *whose* are the accusative and genitive cases of *who* (nominative); and *whence* is the dative of *when*.

By and large, French got rid of most of those complications over the years, although it did develop some of its own. The progressive erosion of the Latin inflection system explains why French articles multiplied at the same time. In Latin the word endings varied not only according to sentence function, but also according to gender and number. When cases disappeared, speakers needed new markers to indicate gender and number, so they created definite articles—*li, lo* and *la*—and indefinite articles—*un, une, uns, unes, des*—features that were totally absent from Latin.

By the tenth century France was a patchwork of duchies, marches, counties and baronies (the estates of different orders of nobles) where a galaxy of vernaculars was spoken that mixed Latin, Frankish and other Germanic languages. By the fourteenth century, scholars had divided these Romance dialects into two broad categories. Those in which "yes" was pronounced *oc*—mostly south of the Loire River—were called *langues d'oc* (*oc* languages). Those in which speakers said *oïl* for "yes"—in the north—were called *langues d'oïl*, a term which came to be used interchangeably with Françoys. *Oïl* and *oc* are both derivatives of the Latin *hoc* (this, that), which at the time was used to say yes. In the south they simply chopped off the *h*. In the north, for some reason, *hoc* was reduced to a simple *o*, and qualifiers were added—*o-je, o-nos, o-vos* for "yes for me," "yes for us" and "yes for you." This was complicated, so speakers eventually settled for the neutral *o-il*—"yes for that." The term was used in the dialects of Picardy, Normandy, Champagne and Orléans. Other important *langues d'oïl* were Angevin, Poitevin and Bourguignon, spoken in Anjou, Poitiers and Burgundy, which were considerably farther south of Paris. Scholars debate who created the designations *langues d'oïl* and *langues d'oc*. The poet Dante Alighieri, in his *De vulgari eloquentia* of 1304, was one of the first to introduce the term *langue d'oc,* opposing it to the *langue d'oïl* and the *langue de si* (Romance from Italy). A fifth important *langue d'oïl* was Walloon, the dialect of the future Belgium.

The *langues d'oc* attained their golden age in the eleventh and twelfth centuries, when groups of wandering musicians, or troubadours, travelled from city to city spreading a new form of sung poem that extolled the ideal of courtly love, or *fin'amor.* This new poetry was very different from the cruder epic poems of the north, the *chansons de geste,* and it enjoyed great literary prestige that boosted the influence of two southern rulers, the Count of Toulouse and the Duke of Aquitaine. Even many Italian courts adopted the *langue d'oc,* which is also known today as Occitan. Wandering poets of the north, the *trouvères* of Champagne, also borrowed and popularized the song-poems of the south.

The influence of the *langues d'oc* and *d'oïl* produced a situation in which French had started exporting itself even before it had become a fully developed language with a coherent writing system. Between the tenth and fifteenth centuries, Romance impressed itself on Europe as the language of worldly business, helping to relegate Latin to the religious sphere, although the latter did remain a language of science and philosophy for many more centuries. In the Mediterranean region, fishermen, sailors and merchants used a rudimentary version of *langue d'oc* mixed with Italian that people called the *lingua franca* ("Frankish language"), and over time this spoken language soaked up influences from Italian, Spanish and Turkish. (Today a lingua franca is any common language used in economics, diplomacy or science, in a context where it is not a mother tongue.)

The Mediterranean *lingua franca* never evolved into anyone's mother tongue, which is why there are very few written traces of it. A rare rendition of it appears in a seventeenth-century comedy by the French playwright Molière, who had been a wandering actor before he entered Louis XIV's Court. In his *Le bourgeois gentilhomme* (*The Would-Be Gentleman*), Molière creates the character of a fake Turk who speaks in *lingua franca* (for obvious comical effect):

Se ti sabir, / Ti respondir;
se non sabir, / Tazir, Tazir.
Mi star Mufti / Ti qui star ti?
Non intendir, / Tazir, tazir.
If you know, / you must respond.
If you don't know, / you must shut up.
I am the Mufti, / who are you?
I don't understand; / shut up, shut up.*

It was the Crusades, which were dominated by the French, that turned *lingua franca* into the dominant language in the Mediterranean. More than half a dozen Crusades were carried out over nearly three centuries. Many Germans and English also participated, but the Arabs uniformly referred to the Crusaders as *Franj,* caring little whether they said *oc, oïl, ja* or *yes.* Interestingly, Arabic, the language of the common enemy, gave French roughly a thousand terms, including *amiral* (admiral), *alcool* (alcohol), *coton* (cotton) and *sirop* (syrup). The great prevalence of Arabic words in French scientific language—terms such as *algèbre* (algebra), *alchimie* (alchemy) and *zéro* (zero)—underlines the fact that the Arabs were definitely at the cutting edge of knowledge at the time.

The greatest export of *langues d'oïl* was to England, and it happened almost accidentally. The English king Edward the Confessor had promised his crown to two men: William, Duke of Normandy, and Harold Godwinson, a duke who had become his right-hand man. When Edward died in 1066, William sailed to Hastings and quickly put an end to any confusion by defeating Harold in battle and seizing the English crown. He made his *langue d'oïl* dialect, Norman, the language of the English Crown and inaugurated a succession of French-speaking

* Unless otherwise noted, all translations are by the authors.

kings that lasted four centuries. The first English king to speak English as a mother tongue was Henry IV (ruled 1399–1413), and his successor, Henry V, was the first to write official documents in English.

French might have foundered in England if William had not been such a competent ruler. He settled his people everywhere, established a new feudal system and instituted an efficient administration that made England the first centralized regime of Europe. The English nobility, civil servants, employees of the palace and Court, and merchant class quickly fell into line and started speaking the language of the king, even those who were born in England. St. Thomas Becket was known in his time as Thomas à Becket, and the ancestors of the poet Chaucer were *chaussiers* (shoemakers). The mixture of a solidly established Romance aristocracy with the Old English grassroots produced a new language, a "French of England," which came to be known as Anglo-Norman. It was perfectly intelligible to the speakers of other *langues d'oïl* and also gave French its first anglicisms, words such as *bateau* (boat) and the four points of the compass, *nord, sud, est* and *ouest*. The most famous Romance *chanson de geste*, the *Song of Roland*, was written in Anglo-Norman. The first verse shows how "French" this language was:

> *Carles li reis, nostre emperere magnes,*
> *set anz tuz pleins ad estéd en Espaigne,*
> *Tresqu'en la mer cunquist la tere altaigne . . .*
> King Charles, our great emperor,
> stayed in Spain a full seven years:
> and he conquered the high lands up to the sea . . .

Francophones are probably not aware of how much England contributed to the development of French. England's

court was an important production centre for Romance litera-
ture, and most of the early legends of King Arthur were written
in Anglo-Norman. Robert Wace, who came from the Channel
Island of Jersey, first evoked the mythical Round Table in his
Roman de Brut, written in French in 1155. An Englishman,
William Caxton, even produced the first "vocabulary" of
French and English (a precursor of the dictionary) in 1480.

But for four centuries after William seized the English
crown, the exchange between Old English and Romance was
pretty much the other way around—from Romance to English.
Linguists dispute whether a quarter or a half of the basic
English vocabulary comes from French. Part of the argument
has to do with the fact that some borrowings are referred to as
Latinates, a term that tends to obscure the fact that they actually come from French (as we explain later, the English worked
hard to push away or hide the influence of French). Words such
as *charge, council, court, debt, judge, justice, merchant* and *parliament* are straight borrowings from eleventh-century Romance,
often with no modification in spelling.

In her book *Honni soit qui mal y pense,* Henriette Walter
points out that the historical developments of French and English
are so closely related that anglophone students find it easier to
read Old French than francophones do. The reason is simple:
Words such as *acointance, chalenge, plege, estriver, remaindre* and
esquier disappeared from the French vocabulary but remained in
English as *acquaintance, challenge, pledge, strive, remain* and *squire—*
with their original meanings. The word *bacon,* which francophones
today decry as an English import, is an old Frankish term that
took root in English. Words that people think are totally English,
such as *foreign, pedigree, budget, proud* and *view,* are actually
Romance terms pronounced with an English accent: *forain, pied-
de-grue* (crane's foot—a symbol used in genealogical trees to mark
a line of succession), *bougette* (purse), *prud* (valiant) and *vëue.*

Like all other Romance vernaculars, Anglo-Norman evolved quickly. At first William's companions were mostly imported from Normandy and Maine, but as the years passed, Picards and Franks (as they called Parisians back then) were also brought to the English court. The English language is an excellent laboratory for examining the different trends that were at work in the formation of French. For the word *château*, the Norman variant *castel* produced *castle*, whereas the Paris variant *chastel* produced *chastelain* and *châtelaine*. There are many other examples; for example, *chasser* (to hunt), which was pronounced *chacier* around Paris, but *cachier* in Normandy, produced *chase* and *catch*. *Real, royal* and *regal* meant the same thing in Norman, Françoys and Latin respectively, but English took them on and gave them each different meanings. The term *real estate* comes from two Anglo-Norman terms. *Leal, loyal* and *legal* followed the same pattern, although *leal* (meaning both "loyal" and "legal") has fallen out of use. *Warranty* and *guarantee* are the same word, pronounced with a Norman and a Françoys accent respectively; this difference in pronunciation also explains how Guillaume became William, *guerre* became *war,* and Gaul became Walloon.

English became the expression of a profound brand of nationalism long before French did. As early as the thirteenth century, the English were struggling to define their nation in opposition to the French, a phenomenon that is no doubt the root of the peculiar mixture of attraction and repulsion most anglophones feel towards the French today, whether they admit it or not. When Norman kings tried to add their French territory to England and unify their kingdom under the English Crown, the French of course resisted. The situation led to the first, lesser-known Hundred Years War (1159–1299). This long quarrel forced the Anglo-Norman aristocracy to take sides. Those who chose England got closer to the local grassroots,

setting the Anglo-Norman aristocracy on the road to assimilation into English. In 1362 the English king went further, with the
Statute of Pleadings, which forbade Anglo-Norman and declared
English the only legal language in the kingdom—this was a century before the French made any such proclamation about their
own language. Curiously, the Anglo-Norman judicial jargon
known as Law French persisted until the eighteenth century. As
well, the motto of the British Crown (*Dieu et mon droit*) and of
the Order of the Garter (*Honi soit qui mal y pense*) are two heraldic
vestiges of the period when the English Crown was French.

In spite of this estrangement, French remained the language of intellectuals and gentlemen for a long time, even in
the English colonies. Some words are a testimony to that; *gentil* was borrowed three times as *gentle* (thirteenth century), *genteel*
(sixteenth century) and *jaunty* (seventeenth century). Chaucer
chose to tell his *Canterbury Tales* in English, but 150 years later
Thomas More published his *Utopia* in Latin with a French
translation; the English version appeared only after his death.
The link between French and English remains strong to this
day: Fourteen million British people visit France every year
(only three million French travel to Great Britain). Statistics on
second-language teaching show that French is doing consis-
tently well in English-language countries (see table 4 and 6 in
Appendix). And the number of borrowings from French into
English remains considerable; *sans, faux* and *garage* are recent
acquisitions that nobody blinks at.

For anglophones, French remains the language of chic,
taste and superiority to this day; as a mark of the love/hate relationship English-speakers tend to have with French, French can
represent these qualities in a positive or a negative sense. The
best-known example is the Harry Potter series. Author J. K.
Rowling, who studied French at Exeter University, gave her
nasty aristocratic characters names that are clearly inspired by

Old French or that have a French etymology: Malfoy (bad faith), Voldemort (flight of death), Lestrange (stranger). William the Conqueror would probably never have believed that his victory would influence the semantics of English for ten centuries.

Back in France, the *langues d'oïl* were about to win a centuries-old Darwinian struggle with the *langues d'oc*. The victory owed much to the rising power of Paris and the Franks, but it was far from predictable. The Frankish ruler Charlemagne's vast empire of a century earlier had not survived his sons' rivalries and the Norsemen's invasion. By the tenth century, French territory was a broken patchwork of principalities. The king of the Franks, who was established in Paris, was theoretically the greatest lord among many others and the ultimate arbiter of justice, but, in fact, his "inferiors"—the lords who ran Flanders, Aquitaine, Burgundy, Toulouse, Brittany and Anjou—were more powerful, and fiercely independent. They had their own armies, currencies and justice systems, and they answered to no one. Things were so bad that by 987 the Kingdom of the Franks had run out of successors. So they crowned one Hugues Capet, a Frank, though he did not speak German; in doing so, they broke with a tradition that dated back to Clovis.

Capet and his successors, the Capetians, played the game of alliances, marriages and war so well that over the next four centuries they enlarged their domain and re-established the precedence of royal justice over that of other lords and the Church. The Franks' power grew, and no one raised an eyebrow when Philippe Augustus (ruled 1180–1223) opened his reign by declaring himself King of France rather than merely King of the Franks—though the significance of his declaration was not yet clear.

It was Philippe Augustus who delivered the death blow to the *langues d'oc,* bringing about their swift decline. The *langues*

d'oc had still been surfing on the popularity of the troubadours, but the wind shifted in 1209, when Pope Innocent III
preached a crusade against the Albigensians, a heretic sect
based around Carcassonne, whose influence was spreading in
southwestern France. It was the first crusade outside the Holy
Land. Philippe saw the attack on the Albigensians as a great
opportunity to flex his muscles and subdue his vassals, so he
offered to help the Pope wipe them out. Much of Toulouse's
wealth was destroyed in the process, and the troubadours
moved to Spain. The *langue d'oc* lost its lustre almost overnight
and became frozen into a set of dialects, which it remains to
this day.

Philippe Augustus grabbed half the territory of present-
day France during his reign and appointed civil servants from
Paris to impose his authority everywhere. These literate bourgeois spoke the language that came to be associated with true
power: Françoys. What makes this period confusing in the
history of French is that labels such as *France, Frank* and
Françoys did not then have clear meanings, and were often
used interchangeably with other terms. Before the first millennium, Françoys was associated strictly with the Franks who
held power in Paris. Since these Franks spoke a northern
dialect of Romance, all *langues d'oïl* dialects came to be called
Françoys. By the twelfth century the term *françoys* also
referred to a manner of writing and speaking that was unique
to the Paris region. By the fourteenth century Françoys
referred to a defined language, distinct from all the other
langues d'oïl; it took another three centuries for *Françoys* to be
spelled *Français*.

By the fourteenth century Françoys was so well-established
that neither the Black Death, which killed a good third of the
population of France, nor the second Hundred Years War, which
almost annihilated the French Crown, could make a dent in its

influence. It was during this century that Marco Polo dictated the first account of his voyages, *Devisement du monde*–in French rather than Italian.

How exactly did Françoys emerge? In the nineteenth century the French linguist Gaston Paris popularized the idea that Françoys was derived from the dialect of Paris; he called it Francien. He believed that this language had taken precedence over all the other Romance dialects because it was the language of the king, and that it had evolved straight into French. It was a seductive theory, taught by generations of linguists, but it turned out to be only half true. In fact, there is no proof that a Francien dialect ever existed.

But there is some truth to Gaston's Paris theory. Paris produced a *scripta,* that is, a writing system, developed to help speakers of the various dialects in the king's domain understand each other. Paris was at the crossroads of four important *langues d'oïl* idioms: Norman, Picard, Champenois and Orléanais. All of these dialects were mutually intelligible, but over time the speakers simply fused the distinctions into a single interregional dialect called Françoys, which became *Français* as the accent changed. By the twelfth century, writers from the regions around Paris–Picardy, Wallonie, Normandy, Champagne and Orléans–were making a conscious effort to eliminate dialectal characteristics in their writing so they could be understood by a larger number of people. However, regional influences did not disappear all at once. For example, Béroul's *Tristan et Iseut* (*Tristan and Isolde*) was the work of a Norman-speaking *trouvère* (a troubadour of the north), whereas Chrétien de Troyes's *Romans de la table ronde* (*Stories of the Round Table*) clearly shows accents of Champagne. Yet their writing shows they purposefully blurred dialectal differences. It was not the last time in the history of French that a group of writers would take the lead in hammering out the language.

According to the French lexicographer Alain Rey, by the twelfth century this *scripta*—which Gaston Paris called Francien—already existed in an oral form among the *lettrés* (men and women of letters). But Francien took much longer to become a mother tongue. Somewhere between the beginning and the end of the second Hundred Years War (1337–1453), a significant part of the urban population of Paris had acquired a sort of common language they called Françoys, and each generation was transmitting more of this tongue to its children. Year after year its vocabulary widened beyond words for trade and domestic life. After millions of informal exchanges at all levels of society over centuries, this *scripta* finally became a common mother tongue.

At the beginning of our research, Jean-Benoît travelled to the island of Jersey, a mere sixteen kilometres off the coast of Normandy in the English Channel. The island is a kind of pastoral dreamscape, with small trails criss-crossing a beautifully unassuming countryside of green vales, medieval castles and Celtic stone monuments. At low tide its surface area extends to a grand total of fourteen by ten kilometres. A dependency of the British Crown, Jersey is a tax haven that harbours five times more foreign capital than Monaco. Like Monaco, it won this role thanks to a combination of handy location, beautiful scenery and unusual historical circumstances. Amazingly, over the centuries this tiny island has managed to retain its autonomy: it's not even considered a part of the European Union. It has managed to hold on to an ancient Anglo-Norman law system that dates back a thousand years, and that financiers and the wealthy find particularly well adapted for sheltering their money.

But Jean-Benoît was there to see—actually, to hear—another remarkable historical relic: the Jèrriais language. The island's English-speaking majority today calls it "Norman

French." To an untrained ear, the language sounds like mispronounced French, but it is effectively a tongue of its own, one of the last surviving examples of the old Norman dialect—one of the source languages of French—that was exported to England in the eleventh century. Jèrriais has its own phonetics, syntax and lexicon. One of its most striking features is its use of the *th* sound, which is common in English but nonexistent in standard French. For words such as *father, mother* and *brother,* Jèrriais speakers say *paithe, maithe* and *fraithe,* rather than the French *père, mère* and *frère.*

Jean-Benoît spent three days with Geraint Jennings, a member of the Société Jèrriaise, an organization dedicated to preserving the language. Geraint spoke in Jèrriais and Jean-Benoît answered in Québécois French—probably much the way such conversations took place between speakers of different dialects around Paris seven centuries ago. In fact, roughly three-quarters of the vocabulary and grammar of French and Jèrriais overlap, which gives the two languages more in common than there is between French and Haitian Creole, for example. For a francophone with a good ear and tolerance for variation, most of the conversation was intelligible, although Jean-Benoît had to ask a few *tchestions* (questions) to clear up some possible *méprînses (méprises,* misunderstandings). Geraint showed Jean-Benoît the island and introduced him to mayors, farmers, business people and church singers. After three days of this Jean-Benoît hardly needed any *aîgue (aide,* help) to find his *c'mîn (chemin,* way) through Jèrriais grammar and vocabulary.

Nowadays Norman is spoken in only three other places: the nearby island of Guernsey and the Contentin Peninsula and Pays de Caux (near Fécamp) in Normandy. In Jersey and Guernsey it is spoken with an English accent, in France with a French accent. Only 2,764 speakers of Jèrriais are left in Jersey, or less than three percent of the island's population—and only 110 use it on a daily basis. As a result, Jèrriais is confined to a primarily rural area around the parishes of St. Ouen and St. Martin, although it is possible to hear it spoken at the market in the capital of St. Helier. By a process that is well-known to sociolinguists, the speakers of the language have sheltered themselves by confining their language to rural traditions, the same process that enabled Cajuns living in rural Louisiana to hold on to their French. This is why Jèrriais is best used for discussions about *vâques* (*vaches*, cows), *pouaîssons* (*poissons*, fish) and *chevrettes* (*crevettes*, shrimp).

Until about a century ago Jèrriais was still part of the modern world, but the language has simply not kept up with the times. Geraint Jennings is conscious that Jèrriais's days may be numbered, and he is working hard to adapt the language to modern realities. As *maître-paître* (webmaster) of his association, he took the initiative of pulling the *souôthie* (*souris*, mouse) out of its hole and adding it to the vocabulary of computers. These improvements are regarded as controversial in a community that has survived because it has let the world pass it by.

Northern Romance dialects, or *langues d'oïl*, fused into Françoys through meetings such as Jean-Benoît's in Jersey, where people "traded" pronunciations and grammar. From studying poetry, linguists can tell that Françoys had developed its particular sound by the beginning of the fifteenth century—emphasis was disappearing from words or moving to the ends of words or sentences. The Latin system of cases had all but disappeared, and the sentence had taken on its standard order of subject-verb-object. The S and Z had changed functions—instead of marking the subject and object cases, they were used interchangeably to indicate the plural. The final E indicated the feminine gender in writing. And French had a complete set of articles (*le, la, un, une*), pronouns (*le mien, le tien*), possessive articles (*mon, ton, son*) and demonstratives (*ceci, cela, ce, cette*). The French language also began to distinguish between the informal form of "you"—*tu*—and the formal *vous*—which is called *tutoiement* and *vouvoiement* (*tu*-saying and *vous*-saying). Old diphthongs and triphthongs such as *au* and *eau*, whose vowels all used to be pronounced, were already fusing into a single O sound. And people were beginning to use inversion to ask a question, although they still hesitated between *veut-il?* and *veut-y?* for "do you want?" They also began to ask questions using the phrase *est-ce que* (equivalent to the English "does" or "do" in questions).

The spelling of French evolved dramatically during this period. Only Latin had a clear written code at the time, and the business of expressing vernacular sounds in writing was very new. This was not easy in the case of French, which used only the twenty-three letters of classical Latin (no J, U or W) to reproduce about forty sounds. The pronunciation of about twenty consonants and twenty vowels differed from one period to another and from one place to another. Until the twelfth century the writing of French had been very phonetic. In such a system, *vit* could mean either "eight" or "he lives," and *vile* was either "oil" or "city." This was fine when only a few people read and wrote and when writing was not vital in day-to-day life, but that changed as the government and business grew. Suddenly, writing inconsistencies were creating misunderstandings, disputes and litigation.

This was why the *lettrés*, primarily notaries and clerks, started introducing unpronounced letters to distinguish words. H was a popular one—they decided to add it to *vile* and *vit*, so "oil" and "eight" came to be written *hvile* and *hvit* to distinguish them from *vile* (city) and *vit* (he lives). Latin etymology was an important source of new letters. That's why a G was added to *doi* and *vint*, which became *doigt* (finger), from *digitus* and *vingt* (twenty) from *viginti*. Since *chan* could mean "field" or "song," it became *champ* (field), in imitation of the Latin *campus*, and *chant* (song), in imitation of *cantus*. This re-Latinization of French was partly the product of the snobbery of clerks, notaries and scholars, who thought that by adding Latin letters to French they would give it more dignity. However, they were not very coherent or consistent about it. To distinguish the number six from *si* (if), they added an X to make *six*, which conformed to the Latin *sex*. While they were at it, they added an X to *di* (ten), although this had no relation to the Latin *decem*. Some of these changes affected the pronunciation of words— such as *six* and *dix*, now pronounced with an S sound at the end to render the X, whereas before they used to be pro- nounced *see* and *dee* (linguists call this process orthographism).

Linguists know that by 1265 people were speaking Françoys in the modern sense. The language by this time was distinct from the dialects that had formed it, and it was a mother tongue being transmitted to children as they grew up, not a mere lingua franca. Françoys by this time was also regarded as superior to the other dialects, both socially and politically. That's one reason why the German aristocracy began learning Françoys in the fourteenth century. However, the spread of this new dialect did not mean the end of the other dialects. Picard, Norman, Champenois and Orléanais continued to be widely used for a couple more centuries before they began to wane. But like Occitan, the dialects were progressively relegated to the status of patois as their social sta- tus eroded, until—as with Jèrriais—their vocabulary stopped keeping up with the times.

Until the sixteenth century French had spread because, in many ways, it was the language of power. But in the sixteenth century this relationship changed, or rather, it was updated. A new kind of king decided to put French to work, not just to expand his own power, but also to build a state. In doing so he made French the official language of the largest and most powerful country in Europe. And he created a relationship between the French State and language that has lasted to this day.

Chapter 2 ~

IN FRENCH AND NOT
OTHERWISE

FRANÇOIS I WAS A RADICAL departure from the two meek
and unimposing kings who had preceded him. Almost two
metres tall, a bon vivant and an excellent hunter, he was
crowned King of France in 1515, at the age of twenty. His reign
began like a crack of thunder, with a military victory against the
"invincible" Swiss mercenaries in Marignano, Italy. While he
inaugurated the modern age of warfare by using artillery,
François still led his charging cavalry like a medieval king, and
even had himself knighted on the battlefield after the victory.
This mixture of chivalric values and modern ideas sparked in
Europe a fascination with and admiration for French kings that
would last until the French Revolution.

François's reputation also spread thanks to his penchant
for sumptuous feasts, but even more important was his Court,
which he filled with *lettrés,* poets and artists. He was a great
lover of the arts, one of the greatest France has ever known,
easily on a par with Louis XIV. Greatly inspired by the Italian
Renaissance, throughout his reign he was bent on modernizing
France and making it a haven of sophistication and refinement. His contribution to the French language was enormous.
François I was the first French king to link language specifically
with the State, a relationship that remains one of the most striking features of French to this day. And, perhaps more important, François's cultural policies helped France—and the French
language—gradually dispense with Latin once and for all.

We visited one of the Renaissance castles that François I built in Villers-Cotterêts, now a sleepy industrial town 80 kilometres north of Paris. The castle was transformed into a retirement home decades ago and, unlike other famous castles François built in the Loire Valley, this one looks rather shabby today. Weeds litter the courtyard and one wing is entirely boarded up. The town of Villers-Cotterêts does its best to honour the memory of writer Alexandre Dumas, author of *The Three Musketeers* and *The Count of Monte Cristo,* who was born here. But any advertising of the significance of the castle is left to a small plaque at its entrance.

As we read on the plaque, it was here, in August 1539, that François I signed the Ordinance of Villers-Cotterêts. This document is often cited as a founding act of the French language. However, the Ordinance was not really *about* language. Its title, *Ordonnānces royaulx sur le faict de iustice (Royal Ordinance on the Act of Justice)*, makes that pretty clear: Its purpose was to give the monarchy more power to organize and administer French society. And it would do so by restricting the power of the clergy to religious matters.

At the time, the Catholic Church, under the central authority of the Pope, was better organized and in some ways more influential and more powerful than many states in Europe. The French king could muster an army and had six thousand civil servants working for him, but this was no match for the army of clerics that ran day-to-day affairs in France. The Church administered canon law, ran tribunals, even delivered the mail. Its clerics not only presided over moral issues, they also dictated the behaviour of kings. Kings would abide by the Church, and if they challenged it, the Church favoured their opponents.

François I understood the threat of the Church better than his predecessors. Absolutism had been a growing trend in

France, but he took it to a new level. A mere week after he was crowned, he coined the motto that French kings would live by for the next three centuries: *Car tel est notre plaisir* (For such is our pleasure). François, the first king to be called *Votre majesté* (Your Majesty), was determined to push the State into the Church's realm and to extend the State's control over French territory. He established his own postal system and he created the Trésor de l'épargne (Royal Treasury), which centralized tax revenues and established a tax collection system throughout France that would help fill the royal coffers and, among other things, finance his campaigns in Italy.

For François, the Ordinance of Villers-Cotterêts was a way of reducing the power of the Church and increasing his own. For the first time the State would set the rules for how officials would be sworn in, how oaths would be made, how witnesses would be heard in court and how judgements would be ruled and enforced. According to the Ordinance, the Church could no longer challenge secular judges. The Ordinance allowed the clergy to keep registers of births, marriages and deaths, but it stipulated that all those documents had to be countersigned by a notary.

So how was language affected? Two of the 192 articles in the Ordinance, numbers 110 and 111, stated that from that moment, all rulings and administrative documents would be produced *"en langage maternel françoys et non autrement"* ("in the French mother tongue and not otherwise"). The "otherwise" referred primarily to Latin, the language of the Church. From here on, all magistrates, clerks and functionaries working in French lands were instructed to use French in official documents. Trials would be carried out and verdicts delivered in French, not Latin. This attack on Latin explains the use of the term *mother tongue* in reference to French. In sixteenth-century linguistics, "mother tongue" is the language spoken at home, as opposed to the *langage paternel* (father's tongue), which here was Latin, the language of the Church (the term *vernacular* appeared in French only in 1765).

With the language articles François solved two problems. First, he reduced the use of Latin, and with it the influence of the Church in legal affairs. But he also put himself in a neutral position between the Protestants and the Catholics. Religious tensions were so acute in sixteenth-century France that subjects declared themselves Catholic or Protestant before any other allegiance. François knew that, to be king of all the French, he couldn't just be king of the Catholics. A considerable part of the aristocracy was converting to Protestantism at the time— including two of his own kin. Protestants rejected Latin and encouraged vernacular languages, both as a refusal of Rome and to reach out to the lower classes. By rejecting Latin and encouraging the use of the French vernacular, François I knew, the Ordinance would appease them.

But Latin wasn't the only target. The Ordinance was also directed at the galaxy of Romance and non-Romance languages that were still being spoken in France. By forbidding official procedures to be performed or official documents to be written in any other idiom than French, François boosted the power of his own functionaries and reduced the power of the counts, dukes and other nobles who were still running France.

The Ordinance did not include penalties for people who did not respect it—the King had no way of enforcing them all over his territory anyway. There certainly was some tacit resistance, but historians on the whole agree that the kingdom accepted it, even though it was never fully applied (as we show in chapter 6, administrators at the time of the French Revolution were still using local languages). The grammarian Pierre de la Ramée (1515–72), known as Petrus Ramus, recorded an amusing anecdote about a delegation of deputies from the

Parliament of Provence who travelled to Paris to convince the King to let them keep using Provençal. The King refused to hear their case in any language other than French, so the delegates spent months learning enough French to make their case. When they came before the King again, he ridiculed them for arguing their case against French *in French*, and sent them back to Provence.

Did the Ordinance help the French language spread? Most historians say it probably didn't have much impact. French had been the language of power for centuries by that time and was spreading on its own. In Brittany, courts had been using French since the eleventh century; it was declared the official language in 1260. In a study on the development of French, Professor Serge Lusignan of the Université de Montréal examined charters copied in France's official registers between 1285 and 1380, and found an important shift in language use in the late 1320s. In 1328 eighty percent of charters were written in Latin. Two years later, eighty percent of them were written in French. (The process was not exactly linear. In 1350 charters were once again being written in Latin; then, ten years later, French returned and was used in the majority of charters copied. No one has an explanation for this, but the trend towards French continued.) The Toulouse Parliament began using French in the early 1400s. In Bordeaux, French replaced Gascon for notary acts in 1444. So by the time of François I, people who wanted power knew they needed French.

Was the French language ready for such an important role? Interestingly, the original text of the Ordinance, as well as the works of other writers of the period, shows that French had taken on most of its modern characteristics by this time. Written examples of sixteenth-century French are hard to read because they use Gothic characters, but the syntax of the language was distinctly French, not Romance. People did not write *cort li roy,* but *la cour du roy* (the king's court). Demonstrative articles such as *cette* or *celle* (this, that) were common—even if people still said *cestui* instead of *celui* (this one). Still, a few confusing matters remained; for example, plurals were indicated by both S and Z—people were still not sure which to use. As in Spanish, if the subject was obvious from the verb ending, pronouns were often dropped; so, for example, *nous voyons* (we see) appeared as just *voyons*. But otherwise, it was modern French—or at least a form intelligible to today's readers.

In some ways the Ordinance of Villers-Cotterêts was not as important to French as other things that François I did to promote the language. Charles de Gaulle's obsession with France's grandeur, Léopold Sedar Senghor's vision of the Francophonie, Pierre Trudeau's Canadian-style official bilingualism, René Lévesque's French-language charter, Jacques Chirac's incantations about the "cultural exception"—all of these contain echoes of François's work. He was the first French king to create a policy for the promotion of culture and to link it specifically to the French language.

Making France a cultural leader in Europe was no small task. At the time France was known for its rich lands, strong military power and religious influence, but the French themselves were regarded as a rather crude and coarse lot. François I may have exhausted the French treasury with endless military campaigns in Italy, but through them he brought the Italian Renaissance to France—starting with Leonardo da Vinci and some of his paintings in 1516. By marrying his son Henri to the Florentine noblewoman Catherine de' Medici, he also brought Italian cuisine to France; she brought her own cohort of Italian cooks, who set a new cooking standard for France. More than any king before him, François welcomed musicians, painters, writers and sculptors to his Court; he encouraged them to innovate, pretended to consult them on important matters and gave them lots of work. He launched an architectural frenzy in France by commissioning eight new castles along the Loire River. He renovated the Louvre palace, which had until then been just a fortress with a dungeon, and he built the Hôtel de ville (City Hall) in Paris. In one of his castles, Fontainebleau, he pushed artists to develop new styles and techniques, including the first erotic representations of the human body in French art, which were widely circulated, thanks to the printing press and the technique of engraving. Through that whole process he raised the profile of his countrymen immensely in Europe.

He also raised France's intellectual stature. François was determined to impress the Humanists, a group of influential thinkers who were in the process of forming the first non-religious, pan-European intellectual elite. Inspired by Italian thinkers, who were in turn inspired by classical Greek literature, the Humanists emphasized human experience over religious and scientific dogma. François founded the Collège royal—today called the Collège de France—where six royal readers taught Greek, Hebrew and mathematics, disciplines the conservative Sorbonne refused to teach. And this teaching was free and open to all. The royal readers were independent of the University of Paris and sheltered from the religious tribunals that rejected everything new.

The Church was so hostile to novelty that it refused to teach Greek. So François I created the Imprimerie royale to publish Greek classics. He also unified his book collections in a royal library, which he opened to thinkers and writers. He even wrote some two hundred poems, beginning a line of artist-kings whose spiritual descendants would include everyone from Louis XIV, a ballet dancer, to Charles de Gaulle, a gifted writer, Georges Pompidou, a connoisseur of modern art, and Jacques Chirac, a collector of primitive art. Renowned novelist and essayist André Malraux was de Gaulle's minister of cultural affairs. Before he became prime minister, foreign affairs minister Dominique de Villepin published an 822-page book of poetry while defending France's position on Iraq at the United Nations (in the eyes of the American media, he's never quite lived down either endeavour). In a way, all of them were merely following an old custom among French statesmen (and now women).

Although François's interest in culture was sincere, he didn't encourage art just for art's sake. It was all part of a carefully designed strategy to influence nascent European public opinion and to compensate for France's weakness compared to the Holy Roman Empire, which controlled Spain, Austria, the Netherlands and their colonies. Did it work? We can't say, but Erasmus, one of the principal Humanist thinkers, often cited François I as an example of a *roi d'élite* (elite king). The English king Henry VIII tried to impress the Humanists with the same strategy. Although Henry was much better read than François, he made the mistake of murdering Thomas More, the author of *Utopia,* after he opposed Henry's break with the Catholic Church; the move was a public relations disaster that didn't hurt the growing influence of French.

While François I ardently promoted French, he did nothing to regulate it. The French of the sixteenth century was not the orderly language it would become in the next century. Its vocabulary was expanding rapidly as French borrowed from other Latin-based vernaculars, including Spanish and, most important, Italian. French picked up and integrated as many as two thousand Italian words, such as *arcade, balcon* (balcony), *concert, cavalerie* (cavalry), *infanterie* (infantry) and *bizarre.* The result was a cornucopia of terms from regional and foreign languages.

For modern readers, the most surprising aspect of sixteenth-century French is its casualness. Most French speakers today, especially the purists, assume that French was born clear and uniform, but until the seventeenth century the language had none of the orderly precision for which it would be famous in centuries to come. During the baroque period, French was indeed baroque. Writers of François I's era treated French like a buffet dinner, helping themselves to words from regional dialects and foreign languages, creating new words as it suited them, using verbs as nouns and basically serving up the language any way they pleased. This large-scale creativity and inventiveness gave writers a verve and a vigour that would never be matched once the cult of *bon usage* (correct usage) took hold in the next century.

François Rabelais (c. 1494–1553) is perhaps the best example of the unbridled creativity of this period. Rabelais, who signed his first books with the anagram Alcofribas Nasier, was a doctor and a former monk who devoted his life to humorous writing—his motto was "*Le rire est le propre de l'homme*" ("Laughter is unique to man"). A true Renaissance man, Rabelais hated superstition and the rigid scholastic teaching of universities, especially the Sorbonne. He published his thoughts in the vernacular so he could reach the greatest possible number of readers. His five-book cycle of the "very horrifying" adventures of the giant Gargantua and his no less "terrible" son Pantagruel is in great part a thinly disguised attack on the Church and the university. As he writes in chapter 8 of *Pantagruel*, "*Je voys les brigans, les boureaulx, les avanturiers, les palefreniers de maintenant plus doctes que les docteurs et prescheurs de mon temps.* (I see brigands, executioners, adventurers and grooms who are more learned than the savants and the preachers of my time.)" He thought the basic rule for monks should be "*Fais ce que veux*" ("Do what you will"). No surprisingly, his five books were all condemned by the Sorbonne.

Though Rabelais's works became classics of French literature, there was nothing classical about them. He freely invented vocabulary, experimented with sentence structure and new
phrases, and adopted foreign words into his writing. In the
scope of his vocabulary and the liberties he took, Rabelais had
more in common with Shakespeare than with later French
writers such as Corneille and Racine. Like Shakespeare, Rabelais
can be difficult to read, not only because his writing is vulgar
even by the standards of the time, but also because his inventiveness knows no bounds. The fourth book of the adventures
of Pantagruel, for example, tells about battles against *andouilles*
(sausages). The overall effect is just short of psychedelic. Like
Shakespeare, Rabelais coined a number of words and lasting
expressions, from *quintessence* and *dive bouteille* ("divine bottle"),
to the racy *"faire la bête à deux dos"* ("make the beast with two
backs," or copulate).

Rabelais owed his success in part to a new technological
innovation that was fuelling the literary activity of his day: the
printing press, invented in Strasbourg in the 1430s. The invention of printing coincided with an abrupt increase in the urban
elites of France, and the relative prosperity of the Renaissance
spawned a middle-class hunger for books that grew throughout
the century. Previously, knowledge could only be acquired by
studying in a monastery or (if you were rich) by hiring a pre-
ceptor who had been trained in one. The availability of books
created a kind of nouveau riche attitude towards the written
word: People didn't need to learn Latin anymore; they could
acquire knowledge by buying books. Naturally this boosted the
use of French. In 1501 only one in ten books published in
France was written in French; by 1575, almost half were.

The rise of the printing press also coincided with the rise
of Protestantism. As a rule, Protestants preferred vernacular
languages to Latin, the language of the Catholic Church. Unlike

the Church, they encouraged people to read the Bible, which
was translated into French in 1530 and 1541. Protestant theologian
Jean Calvin wrote religious treatises in French. Many Lutheran
books were translated into French between 1520 and 1540, and
after 1550, French was considered the language of the Protestant
Church in France. Geneva, Amsterdam and cities in Flanders
that were beyond the reach of religious or royal censorship
became refuges for French-language printers. Over the next two
centuries a considerable proportion of the French urban elite
flirted with Protestantism—a phenomenon that would one day
spread French across Europe.

All this activity had an impact on spelling and grammar. It
was printers who drove the sixteenth-century effort to give
French rules and standards. The business of turning sounds into
written words in French was still relatively new, and spelling and
grammar were progressing by trial and error. Apostrophes were
seldom marked and the article was not separated from the
word; for example, *l'esclaircissement* (the explanation) was written
lesclaircissement. J and U were so novel that most people had not
yet decided whether they were new letters in their own right or
just fancy ways of writing I and V: A word such as *ajouter* (to
add) was written *adiouter.* And most writers used U and V indis-
criminately, so that *oeuvre* (work) read *oeuure.* Until well into the
seventeenth century there were half a dozen different spellings
for the verb "to know": *connoistre, connaistre, cognoistre, cognaitre,
congoitre* and *congnaitre.*

Printers sought concise forms as a means of cost reduc-
tion. In the 1530s Geoffroy Tory, France's royal printer, became
famous for his work in systematizing the French language. In
his book *Champfleury* he promoted the use of accents and the
apostrophe. Keeping costs in mind, he also worked to replace
Gothic characters with roman letters, which were more com-
pact, using up less space on the printed page. The process did

not happen overnight. The S was written as ∫ well into the seventeenth century. Accents were beginning to be introduced into the texts of that time, and Tory promoted the *accent aigu*, as in é (first used in 1530), the *tréma* (as in ë, ï and ö) and the *cedilla*, as in *ça* (it). *Boutique* was written *boutiq̄*. There were still wide graphical variations from text to text, and even within texts; for example, e sometimes appeared as ¢. If one added in all the possible variations, the sentence *"Je suis le sieur"* ("I am the sire") could have been written *"I¢ ∫vi∫ l¢ ∫i¢vr."*

This movement towards systematizing language obviously called for spelling rules. And this forced the question, Would French have phonetic or etymological spelling? In some modern languages today, such as Spanish and Arabic, spellings are phonetic. English and French are both notable for having maintained etymological spellings (that is, based on historic forms of the words), a trend that dates back to the twelfth century in the case of French. In some cases spellings conform to sounds; in others, they reflect the history of the word. This explains why, as writer Bill Bryson points out in *The Mother Tongue*, there are fourteen ways to write the sound *sh* in English. Phonetically, *sure* and *attention* would be spelled *shur* and *atenshun*, but English speakers like to see the history of the word in its spelling. This is why French spellings, like English spellings, make little sense. Even German, with its complex grammar, is much more phonetic than either French or English.

When French printers started attacking the problem of spelling, they had very few models to follow; the only defined languages at the time were Latin, Greek, Hebrew and Arabic. Some printers represented the sounds *in*, *an*, *on* and *un* as ī, ā, ō and ū —not a bad idea. The word *champs* (field) was written *chā*. It could have worked if printers had agreed on standards. But they tended to stick to their own coding systems and used accents in extremely varied ways. One can only assume that each printer's readers got accustomed to his system and that the printers then feared alienating their customers and losing business if they changed (somewhat like early computer makers, who developed languages and operating systems that could be used only by their specific machines, a problem that for some reason took forty years to solve). It took French printers roughly the entire sixteenth century to get rid of variations in spelling and accents, and it wasn't until French grammar books started appearing that real standards took shape.

Besides, old habits die hard, and etymological spellings were already well-established among the *lettrés,* who were the primary consumers of books. Grammarians Jacques Peletier du Mans and Louis Maigret proposed making French spelling more phonetic in their respective books, *Dialogue de l'ortografe et de prononciations françoèze* (*Dialogue of French Spelling and Pronunciations*) and *Tretté de la grammere françoeze* (Treatise on *French Grammar*). While the innovations they proposed all made sense, they were never accepted. Over the next centuries there were several other attempts to make French spellings more phonetic, but they also failed. The reforms would perhaps have taken root if French had had fewer literate speakers and little tradition to speak of. But etymological spelling had already become the norm, and a *norme* is always very difficult to change. It took the Spanish language academy over a century and a half to make their language fully phonetic.

Grammar, previously the domain of monks and royal scribes, became a subject of study on its own during the sixteenth century. Like François I, grammarians (who were often printers) were obsessed with Latin; their chief motivation was not so much to define French as to show how French was distinct from Latin and Italian. The first real grammar of the French language was actually written by an Englishman, in Gothic letters. In 1530 John Palsgrave presented *Lesclarcissement de la langue Françoyse*—a book describing the multiple forms of French words and the grammatical structure of the language—to King Henry VIII and his daughter Mary, who was no doubt a victim of the Renaissance fashion for learning foreign languages. Twenty years later, Louis Maigret published the first grammar in France, his *Tretté de la grammere françoeze*. Dozens of grammars followed but, until the end of the century, spelling and grammar variation was still the rule in French. In fact, French essayist Michel de Montaigne (1522–90) used four different spellings for *à cette heure* (at this time): *à cett'heure, astheure, asteure* and *asture.*

It's hard to imagine a time when French writers were uncertain about the legitimacy and importance of their language, but that was the case in the sixteenth century. French was considered appropriate for vulgar (that is, popular) writing or for old medieval poetic forms such as rondeaux or madrigals, but not for "higher" forms of writing, higher learning or the sciences, which were still the exclusive domain of Latin. While François I didn't regulate French in any way, his policies did legitimize the efforts of the many artists, poets, savants and printers who were trying to dump Latin and make French prestigious by inserting it into the language of state administration, universities and spheres of higher learning such as medicine and poetry.

In some ways writers led the way in this movement. The most militant anti-Latin lobby in France was a group of poets originally called the Brigade who were soon to choose a more poetic name: La Pléiade. They were up-and-coming writers who wanted to position themselves as a literary avant-garde. Their manifesto, *Déffence et illustration de la langue Françoyse* (*Defence and Illustration of the French Language*), was an indictment of Latin in favour of French. It was published in 1549, ten years after the publication of the Ordinance of Villers-Cotterêts. Signed by the poet Joachim Du Bellay, it begged poets to use French for the new-found forms of classic Greek and Latin literature—the ode, the epistle, the elegy, and comedy and tragedy (these were, of course, very old forms, but they were only just being rediscovered after having been forgotten for more than a thousand years). In a chapter titled "Exhortation to Frenchmen," Du Bellay wonders, "Why are we so hard on ourselves? Why do we use foreign languages as if we were ashamed to use our own? . . . Thou must not be ashamed of writing in thy own language." The debate is surprisingly similar to the twentieth-century one in which French musicians wondered if it was possible to make rock 'n' roll in their own language.

François I's policies definitely added weight to the case made by Du Bellay and the Pléiade poets. While Du Bellay's *Déffence* was in many ways a squabble between poets over their art, it also contained a program for the promotion of French in science and art. This influenced a generation of writers to seek originality in language rather than in style. As a result, metaphors and similes multiplied. Using Bacchus, the Greek god of wine, as a symbol for partying and high living was no longer enough. The historian Ferdinand Brunot, author of the monumental twenty-six-volume *Histoire de la langue française des origins à nos jours* (*History of the French Language from Its Origins to the Present Day*), written at the beginning of the nineteenth century, found no fewer than a hundred far-fetched expressions that were being used at the time around the idea of Bacchus, including *triomphateur indien* (Indian victor), *cuisse-né* (thigh-born) and *beaucoup-formes* (many forms).

The professed leader of the Pléiade, Pierre de Ronsard, gained acclaim as "the prince of poets and the poet of princes." Ronsard is famous for developing the alexandrine, a twelve-foot verse form that became the canon of French poetry—

French required longer verses because some of its features, such as the articles (which didn't exist in Latin), added extra syllables. Another member of the Pléiade, Antoine de Baïf, went as far as creating a new, fifteen-foot verse form called the *baïfin*. The freedoms the Pléiade poets took were very similar to those that Rabelais employed in the lowly art of humorous prose. They spent the next thirty years applying their program, developing the language in sometimes very imaginative ways. From the noun *verve* (eloquence) they derived a verb, *verver*, and an adverb, *vervement*. They wanted people to use verbs as nouns—to write *l'aller* (going), *le chanter* (singing), *le vivre* (living), *le mourir* (dying).

In spite of the Ordinance of Villers-Cotterêts and Du Bellay's *Déffense*, Latin remained an important language in sixteenth-century France, especially in education and culture. But things were changing, as the career of Michel de Montaigne shows. Montaigne was the son of a fishmonger turned nobleman who lived in Périgord, east of Bordeaux, who wanted to consolidate his new rank through the proper education of baby Michel. Normally the younger Montaigne's mother tongue would have been Gascon, a *langue d'oc* spoken in Aquitaine. But when he started to speak, his father hired a German tutor, giving him orders to speak to the child only in Latin—in fact, the whole household used Latin. As a result of his intensive immersion program, the young Michel de Montaigne spoke fluent Latin at age six—a skill that left him bored for the rest of his school years while his schoolmates struggled to catch up with him. While rare, Montaigne's Latin immersion remained the ideal scenario, and it produced the desired result: social promotion. He grew up to become mayor of Bordeaux and a special agent to King Henri of Navarre, the future Henri IV.

When Montaigne began his literary career, he chose to write neither in Latin nor in Gascon, but in French, creating a whole new genre of literature. Considered one of the leading lights of Renaissance writing, on a par with Machiavelli and Erasmus, Montaigne invented the personal essay. He is the first example of a writer using literary introspection to create a mental portrait of himself. In *Les Essais* (*Essays*), which he published in 1580 at the age of forty-eight, he describes his feelings, his physical appearance, even his bowel movements, and speculates about the merits of love "in the manner of the Greeks." His famous phrase explaining his friendship with the scholar La Boétie—"*Parce que c'était lui, parce que c'était moi*" ("Because it was him, because it was me")—emphasized the new centrality of human experience, and is still frequently quoted. Shakespeare quoted one of his essays ("On Cannibals") in *The Tempest*. Montaigne's approach and writing are so contemporary in style that it is possible to read them in the original without annotations.

But Latin remained the language of scholarly domains such as theology and philosophy. Students caught speaking French at the University of Paris in the 1620s were flogged. In 1637, nearly a century after Du Bellay's manifesto and the Ordinance of Villers-Cotterêts, philosopher René Descartes (1596–1659) was the first to publish a philosophical treatise in French, the famous *Discours de la méthode* (*Discourse on Method*). Descartes sought to unify all knowledge under a single mathematical principle. He invented coordinate geometry, and his contributions to physics methodology and metaphysics were invaluable. The extended preface of his book, which explains his method—based on doubt—is a classic of philosophy; that's where his famous formula "*Je pense donc je suis*" ("I think, therefore I am") appears. Yet, even in the middle of the seventeenth century, Descartes felt he needed to justify his choice of French over Latin, since many erudite circles still regarded French as too vulgar for science:

If I write in French, which is the tongue of my
country, rather than Latin, which is the
tongue of my preceptors, it is because I hope
that those who use their natural and pure
sense of reason will be better judges of my
opinions than those who only believe old
books; and to those who join good sense with
study, whom I prefer to have as judges, they
will not be, I hope, so partial to Latin that
they will refuse to hear my reasonings because
they are expressed in popular language.

Although Descartes switched back to Latin for his next
two philosophical books, *Metaphysical Meditations* and *The
Principles of Philosophy,* he had broken the ice by using French.
In fact, he and his contemporaries had made a major contribution to the language. They had done the groundwork that
prepared for the next stage in the evolution of French: the creation of the Académie française, the French Academy.

Chapter 3

THE DAWN OF PURISM

IN THE SUMMER OF 2004 we headed out on a three-week road trip down the Mississippi River basin to study the history of French colonialism in the area. On our way back from Louisiana, we stopped in Atlanta, Georgia, to attend a convention of the International Federation of Teachers of French. It was a big event, with 1,300 delegates from 115 countries, including government representatives from France, Canada, Quebec and Belgium. To top it all off, the opening lecture of the conference was given by no less than the *secrétaire perpétuel* (permanent secretary) of the French Academy, Hélène Carrère d'Encausse.

In a Chanel-style skirt suit, with a professorial air, Madame Carrère d'Encausse spoke at great length about the continuing urgency of upholding language standards in France. She discussed the Academy's effort to rid the French of *mots mal faits* (poorly made words) and explained recent attempts to reform spelling in France. At least three-quarters of the conference participants came to hear her—a huge turnout—and she flattered her international public by calling them "pioneers of the French language."

The *secrétaire perpétuel* had her detractors, though. She staunchly opposes feminizing titles, a stance that many in the (largely female) audience found hard to swallow. In French there is no neutral gender, and titles are generally masculine. Carrère d'Encausse herself pointedly insists on being called Madame *LE secrétaire perpétuel* rather than *LA secrétaire perpétuelle*.

Still, the furrowed brows in the audience didn't discourage the barrage of praise she received after her speech. When she stepped down from the podium, dozens of teachers—people from as far away as Korea, central Asia and Africa—flocked to have their pictures taken in Carrère d'Encausse's presence. Her star status had nothing to do with her long career, illustrious though it was (she is a specialist of Russian, not French); people were simply thrilled to be in the presence of the head of the French Academy.

This admiration for the French Academy is very old. The seven hundred or so members the Academy has elected over the past four centuries are still referred to as "immortals," even after they are dead. In France the election of a new member of the French Academy—two per year, on average—is covered on the evening news. France has four other academies, for sciences, fine arts, history and humanities, but only the language academy provokes this lasting fascination, both inside and outside France.

Francophones are not the only ones who cherish their language, but among international languages their attitude is unique (except maybe for the case of classical Arabic, to which many Muslims attribute a sacred value). French speakers not only accept the idea that their language should adhere to grammar and spelling standards, but many francophones even refer to their language as a "monument" or a "work of art." Debates about grammar rules and acceptable vocabulary are part of the intellectual landscape and a regular topic of small talk among francophones of all classes and origins—a bit like movies in Anglo-American culture. The French language does evolve, but it's always against the background of this deeply entrenched idea that some French is good and some is not. "*C'est une faute*" ("It's a mistake") and "*Dit-on ceci ou cela?*" ("Should we say this or that?") are such common remarks that few really stop to think of this attitude towards language as a peculiar cultural trait. It all boils down to norms, or, as francophones say, the *norme*. In the back of any francophone's mind is the idea that an ideal, pure French exists somewhere. And that somewhere is, at least symbolically, the French Academy.

Most people assume that the French Academy created language purism, but it was actually the other way around. The term *puriste* first appeared in French in 1586, decades before the Academy's creation. It referred essentially to morals and was a synonym for puritan. Those writers who chose French in the sixteenth century were free spirits who used the language creatively. But all this had started to change by 1625, when the French tongue was being curbed and *puriste* became associated with language correction. The French Academy was created a couple of years later.

The earliest champion of language purism was a poet whose work very few francophones actually read: François de Malherbe (1555–1628). While there are many cases of literary geniuses whose writing shaped entire cultures—Shakespeare, Victor Hugo, Goethe, Cervantes, Dante, to name a few—there are very few instances of a single person influencing the way an entire people think about their language the way Malherbe did. Almost single-handedly he created a conception of language that fifteen generations of authors and readers, teachers and students, writers and speakers, francophones and francophiles have adhered to and wrestled with.

Malherbe was already a middle-aged lawyer when he gained notice on the French literary scene in the early 1600s. He became famous for his mastery of the alexandrine, the twelve-foot verse that was the standard of French poetry and theatre until the Romantic era. *"Et Rose elle a vécu ce que vivent les Roses, / l'espace d'un matin"* ("And Rose, she lived as live the roses, / the space of a morning") is his most famous line of verse—and a favourite at funeral homes.

Although he became the official poet of King Henri IV in 1605, at age fifty, and retained that status under Louis XIII, it was Malherbe's literary criticism, not his poetry, that gained him repute among his contemporaries and turned him into the French language's first real guru. In his criticism Malherbe preached the values of clarity, precision and rigour. He argued that good writing had to be stripped of ornamentation, repetition, archaisms, regionalisms and hyperbole. Malherbe rejected the idea of synonyms; in his view each word should have a definition, and a definition should apply to only one word. Naturally he abhorred the baroque aesthetic of his predecessors, particularly the Pléiade poets Ronsard and Du Bellay. He considered their use of embellishment and flourishes nothing less than absurd. Above all, he detested the idea of creating new words for the sake of it. His famous follower, the grammarian Vaugelas, wrote, "It is not permitted to anyone to make up new words, not even the King!"

As a pastime, Malherbe edited Ronsard's poetry, removing about half the words. His future biographer, Honorat de Racan, once asked him, "Does this mean you approve of the rest?" Malherbe responded by erasing what was left on the page. Most of his ideas about the French language had been penned by 1606, when he wrote his *Commentaires sur Desportes* (*Commentary on Desportes*), a scathing criticism of his contemporary, the poet Philippe Desportes. "Your soup is better than your psalms," he said to poor Desportes. And to those who defended the poet, Malherbe replied, "Out of your mistakes, I will write books longer than your poetry."

Malherbe was quite possibly the biggest and most brazen language snob the world has ever seen. Biographers describe him as a fretful fault-finder who spent his life attacking, both verbally and in writing, every mistake—or what he regarded as mistakes—he could find and anyone who made one. He wanted to banish the word *vent* (wind) because it was a synonym for fart, and *pouls* (pulse) because it sounded like *pou* (louse). He feared no one, and even reproached King Henri's son, the future Louis XIII, for signing his name as "Loys" rather than "Louys," an inconsistency that many courtiers would not have dared point out had they noticed it. Malherbe hated regionalisms to the point that, when asked whether the best word for "spent" was *dépensé* or *dépendu*, he replied that the former was more French, because *pendu* (which also means "hanged") sounded like Gascon, a dialect of southern France. Malherbe once refused to be treated by a certain Doctor Guébeneau because "his name sounded like a dog's name." On his deathbed he was still correcting the language of the woman who was looking after him.

There's no doubt that Malherbe was a tyrant, especially when it came to vocabulary. But where grammar was concerned he was more moderate, seeking a common ground between principles and the reality of how French was being used. It was Malherbe who imposed the idea that the French negative *ne* should be followed by *pas* or *point*. And his ideal of clarity was not just snobbery: Malherbe rejected the hermeticism that Ronsard and his school fostered, on the grounds that poets used a jargon that was accessible only to other poets. He argued that writers should use plain language so they could be more easily understood by a larger number of readers.

Malherbe's doctrine of clarity gained him support from Henri IV. Because of propaganda about Louis XIV (and later, the nineteenth-century French monarchy), people often associate the ideals of clarity, purity and symmetry with the reign of the Sun King. But it was Henri IV, Louis XIV's grandfather, who started the trend. After fifty years of religious wars between Catholics and Protestants, France was exhausted, and

Henri wanted to make a strong break with the reigns of his predecessors. That meant a departure from the baroque aesthetics of Ronsard and the Pléiade poets, and Malherbe's writing seemed to represent a new age.

By 1615 Malherbe was regarded as not only a master of poetry, but also a master of language. He had become so influential that people created their own academies and salons to either refute his ideas or spread them. As a result of his work and that of his disciples, entire segments of French vocabulary—regionalisms, archaisms, synonyms and duplicates—lost currency and virtually disappeared from the mouths of the well-read and the writing of most authors. As historian Ferdinand Brunot put it, before Malherbe it was common to borrow terms from other languages; because of him, it became a mark of ignorance. That standard would last for the next two centuries, and still remains at the root of the debate over anglicisms.

Not all the writers of Malherbe's time agreed with his doctrine. Archaisms were a strong element in Jean de La Fontaine's fables, and regionalisms were an important aspect of Molière's humour. But almost all of the great writers of the time used plain language, making clarity and precision the "ethic" of French. The fables of La Fontaine and the tales of Charles Perrault (the original author of the *Mother Goose Tales, Sleeping Beauty, Bluebeard* and *Cinderella*) were plainly written and accessible. Racine's language is concise almost to the point of being arid. Molière mocked language purism in his famous satire *Les précieuses ridicules,* but his own writing conformed to the new *norme* as Malherbe had articulated it. The power of purism was such that, by 1661, the new expression for good French usage was "*un français châtié*" ("a well-punished French"), an expression that is still current in France.

How did Malherbe's ideal of language purism become so influential while nothing of the sort ever happened in England?

One reason was that few people in France actually spoke fluent French—less than fifteen percent of the population, by some estimates, and mostly among the urban elite. In comparison, English belonged to all classes of society, making it more difficult for an elitist doctrine of language to prevail. In a famous anecdote recounted to his friend the *fabuliste* Jean de La Fontaine, Jean Racine tells of his attempts to get by with French while travelling south. By the time he reached Valence, he wrote, nobody understood him at all. At an inn Racine asked for a chamber pot and was given a heater. "You can imagine," he wrote, "what happens to a sleepy man who uses a heater for his nightly necessities."

Another factor driving language purism was its "modernity." Given how language purism became associated with stifling linguistic conservatism in the nineteenth and twentieth centuries, it is easy to forget that it was once considered progressive. Malherbe's propaganda, with its powerful ethic of clarity and purity, made French the only living language in Europe, besides Italian, that had normative rules comparable to those of the classical languages, Latin and Greek. (The difference was that French was alive, while classical Latin and Greek were dead, and Italian was not nearly as influential as it had been in the previous century.)

The powerful salon culture that would help turn French into a coveted European language was just developing in France at this time. While it would ultimately help spread the language, purism was also an ideal vector for an elitist view of language. Malherbe spawned another lasting trend: the culture of *remarqueurs* or *remarquistes* (commentators). Alone or in groups, the *remarqueurs* made it their life's cause to assess and comment on the quality of French being used in writing and speaking. The most influential of them, who regarded himself as Malherbe's intellectual son, was the grammarian Claude

Favre de Vaugelas (1585–1650). For better or for worse, Vaugelas gave Malherbe's quest for language purity an edge of elitism that has survived the past four centuries virtually intact and remains unique to francophones. Vaugelas's view was that the language spoken *"par la plus saine partie de la Cour et de la ville"* ("by the best members of the Court and the city") should become the standard. He coined the term *bon usage* (correct, or good, usage), which would become the credo of the soon-to-be-created French Academy.

The French Academy was both a creature of Malherbe's purist ideal and the product of a political power struggle going on at the time. The Academy started out as one of dozens of informal clubs in Paris in the early seventeenth century, where small groups of men and women—many of whom were disciples of Malherbe—gathered regularly to discuss language and read their own poetry. The club hosted by Valentin Conrart, a Protestant financier, bookworm and patron of poets, would eventually evolve into the French Academy, but very little is known about its beginnings. The meetings were secret, and no record was kept of them. Conrart's club of nine friends would probably have faded into obscurity if it hadn't attracted the eye of Louis XIII's prime minister, Cardinal Richelieu, in 1634.

Much of the immediate glory of the French Academy is owed to the character of Cardinal Richelieu. Born Armand Jean du Plessis, into a family of high-ranking civil servants, he distinguished himself early by becoming France's youngest bishop—at twenty-two. By age thirty-nine he was Louis XIII's right-hand man, and he would go on to become one of the most powerful and notorious statesmen in French history. Obsessed with building a powerful French state, Richelieu showed a determination, a sense of purpose and an energy that stunned his contemporaries. He dedicated much of his considerable resources to controlling and eliminating anyone or anything that posed a threat to the power of the French monarch, whether inside France or abroad, including Protestants, aristo-crats, foreign powers of all faiths, and even the Papacy. He became the very embodiment of a novel concept formulated in 1609: *la raison d'état* (reasons of state), according to which the State is the ultimate good—justifying many acts from repression of its own citizens to war. Richelieu was taking François I's Ordinance of Villers-Cotterêts one step farther, and it was a mighty step.

Richelieu was a follower of Malherbe, sincerely committed to the French language and genuinely interested in the literary and linguistic undertakings of the time; his close circle of advisors was composed of writers. The first theologian known to have written in French, Richelieu believed strongly in the innate power of words and eloquence. Early in his career he decided he wanted to imitate the Accademia della crusca of Florence, which had defined clear rules for the literary language of Florentine writers. But according to Louis-Bernard Robitaille, author of one of the rare books on the French Academy, the creation of the Academy had more to do with Richelieu's political ambitions. He wanted to stamp out the literary gatherings at the Hôtel de Rambouillet in Paris, a noto-rious hotbed of aristocratic dissidence that he considered a threat to the regime of Louis XIII. Instead of closing down the Hôtel, Richelieu decided to kill off the gatherings by founding a competing salon, giving it the King's stamp of official approval and, in effect, headhunting the best participants from all the other clubs.

Richelieu heard about Conrart's club from an acquain-tance in 1634, but no one knows exactly why he chose it from among the others. He immediately proposed turning the asso-ciation into a public institution. Conrart and his friends were not particularly enthusiastic about the idea, but they eventually came around (it was never easy to say no to the Cardinal). Although the French Academy is almost always presented as Richelieu's brainchild, Conrart and his friends actually drafted its charter on their own. True to the spirit of Malherbe, they defined its purpose as "*nettoyer la langue des ordures qu'elle avait contractées, ou dans la bouche du peuple, ou dans la foule du palais et dans les impuretés de la chicane, ou par le mauvais usage des courtisans*" ("to clean the language of all the filth it has caught, either from the mouth of the people or in the crowd of the court and tribunal or in the bad speech of ignorant courtiers"). Article 24 of the charter stated: "The main function of the Academy will be to work with all possible care and diligence to give clear rules to our language and to render it pure, eloquent and capable of dealing with the arts and sciences."

Other inspired decisions helped build the institution's prestige. Thinking along the lines of the existing Accademia della crusca in Florence (its name literally means "academy of pure bran," an allusion to separating the wheat from the chaff), Conrart's group considered calling their new creation Académie de l'éloquence (Academy of Eloquence). However, they settled on Académie française. The name was both ambiguous and ambitious—it could mean "Academy of French" or "Academy of France." This ambiguity helped give the Academy an aura of authority unrivalled by any other European language academy. That reputation has lasted to this day, to the extent that many people believe it is the only language academy in the world. In fact, it was one of the world's earliest—and greatest—successes in branding.

The early founders also chose a brilliant motto: *à l'immortalité* (to immortality). The expression originally referred to the immortal and divine power of the king, but it long outlived the monarchy. In 1833 the public began to speak of members of the Academy as "immortals," a title still used today. Hélène Carrère d'Encausse is the Academy's thirty-seventh leader, a position designated in the Academy's charter as *secrétaire per-pétuel*. Grandiose as it now sounds, the title simply reflected the fact that the members elected the secretary for life, but it helped contribute to the special aura the Academy took on. Conrart, appointed at thirty-two years old, was both the youngest and the longest-lasting perpetual of them all—he spent forty-one years on the job (the average has been twelve).

The French Academy was one of the first democratic institutions of the *ancien régime*. One needed neither noble origins nor endorsement from a university to be admitted. It was meant to be a company of cultivated men—lords or commoners, religious or lay—who had an interest in language; literary talent was not a prerequisite. The members were authors and poets but also scientists, generals, politicians, bishops and priests. Early members ranged from Jean-Baptiste Colbert, Louis XIV's prime minister, to François Timoléon de Choisy, an abbot who wrote a history of Christianity (but who was more famous among his contemporaries as a transvestite).

The founding of the Academy raised suspicions in the Parlement de Paris (the high tribunal). The *Parlement* was the turf of the old nobility, who resented Richelieu and feared he was creating a competing form of political representation that would reduce their influence. The Academy's literary mission seemed bizarre to them; they were sure Richelieu had a hidden agenda. After the King had approved the French Academy's charter, *Parlement* refused to register it for two and a half years. According to Paul Pellisson, the Academy's earliest historian, Richelieu decided to stage a publicity stunt to convince *Parlement* that his Academy was strictly about language and literature, nothing else. He convinced the Academy to prove his point by publicly criticizing the most famous theatrical hit of the time, *Le Cid*, by

Pierre Corneille. That did the trick, and *Parlement* registered the Academy a month later, though on the condition that Richelieu's creature would never meddle in anything but language.

So, beyond embracing purism, what was the Academy's actual job? The founders gave themselves a mandate to produce a dictionary of "common usage useful in trades and science" as well as a grammar, a rhetoric and a poetic. These were meant to establish standards for vocabulary, grammar, eloquence and rhyming in the French language. Even before the original members began their work in 1639, they realized that the mandate was too ambitious, so they focused their efforts exclusively on the dictionary. But even that objective was quickly watered down when they realized what they were facing. Their original plan had been to define the rules of usage by quoting authors—an onerous task. So instead of tackling the task of reading and studying the important works of the day, they decided just to make up the rules and invent their own examples. They skipped etymology altogether and decided to drop technical and scientific words, focusing on *le bon usage* as defined by Vaugelas. In other words, they defined only the words used by the "best of society." That's how the Academy's dictionary became a dictionary of an ideal sort of French, not the actual language being used. And so it has remained.

One defect of the Academy's membership criteria was that, opinionated though they were, very few academicians were qualified to accomplish their self-proclaimed mandate of cleaning the French language of its filth. The majority of members has never been made up of authors, and real experts such as grammarians (and later, linguists) have always been a rarity. From the beginning the academicians were in essence a bunch of amateurs, and they have always remained so. This has had huge implications for how the Academy operates and what it has been able to achieve.

All through its history the Academy's work on the dictionary has been plagued by incompetence and delays. In 1642 the Academy decided to pay one of its members, Vaugelas himself, to work full-time on the dictionary, hoping to speed up its pace. He knew his business, reaching the letter I before he died in 1650. During the next twenty years the Academy managed to review what Vaugelas had done but did not move ahead. Colbert, who had no tolerance for their slow pace, instructed his chancellor, Charles Perrault, to pay salaries to all the members, hoping to stimulate their work. The rule was that Academy members who were present at the stroke of the meeting hour would be paid. That led to members spending the first half-hour of meetings debating whether the clock was right. Perrault tried to solve that problem by supplying the Academy with a state-of-the-art clock, but the prolonged, sometimes senseless debates persisted and became a staple of Academy folklore. As an example, early Academy member Antoine Furetière recounted an occasion when two members threw books at each other because they couldn't agree about who should belong to a particular committee.

The task of defining a language in a rational way and setting its standards is enormous. It involves choosing words and deciding on their spelling. In some cases words had competing spellings that reflected different pronunciations. The Academy decided that the proper spelling for "asparagus" would be *asperge,* as some people said, rather than *asparge,* as others did; "to heal" would be *guérir* rather than *guarir*; and "cheese" became *fromage* rather than *formage.* However, in other cases, spelling didn't match pronunciation at all. For instance, the S in *beste* (beast) and *teste* (head)—later to be spelled *bête* and *tête*— was not even pronounced.

The Academy's choices tended to be conservative on the

whole; it generally opted for etymology over pronunciation. Why? According to historian Ferdinand Brunot, members of the Academy steered away from phonetic spellings because they were afraid of looking ignorant of the historical roots of a word. But this orientation was also the expression of a class struggle. The lettered class promoted complicated spellings as a way of holding on to power; by making it hard to learn French, they made it harder for anyone outside their class to enter the circles of power.

Delays in the Academy's dictionary project were such that, in 1674, the Academy was given a monopoly from the King for producing a dictionary of *bon usage,* for they feared that more enterprising lexicographers (dictionary makers) might be working behind their backs. And they were right. In 1680 César-Pierre Richelet managed to publish his *Dictionnaire françoys contenant les mots et les choses* (*French Dictionary of Words and Things*). *Le Richelet,* as it came to be known, was the first monolingual French dictionary without references in Latin. A previous landmark in the field, Jean Nicot's *Trésor de la langue française,* published in 1606, still defined one word in ten by using Latin. With twenty-five thousand entries, Richelet's dictionary stands as the prototype of the general dictionary. It included the Court's best language, but also the language spoken by common people, as well as terms taken from science, the trades and technology, and quotations from authors. *Le Richelet* was a great success and became the standard French dictionary of its time—six editions had appeared by 1735. Strangely, the Academy didn't protest Richelet's stepping onto their turf; he had an excellent reputation, since he had created the first dictionary of French rhymes in 1667. And Richelet was sly enough to print his dictionary in Geneva, out of the King's reach.

Another competitor was less fortunate. Antoine Furetière probably began working on his *Dictionnaire universel* in the

1660s, behind the Academy's back, while attending its dictionary meetings the whole time. Furetière disagreed with the Academy's overall approach for a prescriptive dictionary. In his opinion, the French needed a good general *descriptive* dictionary of French as it was used, not a dictionary of ideal French. But instead of trying to change his colleagues' approach, Furetière went underground. Word got out only because he went to the King to get a monopoly to write a dictionary of scientific and technical. terms, with a promise that it would exclude *bon usage,* the Academy's turf. This provoked a rift, especially when it was discovered that Furetière planned to include definitions of *bon usage* after all. The Academy accused him of plagiarism and dragged him into court. Furetière argued, quite sensibly, that he couldn't possibly define technical terms of navigation or chemistry without defining words such as "sea" and "fire," which were part of the vocabulary of *bon usage.* In the end he lost his privilege and the Academy even expelled him, a very rare case. Ostracized and ill, Furetière sold his work to a Dutch publisher; he died in 1688, two years before his dictionary was printed.

Furetière's *Dictionnaire universel* was far superior to that of the Academy. It was one of the greatest achievements of seventeenth-century lexicography and one of the most remarkable intellectual accomplishments of its time. Working alone, he produced the world's first encyclopedic dictionary, with forty-five thousand entries—in less than twenty years. (Compare the achievement of Samuel Johnson, who wrote his English dictionary, published in 1755, with the help of seven lexicographers over a period of seven years.) While many spelling variations remained from the previous century—*français* was still spelled *françoys*—the language of Furetière's dictionary was modern. The definitions are clear, objective and rarely judgemental. He defines the sexual organs in graphic terms, and his definitions of words such as *cul* (ass) and *merde* (shit) have none of the prudishness one would expect from the priest he was. Furetière was interested in all aspects of human activity, including anatomy, medicine, agriculture, the navy and the sciences. His definition of *sucrerie* (sugar mill) distinguishes those of the West Indies from those in Europe. The author even included a novelty: a thematic index that listed words by trade, for readers who were seeking definitions of specific terms used by, say, butchers or shoemakers. But Furetière's reputation was destroyed by the Academy, and no one ever spoke of *Le Furetière* as they did of *Le Richelet* or would later of dictionaries such as *Le Robert* and *Le Larousse*. Furetière's *Dictionnaire universel* did, however, suffer the ultimate tribute of greatness—it was copied, pillaged and imitated, and it ultimately inspired the work of the eighteenth-century Encyclopedists.

Spurred on by the controversy and the looming prospect of ridicule, the Academy finally published *Le dictionnaire de l'Académie française* in 1694, after fifty-five years of work. Even the King could not quite hide his disappointment when it was presented to him. "*Messieurs, voici un ouvrage attendu depuis fort longtemps*" ("Gentlemen, this is a long-awaited work") was all he had to say. The dictionary impressed no one in France. It had only thirteen thousand definitions. Spellings in the Academy dictionary were similar to Furetière's, but definitions were concise to the point of being curt. Man, for instance, was defined as *animal raisonnable* (animal with reason). Woman was "*la femelle de l'homme*" ("the female of man"). The order of entries was generally alphabetical, but many words were classified etymologically, so that *matrice* (women's reproductive organs) came right below *mère* (mother). The Academy's dictionary was sharper on normative comments, including long discussions of usage, such as the proper use of *moy* (me) and *je* (I). It condemned archaic terms with the comment "*Il est vieux*" ("It's old") after the definition. But the omissions were glaring–the Academy almost forgot to include the word *académie,* and left out the word *françoys* until the third edition, in 1740.

Some of the Academy's choices were frankly bizarre. The word *anglais* (English) was missing from every edition, but is expected to appear in the latest edition, slated for the 2010s. This absence is all the more puzzling since *anglais* is the root of accepted terms such as *anglaise* (a dance), *anglican, anglicanisme, angliciser, anglicisme, anglomane, anglophilie, anglophile, anglophobe* and *anglophobie*–all present in the 1935 edition. But it could have been worse: The word *allemand* (German) was actually removed from the 1935 edition (after being included in the 1835 and 1878 editions), though *allemande* (a dance) remained. The real purpose of the Academy's dictionary was to define an ideal French, and even in this it fell short. The purest of the purists regarded it as extremely vulgar because it contained words in bad taste that were used in the marketplace.

In all, the Academy has managed to produce eight editions, with an average of thirty-seven years between them (the ninth edition has been in the works for seventy years now). The only period during which the Academy showed any semblance of real activity was the eighteenth century, when it produced no fewer than four editions. Members of the Academy at that time included Enlightenment thinkers such as Montesquieu, Voltaire, Diderot and d'Alembert. In the spirit of reform, they set out to remodel the dictionary. The 1718 edition re-established alphabetical order, and the 1760 edition modified the spelling of eight thousand of the eighteen thousand words. But things were still slow to improve. "Woman" wasn't promoted to the rank of "female and companion of man" until the sixth edition, in 1835.

It took the Academy 296 years to complete a grammar, which it published in 1935. Meanwhile, the book that would set the standard for French grammar guides was the *Grammaire générale et raisonnée,* published in 1665 by Antoine Arnauld and Claude Lancelot. Hundreds more would be published before the Academy came out with its own. The plans to produce a rhetoric and a poetic never got off the ground. Even the academicians came to recognize that art and expression evolve in unpredictable ways.

We visited the French Academy to try to understand its role in modern French (more on that in chapters 8 and 17) and how the dictionary project had evolved. The Academy is located in the Institut de France, across the Seine from the Louvre, where it shares its offices with four other academies (of sciences, fine art, history and humanities). The baroque-cum-classical-cum-Italianate building is unmistakable, with its curved façade and oval *coupole* (dome)—coupole became the nickname of the Academy's meeting place. After passing through the front gate we were led through a series of corridors where the staff of the Academy have their offices. The seventeenth-century building was designed before the advent of running water, sewage and electricity; with its peeling wallpaper and threadbare carpets, the overall effect—at least in the office area—is shabby chic, at best.

The two great meeting halls and the library were closer to what we were expecting from this prestigious institution; they were furnished with long polished wood tables and high-backed padded chairs arranged with almost geometric perfection. We were struck by the huge oil painting of Cardinal Richelieu on the back wall of the Red Salon, the hall where Academy members meet to discuss the dictionary. In the portrait (a copy) he is standing in a red robe with his usual ramrod posture and piercing gaze, looking awfully serious for someone who's watching over a discussion of grammar rules. But of course, grammar is serious business here.

The Academy has about forty employees, most of whom are secretaries, ushers, bailiffs and guards. It manages about sixty literary awards and a number of grants, and more than a dozen properties, including several large castles. We didn't run into any of the Academy's forty "immortals" while we were there, and were told that they are rarely on the premises. If they do come, it's only on Thursday, the day of dictionary meetings, and many, we were told, are chronically absent.

The reputation—or notoriety—of the French Academy is owed to a misconception. Outside of France it is seen as a kind of language police. In reality the Academy has never passed laws on language use; it has no authority to. The French government has official language terminology committees that make rules about what constitutes acceptable French and what doesn't (more on this in chapter 18). These committees then run their choices by the Academy for rubber-stamping.

The French Academy's main job is still to create a dictionary. Most of the work on the dictionary is done by eight lexicographers at the Academy who prepare lists of words and definitions for the academicians. On Thursdays the immortals debate definitions and decide which words to include in the next edition of the dictionary, its ninth. As Laurent Personne, the cabinet director of the permanent secretary, and his chief lexicographer, Jean-Mathieu Pasqualini, explained, the ninth edition, which was begun in 1935, was delayed by the Second World War and then by the disruptions caused by the Algerian war of 1954–62 and the student riots of May 1968. The Academy essentially did nothing after that until the appointment of Maurice Druon as permanent secretary in 1980. Since then, progress has been surprisingly swift (they were at the letter R as of early 2006). The new edition will double the number of words to forty thousand.

Although the French Academy still has great symbolic value, its dictionary is not well respected as a language resource.

It has never been widely used in France, largely because, with an average of thirty-seven years between each edition, it can't keep up with the times and is often already outdated by the time it's published. The early editions had considerably more success outside France (more on this in chapter 5). The only exception was the sixth edition (1835), which was used as the reference when the French government defined official spellings for its civil service examinations.

Today, the Academy's new website gets about two million hits per year, compared to fifty million for Quebec's Terminology Bank. But in a way, the dictionary is not really the point. As Laurent Personne explained, the real role of the Academy is to preside over the French language, rather like a House of Lords for culture. Sometimes the Academy does act, as when it accepted spelling reforms in the early 1990s. At other times its inaction is conspicuous, as in 1997, when it refused to accept the feminization of titles (more on these two issues in chapter 17). Personne described the Academy as a *"magistrature morale"* (moral magistrate). "We are not there to decide on rules or establish law, but to consecrate usage," he said.

Fuzzy as it sounds, the idea of consecration is actually what the Academy is all about. If a word enters the Academy's dictionary, its use is indeed "consecrated." That doesn't necessarily mean that anyone uses the word—that's not the point. Consecration means that the word is recognized as part of the ideal French that every francophone is supposed to have in the back of his or her mind. In other words, the French Academy is a place to store the French language in its ideal form—a kind of museum of ideal French. In fact, some Academy members even describe themselves as curators of the French language.

In its four-hundred-year history, the French Academy has had little impact on how French is actually used. But the ethic of purism that inspired the Academy's creation would have a major impact on how French evolved over the centuries. Since the seventeenth century, French authors and grammarians have had the objective of clarity in mind, not just to produce a language that is precise, but also to make French comprehensible to as wide a public as possible. The fables of La Fontaine and the fairy tales of Perrault are monuments of that century that are still read today because of the genius of authors who wanted to write for all of humankind. In the eighteenth century the doctrine of purism made it possible for French writers to export their work and spread their influence over the entire European continent (the subject of chapter 5). In fact, most French authors remained obsessed with clarity and precision until the twentieth century.

But first and foremost, this purist ethic shaped how francophones put together their dictionaries. The French lexicographic tradition is far more prescriptive than the English. There is no equivalent in French of the *Oxford English Dictionary*. From its inception, the OED was meant to be a vocabulary collection and a great inventory of archaisms and regionalisms—almost half the words on any given page are no longer used. In comparison, French lexicographers do their spring cleaning regularly so that the language doesn't hold on to words it doesn't need. Ever since Malherbe's time, synonyms, neologisms, regionalisms and archaisms have been weeded out on a regular basis and pushed into obsolescence. Sometimes, however, archaic terms are rescued from limbo and repopularized by an author or public figure. Charles de Gaulle is famous for labelling the May 1968 rioters *la chienlit* (shit-a-bed), resurrecting a sixteenth-century insult that hadn't been heard for centuries.

The logic of French purism since Malherbe has been that each word should have a precise definition; no two words are perfectly synonymous. In Webster's English dictionary the word *tolerate* has a definition. But *put up with* is defined merely as "tolerate," without further explanation. No French dictionary would ever do that. A French dictionary of synonyms goes much further than an English thesaurus, which merely lists the synonyms. It will either give precise definitions for each equivalent, categorize the synonyms as literal, analogous or figurative, or differentiate them in some other way.

The French tradition seems to have convinced everyone that there are fewer words in French than English. A popular statistic of comparison is the *Oxford English Dictionary*'s six hundred thousand entries as compared to *Le Robert*'s hundred thousand. Yet half the vocabulary in the OED is never, or almost never, used. At the time of its creation the OED was meant as an inventory of English words not listed in any other dictionary. In 1987 linguist Henriette Walter disproved the old, false misconception about the paucity of French vocabulary. She simply added 175,000 terms found in literature of the nineteenth and twentieth centuries, plus half a million technical terms, plus a couple of hundred thousand new words created since the 1960s, and came up with a total of 1.2 million different words. And this is a conservative estimate, since it excludes archaic and technical terms that fell out of use before the nineteenth century. Quebec's *Grand dictionnaire terminologique,* created by the Office québécois de la langue française (French Language Commission), lists a million French terms used in two hundred fields of science, industry and technology. According to Sherbrooke University professor Pierre Martel, who is currently working on the first modern dictionary of Quebec French, twenty to thirty thousand new terms are created in French every year "if you consider all regional varieties, all fields of research and all slangs," although, according to Martel, "Most of these terms are short-lived and used by very few people, sometimes as few as half a dozen." The real difference between English and French dictionaries is one of spirit. Because they exclude things such as technical and scientific vocabularies, French dictionaries have fewer words. On the other hand, the definitions are infinitely more precise. If French dictionaries included all words—the way English dictionaries do—the number of entries would be much larger. But they don't, and that's because of the principle of *bon usage,* according to which only words that are used (or deemed useful) find their way in; the rest are relegated to specialized dictionaries. In other words, if the English dictionary is like an inventory, the French dictionary is like a toolbox, with words divided up into categories, each with specific instructions about how to use it. The mandate? To help users speak pure French.

The dictionary question aside, the purist approach had two hidden traps, and over the centuries French speakers have fallen into both of them. The first was that the plainness they sought led to extreme dryness. That's the term that comes to mind when one reads French poetry from between the 1600s and the arrival of the Romantic movement in France in 1830. Before 1600, French poetry had been praised for its refinement and inventiveness. But the influence of Malherbe led creative people to eschew the very things that help a language develop, such as wordplay and neologisms. In other words, *bon usage* had a castrating effect. "*On a appauvri la langue en voulant la purifier*" ("The language was impoverished in our effort to purify it"), wrote French Academy member Henri Fenelon in 1716. His observation came fifty years too late, and it raised very few echoes in the next century. The damage had been done.

The other trap of purism was to create a gulf between *bon usage* and scientific and technical language. The seeds had already been planted when Furetière was quarrelling with the Academy. He maintained that "an architect speaks as good French when he uses technical terms like plinths and stylobate . . . as a courtier who speaks of alcoves, stands or lustres." But his view did not prevail. For the next two centuries the Academy put cultural and court language on a pedestal and relegated scientific language to a sort of linguistic ghetto. The problem that promoters of French had with scientific language came mainly from their opposition to jargon and their anti-Latin stance (the influence of Latin was strong in scientific circles). Language promoters also dismissed legal vocabulary as outdated, as much of it had been created along with the Ordinance of Villers-Cotterêts. French science remained strong throughout that period, but the separation between the idea of *bon usage* and the rest of society meant that the people at the top didn't pay any attention to what was going on below them. So the Academy inadvertently deprived French elites of a major source of linguistic and cognitive renewal.

Yet the prescriptive approach of French dictionaries had one positive outcome: What "pure" French lost in lexical richness, it gained in lexical precision. Because it was defined, French in the seventeenth and eighteenth centuries was regarded as easier to learn. People using *Le Richelet* and *Le Furetière* and the *Grammaire raisonnée* of Lancelot and Arnauld could pick up the basics of the language. For that matter, the Academy's dictionary had much more success outside France than inside, because it allowed people with no access to the French court to get a good idea of the correct usage that was the rule there. Because French was the first European language with a fully developed written system of spelling and grammar, France was also the first country to develop a group of literary stars (later called philosophers or intellectuals), a phenomenon that would help boost the great admiration that Europe developed for the French language.

One effect of this success was that most of the courts of Europe (and overseas) wanted to develop their own clones of the French Academy. Berlin, Vienna, Madrid, Lisbon, St. Petersburg, Stockholm and Philadelphia all created academies modelled on the French Academy. The most successful clone, Spain's Real academia española de la lengua (Royal Spanish Language Academy), became a model of effectiveness, and remains so. Created in 1713, it issued its first Spanish dictionary after thirteen years of work; the twentieth edition was delivered in 1984. Better still, it published eight editions of a Spanish grammar between 1741 and 1815, accomplishing a complete reform and rationalization of the Spanish language. The French Academy never got close to those results. Over the centuries most countries would establish their own form of language institution, whether they called it an academy, an institute, a commission or a committee.

One of the great enigmas of the period is why the English never followed the trend and created an academy—all the more so since many of them viewed the French Academy with envy. The English intelligentsia complained bitterly about the corruption of their language, from about 1660 until publication of Samuel Johnson's dictionary in 1755. People wrote as they spoke; nobody seemed to follow any fixed rules. This was perceived as a great problem by men of science, and the Royal Academy of Science created a committee to tackle it. Many writers joined the movement. Jonathan Swift, the most outspoken promoter of an English academy, wrote: "Some method should be thought for ascertaining and fixing our language for ever." Daniel Defoe went even further, at least rhetorically, writing that it was "criminal to coin words as money."

Yet the project of an English academy never materialized, probably because it went against the grain of society. Unlike the French, the English never felt it necessary to define their language (or their civil law, or even their constitution, for that matter). After they gained their independence, the Americans toyed with the idea, but rejected it as a royalist institution. Robert McCrum suggests in his book *The Story of English* that plans for an English academy may never have materialized simply because the idea was so obviously French. That explanation is a bit reductive, since most languages have some form of academy, but the concept of a language academy would become a classic illustration of the different spirits of English and French.

In the same century that the French Academy was created, the age-old rivalry between English and French would be carried over land and sea. And it would determine the fate of French on an entire continent.

Part Two ~

SPREAD

Chapter 4

FAR FROM THE SUN

A SWIFT TWENTY-MINUTE FERRY ride from Senegal's capital city, Dakar, the island of Gorée is an ideal place to get away from the commotion of the West African metropolis for an afternoon. Tourists and well-off Dakar residents flock to this peaceful, sandy haven to admire its steep rocky cliffs, historic forts and the hundred or so colourful colonial houses that line its cobblestone streets. The tiny island is dense with history and activity. On one side, residents have transformed two Second World War bunkers into dwellings. In the centre is an exclusive college where young girls study under the chubby silhouettes of baobab trees. Near the port, children swim and play on the beach all day while their parents sip sodas at quaint beachside cafés.

The idyllic atmosphere is almost enough to make one forget the island's turbulent and horrific history as a slave port. The Dutch first claimed Gorée in the seventeenth century; its name comes from the Dutch *goede raede* (good harbour). It was later claimed by the Portuguese, Danish and English, finally ending up in French hands. The Europeans vied for Gorée because it was an ideal location for holding slaves and as a stopover before the journey across the Atlantic. It had plenty of water and was close enough to the shore to allow commerce with the mainland, yet far enough to be protected from threats from the continent. Most visitors who arrive there today are herded straight from the ferry to the Maison aux esclaves (slave house), where a local guide recounts a short history of the island's role in holding slaves and shipping them to the Americas. Although Gorée's real importance in the slave trade is a matter of controversy among historians, the island has become a kind of living museum of the two-hundred-year period when Europeans tore apart African society to supply labour to their colonial plantations.

In writing the history of the French language (or of any European language), authors tend to brush over colonialism and skip the European slave trade, probably because the issues seem too painful to be reduced to episodes in the story of a language. We are not writing an apology for French colonialism or its methods, but the subject cannot be avoided. If French became not only a European but also an African, Asian and American language, it is because France became an important colonial power.

The first colonial push, from the beginning of the seventeenth century to the French Revolution, was not even remotely about exporting language (unlike the second colonial push, in which Europeans attempted to export "civilization," as discussed in chapter 9). Early colonialism was strictly about importing (often stolen) wealth. Throughout the colonial period the nature of the treasure changed according to fashion and new tastes—from gold to beaver fur to luxury products such as coffee, cocoa and, of course, sugar. Europe's crowned heads saw the world as a zero-sum game: Whatever territory they didn't snatch, others would surely scoop up in their place. But no one had a master plan. They started out by sending adventurous trader-explorers and giving them charters—basically trade monopolies—in exchange for a cut of their profits and a promise to take settlers to the new territories. In effect, the entrepreneurs were given royal charters to loot and plunder the local natives and raid their competitors.

The French were no exception to this pattern, even though, like the English, they got started relatively late. Both countries sent merchants, navigators and pirates overseas during the sixteenth century, but neither established trading posts or permanent settlements until the beginning of the seventeenth century, a good 110 years after the Spaniards and more than 150 years after the Portuguese. In the seventeenth century the French pushed with some success into Africa, India and the Caribbean. They occupied Île Bourbon (present-day Réunion) in 1638, then opened their first trading post in Senegal and began sending colonists in 1687. They opened a trading post in Pondicherry in 1674—few people know that this section of India remained French until 1954. They colonized Île-de-France (present-day Mauritius), off the coast of Mozambique, in 1712.

By the time the French got to the Caribbean, the Spanish and the Portuguese had already claimed most of the islands. All the French could do was grab what was left over and try to seize territory from their European rivals. In the end, some islands changed crowns a dozen times. The French occupied Guadeloupe and Martinique in 1635, but the real prize was the western part of the island of Hispaniola, present-day Haiti, which the French called Saint-Domingue. In 1665 Saint-Domingue became a formal colony of France, and in 1697 the island of Hispaniola was formally partitioned between France and Spain (into today's Haiti and Dominican Republic). Nobody suspected it at the time, but this was quite a coup for the French; Saint-Domingue would turn out to be the most profitable of all European colonies during the eighteenth century.

By the seventeenth century the quest for gold bullion was already giving way to the market for exotic goods and commodities. The political economy had evolved, and the development of trade routes had made bulky items such as tobacco and fur profitable. New products—indigo, coffee and cocoa—became popular in Europe, but when Europeans decided they preferred their cocoa and coffee drinks sweetened, there were not enough bees and berries in Europe to produce all the sugar they needed. This sudden change in taste hastened the development of slave-based sugar plantations and, with them, slave trading and an interest in places like the island of Gorée.

Sugar cane is not actually native to the Caribbean. The Arabs discovered it in Egypt—the word *sucre* (sugar) is derived from the Arabic *sukkar*. Christopher Columbus picked it up on a stopover in the Canary Islands. As Europeans discovered, the Caribbean was perfectly designed for sugar plantations, as the islands were sparsely populated and the weather was the same all year round. The Spanish began building sugar mills in the mid-1500s. After local populations in the Caribbean had been decimated by European-imported disease, the Spanish went looking for manpower, and discovered that African slaves were more resistant to diseases such as smallpox, yellow fever and malaria than the local natives or the *engagés* (European contract workers).

The French were late getting into the sugar trade, but they took to it with a vengeance. The French colonies of the Caribbean soon became part of a single system that linked them to half a dozen African slave-trading posts in Congo, Angola, Guinea, Senegal and Benin (which also supplied slaves to Brazil and the American colonies). Because it was the shortest distance across the Atlantic from the Caribbean, West Africa was hotly disputed between the French, English and Dutch. The French soon got the upper hand. After establishing trading posts on the west coast of Africa, they began building fortresses and warehouses and founded the city of Saint-Louis in 1659. By 1750 they controlled a quarter of the slave trade.

Caribbean plantations produced coffee, cocoa and cotton in vast quantities, but sugar was the backbone of the trade, to the point that the French called their possessions the *Îles à Sucre* (Sugar Islands). Saint-Domingue produced more sugar than all the other islands combined, even Jamaica, and became the prize that everyone was after–it was dubbed *la perle des Antilles* (the pearl of the Caribbean). Saint-Domingue was the biggest sugar producer in the world by 1750. In the eighteenth century the settlers of Saint-Domingue were rich enough to build theatres, where they watched French plays, and to send their children to school in Paris. For a brief period they even had a local newspaper, the *Gazette de Saint-Domingue*. The colony was also notable for being the Caribbean island with the highest concentration of slaves relative to planters, as the white people called themselves (most of the land was controlled by absentee landowners, so few of the planters owned their land; the majority were artisans, overseers, administrators and the like). This imbalance would have important consequences for the history of French (as we discuss in chapter 7).

This early form of globalization spawned new words, and the effect on the French language was immediate. The Spanish borrowed from the South American Tupi people the word *boucan* (a meat-smoking process), which became the French word *boucanier* (buccaneer)–Quebeckers still use *boucane* colloquially for *smoke*. Other words, such as *igname* (yam) and *macaque* (a kind of monkey) came through Portuguese, whereas *tomate* and *chocolat* came from the Aztecs via the Spanish language. The word *maringouin* (a type of mosquito), which French Canadians swear was coined in Canada, is in fact a borrowing from the Tupi and Guarani languages of South America that was first adopted in the Antilles (French Caribbean), where it is still used today. Hundreds of similar terms from Peru or

Brazil came into French via Spanish—for example, *chinchilla, caïman* (cayman)—or Portuguese—*caramel, fétiche* (fetish), *marmalade, ananas* (pineapple). There were also borrowings from Africa, such as *zèbre* (zebra), which entered French via the Spanish *cebra* (meaning a wild donkey, as Spanish explorers couldn't think of a better word for these strange striped horses). *Banane* (banana) is a Bantu word that became French via Portuguese. And *vaudou* (voodoo) is a word from Benin that became French—and was later borrowed by English through Louisiana French.

The new industries of the time generated terms that were copied freely into all languages. *Sucre* gave *sucrier* (sugar bowl or sugar maker) and *sucrerie* (sugar mill). *Nègre*, borrowed from the Spanish *negro* (black) in 1529, produced *négresse* (black woman), *négrillon* (black child), *négrerie* (a place where slaves were held) and *négrier* (slave trader); racist policies also spawned terms such as *quarteron* (quadroon) for mulattos.

But the Caribbean colonies' main impact on the French language was the creation, almost overnight, of French Creole. The term *créole* came from the Portuguese *crioulo*, which referred to Brazil-born mulattos. No one knows exactly how the term came to refer to the language of the slaves (there are many widely divergent theories). The term travelled to the New World on slave ships leaving Senegal, which had been a Portuguese colony before the French occupied it. The Spanish, and later the French, used the term for anyone born in the colonies. It generally referred to whites, but later became the name for the jargon that developed among slaves.

A Creole language is born when populations of different origins combine elements of their languages to form a new one. Properly speaking, it becomes a Creole when it evolves into a mother tongue, transmitted from parents to children—that's what distinguishes it from a lingua franca or a pidgin (trade jargon). Of the world's 127 Creoles, thirty-five are English-based and fourteen are French-based. There are more speakers of French-based Creoles than all other Creoles combined (including English), thanks mostly to Haiti, the biggest Creole-speaking nation in the world, with a population of seven million (where both Creole and French are official languages), but also Mauritius, with a population of one million. The four other main centres of French-based Creole are Réunion, Guadeloupe, Martinique and French Guiana, which account for another million speakers. Together, the population of these lands is larger than the two biggest centres of English-based Creoles—Jamaica and Suriname—combined.

All French-based Creoles were created during the slave trade, when African slaves communicated among themselves by using colonial French terms with a simplified grammar. Most Creoles were strictly oral languages until recently and evolved without a fixed grammar system for two or three centuries. Words are very often similar to the French spoken in France at the end of the seventeenth century, but spelled phonetically, which blurs the resemblance. The Creole word for *étudiant* (student), for instance, is *étidyan*. Many terms can be understood if they are sounded out, but it sometimes takes a bit of imagina-tion—*comprendre* (to understand), for example, is *konprann*.

No one knows exactly how French-based Creoles devel-oped, partly because slaves couldn't write and because slave masters didn't care much about what their slaves were saying. Today, speakers of these different French-based Creoles can generally understand one another, which shows how strongly Creoles are related to French. Most francophones would be able to understand a phrase like *"Mwen palé on ti kal Kreyol"* ("I speak a bit of Creole") if it was clearly enunciated, but probably not *"Ki sa wap etidye?"* ("What are you studying?").

While French-based Creoles have features remarkably similar to the French spoken in the colonial period, the grammar and phonetics are often typically African. Verbs like *voir* (to see) and *boire* (to drink) are pronounced *vwè* and *bwè*, while *ici* (here) is pronounced *isit*, as it was in the seventeenth century. Colloquial French in North America has also retained these features. But whereas the French of the time rolled the R, Creole speakers often drop the R, which is why they say *vwé* and *bwé*. Nasalization is typically African—*aimer* (to love) is pronounced *enmé* in Guadeloupe and *renmen* in Haiti. Grammatically, gender disappeared and all words became neutral. The five articles usually follow the noun; *la pomme* (the apple) is *pom-la*. Verbs are not conjugated (with endings, as in French), but constructed, like most English tenses, with a pre-verb marker to indicate the tense. In Guadeloupe, Martinique and French Guiana, for instance, they use *ka* for the present, *té* for the past, *ké* for the future and *téké* for the conditional. There are a number of Africanisms in the vocabulary, and not just for voodoo-related terms. In Martinique and Guadeloupe the native whites are called *békés*, but in Haiti they are called *blan*, from the French *blanc*. The present meaning of Africanisms is often far removed from the original meanings in African languages—*zombi* originally meant *god* in Bantu (spoken in the Congo area).

French Creoles are actually separate languages, not dialects of French. But despite the high numbers of speakers, they never had much impact on French during the colonial period, not even on the French of Haiti, despite the fact that half a million people spoke Creole. The impact of Creoles may become greater with the rise of francophone literature today (which we discuss in chapter 19). The strong normative attitude of francophones has always been an obstacle to contributions from Creole, aside from a few terms such as *vaudou* and *zombi*. The same attitude would also shut Canadianisms out of mainstream French for two centuries.

In North America, French exploration and settlement were all about fur. When beaver hats became fashionable in the sixteenth century, the craze for fur encouraged François I and, later, Henri IV to send explorers to Canada. French explorer Jacques Cartier visited Canada twice, in 1534 and 1535 (with mixed motives—still in the gold bullion era, he was seeking a northwest passage to the Pacific). But Cartier's forays into the North American continent didn't amount to much. The winters were harsh, there was no gold, scurvy decimated his men and he had trouble seeing how he could make a profit out of the whole business.

It was Samuel de Champlain who ushered in France's first colonial push into the New World. He established the longest-lasting French settlement in North America in 1608, at a time when he had more than a few grey hairs under his wig. He called the settlement *l'abitation* (the habitation). He was tireless, crossing the Atlantic no fewer than twelve times and running the colony until his death in 1632. In the explorer's first winter in Canada, scurvy killed two-thirds of his men, yet Champlain survived. He went on to gain control of the continent's main waterway, the St. Lawrence River. To solidify France's presence in America, he set out to create alliances with the Natives; his favourites were the Hurons, so called by the French because the men's hair resembled a *hure* (a wild boar's mane). To bolster his alliance with the Hurons, Champlain joined a campaign against their enemies, the Iroquois, in 1609. The Natives' help would make it possible for the French to explore a huge swath of land that spanned the American Midwest and the Mississippi River basin.

Champlain understood that language was a key to building alliances with the Natives, and he established a tradition of learning Native languages that became the trademark of French expansion in North America. In 1610 he sent an eighteen-year-old colonist, Étienne Brûlé, to spend the winter among the Algonquin (allies of the Hurons), with instructions to learn their customs and master their language; he also brought a young Algonquin to live among the French. Champlain's plan was to turn Brûlé into a *truchement* (interpreter). The word was a corruption of the Turkish word *tergiman* (interpreter), which the French had picked up when François I struck up an alliance with Suleiman the Magnificent in the 1520s. The next summer, Brûlé returned to Quebec "dressed as a savage" and speaking fluent Algonquian.

After the success of this early experiment, the French began sending children as young as nine or ten to learn Native languages from tribes as far away as the Illinois (in the American Midwest) or the Natchez (in present-day Alabama). French missionaries all learned at least one aboriginal tongue; it was considered the most efficient road to converting the Natives. Father Jacques Marquette, a missionary who accompanied explorer Louis Jolliet down the Mississippi River, spoke six Native languages. In contrast, early English explorers and colonists did not make a habit of learning Native languages.

Brûlé turned out to be a brilliant scout. He was the first in a long line of bold, larger-than-life French characters known as *coureurs des bois* (bush rangers). During the five years he lived among the Hurons, on present-day Lake Huron, he canoed south to Lake Ontario and the present site of Buffalo, New York. He was the first European to see Niagara Falls. He roamed the inland territory of Pennsylvania and had explored Lake Superior by 1622. Brûlé recorded none of his observations, but spoke widely of them to other colonists. He was a controversial character; one early missionary criticized him for adopting the "licentious" way of life of the Natives, and he later sided with the English against Champlain. His life ended tragically when he was murdered and eaten by his adoptive tribe for reasons that no one has established.

At the end of the seventeenth century more than eight hundred *coureurs des bois* were spread over the continent, an impressive number considering that there were only ten thousand French settlers in North America at the time. The French missionaries were their harshest critics; they particularly disapproved of the custom of paying for furs with alcohol. And the French authorities didn't think much of this group of free spirits because they were loose cannons. As an example, two famous *coureurs des bois,* Médard Chouart des Groseilliers and Pierre-Esprit Radisson, were instrumental in the founding of the Hudson's Bay Company in 1670, after they switched allegiance and sided with the English.

French explorers have become a mere footnote in American history. Yet they were the ones who really opened the path for British and American settlers, founding cities such as Minneapolis, Detroit and St. Louis. The European dream of finding a continental route to China died a slow death. One French explorer, René-Robert Cavelier de La Salle, who came to New France in 1667, was so obsessed with finding the passage to China that his seigneurial estate east of Montreal was dubbed *La Chine* (now called Lachine). On his way down the Mississippi Lasalle realized that he was actually headed for the Gulf of Mexico. He was the first to link the territory at the lower end of the Mississippi, first explored by Hernando de Soto, to the upper Mississippi, which had been explored by Jacques Marquette and Louis Jolliet. By 1743 the La Vérendrye brothers were walking the Black Hills and they allegedly saw the Rockies.

The impact of this expansion on the French spoken in the New World was immediate. The French named most of the continent and the natural phenomena they observed there. Many French terms were picked up later by English colonists and slipped straight into English, for example, *butte, levée, depot, bison* and *Sioux. Gofer* (gopher) is a deformation of *gauffre* (waffle), which described the waffle-like holes that prairie dogs dug. *Mush,* a familiar command of dogsled drivers, comes from the French *marchez* (walk). Many names of Indian tribes in English are deformations or translations of French names, including Cheyenne, Blackfoot, Fox, Creek and Iowa, which were formerly Chiens, Pieds-noirs, Renards, Crics and Ayouhais. More than five thousand places were named by the French; most of the names were translated, like the Ozark Mountains, formerly Aux Arcs (itself short for Arkansas).

Settlers in New France borrowed from the tribes they were friendly with—Algonquin, Hurons and Montagnais—picking up words such as *caribou, carcajou* (wolverine), *mocassins* (moccasins), *achigan* (bass) and *sagamité* (a type of corn soup). The Iroquois contributed the name for a new sport, *lacrosse. Tabagie,* now the word for a smoke shop, came from the word for an Algonquin feast. Many of the terms the settlers picked up are still used in French Canada today, although *mocassin* became a common term in French only in the nineteenth century, under the influence of English literature.

The New World experience also led to new variations of old words. The term *sauvage* (savage) existed, but colonists and explorers soon started using terms like *sauvagesse* (a female savage) and *ensauvagement* (returning to the wild). The French names for animals such as the *chat sauvage* (wildcat) and *bête puante* (stinking beast, or skunk) have remained in use in Canada, although Canadiens also developed their own terms, such as *raton laveur* (washing rat, or raccoon) and *mouffette* (skunk). Settlers called snowshoes *raquettes* because they looked rather like the rackets of a new sport, *le jeu de paume,* French for "tennis"–a game borrowed from the French and named after the server's call, "*Tenetz!* (Take this!)" However, while exploration brought new words, it had very little impact on the structure of the French spoken in France, which was settling down during this period, though not quite set in stone.

In New France a linguistic phenomenon was taking shape that was almost the opposite of Creole. In its early days the colonists were reputed to speak French as well as or better than it was spoken in France–this comment is almost universal in accounts of early French colonialism. Ninety percent of French people at the time lived in the countryside and spoke only a local dialect. However, unlike the slaves who were shipped to French colonies, the majority of colonists in New France came from roughly the same places–either around Paris or the major Atlantic ports of La Rochelle, Nantes and Bordeaux. The French kept thorough records of who was sent to the New World, so historians know that ninety-two percent of the colonists came from *langue d'oïl* regions. Most of them spoke Picard, Norman or Orléanais as well as French. Half the new settlers had also been city dwellers, making them a more literate and cultivated group than most French people at the time (meaning that they spoke at least some French in addition to their regional dialect). Illiteracy was still the norm in France, but most of the colonists could at least sign their names.

Today the descendants of original French settlers in North America are reputed to speak not a "pure" French but, quite the contrary, an old if not archaic French. Although this view is now greatly exaggerated, Canadian French has retained some expressions and pronunciations that in purist circles are regarded as archaisms. Quebec French would even come to be called (falsely) a patois (discussed in chapter 10). That's not surprising, given that French speakers in North America were almost completely cut off from France near the end of the eighteenth century, and would remain that way until the middle of the twentieth century.

In a way it's surprising that French even survived in New France. The French never did send enough colonists to the New World. In 1600 France's population was four times larger than Britain's. But in the New World, British settlers far out-numbered the French, right from the start. In 1620 there were already a thousand Virginians while French settlers numbered no more than a hundred in Quebec and Acadia combined. By 1700 New France had attracted only ten thousand colonists, compared to some 150,000 settlers spread out among the thir-teen British colonies. In 1750 France still had more than twice Britain's population, but New France, Acadia and Greater Louisiana had only seventy-five thousand French inhabitants, while New England had 1.5 million (including three hundred thousand slaves). In short, one British subject in six lived in the colonies, compared to one Frenchman in three hundred.

What exactly was holding the French back? The first answer is that they weren't that interested in colonizing. At best their overall interest in naval affairs was sporadic. It's not that the French lacked vision; rather, geography forced them to focus on Europe. Unlike Spain and Britain, France's borders were not guarded by natural obstacles. While Britain was aggressively building New World colonies, France was obsessed with fending off the Hapsburg Empire. Because France had its capital right along its longest open border, its foreign-policy priority was to keep its neighbours weak and disunited, by either diplomacy or war. In the seventeenth and eighteenth centuries the conquest of Savoy, Alsace, Lorraine and Franche-Comté allowed France to roll back its borders to natural bar-riers of mountains and rivers. Colbert and Richelieu knew that the solution to France's poor colonial record was to build a strong navy. When Colbert came to power in 1661, there were twenty-six thousand merchant vessels in Europe: thirteen thousand Dutch, six thousand English, and only two thousand French. Colbert planted entire forests of oak, hoping that future generations of the French would build more ships, but he himself was sucked into European conflicts and diverted from New World issues.

France's colonial model, which was based on charter companies, also discouraged settlement. The charter companies were supposed to bring in settlers, but to keep their costs down they brought as few people as possible and invested little in infrastructure to keep them there. The very nature of the fur trade also worked against settlement. Fur trading depends on unspoiled nature and good relations with the Natives, who act as the harvesters. The highest grade of beaver skin was dubbed *castor gras* (greasy beaver) because it had been worn by a Native for two years. Such an economy doesn't encourage settlement—agriculture displaces wildlife. The companies preferred hiring single men for short contracts. By 1617, nine years after the foundation of Quebec, only one French family had settled in New France, that of Louis Hébert, an apothecary, who came to Quebec with his wife and three children. Hébert's daughter gave birth to the first (French) native of New France in 1620, twelve years after Quebec was founded. Meanwhile, Virginians and Bostonians had arrived with families and started multiplying the minute they set foot in the New World. Until 1660 there were seven males for every female in New France. Colbert changed the ratio when he emptied the Parisian orphanages of nubile girls—the so-called *filles du roy*—and shipped them to Canada to marry the settlers, but the initiative was too little, too late to offset the demographic imbalance with the American colonies.

And, of course, the French themselves weren't particularly drawn to the idea of moving to the colonies. The French have

never migrated en masse to any colony, the only exception
being Algeria. In Britain in the same period, the Enclosure
provoked a rural exodus to the cities—and the New World was
there to soak up surplus labour. The French, meanwhile, were
obsessed with demography and terrified by the idea of letting
too many people go—they were the first people to practise
birth control in Europe, a phenomenon that had created a
serious population slump by the 1800s. The colony of New
France also had many built-in disincentives such as scurvy,
mosquitoes and cold, not to mention the dangers of the trip
over. The Iroquois wars that lasted from 1641 to 1660 also discouraged settlers, right at a time when the demographic imbalance could still have been corrected.

France also missed the boat with one group of potentially
dynamic colonizers: the Huguenots (French Protestants). In 1598
Henri IV had passed the Edict of Nantes, which guaranteed
freedom of conscience and protection to Protestants. These
rights were progressively eroded until Louis XIV completely
revoked the Edict in 1685. Fleeing persecution, three hundred
thousand French Protestants left France for neighbouring
countries, and they turned out to be industrious settlers when
they went overseas. Many Huguenots had been skilled trades-
men, merchants and artisans in France. In exile they tended to
turn to professions such as journalism, publishing, editing and
teaching French. London-born Peter Mark Roget, author of
the famous thesaurus, was a descendant of Huguenots.
Champlain himself was a converted Huguenot, as was his boss,
Pierre Du Gua de Monts. Pieter Minuit, famous for buying the
island of Manhattan for sixty guilders, founded a prosperous
Dutch colony in which French Huguenots were prominent.
Other famous Huguenots include Paul Revere (formerly
Revoire) and Davy Crockett, whose ancestor, Monsieur de
Croquetagne, had been a captain of Louis XIV's Guard. In

Canada, famous Huguenot descendants included John Kinder Labatt, founder of the brewing company, and Laura Secord, a Loyalist heroine whose name would be given to a chocolate empire.

Yet relatively few Huguenots travelled from France to New France. Richelieu forbade them to emigrate to the New World; he feared, with reason, that they would side with fellow Protestants when they got there and switch allegiance to the British Crown. Of the three hundred thousand Huguenots who left France, about a third went to the Netherlands, a quarter to Switzerland and some German states—Berlin was founded as a refuge for Huguenots—and only a third to England, Ireland and the Americas combined. In the end, it seems, the Huguenots were no keener on the cold, mosquitoes and scurvy than French Catholics were.

Other French values worked against colonialism. Like their fellow Europeans, the French were curious to hear stories of adventure from the New World, but an important segment of the elite was simply not interested in questions of industry, science, technology, money or markets—issues that were vital to the development of a trading empire. The French Academy, of course, completely ignored scientific and technical vocabulary (as well as new vocabulary from the colonies). Unlike the English Puritans, French settlers were not driven by the idea of building an ideal French society, except maybe as an after-thought. The French Crown instead created an absolutist society that did not encourage free enterprise or local initiative. In New France, colonists were forbidden to establish towns; only parishes were allowed, which is why so many towns in Quebec have saints' names. Finally, France's colonial adventure was a victim of France's growing brilliance. When the very capable General Frontenac started showing some initiative in New France, Colbert reprimanded him: "Even if Canada may seem far from the Sun, nobody should undertake things without the King." Indeed, who wanted to be so far from the Sun?

Contrary to what most North Americans have come to believe, France's loss of America was not inevitable. At the time of the Treaty of Utrecht in 1713, demographics definitely favoured the British, at a ratio of twenty to one. By 1750 the New World held 1.5 million British, compared to about fifty-five thousand Canadiens, thirteen thousand Acadians and no more than a few thousand settlers in Louisiana. Yet militarily the French were much stronger, to the extent that it was the thirteen British colonies that felt threatened. Until the middle of the Seven Years War (1756–63) France invested proportionately more in military resources in New France than the British did in the Thirteen Colonies, and the French controlled the main waterways. The very organization of New France was fundamentally military. Many of its first settlers were former soldiers. Houses and farms were organized in a way that favoured defence and the mustering of forces—a layout that is still obvious today. France's strong militia, seasoned in wilderness tactics and guerrilla warfare, fought and moved like the Natives, allowing the French to accomplish much more with far fewer people over a territory twenty times larger than that controlled by the English.

To compensate for their numeric inferiority, the French became exceedingly skilled at building alliances with the Natives. In some years the small colony could spend as much as eight to ten percent of its budget buying the loyalty of Native chiefs with guns, alcohol and lavish meals. Rare was the chief who did not possess a medallion of the King of France, the French "father." In 1701 *La Grande paix* (Great Peace) of Montreal was signed by more than sixty First Nations. The thirteen British colonies, meanwhile, were suffering from infighting, lack of unity and poor military organization.

The wind might have continued to blow favourably for the French had it not been for the providential character of William Pitt the Elder (1708–78). Pitt became minister of war after the British suffered a series of military disasters in the early stages of the Seven Years War. Grandson of a former governor in India, he had colonialism in his blood. In Pitt's view, Britain had spent too much energy on battles in Europe. He redirected England's military objectives towards the seas, with the objective of destroying French trade and ousting the French from India and America. While France committed heavy resources to the battles in Europe—as many as a hundred thousand men—Pitt put all he had into America. He chose competent generals and admirals, and finally convinced the Thirteen Colonies to coordinate their efforts against Quebec.

For the first time, all of Britain's advantages came together: huge American colonies, a massive navy, good naval policy and some good luck. The Royal Navy generally had better training, a better sense of the sea and more heavy ships of the line— although the differences were not as great as is generally assumed. In the summer of 1759 a quarter of the British fleet was anchored in front of Quebec City. The French lost the battle of the Plains of Abraham in September 1759, then actually won a lesser-known second battle of the Plains and retook Quebec City the following April. The exhausted French expected reinforcements that never came, and then had to abandon Quebec when more British sails appeared on the horizon.

Even then, however, America was not lost to France. An odd thing happened during the peace negotiations. In 1763 the British offered to let France keep either Canada or the Sugar Islands (Saint-Domingue, Martinique and Guadeloupe). The offer was surprising, given Britain's victories in Canada and India. What did they have to gain from making concessions to France? In fact, their victory was fragile. Britain was exhausted from fighting the Seven Years War, and near bankruptcy. It could not really afford to destroy France's overseas commerce, because in doing so it would have delivered a larger blow to the economy of Europe than Britain's economy could withstand.

With what today seems like an absolutely stunning lack of foresight, the French chose the Sugar Islands over New France. They were able to hold on to their Caribbean islands and five trading posts in southeast India—in Pondicherry and Chandernagore, which they would keep until 1954—but abruptly ended their 160-year presence in America. France also kept the island of Gorée, off the coast of Senegal, which was still an essential slave-trading transfer point. We visited one of the former Sugar Islands, Guadeloupe, now a French overseas territory. Wandering past the tumbledown apartment blocks in its capital city, Pointe-à-Pitre, and gazing at the meagre remains of the island's once-flourishing sugar and banana plantations, as Quebeckers we were stunned to think that the French had traded Canada for this place. Although it's better off than many of its Caribbean neighbours, the island's economy is largely dependent on mainland France.

The choice may now seem short-sighted, but at the time it was rational. The French Antilles represented twenty percent of France's total external trade. The islands—in particular Saint-Domingue—were the richest colonies in the world. Canada, by comparison, was a money pit. The influential Encyclopedists of eighteenth-century France believed strongly that only trade, not conquest, could produce wealth. They were convinced France would be better off without America, and they convinced many others as well. In his philosophical tale *Candide*, Voltaire dismissed New France as "a few acres of snow," not worth the money France had already spent on it.

———

Yet French didn't disappear with France's departure from America. It survived, largely thanks to the work of French colonial mastermind Étienne François, Duc de Choiseul, Louis XVI's naval minister (1761–66) and then war minister (1766–70). With his vision and sense of purpose, Choiseul was a match for Pitt. The French had begun settling in Greater Louisiana at the beginning of the eighteenth century, founding villages and building forts. Most of the settlers up the Mississippi were domesticated *coureurs des bois* who had turned to farming the rich land of the upper Illinois (now Missouri). At the time Louisiana encompassed what are now fifteen states west of the Mississippi, right up to the Canadian border. Choiseul knew the French were going to lose anyway, so in 1762 he secretly ceded Greater Louisiana to Spain, as payback for siding with France in the Seven Years War and as a way of keeping it out of British hands.

Spanish rule over Greater Louisiana turned out to be so mild that it hardly made a mark on the French culture there. French settlers moved over to the west bank of the Mississippi to avoid British rule. Over the next seventy-five years this group would be constantly reinforced by French Canadians from Quebec who joined in the fur trade—to the point that most of the early legends of the American frontier were French (more on this in chapter 10). Even in the state of Louisiana, French was sheltered. The Spanish regime was not anti-French and not interested in assimilating the different groups that lived under its rule. The Spanish even invited Catholic Acadian colonists to Louisiana to help them defend the west bank of the Mississippi against the British, and later against the Americans. French speakers were a resilient group in Louisiana; they were the assimilators, soaking up Spanish, German and Portuguese immigrants, whose cultures would be absorbed into the French-speaking Cajun culture, with its unique music, food and language.

With Louisiana safely in Spanish hands, Choiseul worked on improving the French navy. He modernized the French artillery, increased the number of warships, developed military engineering, created military academies and abolished the right to purchase military rank. Choiseul purchased Corsica from Italy in order to give France a base in the Mediterranean. (Through that purchase, a certain Corsican family by the name of Buonaparte became French.) As a result, Britannia ruled the waves but was feeling the heat from France. In 1785 commerce over the Atlantic was thirty-four percent British and twenty-eight percent French. France had become a strong enough naval power that American insurgents sought its aid when they revolted against the British. In the end, the French spent more money helping the Americans than they had defending New France: one billion pounds. By 1781 the French had sent twelve thousand troops and thirty-two thousand sailors to America. In America, the French won a place in the heart of the people (or some of them, at least) that they had lost on the continent.

In Canada, as it turned out, the British couldn't afford to wipe out the French language any more than they could afford to cut France out of global trade. In 1763, when France officially gave up New France, fifty-five thousand Canadiens were living there. The British simply didn't have the manpower to assimilate them, even with the help of the six thousand Scottish merchants who came to Canada over the next ten years. These merchants tried to strip the French-speaking Catholics of their rights in any way they could. They refused to allow Catholics to occupy positions as civil servants and forbade contracts to be written in French or local justice to be administered in French; they were even against the French system of land allotment. But the Canadiens resisted, so much so that the British had to hire French Huguenots as administrators to deal with them. In the meantime, trouble had started brewing farther south, in the thirteen British colonies. The British just could not afford to bring in any more troops to deal with Canada.

So the British compromised. In 1774 they passed the *Quebec Act,* which allowed Catholics to hold positions in the civil service and in public office without renouncing their faith. The Act also kept the French civil justice system in place and preserved the seigneurial land tenure system, physical traces of which—such as close-together villages and narrow plots—can still be seen in Quebec today. The *Quebec Act* also allowed some Catholic involvement in the colonial council and promised that Quebec could have its own elected Parliament, which was created in 1791. The deal, of course, enraged the Scottish merchants of Quebec and Montreal—a small but powerful minority—as well as American colonists in Boston, who detested the French-speaking Catholics. But ultimately the *Quebec Act* ensured the survival of French.

Ironically, British North America (before it was Canada) turned out to be almost a sanctuary for French. The fifty-five thousand Canadiens would have had little chance of hanging on to their language if they had been thrown in with 1.5 million Americans. When American insurgents defeated the British in 1783 and the continent was divided, British North America protected French speakers from disappearing into the American melting pot. In Canada, French persevered, in spite of successive waves of immigration and in spite of being cut off from France. Part of the explanation is Canada's smaller population. As early as the 1780s, some fifty thousand British Loyalists fleeing America arrived in Canada and nearly over-whelmed the Canadiens, but French speakers made up more than half of the population of Canada until the 1830s. Today they account for a quarter of the Canadian population. In Quebec and New Brunswick they respectively make up eighty-one percent and thirty-three percent of the population (more on how they survived in chapter 10). The proportion of French speakers in Canada in the eighteenth century was large enough to allow them to survive after being cut off from mainstream French, which happened just when French was about to become the universal language of Europe.

Chapter 5

THE LANGUAGE OF GENIUS

"How has French become the world's universal language?" There was nothing presumptuous about this question when the Berlin Academy chose it for an essay contest in 1782. By the late eighteenth century, no one in Europe would have challenged the idea that French was the world's lingua franca. But to win, candidates in the essay contest had to go beyond merely stating the obvious. They had to explain why French had become pre-eminent in the first place and why it was maintaining this status, and to speculate on whether its supremacy would last.

The Academy received twenty-two entries and awarded two first prizes, one to Antoine de Rivarol, a Frenchman and a protégé of the famous writer Voltaire, and the other to Jean-Christ Schwab, a German professor at the Academy of Stuttgart.

The winners made radically different cases. While providing a good synthesis of the history of the French language's development, Rivarol basically built his case around a foregone conclusion, that French had gained its status because it was clearer, simpler and more concise than any other language; he even argued that French was the best language for doing business. In a famous line he writes, *"Ce qui n'est pas clair n'est pas français"* ("If it's not clear, it's not French"). To contemporary readers, Antoine de Rivarol's argument might sound strangely familiar—he said the same things about French that many commentators today say about English. In Rivarol's view, no other language could even hope to compete with French, including Spanish, Italian and English.

While Rivarol is still widely quoted today, few recall his co-laureate, Jean-Christ Schwab (1743–1821). Yet Schwab's analysis was far more penetrating. Like Rivarol, he argued that the prestige and popularity of French culture had helped make French the preferred language of theatre, poetry, essays, history and science. But in his view the popularity of French had nothing to do with a supposed "genius" of the language. According to Schwab, political conditions, not linguistic qualities, had made French the dominant language of Europe. France's political superiority and spirit of conquest had made the language appealing to foreigners. French had "agents" spreading it through Europe and beyond, in the form of colonizers, diplomats and Protestant refugees who had fled France in the previous century.

In Schwab's view, its linguistic features reinforced the supremacy of French. European nations needed a common language, because what Schwab called a "spirit of communication" had appeared among them in the eighteenth century. French was perfectly adapted to fill the need for a common language because, thanks to the work of the French Academy, it had been given a systematic grammar, making it what he called a "finished" language. That made it easier to learn. And that, in turn, explained why French had prevailed over other European vernaculars; Italian, for example, had the right civilization behind it, but the language had not yet been systematized.

In a way, both authors were right. But they had overlooked another important phenomenon. As with all of France's successful exports, one of the secrets behind the spread of French was strong local consumption. The eighteenth century in France was a time of peace; for the first time in centuries the

French weren't using up their energy fighting one another. France was the biggest country in Europe, the central country in the European balance of power, and it had a huge army. Paris, with six hundred thousand inhabitants, was also the biggest European capital after London. The income of both aristocrats and bourgeois was on the rise, and life was good for the fortunate classes.

This prosperity had a curious effect on the language. As France's middle class increased and the country became wealthier, the French aristocracy was no longer satisfied to distinguish itself strictly by status and title. It was looking for a new way to set itself apart from the masses. Slowly, manners and style, respect for culture, refinement and elevated ideas became the mark of the upper class. To shine in the salons one needed a sharp mind, a sharp tongue and a sharp quill. So language skill became a tool of social advancement.

The salons were not new. The Marquise de Rambouillet (1588–1665) created the first great French salon in the first decade of the seventeenth century. A young noblewoman, married at the age of twelve, she had grown tired of the intrigues and vulgarity of the Court of Henri IV. Before she turned twenty she had refused to go to the King's receptions and had started hosting her own, inviting the best minds of France to her home, the Hôtel de Rambouillet (this was the salon Richelieu was hoping to stamp out by creating the French Academy, as discussed in chapter 3). She even had the house redesigned as a succession of small rooms that were ideal settings for intimate conversation. Being gifted in many art forms (though brilliant in none), the Marquise attracted the cream of the crop of princesses, nobles and men of letters. The Hôtel de Rambouillet quickly became the salon of choice for the French nobility and *lettrés,* and remained so, well into the 1650s.

The Marquise de Rambouillet's salon is credited with raising conversation to the level of a fine art. She had countless imitators—Madame de Scudéry, Madame de La Fayette and, later, Madame de Staël. By the eighteenth century even small provincial cities had salons to which women invited famous (or less than famous) writers, artists and thinkers to discuss ideas and practise the art of conversation. The salons had different formats—some were weekly dinners, some were held many times a week and some were sporadic. They could include singing, theatre, dancing, debates or lively verbal sparring. Some specialized in the arts, writing or philosophy; others had different nights for different types of entertainment—serious, entertaining or frankly libidinous. But no matter what their form, salons sought one feature: *esprit,* a difficult concept to translate that is a combination of wit, cleverness, eloquent rhetoric and liveliness. The art of conversation required speakers to be playful, to make witty comebacks and offer sudden and surprising insights. Under the influence of the salons, the French language became associated—both inside and outside France—with sociability in its highest form. Etiquette, a form of regulation within salon culture, became a prestigious art strictly associated with the French.

In the 1680s a famous French publisher based in Holland, Pierre Bayle—he would print Furetière's *Dictionnaire universel*—published a magazine called *Les nouvelles de la république des letters* (*News from the Republic of Letters*). The name described perfectly what salons were all about: a sort of intellectual community where class origins mattered less than skilful use of language. One of the reasons for the success of salons in France was that they managed to mix the best literary minds—commoners, for the most part—with the highest nobility. Military men, bourgeois and even women were welcome if they could display some wit. Women enjoyed much greater freedom in the salons than they could outside them; they were allowed to broach any topic they wanted, and if they had *esprit* they were considered to be on equal footing with men. Only verbal dexterity, not social status, secured reputations in the salons. So, in a way, language acted as a great equalizer in French society, a role it still plays in modern France. (This intellectual intermingling of men and women led many to believe that salons were places of licentiousness and scandal. In fact, they were a new form of entertainment that had its stars, its public and even a tabloid press, in the form of gazettes that reported debates, controversies, findings and trivia.)

By the eighteenth century, French salons were being imitated all over Europe—in French. They were considered the epitome of the French nobility's *art de vivre* and the height of fashion—the word *mode* (fashion) appeared in French at this time. The hostesses of salons were usually dressed in the latest styles and their houses were sumptuously decorated—again following the example of the Marquise de Rambouillet, who was famous for provocatively painting her bedroom blue rather than the usual red or light brown. Nobles all over Europe were attracted by the festive spirit—sometimes veering towards debauchery—that reigned among the French aristocracy, and the mystique of the salons lasted well into the nineteenth century.

The effect on French? It came to be considered the *entrée* to everything the salons represented, much the same way that English is considered today's door to the future. French became a desired commodity that was indispensable for practising the art of communication—whether spoken or written—and the undisputed medium of culture and refinement. As French historian and member of the French Academy Marc Fumaroli put it in *Quand l'Europe parlait français* (*When Europe Spoke French*), in the eighteenth century the French language, with its trappings of prosperity and leisure, represented all the happiness that could be had.

There was much more to the growing reputation of French than fluff and *petits-fours*. Behind the window dressing of the salons, France was making important scientific, intellectual, cultural and industrial achievements. In the eighteenth century France was already famous for producing crystal, mirrors, fine foods, perfumes and wines. Although England was a major contributor to scientific and intellectual production, the French also made significant advances, as the creation of the *Journal des savants* in 1665 suggests. As early as the seventeenth century, Blaise Pascal had created the first calculating machine. Another technical genius, Denis Papin, invented the pressure cooker in 1679, demonstrated the power of steam in 1687, dived in the first submarine in 1691 and built the first paddleboat on the Rhine River in 1707 (competitors later destroyed the machine). Inventor Jacques de Vaucanson stunned his contemporaries in 1737 with his automatons, or mechanical toys: a flute player, and a duck that could eat, drink and swim. In 1746 Vaucanson invented the automatic loom, which was operated with a system of punch cards and powered by the force of water (nobody cared much about it until it was rediscovered by Jacquard at the beginning of the nineteenth century and became a main feature of the Industrial Revolution). The crowning technical achievement of the French was the *montgolfière* (hot-air balloon), named after its inventors, the brothers Joseph Michel and Jacques Étienne Montgolfier. After a series of experiments, the brothers amazed the Court in 1783 when they sent a sheep, a rooster and a duck on a short flight in a paper balloon. People were stunned; they hadn't thought it was possible to breathe up in the sky. Two months later François Pilâtre de Rozier boarded a Mongolfier balloon and made a twenty-minute trip across Paris's Left Bank, the first human flight in the world.

The French made important scientific advances during the eighteenth century. Pierre Fauchard inaugurated modern dentistry. René de Réaumur refined the process of steelmaking and invented one of the first working thermometers. Claude Berthollet was famous for his studies of chlorine and chlorides. Georges de Buffon theorized on scientific experimentation, proposed a model for the classification of species and wrote a thirty-six-tome *Histoire naturelle* (*Natural History*). Joseph Louis de Lagrange is famous for his theories of mathematics. One of the luminaries of the century was Antoine de Lavoisier, who demonstrated the composition of water (H_2O) and created the first periodical chart of the elements. Abbé Jean Antoine Nollet invented the first electroscope and observed the transmission of sound in liquids. A family of Swiss mathematicians and physicists, the Bernoullis (Jacques, Jean and Daniel), developed a number of theories in the fields of calculus, statistics and oscillation, one of which proved essential for designing the wings of an airplane.

But it was unarguably the ebullient intellectual climate of eighteenth-century Paris that turned French into Europe's universal language of communication and scholarly exchange. In France the eighteenth century is known as *le siècle des lumières* (the century of light and knowledge, or the Enlightenment). During that century, universities were still controlled by the conservative Catholic Church, but free discussion began popping up in salons and cafés, and arts and science academies were sprouting up throughout the country. Paris already had cafés in every neighbourhood (the most famous, Le Procope, is still operating, though in a different location) and there were dozens of bookstores in the Latin Quarter alone, mostly along the Rue St-Jacques. The press in France was still censored by the government, but it was very active.

The salons created a climate of intellectual rebellion, notably by encouraging the philosophes, a group of French thinkers (also called the Lumières) whose influence reached its peak in the 1750s. Many of the philosophes attended salons or were directly supported, if not actually protected, by their hostesses. Madame de Pompadour, the famous mistress of Louis XV, was considered a great friend of these philosophers.

The philosophes believed that empirical investigation could be used to question matters that had previously been explained by religious dogma. They were interested in many subjects, from science and the trades to literature and social criticism, and were really united only by their approach, which was reformist, anti-despotic and anti-authoritarian. They were optimistic thinkers whose central interest was human happiness. They believed that man (feminism was not part of the program) was born free and that his liberty was inalienable. Political authority was something he submitted to willingly.

One of their central tenets, which was extremely radical at the time, was that a government could not justify its existence merely by divine right to rule. To be legitimate, rulers had to contribute to the happiness of their subjects. The challenge was, how do people retain their liberty and reconcile their competing interests in order to live happily together in a single society? The philosophes believed that, in one form or another, reason and natural laws would solve this dilemma by allowing men to find a better way of organizing society. This triumph of reason and individualism over tradition and religion fed a climate of almost constant intellectual research, not just in philosophy, but also in science, technical knowledge and political thought.

One of the great intellectual undertakings of the century was the *Encyclopedia*. The project was the life's work of Denis Diderot (1713–84). Educated by the Jesuits, Diderot had set out to become a priest, but instead ended up in Paris in the late 1720s and began writing essays. He wasn't too successful, so in 1728 he switched genres and set out to create a catalogue describing all the arts and sciences and vocations being practised in France at the time. The idea had been kicking around for a while—Diderot was inspired by the *Universal Dictionary of Arts and Sciences,* which had appeared in London in 1728 (itself inspired by Furetière's 1690 *Dictionnaire universel*). Such a concept was considered revolutionary because an encyclopedia would enable anyone to gain knowledge about almost anything, allowing individuals to circumvent schools or masters of trades, who up until then had a monopoly on knowledge. The *Encyclopedia* was an attempt to organize all the fields of knowledge into a single system and to show the relationships between them. It put noble arts such as poetry on the same footing as common trades such as tanning or *chaudronnerie* (boilermaking).

Diderot, like Voltaire, was jailed more than once for his writing. Ultimately it was their extraordinary celebrity that saved them both. The first volume of the *Encyclopedia* appeared in 1759, after Diderot had been thrown into prison for three months for his writings on religion (it was salon hostess Madame de Chatelet who reportedly got him out). The influence of the *Encyclopedia* was such that the Empress of Russia, Catherine II, a friend of Voltaire, bought Diderot's library in 1765, allowing him to use the books while supplying him with a fifty-year salary so he could complete the *Encyclopedia*. The project was finished in 1778 and had twenty-eight volumes. Both Jean-Jacques Rousseau and Voltaire contributed articles to it—Rousseau on music and Voltaire on history. In one article Voltaire defined history as "an account of facts given as true, contrary to fables, which are the account of facts given as false." He divided history into sacred and profane; in the entry for sacred history he saucily wrote, "No comment." He divided profane history into "what you can know because there are physical traces left of it, and what you can't (like the lost language of ancient Egypt)." As an irreverent warning to his readers, he noted that historical profiles were often written to "make people shine" rather than to instruct the reader.

Better known as Voltaire, François-Marie Arouet (1694–1778) was one of the strongest intellectual forces pushing French across the Continent. His pseudonym is an anagram of *AROVET* Le *Ieune* (Arouet the Young) as it was spelled in the early eighteenth century—U and V, J and I were still interchangeable. Voltaire, born into a prosperous Paris family, went on to become the most influential French philosopher of the eighteenth century—much more famous at the time than he is even today for his essays, historical works, poetry, novels, plays and philosophical tales. He was the rock star of salon culture. A brilliant polemicist, he became a correspondent and confidant of kings and queens such as Frederick II of Prussia and Catherine II of Russia; he wrote more than eighteen thousand letters in his lifetime. But he did not invent ideas so much as popularize them. He imported the ideas of Newton and John Locke and popularized the philosophes' love of clearly expressed ideas, their faith in human experience, criticism of the structures governing society and opposition to absolutist rule. He was outspoken on every issue and used any opportunity he found to attack authoritarianism and traditionalists of all types. He even led a campaign against France's keeping the colony of Canada (being outspoken did not always make him right).

It was Voltaire who popularized the idea that the French language had a particular genius for conveying ideas. He wrote, "What we call the genius of a language is its ability to express, clearly and concisely, and in a harmonious manner, what other languages express in a poorer fashion." In retrospect, he was probably confusing language with an attitude towards language. If anything, the philosophes themselves were the source and vehicle of this attitude about French. Their writing was clear and concise and they valued language as a tool for making ideas understandable. In other words, they fulfilled Malherbe's doctrine of clarity and precision, and brought it to new heights. But brilliant as he was, Voltaire was primarily a communicator. As a thinker he was much less original than two of his peers who each made a mark on political theory that is still felt to this day: Montesquieu and Rousseau.

The Bordeaux judge Charles de Secondat, Baron de la Brède et de Montesquieu (1689–1755), was a regular at the Paris salon of Madame De Lambert from 1724 on and was also known to frequent those of Madame De Tencin and Madame de Deffand. In 1721 Montesquieu arrived on the French literary scene with his *Persian Letters*, a fictional account of a faux Persian living in France who observes the country's social customs, manners and political institutions with the eye of an outsider. In a loosely concealed criticism of the French monarchy, Montesquieu's hero naively describes the absolutist king as a magician who has a magical ability to get people to agree with him—his take on authoritarianism. His criticism of religion was just as harsh. He wrote, "If triangles had a god, they would give him three sides." Montesquieu was perceived as a comic writer, and many French people can still quote humorous lines such as "Heirs prefer doctors to confessors" and "Frenchmen rarely talk about their wives; they fear speaking in front of people who know them better."

Outside France, Montesquieu is best remembered for his political essay *De l'esprit des lois* (*The Spirit of Laws*). In this groundbreaking work he introduced a new classification system for governments—those that governed by consent, by honour or by fear. His most famous chapter, on the separation of powers, inspired the U.S. Constitution, thus earning Montesquieu a solid place in the pantheon of American political philosophy.

Jean-Jacques Rousseau (1712–78) was the other political thinker who made his mark in the eighteenth century. Born in Geneva, the son of a watchmaker and fifth-generation Protestant who had converted to Catholicism, Rousseau had an unhappy childhood that turned him into an unstable, paranoid character. His mother died shortly after he was born and his father abandoned him when he was ten; later in life he became obsessed by the idea of lost innocence (though he himself abandoned the five children he fathered out of wedlock with his maid). An accomplished musician who began writing in the 1740s, Rousseau shot to fame in 1750, when he won an essay contest sponsored by the Dijon Academy. The question was, Have the arts and sciences purified or corrupted manners? Rousseau argued that progress in the arts and sciences had "denatured" the soul of man. Although he never actually used the term "noble savage," this notion has forever been associated with him.

Rousseau's main preoccupation was not government per se, but the more strictly philosophical question of how to reconcile man's natural, psychological and moral qualities with his life in society. There is still much debate over whether Rousseau considered people to be inherently "good" or not. What's clear is that he launched the idea that people are born with something natural and inalienable, some potential that is either realized or thwarted by society. In his widely read treatise *Émile*, published in 1762, he outlined an ideal education that could preserve a child's essence while turning him into a citizen. In *The Social Contract*, published the same year, he argued that to reconcile "good" people with institutions, society must ensure that human security and liberty are both preserved. Rousseau rejected the idea of authority based on mere privilege or might, arguing that only the people are sovereign, and that only common agreement of the members of a society can form a legitimate basis for authority. Rousseau's later criticism of religion enraged the conservative Sorbonne, and he was forced into exile in England, returning to France only for the last few years of his life. But his thinking, and that of the philosophes, established an association between French and anti-conformist, universal thinking that would last until the present day.

The philosophes spread and sealed the reputation of French as the language of the future, both through the influence of their writing and by travelling to the European capitals. Rousseau was widely read and particularly influential in England, where *Émile* was very popular. Montesquieu and Diderot visited Holland. Voltaire travelled to Holland five times, as well as to Berlin, and lived in exile in England for two years in the late 1720s and in Geneva a number of times. Their influence, along with the mystique of the salons, explains why the Swedish, German and Russian languages became sprinkled with French expressions during this period. Russians used words such as *coquetterie* and *gallant*. Dutch speakers picked up numerous Gallicisms, especially in the arts, public life and social life. The English, who were particularly susceptible to French influence because of their proximity to and long rivalry with France, picked up hundreds of words during this period, including *elite, avalanche, reservoir, bouquet, engagement, salon, buffet, liaison, caprice, façade, fanfare, pirouette, maladroit, bourgeois, éclat, manoeuvre* and *debut*. French expressions also came into use in England, including *bon vivant, coup de grâce, beau monde* and *tête-à-tête*.

During the eighteenth century, French spelling and grammar took on the written forms that make the language instantly recognizable to modern readers. The logical order of subject-verb-object became fixed in French sentences. The letters

I and J, as well as U and V, became completely distinct, largely thanks to spelling reforms undertaken by the French Academy in 1760. French language theorists also continued their work of codification. A hot debate erupted over whether past participles should remain neutral or *s'accorder* (agree with the gender and number of the nouns they relate to). In the end, some would agree and others would do so only under special conditions, but at least the situations were defined. Pronunciation evolved little during the century, except that some class differences became more marked; aristocrats tended to say *moi* and *anglois* as *mway* and *anglway*, while the populace, especially in Paris, said *mwa* and *anglay* (as they do now).

While theorists and purists were busy establishing rules for French, the language itself kept evolving in order to assimilate the new realities of science, industry and exploration. New words such as *usine* (factory), *bureaucratie*, *économiste*, *gravitation* and *azote* (nitrogen) came into usage. The French developed new adjectives such as *alarmant* (alarming) and new nouns such as *moralisme* (moralism) to describe the new philosophy and new sensibilities. *Ingénieur* (engineer) and *facteur* (mailman) took on their modern meanings. During the eighteenth century English words such as *challenge, toast* and *ticket* (originally imported from Old French into English) re-entered French, sometimes with new meanings. The influence of British parliamentarianism brought the new words *officiel* (official), *législature* (legislature) and *inconstitutionnel* (unconstitutional) into usage, as well as *club, vote, pétition* (petition) and *majorité* (majority). There were many other foreign influences on French at this time; Rousseau's *La nouvelle Héloïse* (*The New Eloise*), for instance, popularized an old Swiss term, *chalet*, which meant "shelter" in the Franco-Provençal dialect spoken around Geneva at the time.

—

It was during this period that French replaced Latin as the language of European diplomacy, although this was never stated anywhere in international law. Until 1678 almost all European treaties were written in Latin, which was considered a neutral language. That began to change after the Treaty of Westphalia of 1648, when the Austrians, who controlled the defeated Holy Roman Empire, claimed it was their prerogative that treaties be written in Latin. For the first time Latin became associated with a specific nationality. French was a defined language, so its corset of rules and definitions meant that whatever was written in French would not change its meaning a couple of years later. In 1678 the Treaty of Nijmegen was written in both French and Latin. The Treaty of Rastatt and Baden of 1714—one of three that ended the War of the Spanish Succession—was the first to be written completely in French, even though France had lost the war. The French plenipotentiary, the Duc de Villars, knew only French, so his imperial counterpart, Prince Eugene of Savoy, who knew French, accommodated him. According to Professor Agnès Walch, of the University of Artois in France, the negotiators introduced a clause specifying that although the treaty was negotiated in French, that did not constitute a precedent. This clause reappeared in other treaties in 1736 and 1748. But by the time of the Treaty of Paris in 1763, the clause had disappeared, and the entire treaty was negotiated and written in French—even though the French had lost. From then on, all treaties were negotiated in French. In most European countries, with the notable exception of Britain, even diplomatic notes were written in French.

French became the language of diplomacy in Europe less because of the power of France than because of the power of French. A class of career diplomats had begun to appear at the time. Many of them were also career soldiers, and soldiers, who usually joined the military at a young age, rarely knew Latin. These career diplomats started bringing their wives to diplomatic conferences, and women of high society spoke French, so salon culture gradually spilled over into the meeting rooms. (The participants also spoke French among themselves so the servants could not understand them.) No decree ever made French the diplomatic language of Europe; its status was never official. It was all a question of usage. French remained the sole language of high diplomacy in Europe until 1919.

Social conditions also favoured the international pre-eminence of French. In the political system of Europe, based as it was on marriages among different dynasties, all communication between princes and princesses, people of rank, writers, and their lovers and mistresses—what Marc Fumaroli calls the "politico-diplomatic machine of the century"—was done in French. From Spain, Italy and Portugal to England, Germany, Holland, Russia and Sweden, the crowned heads studied French, corresponded in French and looked to France as an example and a model.

Young Swedish nobles had been travelling to Paris for their education for a good century before Gustav III (who ruled 1771–92) came to power, but he would become the king of francophiles. A great admirer of Voltaire, as well as of Jean Racine, Gustav had been raised in French; he read French books and spoke no other foreign language. During his reign he introduced French theatre to Sweden, where it played to full houses, and he brought in French artists to decorate his castles. He was kept abreast of the news from Versailles through Madame de Staël, the Swiss wife of a Swedish ambassador and the daughter of Louis XVI's last finance minister, who became famous for her novels and essays. Gustav III paid an incognito visit to King Louis XVI and Marie-Antoinette in Versailles in 1786 (during the French Revolution he would try in vain to arrange exile for them). Shortly after this visit Gustav resuscitated the Swedish Academy (an earlier one had been founded in 1753). The Swedish Academy is still in operation today. Its motto is "Talent and taste" and its mandate is "to further the purity, vigour and majesty of the Swedish language."

Gustav III was an extreme case, but his taste for French was not uncommon among Europe's crowned heads. Catherine II of Russia (ruled 1762–96) was an avid reader of the works of Voltaire and Montesquieu before she took power. For fifteen years during her reign she exchanged letters with Voltaire in which they discussed European and world events (her French was full of mistakes—it was her third language after German and Russian). Like Gustav III, she founded an academy based on the French model, for Russian writers. Historians still debate whether she was an enlightened despot or simply a tyrant. In either case, she worked hard throughout her reign to increase the grandeur of the Russian Empire and looked towards France for ideas. She imported French intellectuals, scientists, artists and industry leaders, sent teachers of French to Paris to complete their studies, imported French teachers and hosted French theatre evenings in her castles. Most of Russia's nobility spoke French well into the nineteenth century—the nobles in Tolstoy's *War and Peace* make comments in French on almost every page. And the link between France and Russia remained strong until the Russian Revolution of 1917.

The case of Prussia's Frederick II (ruled 1740–86) was more complicated. He was easily as passionate a francophile as Catherine II, and he only ever wanted to learn and write in one language: French. He built a new castle, Sans Souci ("free of care"), modelled on Versailles, and peppered his Court with French speakers. He had French soldiers in his army and French bureaucrats in his civil administration; he wanted to hear only French actors and plays and wrote poetry in French.

He was known for including French witticisms in his messages to Voltaire during their long correspondence, like this cryptic dinner invitation:

_p_ à   _ci_
venez   sans

Translation: *Venez sous p* (*venez* below P) *à sans sous ci* (*sans* below *ci*), which in French reads phonetically as *Venez souper à Sans Souci* (Come to dinner at Sans Souci).

At the beginning of Frederick's rule he reorganized the Berlin-Brandenburg Society of Scientists in Berlin on the model of the French Academy, and it was this academy that hosted the essay contest that Rivarol and Schwab won in 1783.

But his francophilia didn't prevent Frederick II from going to war with the French and the Russians. His ruthless expansionism, especially the way in which Prussia—along with Russia and Austria—dismantled Poland, made a serious dent in his reputation in Europe. Some historians argue that Frederick II was using the philosophes for the same purpose François I had used the Humanists for: trying to get the endorsement of public-opinion makers in order to boost his nation's international reputation at a time when it was in an unfavourable light. In the end, Frederick's aggressive foreign policy spelled the end of his friendship with Voltaire, and an end to the witty invitation cards.

The British were among the most ambiguous regarding their love of things French, not surprisingly, since their national identity had been built on England's four-century-long competition with France. Yet French retained an undeniable cachet among England's upper classes. A couple of years before defeating the French outside the walls of Quebec City, the young officer James Wolfe was sent to the City of Light for five months to dance and fence, ride and go to the opera, and improve his French. Most British officers in Quebec spoke French. Horace Walpole and David Hume wrote much of their correspondence in French. British aristocrats and members of the gentry sent their offspring on an extended journey through Europe to Italy, when they were expected to develop their taste and manners and be exposed to civilization. France, a mandatory stage of the trip, often became the sole destination.

During the eighteenth century the grand tour became a target of satirical travel writing in England. In *A Sentimental Journey* Laurence Sterne (who lived in France in 1762–64 and 1765–66) calls France a "polished nation," though "a little too serious." Over the course of a light-hearted romp through France, the novel's hero turns out to be not so much widening his cultural horizons as chasing after a married woman, but through the process he encounters all the characteristics associated with the French of the period: refinement, debauchery, gallantry, wit, urbanity and self-assurance. Interestingly, the word *sentimental* entered French under Sterne's influence; the adjective didn't yet exist in the language, so the French translator and publisher just used the English word.

British admiration for France and French had its limits. In his *History of the French Language,* published in the nineteenth century, Ferdinand Brunot argued that the British accepted French as the language of Europe in the eighteenth century, but never accepted the idea of French cultural superiority, as many other countries did. In Britain, Brunot says, French was considered simply a "universally useful language." The works of many British thinkers and scientists spread throughout Europe thanks to wide dissemination of their works in French translation. The philosopher John Locke became known in Italy through a French translation of his *Essay on Enlightenment,* which appeared in 1736, and the writings of Hobbes also spread through Europe in French. French started being taught as a second language at Oxford University in 1741. But according to Brunot, the English really just "wanted to learn a European language, not French per se."

More than anything, it was this quest for a European language that drove people outside of Europe's upper classes to learn French. Throughout the century, noble and middle-class families scrambled to find ways to enter the French-speaking world. Many French dictionaries and grammar guides were designed specifically for the provincial bourgeoisie and nobility of France, but readers outside those circles also picked them up. In the German principalities many people thought that German was good only for speaking to their horses. Parents sent children to school in French, and the schools run by Huguenots were especially popular; in a century and a half these would form the backbone of a network of *collèges* and *lycées français*. Families also imported French-speaking nannies from either France or Switzerland. In many places in Europe the French language made progress independently of any contact with France or its people. French books or French translations and French theatre were widely available in the European capitals. Francophiles were able to keep abreast of the news in France by reading one of the dozen French-language papers called *Gazette de Hollande*. According to Clyde Thogmartin of the University of Indiana, the title described any international French paper, whether it was published in London, Berlin, Monaco, Luxembourg or Geneva. (The label was a tribute to the fact that most cities in Holland had a newspaper in Dutch and another in French. The oldest version, the *Gazette de Leyde*, was founded in 1639.)

But the seeds of francophilia were spreading even beyond Europe. French made remarkable progress during that period in a region of Moldavia and Wallachia that was under Turkish influence, the future Romania. Romanians already spoke a Romance language, making it easier for them to master French. The language gained wide currency through their contacts with francophile Russians and the Greek administrators of the Ottoman Empire, who were also ardent francophiles. In 1859 Napoleon III helped bring about the union of Wallachia and Moldavia to form modern Romania. And in the first decades of the twentieth century, France's support and the strong franco-philia of the Romanian elites were critical in establishing an independent Romania. The Romanians as well as the Moldavians would retain strong emotional links to French even while they were under Soviet rule.

Although Antoine de Rivarol wrongly argued that English was the last language that would ever displace French (because, he said, it encouraged "disorderly thinking"), some learned observers of the time were already predicting that English would one day become the world's universal language. According to Ferdinand Brunot, there was more interest in English ideas than in the language itself, but it was already showing signs that it could rival French. Jean-Christ Schwab believed that even if English lacked in appeal—he said it was not "polite" or "man-nered" like French—it was one of the easiest languages to learn (from a German point of view). The main problem with English, Schwab wrote, was that it hadn't succeeded in spread-ing itself. But he predicted that that would change when English acquired its "prodigious empire" in America.

Schwab would turn out to be right, but by that time the reputation of French would no longer based be exclusively on refinement, or even on international influence. French was about to take on a new personality—as the language of revolution.

Chapter 6 ~

REVOLUTIONARY FRENCH

IN AUGUST 1790, a year after the French Revolution began, France's new National Assembly commissioned the world's first language survey. They appointed Abbé (Father) Henri Grégoire, a popular revolutionary priest, to carry it out. Grégoire sent fifty doctors, lawyers and professors to villages all over France to see whether people were speaking French, other languages such as German and Italian, or a patois—a pejorative term for local dialects. If they spoke a patois he wanted to know what it was like, whether it was similar to French, how vulgar or repetitive it was, whether children in the villages were schooled in it and whether priests preached in it; he even wanted to know if people swore in patois.

The project was ambitious, but Grégoire managed to compile his answers and present a report in four years. It was a stunning achievement considering the scale of the survey and the detailed information he had to process, not to mention the fact that the country was in the middle of a revolution and small-scale civil war the whole time he was gathering his data.

Grégoire's report, submitted to the National Assembly in 1794, paints a picture of France that still surprises foreigners today. France in the 1790s was a potpourri of different cultures and languages. Of a population of twenty-eight million, only three million French citizens spoke French well, and even fewer wrote it. Another six million could carry on a conversation, and at least six million didn't speak French at all. The thirteen million others probably had a shaky understanding of French at best. Grégoire discovered no fewer than thirty dialects being spoken across France. And more than two centuries after the Ordinance of Villers-Cotterêts was passed, French still had not pushed other languages out of the state apparatus. On the borders with Italy and Germany, Italian and German were used for everyday communications, in courts and in the administration. In other words, the young Republican general Napoleon, who learned French only when he was fifteen and spoke it with a Corsican accent all his life, was typically French.

The impact of the Revolution-and-Empire period on the French language was tremendous. It spawned a vast new vocabulary to describe new political categories and institutions. The function of French in France also changed radically, and practically overnight. During the Revolution, language became a tool that the French government would use to centralize the country. And through this process the French language became, for the first time, the foundation of a French national identity. The Revolution also changed the role of French outside of France, giving it a double personality: It reinforced the status of French as an elite language while giving it the new label of "universal language of liberty." And all this happened while France was being crippled by civil and foreign wars and Napoleon was draining France's resources in a vain attempt to carve out a French Empire in Europe.

Although decades—some even argue a century—of political conditions in France explain how France ended up with a revolution, its outbreak was sudden. The Revolution is widely considered to have begun with the storming of the Bastille on July 14, 1789; the political crisis that provoked it began ten weeks earlier, in May. At the time Louis XVI was staring bankruptcy in the face. After three years of bad harvests his subjects were rioting, so raising taxes was no longer an option. He had no choice but to consult the Estates General, a parliament composed of three distinct estates, or chambers, with representatives of the clergy, the nobility and the commons. The Estates had not been summoned since 1614, and their gathering unleashed a wave of recrimination, especially on the part of the commons, who resented not only the privileges of the aristocracy and the clergy, but also the arbitrary rule of the King himself.

The commons, which had already declared itself the sole representative of the people, forced the French regime to transform itself overnight. On June 20 the commoners swore an oath that they would not disband until they had a constitution to define their rights, and they proclaimed themselves to be the National Assembly. Six weeks later, this National Assembly—which had also attracted progressive members of the clergy and the nobility—abolished aristocratic privileges, destroying the feudal regime. A violent chain of events followed that would draw France into civil war, dictatorship and imperial conquest.

Historians still argue about how the French Revolution actually unfolded. Between 1789 and 1815 the country went through roughly five phases. From 1789 to 1792 France was a constitutional monarchy. During that time Louis XVI came to be seen as a despot, and in 1792 he was tried and beheaded. That marked the beginning of the most radical period of the Revolution, called the Terror, when France was run by the Comité du salut public (Committee of Public Safety), headed by Maximilien de Robespierre. Robespierre quelled civil war within the country and waged war on the neighbouring countries hostile to the Revolution. Some seventeen thousand opponents of his regime were beheaded and another thirty-five thousand jailed, but in 1794 Robespierre himself was led to the guillotine in a counter-coup.

In 1794 things calmed down under the bourgeois (but increasingly corrupt) government of the Directoire (Directory), until 1799, when a young general and popular hero, Napoleon Bonaparte, seized power and declared himself first consul, or dictator for life. Napoleon ran things competently for five years and re-established order in France. But in 1804 he decided to crown himself Emperor of France and wage wars of conquest to expand his country's territory. Napoleon's regime became increasingly despotic until the British defeated him once and for all at Waterloo in 1815; he was sent into exile on Saint Helen's Island to finish out his days.

This close succession of revolutionary and imperial governments between 1789 and 1815—more appropriately called Revolution-and-Empire—was a period of almost constant political, economic and military crisis that brought out the worst and the best in people. Maximilien Robespierre thought terror was the only way to deal with political dissent and preserve the Republic. At the same time he was an ardent democrat and defender of human rights, supporting the abolition of slavery no matter what it would cost France. Napoleon was a dictator and imperialist who did his best to reinstate slavery, yet he created such institutions as the Civil Code and a system of public administration, which are still in place in France and went on to become models for nations across the world. Then there were characters such as Charles Maurice de Talleyrand, who simply kept reinventing himself in order to ride France's political roller coaster. Talleyrand was Bishop of Autun (in the Loire Valley) when he joined the Revolution. When things got extreme, he went into exile. In 1797 he returned, became foreign minister under the Directoire and remained there under Napoleon. But in 1807, as Napoleon's ambitions began to become alarming, Talleyrand turned against the Emperor. In 1814 he represented France during the

peace negotiations of the Congress of Vienna, as foreign minister during the brief reign of Louis XVIII. And in 1830, after a
long period of retirement, he returned to advise King Louis
Philippe during the July Revolution (when the latter seized
power from Charles X). He ended his career as France's ambassador to London.

Abbé Henri Grégoire was perhaps one of the most prin-
cipled and consistent personalities of the Revolution. He was
well-known for writing a progressive essay titled "The
Regeneration of the Jews" in 1788. His tremendous intellectual
energy led him to support causes ranging from the Bureau des
longitudes (Navigation Office) to the emancipation of Jews
and slaves. As a clerical representative to the Estates General,
he was one of the first to cross over to the commons side when
they created the National Assembly. During the Revolution he
was an ardent nationalist and republican who insisted on
being the first cleric to pledge allegiance to the Republic.
When clerics were being dragged to the guillotine during
Robespierre's Reign of Terror, Grégoire brazenly walked the
streets in his priest's gown. He defended the nationalization of
the Catholic Church and later openly opposed Napoleon's
reconciliation with the Vatican. At Grégoire's funeral, students
unharnessed the horses and pulled the carriage themselves,
leading a procession of twenty thousand mourners.

Within months of the creation of the National Assembly, its
members already understood how important language was to
their project. In fact, the issue came up as soon as the revolutionary government tried to impose its authority. To be understood by as many people as possible, the National Assembly
initially decided to translate its decrees and laws into the local
languages spoken across French territories: German in Alsace,
Breton in Brittany, as well as Catalan, Italian and others. But

there were many problems with this approach, not least of which was the fact that many regional languages did not have clear rules, grammar or a defined vocabulary. But more important, the National Assembly really had no idea what people spoke or where. The initial reason they asked Grégoire to carry out the language survey was simply for him to assess France's linguistic situation and make recommendations on how the National Assembly should proceed with respect to the question of language.

But thinking on the issue evolved quickly. For one thing, the National Assembly did not have the means to translate all its decrees and laws. It also realized that, for practical reasons, it needed to establish a common tongue in order to enforce the new values of the Republic and its laws. In 1791, long before Grégoire's results were in, Talleyrand—then a parliamentarian—declared, "French must become the universal language used in France."

National Assembly members quickly began to see language as a way to create and solidify a national identity. In the *ancien régime,* the king had inspired such loyalty that the nation held together even though it was in effect multilingual. Now the legitimacy of the regime was based on popular support (that is, in the ideal scenario—this new democracy would switch modes several times, from monarchy to dictatorship to empire, before it became a reality). To win that support, the National Assembly set out to turn the French language into something with which all French citizens would identify—in other words, to make it into a French institution, on a par with the National Assembly itself.

When we lived in France, we were a little puzzled to hear people refer to the French language as an institution. To us the term applied to public services, buildings, corporate entities or foundations. But of course, in its pure meaning (even in English), *institution* really refers to anything that has been instituted: established, set up or put in place. And that's exactly how the French came to see their language—as a fixed and immovable part of the state apparatus. This view goes to the heart of one of the most fundamental cultural differences between English speakers and the French. The British tend to understate their institutions; their constitution is unwritten and their legal system is not codified into a whole. Strangely, their attitude towards language reflects this. The English language has rules (and many exceptions), but English speakers downplay the rules, especially when they are comparing their language to French. The French, meanwhile, proclaim and embrace their institutions with all their officialdom—and their language with all its rules.

French revolutionaries soon understood that to make French an institution, they had to get people to speak it. They quickly homed in on education as the means to this end. Article I of the first constitution, written in 1791, defined the "principal social goal" of the Republic as public education, available to all citizens for free. The National Assembly then created a Committee for Public Instruction. The main objective was to teach children to read and write in French. Through education, French would become *institué* (made into an institution), so teachers were known as *instituteurs*—a word used for primary schoolteachers in France to this day.

The plan had the added benefit of taking teaching out of the hands of the clergy and reducing their power—outside Paris, the clergy were predominantly monarchist and anti-revolutionary. Revolutionaries also hoped that by "instituting" French, they would get rid of the galaxy of patois and *idiomes* (foreign languages) spoken across French territory. Local languages had been labelled as patois long before the Revolution. A century earlier, in his *Dictionnaire universel*, Antoine de Furetière had defined a patois as "corrupt and vulgar language, such as used by peasants and children who don't know how to speak properly." In fact, patois were not seen as languages in themselves but, falsely, as corruptions of French. Although most regional languages were not just mispronounced French but languages in their own right, the term *patois* threw them all into the same bag and labelled them a sign of ignorance. Until the 1980s the idea remained ingrained in the French psyche that regional languages were corruptions of French, not its source languages, as they in fact are.

During the Revolution, patois took on a new significance. They were prevalent in the countryside, where support for the monarchy and the counter-revolutionaries was strong. Talleyrand claimed—and many believed—that if the revolutionaries could get rid of the patois spoken in the countryside, they would get rid of the prejudices of the people who lived there as well, and quickly convert them to the values of the new republic. Abbé Grégoire would later agree. In his report he wrote that imposing French would "smelt citizens into a national mass" and "replace their prejudice with universal truths and virtue."

Many plans were made during the revolutionary period to establish a system of free primary schools throughout France. But the results were meagre; it was partly a problem of manpower and partly the result of general political chaos. In many French towns there were no teachers who spoke French, and few towns had the resources to train new ones. The National Assembly came up with a vast plan to produce and distribute teaching books in French, but amid the political and social upheaval of the Revolution, the books never got printed. In 1794, seeing the poor results of the Committee for Public Instruction, the revolutionary government decided to create a teacher-training school in Paris, the *École normale* (teachers' college, a term still in use). Each of the *Départements* (administrative territories created during the Revolution) had orders to send four individuals "with a disposition for teaching" to Paris, where they would be provided with accommodation and paid during their training. But even that wasn't enough to get universal education off the ground. France would have to wait until the middle of the nineteenth century for a universal primary education system to be established (more on this in chapter 8).

French spread rapidly during the Revolution, but by other means. Administrators were sent all over France by the central government, with the result that men from different regions were mixed together and had to use French as a common language. Mass conscription, which began under Robespierre, also mixed soldiers from different regions in France, forcing them to adopt French as a common language.

Of course, there was plenty of resistance to the Revolution, both inside and outside France. As early as 1791, rebellions had reached the scale of civil war. In the Vendée, southwest of Paris, fighting was so brutal that one representative of the revolutionary government, Jean-Baptiste Carrier, went so far as to execute opponents by drowning them en masse from barges in the Loire. Meanwhile, Europe's other monarchs had awakened to the threat (and the opportunity) posed by the French example. Austria and Prussia attacked France, and Britain joined in when it realized that France might win. The French people, who feared losing their newly acquired rights, mobilized quickly. The war song of the Army of the Rhine, popularized by soldiers from Marseilles, became known as the "Marseillaise," and was adopted as the national anthem in 1795.

When the nation was being threatened, language became a means of defining the enemy. Revolutionaries came to regard the languages spoken in regions such as Basque country or Brittany and foreign languages in the border areas of France, including German, Italian and Catalan, as seditious by definition. They viewed people in the east who spoke German, and the Basques on the border with Spain, as natural conspirators against the republic. In a 1794 report to the Committee of Public Safety on idioms, Bertrand Barère (1755–1841) declared, "Federalism and superstition speak Breton, emigration and hatred of the Republic speak German, the counter-Revolution speaks Italian and fanaticism speaks Basque."

As early as 1793 the revolutionary government introduced laws banning the use of languages other than French. Members of the French administration who used a local language to carry out their functions could be imprisoned for six months and lose their jobs. The decree finally gave teeth to the Ordinance of Villers-Cotterêts, some 250 years after it was passed. The Committee for Public Instruction ordered a ban on Latin in secondary teaching. They tried to force priests to stop using Latin for Mass, but the clergy refused to obey. During the nine months of Robespierre's dictatorship, functionaries who spoke a language other than French risked being deported. But these repressive measures never really worked, and the so-called patois remained strongly entrenched until the Second World War.

Starting in November 1792, the National Assembly forbade the appointment of new academicians. By the summer of 1793 the guillotine, exile, jail and death by natural causes had reduced the number of Academy members from forty to seventeen. That same year, the Academy was shut down on the basis that it was a monarchist institution. The argument was questionable at best. On one hand, Academy members included a number of nobles, clerics and aristocrats, and the King had been the Academy's protector. But it was still dominated by the philosophes, who strongly believed in the ideals of the Enlightenment that had fuelled the Revolution in the first place. Academy member Abbé André Morellet was such an ardent supporter of the rebellious philosophes that Voltaire nicknamed him *Mords-les* (Bite-Them).

The National Assembly also closed the four other royal academies. Morellet, who was interim permanent secretary of the French Academy before it was closed, managed to save the Academy's archives and some eighty oil paintings by hiding them in his home (sacking and looting of monarchist institutions was common during the Revolution). But the French evidently missed their academies. Two years after they had been closed, the government created the Institut de France, with four branches dedicated to science, fine arts, history and humanities, and although there was no specific section for language, the Institut published the fifth edition of the French Academy's dictionary in 1798. In 1803 the French Academy was resurrected in all but name, when Napoleon created a fifth section of the Institut dedicated to language and literature. In 1816 it reopened as the French Academy.

French phonetics and grammar were not much affected by the Revolution, mostly because it unfolded over such a short period of time. Some aristocratic pronunciations disappeared, along with the aristocrats who had used them, but such changes were quite minor compared to the tremendous impact the Revolution had on French vocabulary. New words had to be created to describe the new political reality, new institutions and the radical experiments of different revolutionary governments.

Some existing terms took on new meanings. In the Middle Ages, the word *révolution* had applied to astronomy, and had meant a cycle. The French borrowed the sense of "toppling a government" from England, which had been through its own revolutions a century earlier. They then created a flood of derivatives such as *révolutionner* (revolutionize), *révolutionnaire* (revolutionary), *anti-révolutionnaire* (anti-revolutionary), *contre-révolutionnaire* (counter-revolutionary) and even *révolutionnairement* (revolutionarily). Ultra-revolutionaries were dubbed *enragés*, an old term that had meant "rabid" but during the Revolution took on the sense (now common) of fanatic, crazy or furious. *Nation*, which had previously referred to a linguistic group, came to designate a collectivity that lived in a territory (both meanings were soon merged). The Revolution also created *nationalisation* and *nationalité*. The centralizers were called *Jacobins*, while *Girondins* described those who were *fédéraliste* (federalist). The latter term took on a pejorative meaning in France (which it still has), as did *bourgeois*, which had previously referred to the urban middle class—now perceived as reactionary by definition. The most radical lower-class revolutionaries were called *sans-culottes* ("without knee breeches"). *Sans-culottes* produced *la sans-culotterie* (their behaviour), *le sans-culottisme* (their principles), the adjective *sans-culottique* and even *les sansculottides* (an untranslatable term applied to leap days in the revolutionary calendar—a curious honour).

Some of these creations didn't survive the excesses of the revolutionary period, but some had longer careers and were picked up by other languages. *Vandalisme* (vandalism), *anarchisme* (anarchism) and *terrorisme* (terrorism) all took their present meaning in English from French terms coined during the Revolution. Some terms disappeared, at least temporarily. *Parlement* (parliament) was abolished as a royalist institution in 1790 (it referred to the high tribunal in the *ancien regime*); after several generations it reappeared in France with the English meaning of the term.

Commoners also influenced the language. In the early days of the Revolution, Joseph-Ignace Guillotin, Louis XVI's doctor, actively promoted reform of capital punishment. Before the Revolution only criminals of high rank and nobles were executed by decapitation, which was more humane than hanging, strangulation or quartering. Guillotin's machine for beheading was almost named the *louisette* or *louison,* after the surgeon Antoine Louis, who perfected it with the help of a German mechanic (Louis XVI himself suggested making the blade angular so it would cut better). In 1790 it was named the *guillotine,* though it was also known simply as *la veuve* (the widow). Guillotin was jailed during the Terror along with many high-profile reformers (on the basis that they were not revolutionary enough), but he escaped his invention and died a natural death in 1814.

Although Napoleon was notoriously uninterested in the French language itself, he had a huge impact on it. Under his reigns both as consul and later as emperor, a mass of official terminology was created to describe the new apparatus of the State and the institutions he created, from Conseil d'état (State Council) to *préfet* (prefect) and *lycée* (college), all of which are still used today. His Code Civil (the Napoleonic Code) and his centralized administration called for hundreds of new words such as *département* (department), *arrondissement* (city district) and *commune* (town), as did other creations such as the Bank of France and *chambres de commerce*—a French invention.

The period also resulted in an almost total reinvention of the French military, creating new vocabulary such as *levée en masse* (mass recruitment) and *tirailleurs* (skirmishers). A French engineer, Claude Chappe, proposed translating the old military system of visual signals into a visual code using flags, which he called *sémaphore.* He convinced authorities to invest in a network of towers equipped with signalling systems and state-of-the-art optics. His *télégraphe* (he coined the term) system was so successful that the French army could relay messages from Paris to Toulon, on the south coast, in twenty minutes. It played a crucial role in Napoleon's ability to lead campaigns and coordinate efforts hundreds of kilometres away.

The revolutionaries were bent on modernizing all aspects of French society. In 1795 the existing currency, the *livre,* became the *franc,* and was subdivided into a hundred *centimes.* God, whose existence had been temporarily denied, became the *être suprême* (supreme being). One of the revolutionaries' most ambitious undertakings was to overhaul France's chaotic weights and measures system. The British had succeeded in unifying their system in 1496, but the French had still not gotten around to it, partly because France was so big. Each region had its own system, so a pound of flour and a pound of bread were not the same from one region to another. Talleyrand first proposed unifying the system. In 1791 the Academy of Science (which had not yet been closed down) recommended the *mètre* (metre, from the Greek for "measure") as the fundamental unit of measurement.

The Academy of Science decreed that a metre would be one ten-millionth of a quarter of a meridian of the Earth. To determine this, they needed an exact measure of the distance between Dunkirk and Barcelona in order to extrapolate the distance between the North Pole and the Equator (which they would then divide by ten million to get the metre). It took two teams of surveyors six years to finish the measurement, as their work was somewhat disrupted by civil unrest and war. The length of the metre was crucial because all the other measurements of volume, weight and surface area were derived from it. For example, a *tonne* was the weight of a cubic metre of water, consisting of a thousand litres, which each weighed precisely one kilogram. The system was decimal (that is, based on factors of ten). Prefixes denoting quantities were uniform for measures of mass, length and volume; *kilo,* meaning a thousand, was taken from Greek. The system became official in 1795, although with a temporary estimate of the metre, since they needed three more years to measure the distance between Dunkirk and Barcelona (the surveyors ended up with an error of three kilometres). Then it took France another forty-five years to overcome entrenched customs and make the new system mandatory for daily life.

This modernizing spirit was less successful with the Republican calendar. In their desire to blank-slate everything, the revolutionaries decided to get rid of the Gregorian calendar, with its religious undertones that included pagan and Christian names for days, months and celebrations. While they were at it, they decided to make the calendar decimal. The new calendar still had twelve months of thirty days each (plus five or six supplementary days at the end of the year), but the weeks had ten days and the days had ten hours of a hundred minutes each.

The revolutionary government hired the poet Fabre d'Églantine—better known for his bedtime song "*Il pleut, il pleut, bergère*" ("It's raining, it's raining, shepherdess")—to come up with new names for the days and months. D'Églantine was inspired by the weather and natural cycles, so he used different suffixes for each season, attached to Latin words that corresponded to the typical weather for each month. The fall months were Vendémiaire, Brumaire and Frimaire; the winter months were Nivôse, Pluviôse and Ventôse; the spring months were Germinal, Floréal and Prairial; and the summer months were Messidor, Thermidor and Fructidor. D'Eglantine wanted to rename the days after vegetables, animals and farm tools, but the National Assembly probably realized that they were already pushing their luck by trying to name the days after Latin numbers (*primedi, duodi, tridi* and so on).

This poetic approach had problems, the biggest being that

the previous calendar worked (even if the revolutionaries didn't like it) and everyone was used to it. In spite of its universal pretensions, the revolutionary calendar was based on the seasons around Paris, and it didn't apply well to other areas of France such as the Alps. And the revolutionaries didn't exactly make the calendar easy for people to use: Day 1 of Year I was September 22, 1792, the day the monarchy had officially ended. That meant that January 1 fell on 11 Nivôse. Robespierre, for instance, was ousted on 9 Thermidor An II (July 27, 1794)–which is why the episode is still known as Thermidor. The promoters also shot themselves in the foot by allowing only one day of rest in ten, rather than the one in seven of the old system. Napoleon abolished this impractical and unpopular calendar on 11 Nivôse An XIV–January 1, 1806. But French laws established while it was in use are still referred to by their republican date.

The Revolution also contributed to the spreading of French outside of France. From the outset the revolutionaries were bent on exporting their ideas, by force if necessary. As Oxford University professor and author Theodore Zeldin put it in an interview, the English invented liberty for themselves while the French invented liberty for all of mankind. Although the American Revolution, like the French, was carried out in the name of freedom, American revolutionaries never tried to export their new political concepts, with the exception of Benedict Arnold's foiled invasion of Canada in 1775–76. The French intended their new ideals about the rights of man to be universal, to apply to everyone. Although this campaign eventually evolved into a justification for imperial conquest, the French Revolution became the blueprint for all revolutions to come. It also inspired a generation of insurgents in the Spanish colonies, all of whom were francophiles, including South American revolutionary Simón Bolívar (1783–1830).

The influence of the Revolution's ideas was also important in Romania, which was still under the rule of the
Ottoman Empire. Romanian students who returned to their
mother country came to be known as *bonjouristes* for their preference for French. Links between France and Romania became
strong in this period, and even stronger when the French
actively supported the creation of an independent Romania.
At the same time, "La Marseillaise" became a hymn of freedom in Europe; it remains one of the best-known national
anthems today.

In its early years European monarchs greeted news of the
Revolution favourably, partly because they expected it would
weaken France, and partly because it was the first real-life application of the principles put forward by the universally
acclaimed philosophes. Many writers, particularly in Germany
and England, believed that the French had succeeded in creating
an ideal society. German philosopher Immanuel Kant called
France a nation of "superior organization." Hegel congratulated
France for "organizing reality around ideas." In England the
Revolution inspired Romantic poets such as Coleridge and
Blake. The Portuguese government was spurred to implement
reforms in imitation of France's. As late as 1804 Ludwig van
Beethoven was considering dedicating his Third Symphony to
Napoleon (he changed his mind when Napoleon crowned himself emperor that year, and dedicated it merely to the "memory
of a great man"). Reality sank in only later, as princes, dukes and
all the privileged classes—in particular, the autocrats—woke up
and realized how threatened they were by the ideas of the
Revolution. Its neighbouring countries soon attacked France,
starting with Austria and Prussia in 1792.

Outside France, the mass exodus of some 250,000 French
nobles, royalists and *réfractaires* (resisters) during the Revolution
buttressed the exiled Huguenots in many parts of Europe,

including England, Switzerland, northern Italy, Belgium, the Netherlands, Germany and Austria. About forty percent of the émigrés later returned to France, but sixty percent stayed. Stripped of their privilege and income, many took to teaching or other vocations, opened bookstores or became printers. Many also occupied important positions in foreign countries and contributed to maintaining the influence of French among the elite there. The Revolution-and-Empire and even Napoleon's ultimate defeat couldn't make a dent in the status of French as Europe's diplomatic language, at least immediately. The result was that many French émigrés ended up as administrators and diplomats for foreign governments.

The language also spread as France's territory expanded during the revolutionary wars—though not simply because conquered citizens were forced to speak it. Citizens of more than twenty nations fought in France's armies and thus learned French. By 1803 France had integrated all of what is now the Netherlands and Belgium, most of Italy and a good half of Germany, and many reforms of the Revolution-and-Empire period took root there, particularly the Civil Code. At the height of the Empire, France had doubled in size and population; the new lands acquired were run under French law. And language was no obstacle to French designs in Europe—elites everywhere still spoke it.

Ultimately, however, Napoleon's conquests would work against French. In countries such as Germany, Italy and Spain the French Empire produced an anti-French backlash that would favour the development of national languages. Napoleon himself unified the patchwork of hundreds of German principalities, city states and kingdoms into a more rational thirty principalities. And this merely nourished a movement that had been underway among writers since the 1760s to create a national literature and culture of their own—in

German. Some authors—for example, Goethe and Schiller—had tried to convince Germans that their own language was as good as or better than French. Such nationalist sentiments were still only tentative in the Europe of 1800; their full impact on the influence of French would be felt only in the 1870s.

Meanwhile, the Revolution was about to have unforeseen but important side effects for French, both in Europe and beyond. By 1800 the ideal of liberty had spread like wildfire to Haiti and exploded into a full-scale revolt that would lead to the creation of a new French-speaking republic. And in the decades that followed, European powers would unwittingly create not one, but two new French-speaking nations.

Chapter 7 ~

NEW SANCTUARIES

When we met Bernard Pillonel, the Swiss consul in Montreal, to talk about his country's place in the history of French, he strongly objected to the idea of discussing Switzerland and Belgium in the same chapter. He probably would have objected even more had he known we were including Haiti as well. But in the story of French the three histories are linked. Each in its own way is a by-product of the imperial wars that Napoleon waged after the French Revolution. In the nineteenth century the three countries became new *foyers* (centres) of French, and their citizens would go on to shape the fate of the language beyond French borders.

After the French Revolution began, it didn't take long for slaves in the plantation colonies of the Caribbean to pick up the cue and demand their own freedom. This put the National Assembly in a curious dilemma. Although they had passed the Universal Declaration of the Rights of Man in 1789, the new republic could hardly afford to destroy the economies of its extremely profitable slave-based colonies in the Caribbean. The revolutionaries decided against abolishing slavery, but revolutionary ideals were spreading beyond their control by this time. Within a year the French faced full-scale slave revolts in Martinique, Guadeloupe and Saint-Domingue.

Saint-Domingue in particular had been a ticking time bomb. The thirty-two thousand whites there made up only seven percent of the population—about the same number as the *affranchis* (free people of colour) and mulattos, who enjoyed no civil rights but could own slaves. The rest of the population, a huge majority of roughly half a million people, were slaves, and the colonial government often had to repress violent rebellions among them. The National Assembly took baby steps by granting citizenship to the wealthiest *affranchis* in May 1791, and then, a year later, to all *affranchis*. This alarmed the white planter class, who forced the French government to reverse its position. But the move backfired; capitalizing on yet another slave revolt, the *affranchis* and mulattos decided to join the slaves in a full-scale revolt the same year. The whites received support from the Spanish and the British, but when the French realized that the British were attempting to take advantage of the situation and take over the colony, they threw in the towel and granted civil rights to Saint-Domingue's former slaves.

At this point Saint-Domingue's prospects as an independent nation were promising. It was a rich colony, the *affranchis* were running the show. One of them, a military genius, General Toussaint L'Ouverture–who knew how to read and write, a rarity–had assumed leadership. Before the revolution, Toussaint had run his master's entire estate, worked twenty hectares of his own land and owned thirteen slaves. He turned out to be the most capable leader of the Haitian Revolution and by far the shrewdest, carefully manoeuvring among the European powers to push them out. By 1800 Saint-Domingue had a government. It wrote a new constitution in 1801 and proclaimed Toussaint L'Ouverture governor for life.

In the meantime, the French had begun to think twice about letting their profitable colony go. In 1802 Napoleon sent his brother-in-law General Leclerc to Saint-Domingue with thirty-five thousand men and ninety-six ships. It was France's biggest expeditionary force ever. The same year Napoleon decided to re-establish slavery–some say at the insistence of his wife, Josephine, who came from the planter class of Martinique. But in reality he had more strategic considerations: Napoleon wanted to regain control of the island's sugar production and turn Saint-Domingue into a base for the development of Greater Louisiana, which Spain had promised to return to France. Toussaint L'Ouverture was captured and died in a French jail. Although General Leclerc later died of yellow fever, along with most of his men, and the French were routed, the loss of Toussaint stripped the nascent republic of its most capable leader.

Haiti (the name means "mountainous country" in Arawak, the local Native language) proclaimed its independence in 1804. And from then on it was on its own, quite literally. No country would support it, and the French crippled the new country's economy by demanding 150 million francs in reparations. France didn't recognize Haiti until 1838, and the American government did so only in 1862, when the United States decided that the Civil War was really about slavery. Haiti would remain the only "negro republic" (as it was often called then) during that century, but it went on to be run by a series of emperors, kings and dictators, each more corrupt and incompetent than the last, and it remained bogged down by rampant racism between the black and mulatto classes.

The creation of Haiti had an immediate impact on the future of French. Some ten thousand refugees (planters and free people of colour alike) fled from Haiti to Cuba and then to New Orleans after 1804, where they strengthened the local French culture for another two generations, bringing new blood, new money, know-how and cultural artifacts such as *vaudou* (voodoo). But France, which had got Louisiana back from Spain, couldn't make a go of this vast territory without the rich colony of Saint-Domingue to supply it with men and money and serve as a base, so Napoleon decided to sell Louisiana to the

American government. President Jefferson had asked only for New Orleans and Florida, and his negotiators were much surprised when Napoleon decided to throw in the rest of Louisiana for fifteen million dollars. The price sounds ridiculously low today, but at the time it amounted to a large part of the entire annual revenue of the United States government.

Economically the Haitian people made slow progress after independence. And since the population had no tradition of industry and literacy, things went from bad to worse. Yet Haiti became a vibrant centre for painters, writers and poets. The country also adopted French as an official language—a phenomenon that would prove crucial when the United Nations was created in the next century. (Haiti would also give Canada its present Governor General, former journalist Michaëlle Jean.) Creole would not be regarded as a legitimate language until the beginning of the twentieth century, and Haiti did not make Creole an official language until 1987.

The Haitian elite have always been strongly francophone. Haitian writers have a strict sense of correctness in their use of French, but Creole grassroots add a flair to their language use, and an unbridled creativity, particularly in the use of metaphors. One of Quebec's greatest contemporary authors, Haitian writer Dany Laferrière, told us, "The French language is *notre butin de guerre. C'est à nous, on en fait ce qu'on veut*" (". . . our war booty. It's ours, and we do what we want with it").

The most famous writer of Haitian origin was Alexandre Dumas, who was a quarter black. His life was as dramatic as his novels. His grandfather, Antoine Davy de la Pailleterie, ran a slave plantation in Saint-Domingue near a place called Montecristo (the origin of Dumas's famous novel's title was a mystery until his background became known). De la Pailleterie's wife, Cézette du Mas, was a slave who bore him four sons (her surname means "of the house" in Occitan, although some

claim it was a Frenchified version of *dûma,* which means "dignity" in Fang, a language of Gabon). In 1770 de la Pailleterie ran
into financial trouble and sold his wife and sons; later he
bought back his favourite, Thomas-Alexandre, the father of
Alexandre Dumas.

Thomas-Alexandre, as a mulatto, was denied a noble title,
so he assumed his mother's name, Dumas, instead. He started
out as a soldier in France and rose to become a general in the revolutionary army in 1793. Nine years later he fathered Alexandre,
and died shortly after. This romantic family history certainly fed
Dumas's love of historical literature. Of the 250 books he wrote,
the historical novels are by far the best, displaying an inimitable
flair in the writing, especially the Three Musketeers' famous
rallying cry, "One for all, and all for one."

Like Haiti, Belgium and Switzerland both owe their existence
to Napoleon's military failures. Napoleon's stunning victories
and powerful propaganda overshadowed the fact that his battles were getting costlier and costlier as time went on. By 1805
he had lost command of the sea. Because of diplomatic blun-
ders, his allies had turned against him. He lost the Russian
campaign in 1812 and his final battle, at Waterloo (in what
would become Belgium), three years later. At the 1815 Congress
of Vienna that followed his defeat, European nations looked
for a way to ensure general peace in Europe; they settled on
the idea of creating neutral buffer states. According to the original plan, the Netherlands and Switzerland were supposed to
play this role, as well as keep France in check.

Belgium was never meant to be. The region, known as
Flanders or the southern United Provinces, had been hotly disputed by France, Holland, Austria, Spain and England over the
centuries, but the locals had proven themselves remarkably
resilient by remaining autonomous. At the Congress of Vienna

Belgium was simply handed over to the northern United Provinces (the leading one being Holland). The problem was that the population of Flanders was not willing to be traded so easily. The francophones along the French border and the Dutch-speaking Flemish in the north were all Catholics, and they fiercely opposed the idea of being ruled by Protestants from Amsterdam, especially since they were more numerous, at four million, than the three million people in Holland.

In 1830 the Belgians rebelled and founded their own state. The British, thwarted in their scheme to create a strong buffer nation north of France, reacted somewhat as the French did towards Haiti. They recognized the new state but saddled it with harsh conditions, including a large chunk of the Netherlands' debt. They also forced Belgium to be neutral so it could fulfil the original objective of the Congress of Vienna—to form a buffer state against the French. The British went as far as refusing to allow a French prince to become King of the Belgians; instead they imposed a German-British prince, Leopold of Saxe-Coburg-Gotha, who would become Leopold I.

The French language fared surprisingly well in newly cre-ated Belgium. At the outset French speakers made up about half the population. But thanks to the enduring prestige of the language in Europe, the Flemish nobility, bourgeoisie and pros-perous classes all spoke French, tipping the linguistic balance of power. Belgium's constitution was written in French. The French-speaking Belgians even hoped to turn Belgium into a unilingual French state, but the plan failed. Contrary to the situation in France, where French competed with a dozen regional languages, in Belgium it had to compete with a single language whose speakers formed a united bloc. The Flemish were embarking on a linguistic revival at the time, similar to the Occitan revival that was happening about the same time in

France. Oblivious, the francophone elite pushed their linguistic agenda anyway. Their intransigence was the main factor in transforming the Flemish renaissance into a separatist movement that has lasted to this day.

But for the first 120 years of the state of Belgium, French remained politically dominant. In 1832, against the wishes of the British, King Leopold I married a French princess, Marie-Louise d'Orléans, the daughter of the King of France. French was so powerful, politically and economically, that the population of the capital city of Brussels slowly adopted it. Brussels was only fifteen percent French in 1830, but it is now thought to be eighty-five percent French, although the statistics are unreliable (since 1947 the Flemish have refused to conduct language surveys, still believing that Brussels is their city, and the lack of reliable data to the contrary keeps their argument alive). To this day, many more Flemish learn French as a second language than French-speaking Belgians learn Flemish. The famous Belgian accent, much derided in France, is often the accent of Flemish Belgians speaking French as a second language rather than that of native francophone Belgians.

Belgium went on to become an impressive industrial powerhouse. Jean Chrétien, the former prime minister of Canada, was fond of reminding everyone of his modest origins in the Quebec town of Shawinigan, located between Montreal and Quebec City. During the first half of the twentieth century the town became famous as a centre for high-tech research in hydroelectric power and paper production. Few people recall that the city's first paper plant was Belgo-Canadian Pulp and Paper, the creation of a Belgian engineer and industrialist, Ferdinand-Charles de Bruyssels.

It was in Belgium that the Industrial Revolution started on the Continent. Among other things, the Belgians were renowned for building roads and railways, which they needed to move their abundant stocks of coal and steel. When coal production dropped, the Belgians simply enlarged their ports to handle new types of trade. Faced with a tiny domestic market, they decided to export their talent for engineering, and went on to build turnkey projects all over the world, especially railways. Their industrialists invested in raw materials from as far away as the Americas, Asia and Russia. They built trains for France, Austria and Germany, and later for Spain, South America, the British Indies, Russia and China. The Belgian industrial baron Édouard Empain was responsible for digging the first Paris subway line and was the first to build high-risk turnkey steel plants in Russia. In fact, Belgium was the most dynamic industrial power on the Continent throughout the nineteenth century and until 1914.

Belgian scientists and inventors stood at the forefront of research and participated in the great wave of discoveries in the nineteenth century (more on this in chapter 11). They were particularly active in fields such as mechanics, optometry and engineering, and one inventor of note, Adolphe Sax, patented a new musical instrument—the saxophone.

Belgium owed much of its economic dynamism to its colony in the Congo. In fact, this tiny country probably benefited more from the second wave of colonialism than any other power in Europe, all things considered. Though the methods of Belgian explorers and colonists are alleged to have been among the most brutal, racist and exploitive ever used, there's no disputing the fact that Belgium was an effective colonial power, much more so than Germany (some of whose African colonies Belgium inherited after the First World War). Ultimately, Belgium contributed greatly to the spread of French in equatorial Africa, particularly around the Congo River basin.

Like the rest of the world, the Belgians became interested in equatorial Africa after hearing stories of the legendary Scottish missionary David Livingstone, who was famous for his exploration of vast swaths of central Africa. When Livingstone disappeared in 1866, an ambitious New York reporter, Henry Morgan Stanley, was sent to find him. He finally discovered him at Lake Tanganyika in 1871. His first question, "Doctor Livingstone, I presume?" became the most famous line from the whole African colonial era. In a curious twist of history, explorations by the Welsh-American Stanley would help the French language establish a large and permanent presence in equatorial Africa.

After discovering the Congo, Stanley couldn't find a country willing to finance further explorations, so he accepted offers from the eccentric (and, as it would later turn out, monstrous) King of the Belgians. Leopold II (ruled 1865–1909) never set foot in Africa, but from the beginning of his reign he had been bent on purchasing some exotic foreign territory to create a personal domain and then get rich extracting priceless treasures from it. Thanks to Stanley, he settled on Africa. Deranged as he was, Leopold II knew he needed to establish an appearance of legitimacy in order to explore Africa, so he created the Association internationale africaine (International African Association) and camouflaged it with supposedly humanitarian objectives. In fact, all he wanted to do was strip Africa of all the wealth he could get his hands on.

Stanley worked for Leopold from 1879 to 1884, signing treaties with chiefs on the left bank of the Congo, constructing roads and forts and organizing river navigation. By the turn of the century Europeans had heard about what Leopold and Stanley were really doing: forcing Africans to work in appalling conditions, often under torture, to hunt for ivory and later to harvest rubber. But until the word got out, Leopold II managed

to convince Europe's leaders that he was bringing "civilization" to Africa. And the argument worked; in 1885 they handed
over to him part of the territory south of the Congo River,
which he cynically named the Congo Free State. Millions of
Africans died under the rule of Leopold II. Joseph Conrad
based his novel *Heart of Darkness* (published in 1902) on the
Belgian Congo; it tells the story of a search for a deranged
company agent whose dealings with the locals have become
savagely abusive.

The Belgians reappear in different episodes of the story of
French. Whether in Africa or Europe, Belgium was a dynamic
centre, quite autonomous from France and the British, and it
played an important role in spreading the French language and
fostering its international influence. In the twentieth century
Belgium would become a founding member of the United
Nations, and later Brussels would become the capital of a new
form of internationalism: the European Union. An early sign of
this trend was the creation, in 1913, of the Union of International
Associations, still active today.

Belgium has always been part of the original domain of
French. The language is as native to Belgium as it is to France.
Some parts of Belgium could even make fair claim to being epi-
centres of the melting-pot process by which Romance dialects
evolved into modern French. Belgium was the centre of the
kingdom of the Franks before they moved their capital to Paris.
The Frankish king Charlemagne, who became Holy Roman
Emperor, was born in the Belgian city of Liège in 742. He spoke
Frankish, not Romance, but he certainly played a part in the
political rise of northern France and, consequently, of the
langues d'oïl. Although the oldest original document written in
Romance, the poem of St. Eulalie, is stored in an abbey in
Valenciennes, on the French side of the Belgian border, it was

probably written on the Belgian side, between Liège and Tournai. Two *langues d'oïl*, Picard and especially Walloon, were firmly established, and they both went into the historical melting pot that created French, although the extent of this contribution is debated among scholars. The great Belgian linguist Jean-Marie Klinkenberg characterizes Belgium as a linguistic suburb of France, a satellite. Indeed, the symbol of Brussels was, and remains, the same as that of the kingdom of France—the fleur-de-lys—even though, historically, Brussels has more often been outside the kingdom than within it.

"*Vous êtes Belge?*" ("You're Belgian?") is a question Jean-Benoît is often asked in France, though more often in the south than in the north. He knows enough not to be flattered. For some reason the French love to laugh at Belgians. Belgian jokes are like Newfie jokes in Canada or Vermont jokes in New England (we can testify that the same cookie-cutter stories circulate freely between languages). But there is at least one legitimate reason why some French confuse Belgians and Quebeckers: Both produce diphthongs (combinations of two vowel sounds) for certain vowels and drag other vowels out in a way that Parisian French no longer does. The pronunciations of Belgians and Quebeckers are actually quite different, but years of language purism have dulled French ears to the nuances that distinguish Belgian and Quebec diphthongs. Typically, Belgians add an I after the sound É so that *aller* (to go) sounds like *alleï*. In words like *bière* (beer) they stretch the E (*bee-ehr*). Quebeckers typically stretch the E *and* the diphthong, which results in a pronunciation something like *bee-ah-air*. Belgians also tend to use the resources of French differently from French people, distinguishing between words that the French pronounce the same way, like *brun* (brown) and *brin* (twig) or *bout* (end) and *boue* (mud).

Belgians themselves disagree on what exactly constitutes the so-called Belgian accent. The strongest examples come from either native Flemish speakers who use French as a second language, or citizens of Brussels, where the Flemish influence is by far the strongest. Elsewhere, native Belgians speak very normative French under the influence of Picard and Walloon, two dialects spoken on both sides of the Franco-Belgian border and therefore not specifically Belgian. The universally distinct trait of Belgian French is found in its vocabulary, a result of the influences of Flemish, Picard and Walloon. Belgians have different terms for institutions; they do not speak of the *maire* (mayor) and *lycée* (college) but of the *bourgmestre* and *athénée*. They use terms such as *wassingue* (floor cloth) and *drache* (heavy rain). Germanic influence has led Belgians to use terms such as *une fois* (once), which is a calque, or loan translation, of the Flemish *eenmaal.*

Belgians also count differently. Whereas the French have come to say *soixante-dix* (literally "sixty and ten," for seventy), *quatre-vingts* ("four twenties," for eighty) and *quatre-vingt-dix* ("four twenties and ten," for ninety), the Belgians kept the more sensible *septante, huitante* and *nonante,* which are calqued on the French *quarante* (forty), *cinquante* (fifty) and *soixante* (sixty). For *eighty* some Belgians say *octante,* but more prefer, *quatre-vingts.* Although it sounds more modern to say *septante* or *nonante,* the terms actually come from an older system of counting.

Apart from these few exceptions of vocabulary and usage, Belgians, like the French, on the whole embrace a very purist conception of language. The main reason is that their education system was strongly influenced by the French system (more on this in chapter 8). So, unlike Quebeckers, many Belgian writers and intellectuals enter the French cultural sphere quite seamlessly. It was a Belgian schoolteacher and scholar, Maurice Grévisse, who published the definitive grammar of French, *Le bon usage,* in 1936.

———

The history of Switzerland is far more complex than that of Belgium. It started as a confederacy of German-speaking cantons in 1291, but France's influence on Switzerland has always been strong. When François I crushed Swiss ambitions in Italy at the battle of Marignano in 1515, he gave the Swiss trading privileges with France, and France remained their main market until the French Revolution. The western, francophone cantons of Vaud, Valais, Fribourg, Neuchâtel and Geneva were originally outside Switzerland, although they frequently allied with the Swiss to defend themselves against the Duchy of Savoy, France, Italian city states or German principalities. These francophone and semi-francophone cantons progressively joined the confederation until 1815, when the Congress of Vienna formally integrated them into Switzerland. During the same negotiations, Switzerland's neutrality was recognized, making it a virtual sanctuary of peace in the middle of Europe.

Unlike Belgium, which influenced French because of its economic and cultural dynamism, Switzerland's impact on French came about through the peculiar fate of one city— Geneva. In the history and geography of Switzerland, Geneva sticks out like an appendix, sharing about 118 kilometres of its border with France but only seven with Switzerland. During the Protestant Reformation, the exiled French theologian Jean Calvin established the political and religious doctrine that transformed Geneva into an autonomous city state. Calvin preached an ascetic form of Protestantism that became very influential in England and America among the Puritans (who called him John Calvin). During the wars of religion in the sixteenth century, Geneva became a refuge for the French Huguenots. The first wave of eight thousand doubled the population of the city between 1549 and 1587, followed by a second wave after the revocation of the Edict of Nantes—after which Geneva became the centre of French Protestantism.

The Geneva Huguenots became important in the textile industry, and as goldsmiths and watchmakers.

Over the centuries, business got so good that Swiss banks in Geneva (as well as in Zurich and Basel) accumulated huge reserves of capital. In the eighteenth century Geneva developed a reputation as a banking centre. Swiss bankers demonstrated an uncanny talent for investing abroad. One of them–Jacques Necker, Louis XVI's last finance minister–was the father of Madame de Staël, and she held a famous salon on the shores of Lake Geneva (in French, Lac Léman), which was already a refuge for the rich and famous. This had a spillover effect all the way to Lausanne, in the canton of Vaud, which was also on the shores of Lake Geneva–an area still known as the Swiss Riviera. The accumulation of wealth transformed Geneva into an important intellectual centre. As a printing centre, Geneva was not as important as Holland, but it did remain French, whereas the Huguenots in Holland assimilated in the eighteenth century. Jean-Jacques Rousseau was born in Geneva, and returned there in 1754 after he became famous in Paris. Voltaire was frequently seen in Geneva as well; he went there seeking refuge from the French authorities, who often threatened to jail him for his irreverence.

Although there have always been far fewer francophones in Switzerland than in Belgium–today about 1.4 million, compared to 4.4 million in Belgium–Switzerland's francophones, especially Genevans, have played a remarkable role in the development of internationalism. Geneva's prestige in watch-making and industry was eroding by the mid-nineteenth century, so the city reinvented itself by creating a completely new form of international activity–humanitarian aid. Geneva had long been a popular travel destination for the French and English elite. Its neutrality also made it an ideal location for representatives of countries such as France, Germany and

England—always rivals—to meet to consider their common interests. Starting in 1853, the International Sanitary Convention (which later became the World Health Organization) and the World Meteorological Organization were established in Geneva to find ways to control epidemics and coordinate efforts on weather forecasts.

Henri Dunant (1828–1910), the founder of the International Red Cross, was an important player in developing Geneva's new international vocation. His story is a film waiting to be produced. Although a Genevan, he left Switzerland in the 1850s to run a colony of Swiss citizens living in Algeria. In order to get the proper papers to open a grain mill in the colony, he tracked down Emperor Napoleon III (Napoleon's nephew, who was briefly president and then France's second emperor from 1852 to 1870), following him all the way back to Italy, where he was fighting the Austrians. In 1859 Dunant arrived in the wake of the battle of Solferino, where forty thousand men died, mostly because of lack of medical care. In 1862 he published *Un Souvenir de Solferino* (*Memories of Solferino*), which recounted the horrors he had witnessed. In this book Dunant called for an international body for the care of the wounded.

The idea snowballed, and by 1863 the International Committee of the Red Cross had been created, thanks to the support of four influential Geneva francophones, including General Dufour and Gustave Moynier, who would run the organization for its first forty years. The next year, sixteen countries signed the first Geneva Convention. This accord obliged signatories to take care of the wounded and to protect medical personnel, regardless of their nationality, during conflicts. It was the first move to civilize modern warfare and has remained the basis of humanitarian law ever since. Dunant went bankrupt the same year and lived in obscurity until a journalist rediscovered him in a poorhouse in the late 1890s. He won the first Nobel Peace Prize in 1901.

The spillover effect of this burgeoning internationalism was almost immediate. In 1865 Geneva was made the headquarters of the International Telegraphic Union. Berne became host of the Universal Postal Union in 1874 and the World Intellectual Property Organization in 1886. In 1915, as the First World War was raging, Pierre de Coubertin moved his International Olympic Committee from Paris to Lausanne, where it enjoyed the protection of Swiss neutrality. Geneva has gone on to attract some 250 other international organizations of all sizes.

All Swiss francophones—a fifth of the population, known as Suisses Romands—are spread over half a dozen cantons, and there is not really a unified Swiss Romand dialect. Historically their cantons belonged to a dialectal area known as Franco-Provençal, a Romance dialect spoken in a pocket around Geneva, but stretching into Besançon, Lyon, Grenoble and Val d'Aoste. (Franco-Provençal is in a category of its own, neither *langue d'oc* nor *langue d'oïl*.) For instance, Genevans spoke a Franco-Provençal dialect related to the dialect spoken in Savoy. Language purism is strong among Swiss francophones to the extent that many outsiders believe the Romand dialect is dead. In fact, the Swiss tend to present a very standardized French to the outside world while maintaining their dialectal variations among themselves, especially in rural areas.

Like the issue of the Belgian accent, that of the Suisse accent is complicated. Many French people swear that there is a typical Swiss accent. In fact, what is assumed to be a typical Swiss accent is actually the accent of a German Swiss speaking French as a second language. As for the Suisses Romands, they have roughly the same accent that one would hear in France near the Swiss border. They have a reputation for speaking slowly, but the real difference is where they put the emphasis in their words and sentences. Whereas standard French stresses the last syllable of words and sentences, Swiss French stresses the penultimate (second-last) syllable. This produces a musicality that is instantly recognizable, though it is more typically Franco-Provençal than Swiss per se. Like Belgians and Quebeckers, Swiss francophones also pronounce vowels in a way that distinguishes homonyms (Belgians and Quebeckers distinguish vowels sounds too, but different vowels). Words like *peau* (skin) and *pot* (pot) sound the same in Paris, but in Switzerland they are differentiated as *po* and *pah*.

Features that are more genuinely Swiss than French are primarily in vocabulary. The German influence is obvious although not as great as one might expect. The Swiss say *chlaguer* (from *schlagen,* to smack) and *poutser* (from *putzen,* to clean). They say *rösti* for the grated-potato pancake and *foehn* to describe a warm wind, and also a hairdryer. Swiss purists decried the use of Germanisms in the early twentieth century, blaming constructions like *"Il a aidé à sa mère"* ("He helped his mother") on Germanic influence. In reality, the use of the preposition *à* is merely an old form of French. As we saw in the case of pronunciation, the Swiss, like the Belgians, use resources that the French have forgotten. For instance, they say *"Il veut pleuvoir"* ("It wants to rain") to mean "It's about to rain." Like Belgians, they use a specific verb tense called *passé surcomposé* (the equivalent of the past perfect) to mark a past action that has ended, as in *"Il a eu neigé"* ("It had snowed"); Parisians regard this construction as weird. Rousseau sometimes pointed out the Swiss French "mistakes" in his own writing, though in *The New Eloise* he came to the conclusion *"Qu'aurait-on à gagner à faire parler un Suisse comme un académicien?"* ("What have we got to gain from making a Swiss speak like an academician?").

Because they use some of the same vocabulary to talk about very different political systems, political conversations between Belgians and Swiss (not to mention Quebeckers and

French) are minefields for misunderstanding. *Fédéralisme* doesn't have the same meaning in Switzerland as it does in France, Belgium or Canada. For the French it evokes medieval anarchy; for Belgians it describes the separation of powers between the Walloons and the Flemish. For the Swiss it refers to the integration of different parts into a whole. There are less confusing examples of Swiss institutional terminology. In Switzerland a vote is *votation* instead of *vote,* as in France and Quebec. Rescuers are called *samaritains* rather than *secouristes. Lycées* (the equivalent of grades eleven to thirteen) are called *gymnases,* like the German *gymnasium.* And the diploma given at the end of high school is not a *baccalauréat* but a *maturité.*

The Swiss have preserved a number of old French expressions, such as *dent-de-lion* (dandelion), long replaced in France by *pissenlit.* One of their most endearing regionalisms (except to Parisians) is the Swiss term for Parisian French: *françouillon,* a derogatory term that evokes Belgian expressions such as *Franskillon* and *Francillon.* They also count the way Belgians do; in fact, they have fully rationalized their numbers and more commonly say *huitante* instead of *quatre-vingts* for eighty.

In spite of the ways in which the Swiss, the Belgians and even the Haitians have shaped the story of French, it's surprising that they have been able to hold on to their own idiosyncratic pronunciations and vocabulary. The same century that saw the birth of these new homes for French also saw the birth of a powerful new home for language purism: France's national education system. Through the education system, language purism would reach new heights and gain new influence, beyond anything the seventeenth-century purists could have dreamed of–to the extent that virtually no francophone on the planet today can escape its influence.

Chapter 8 ~

FRENCH WITHOUT *FAUTE*

DURING OUR STAY IN Paris we decorated our offices with cheap artifacts of French culture. The most interesting were a series of large colour posters we purchased in Lyon. These quaint illustrations of episodes from French history were at least fifty years old and had been created to hang in school-rooms. Each contained a moral and was clearly designed to drive a principle of the French Republic into young minds.

Our favourite was called "A School before Jules Ferry." It depicts a group of children of various ages receiving a math lesson. The classroom is a shack and the scene is one of dis-order and chaos, with chickens and dogs running around among the students. In the foreground a schoolmaster appears to have been carving wooden clogs while delivering the day's lesson. He is swinging a stick at a child who is trying to perform an addition exercise at the blackboard, either as punishment for getting the wrong answer or, more likely, because he is irri-tated at being interrupted in his work. At any rate, the mes-sage of the poster is clear: School before 1880 in France was a disorganized, unprofessional business, and French children should be thankful for the work of France's first minister of national education, Jules Ferry, revered for putting in place France's public school system.

Education had been one of the great obsessions of the revolutionary period, but because of lack of teachers, resources and interest, many projects fell flat, and teaching effectively remained in the hands of the Church in the decades that followed. In addition, France was still predominantly an agrarian society where children were required to work, so few could be spared for studies. Under Jules Ferry, teaching became "universal" in 1881. The national education system would be the greatest tool for spreading French inside France. Yet its approach was anything but neutral; France's education system was put in place during a return to the ideals of classicism and language purism, and French would bear the imprint of this influence from then on. Under national education, purism entered the schools and spread throughout the French populace. That's why French writer André Gide (1869–1951) would later write, "*En chaque Français, il y a un Vaugelas qui sommeille*" ("There is a dormant Vaugelas within every Frenchman"), referring to the famous seventeenth-century grammarian who created the central doctrines of purism and *bon usage* (see chapter 3).

Although Jules Ferry made public school mandatory in 1880–81, the poster should actually be called "A School before François Guizot." Fifty years before Ferry, it was Guizot (1787–1874), the most important minister of the last French king, Louis Philippe, who took the first crucial steps towards creating a universal school system in France. Guizot was minister of public instruction between 1832 and 1837. A historian and a Protestant, he understood that reading skills were necessary to unleash the potential of a nation in the middle of an industrial revolution. He also understood that to build a state, the French needed a competent bureaucracy, and for that they needed schools.

Guizot began his program by making reading and writing skills a requirement for all public jobs. In 1833 he passed a law that required all towns to build a primary school for boys, and all Départements to have a teacher training college to transmit basic knowledge, including religious and moral instruction, reading and arithmetic. He made school obligatory for boys, opened up education to all classes of society (including girls), and created a body of school inspectors. His successors maintained the program, and by 1880 the number of primary schools had grown from 1,700 to 75,000. The number of *instituteurs* had risen to 110,000, and 6.5 million boys and girls were attending school. So by the 1880s, most French children had been exposed to at least some French.

In 1880–81 Jules Ferry, a pillar of the newly formed Third Republic, created the Ministry of National Education and made public school mandatory, free and secular. Schooling was organized into three cycles: primary, secondary and *lycée*. Part of Ferry's objective was purely *républicain*–he wanted to get the clergy out of public-school teaching for good. Even after the Revolution the Church had been encouraged to run schools, but clerics were known for rejecting the values of the Republic and advocating autocratic rule. In many regions, Brittany in particular, the clergy maintained and even encouraged local languages as a form of resistance to the Republic. Ferry's secular teachers came to be dubbed *les hussards noirs de la République* ("black soldiers of the Republic"), partly for their severe black uniforms, but mostly because they were trained to fight obscurantism and actively promote the values of the Republic.

Although Ferry was really building on the work that Guizot began, there is a reason that the French today speak about school before and after Jules Ferry rather than Guizot. Guizot was a conservative who thought that democracy should be limited to the landowning class (that is, those who paid at least two hundred francs in income tax–a fortune). He also advocated a strong role for the clergy in education. Ferry, on the other hand, favoured the modern, secular conception of the Republic, where everyone would vote and where the clergy would be relegated to running churches–ideas that are fundamental to the French Republic to this day. So Ferry went on to become an icon of republican education and Guizot didn't.

Thanks to both their efforts, however, education dramatically increased the number of people who had some understanding of French. At the time of the Revolution, not even half of France's population spoke French fluently, and another twenty-five percent had no understanding of it at all. By the Second World War virtually all of the French understood the language, and most of them spoke it well—although fifty percent of the population still spoke their regional language as a mother tongue. The switch to French strengthened the French state and democracy, and dramatically increased the size of the public that both French writers and the media were able to reach. That created a powerful French popular culture in the nineteenth century, a novelty in the history of a language that had been confined to urban, aristocratic and bourgeois circles for centuries (more on this in chapter 11).

National education not only taught French but also largely determined how the French—and, by extension, all francophones—came to see their language. After the abuses of the Revolution-and-Empire period, the French monarchy, which was reinstalled in 1815, strengthened both the academies and their thinking (known as *académisme*). The monarchy pushed the notion of classics and classicism partly because they were comforting and not challenging. Authors such as Molière, Racine, Corneille and Pascal, who were believed to conform to these standards, soon came to form the canon of French literature. Their language was thought to be pure and their ideas did not challenge the monarchy. More than ever, the Academy of Fine Arts and the French Academy were setting the standards for beauty and language use.

This return to purism was happening precisely when Guizot began building the education system. Between 1820 and 1840 most French people still did not speak French, so French teaching in schools was literally second-language teaching and, as a result, highly normative and rule-based. The influence of the new academism amplified this tendency. Between 1800 and 1860 no fewer than a thousand French grammars were published. The most influential was *La nouvelle grammaire française,* by François Noël and Charles Pierre Chapsal, published in 1823. It was followed by an abridged version, and the book went through more than eighty editions, including two translated American versions, one abridged and the other full-length.

In the early decades of the nineteenth century the flurry of activity in language instruction materials was phenomenal. In 1834 the Bescherelle brothers came out with another grammar, *La grammaire nationale.* Although *Le Bescherelle* now specializes in verb conjugations, it is still one of the most important names in French grammar. In 1849 an enterprising school director, Pierre Larousse, came out with the *Lexicologie des écoles primaires,* the first full method for teaching French grammar and spelling ever published. Three years later he published the *Dictionnaire complet,* which bore the motto "A dictionary without examples is a skeleton." At about the same time the lexicographer Émile Littré published the *Dictionnaire de la langue française.* With its original definitions, etymology and examples from authors, it set a new standard in the field. Larousse and Littré are still among the biggest names in today's dictionary business, and until the creation of *Le Robert* in 1967, *Le Larousse* enjoyed a virtual monopoly in schools.

In 1835 the French Academy published the sixth edition of its *Dictionnaire,* which got its usual lukewarm reception. However, partly because of Guizot's influence, the French government decided at this time that candidates for the civil service had to pass written and oral tests. That meant that the government needed a standard, so it turned to the French Academy. This was the first (and only) time the work of the Academy took on a genuinely official character and, predictably, this became the heyday of its influence. Lexicographers even published unauthorized versions of the Academy's dictionary on their own. In 1836 and 1837 no fewer than four of these abridged (basically bootleg) editions of the dictionary came out. Joining the movement, publishers edited and republished the classic French authors, including Molière, Racine and La Fontaine, with the new, official spellings. Ever since then, francophones have entertained the myth that classic French authors wrote exactly like the French bourgeois of 1830. This linguistic revisionism fed (and still feeds) a quasi-religious belief among francophones that the French language had been *fixé* (set) since the time of Louis XIV. That's patently false, but most French speakers and many foreigners believe it.

While the Academy's work had achieved official status, the real drive behind the purist movement came from the schools. Possessed by the idea of a pure language, teachers began pushing an idealized, bourgeois version of French on schoolchildren. They started a tradition of drilling generations of kids to write purely and perfectly by imitating the classics. This is why francophones—particularly, but not only, the French—are known for trying to speak as they write (formally, with rules), rather than write as they speak (informally, favouring effective communication, an approach widely associated with the writing of English speakers).

Although language purism has been drilled into the French for centuries through education, it is by no means exclusive to them. But francophones outside of France are perhaps more tolerant of linguistic variation, mostly because the French they speak differs from the *norme* imposed by

French education. North American francophones are also influenced by a cultural tolerance for language mistakes that is more typical of the English-speaking majority around them, who tend to value communication over form. Yet all francophones—and even non-francophones—are subject to the pressures of purism.

The ideology of purism was so strong that it crossed the language barrier. Many French teachers in the United States accept as an article of faith that the French spoken in France is "purer" than that in, say, Belgium or Canada. Even the hundreds of thousands of English-speaking Canadian parents who go to the trouble of educating their children in French immersion programs (ironically, to make them more employable in Canada) tend to think there is an ideal French spoken somewhere else, and they imagine it is in France—more specifically, in Paris. What they are reacting to is the power of the *norme*: an ideal French that nobody really speaks. In fact, purism has never been able to eliminate accents and regional variations, because its primary object is the written word, which is why French is so uniform wherever it is written. No place or group speaks pure normative French; there is only a broad range of speakers across the planet who adhere to the ideal in differing degrees. For instance, we met many Africans who speak extremely normative French—at least they did with us, in public— and we responded in kind. But we don't speak that way at home, and neither do they.

More than anything, this attitude is explained by a particular concept that developed in the nineteenth century: *la faute* (fault). A *faute* in French is not just a mistake (which is literally translated as *une méprise*). *Faute* has a moral stigma, contrary to *erreur,* which is more neutral. Until about the fifteenth century the term referred to the sins of the flesh, as in "original sin." In the seventeenth century, language purists gave the connotation of sin to mistakes in speech or writing, and it became common to speak of a *faute de goût* (error in taste). In the eighteenth century Jean-Jacques Rousseau still spoke of his language *incorrections* (improprieties). It wasn't until the nineteenth century, when the French built their education system around a very strong purist doctrine, that the stigma of *fautes* was implanted in the minds of millions of French speakers, where it remains to this day.

The stigma was reinforced during that century by the introduction of *la dictée* (dictation exercises), a technique that has survived until the present. All cultures use dictation as a language-teaching method, but francophones rely on it, and until quite far along in their studies (Jean-Benoît did his last dictation in college when he was nineteen). French TV personality Bernard Pivot turned dictation into a sport throughout the francophone world when he began his famous annual dictation contest in 1986. Literally hundreds of thousands of people from dozens of countries competed to win the Dico d'Or (Golden Dictionary) prize. Pivot's dictations are really a series of grammar and spelling traps that have very little to do with how French is actually used. But usage is not the point. The whole idea of dictation is to prove that one can write *sans faute*—even at a level of language and vocabulary that has no use in the real world of conversation, culture or work (unless you're a lexicographer).

An anecdote told by author Christophe Traisnel shows that changes in how people wrote took longer to develop, in spite of the strong ideology of purism. He tells of a boring reception at Fontainebleau in 1857, during which Empress Eugénie asked her friend the author Prosper Mérimée to organize a game. Mérimée came up with the idea of a dictation. The results were surprising—the Emperor had seventy-five *fautes*, his wife sixty-two, and Alexandre Dumas twenty-four. It was the

Austrian ambassador, Prince Metternich, who won, with only three mistakes! Purism was obviously not a monopoly of the French; evidently even second-language learners had adopted a strong sense of correctness.

For generations now, French has been taught with an emphasis on exact spelling and grammar and avoidance of *fautes*. Francophones constantly remark on, or correct, one another's speech and writing. Where language is concerned, they can demonstrate a righteousness that is quite similar to the way the Puritans confronted (as some puritans still do) the notion of sin. Like sin, *fautes* are inevitable. So the idea functions as a kind of regulating principle that makes speakers nervous about how their transgressions will be perceived. It takes a particularly strong personality to free oneself from the fear of committing a *faute*. As professional writers we can testify that one of the strongest factors inhibiting francophone writers everywhere is the fear of making *fautes*, which is seen as being not only unworthy of the language, but even a traitor to it.

Francophones can be divided into those who are forgiving and those who aren't. Purists are not forgiving, and they have set the standards since the nineteenth century, so francophones learn to spell rare words and deal with cunningly complicated grammatical traps. The overall effect has been to produce an elite whose command of the language is magnificent and whose dictates tend to be regarded as absolute truths—even if no one entirely respects them.

The new emphasis on *bon usage* transformed what was once an extremely progressive concept—purism—into an extremely conservative one. By giving French rules, the purists of the seventeenth century had made it into the Latin of the moderns. But in the nineteenth century, with its ideology of the *faute*, purism rejected innovation, novelty, new rules, new pronunciations and, especially, new spellings. Purism also gave francophones the idea that the language *is* its spelling, to the extent that any attempt to change spellings was seen as an attack on French.

This new attitude came into focus when the French Academy attempted to reform spelling in the early decades of the nineteenth century. In 1835 the sixth edition of the Academy's dictionary modified a number of spellings. Some of the reasons were bizarre; for example, *enfan* became *enfant* (child) for etymological reasons, to conform to the verb *enfanter* (to give birth). But on the whole, the changes were accepted with little protest. This is when words ending in *-ois*, such as *françois*, became *français*. However, in 1900, when the Academy again considered reforming the spelling of some words, the purists screamed. How could anyone think of writing *psycologie* instead of *psychologie?* They argued that such changes would make French look ridiculous and it would be impossible to read the classics—an absurd claim, since their spellings had been thoroughly modernized just sixty years earlier. A compromise was struck. In 1901 the French Academy made some proposals and the French government published "edicts of tolerance" in which it declared the recommended modifications—without replacing the old spellings. Large-scale grammar reform has been frozen since the nineteenth century because the purists have allowed spelling modifications to be carried out only one word at a time. And that is why francophones still have to deal with complicated and untranslatable rules about such topics as the *accord* (agreement) of past participles (more in chapter 17).

Language purism rears its head every day in the professional life of francophones. For the French edition of our earlier book, Jean-Benoît proposed back-cover text that included the word *mondialisateur* (globalizer). The words *mondialisation* (globalization) and *mondialiser* (to globalize) are both in the dictionary, but not *mondialisateur*. It didn't seem like such a stretch to him, but our (French) editor refused to print the word on the basis that "*Cela ne se dit pas*" ("It's not said"). Why not? "Because it's not French," she told him.

Our publisher was a modern young woman who liked challenging ideas, but where language was concerned, like most French professionals, she preferred not to rock the boat. The root of her hang-up was that *mondialisateur* was a neologism—a new word. Neologisms are the great evil of purism, which dictates that each word should have one definition and that there should be only one word for any given definition. This shows how conservative purism has become a handicap. To language purists, all innovations in grammar and pronunciation are, by definition, *fautes*. Borrowing words from another language or making up new words is a sign of ignorance—this is the moral underpinning of the issue of anglicisms. Wanting people to conform to what French supposedly *is*—in lexicon, in grammar, in phonetics—makes it very difficult to find words to describe new realities.

In many cases, by the time the purists change their minds the world has already passed them by. In the sixth edition of its dictionary the French Academy explained what a *bateau à vapeur* (steamboat) was under the entry for *vapeur*. By the time the next edition came out, in 1878, people were using *un vapeur* (masculine gender) to talk about the boat and *une vapeur* (feminine) to talk about steam. The Academy refused to include the new meaning and the new masculine version, arguing that it was a neologism—in this case, giving a new meaning to an existing word. By the time they had decided to include the concept (in 1935), steamboats were no longer being used! It's something of a caricature, but this example shows how the purists have always had difficulty integrating new discoveries, new inventions, new realities and new attitudes into French.

French doesn't lack the resources—as the example of *mondial-isateur* shows—and it is not inherently less adaptable than English. The root of the problem is the purist mentality that has dominated French for the past two centuries.

Things are changing, though. Purists now distinguish between what they call "new words" and neologisms. A new word describes a new reality, whereas a neologism is a new word that describes a reality for which there is already an existing word. However, this almost theological nuance still doesn't solve the problems that result from the stifling influence of purism. For instance, the French Academy refuses to include the word *récré* (short for *récréation,* recess) in its dictionary. The Academy claims that *récré* is a neologism and is worried that it would set a dangerous precedent; it would then have to accept *gym* for *gymnase* (gymnasium) and *prof* for *professeur.* For some reason the Academy does not consider these terms to be acceptable French, despite the fact that everyone uses them. Fortunately, all other French dictionaries recognize them. Of course, these examples also show that French evolves no matter what the Academy thinks, but purists will probably continue to fight their rearguard battle—no matter how popular usage evolves.

At the height of purism's glory, other realities were shaping the language, including regional languages, Romanticism and slang.

Since the French Revolution, regional languages had been relegated to the status of patois. Yet these patois held their ground for a century after Guizot—to the point that teaching in patois had to be formally forbidden in 1853 and again in 1880. Like all European societies in the nineteenth century, France was experiencing massive population move-ment from the countryside to the cities. This mixing, along with education, gradually forced people to adopt French as a common language. At the same time, though, few French people abandoned their local languages, so most of them were bilingual. In 1900 most of the French spoke patois eighty percent of the time. According to the National Institute of Statistics, a third of French people born before 1920 still spoke their regional language to their children.

As a result of the nineteenth-century rural exodus, many patois terms entered the mainstream. *Spirou* (squirrel) came from Ardennes; *gones* (children) from Lyon; *cabochon* (stubborn) from Beaujolais; *tartifles* (potatoes), *pitchoune* (cutie, referring to a child) and *fada* (crazy) from Provence; *galette* (buckwheat crepe) from Bretagne; *arnaquer* (to sting) from Picardy; *dégoter* (to find) from Angers; *mouise* (shit) from Jura. This short list doesn't do justice to the depth of the borrowings, which number in the hundreds, if not the thousands.

However, the rate of borrowings slowed down as French became more solidly established as a mother tongue. By 1900 most of these languages had entered a phase of decline. It was not schooling that hastened the waning of regional languages in France so much as compulsory military service and, later, the development of mass media. Few patois had up-to-date lexicons or grammar. As the common language, French took on the job of naming modern concepts, which meant that the patois were relegated more and more to traditional spheres of activity and private life—the classic prelude to assimilation.

During the nineteenth century a number of poets and thinkers in France took up the cause of saving local languages. The most successful was the poet Frédéric Mistral, who worked to revive a variety of *langue d'oc* (or Occitan, as some call it) that he dubbed Provençal. He created an association, the Félibrige, to rejuvenate the language, and updated its spelling system, which had not kept up with the times. Mistral even wrote poetry in Provençal, and was the first writer in a minority language to win the Nobel Prize for literature, in 1904. Unfortunately, of all the pre-French dialects that survived, Provençal is not faring the best today.

In a 1999 survey, twelve percent of the French population—seven million people—claimed they still spoke a regional language. Another survey determined that seventy-five regional languages were spoken in France, although this included ethnic languages of the overseas territories. In continental France about two dozen local languages are still spoken, some as obscure as Poitevin-Saintongeais or Bourguignon-Morvandiau. The ones that are doing best are *langues d'oc* (two million people), Alsatian (about 900,000), Breton (200,000), Corsican (125,000), Catalan (100,000) and Basque (40,000). All of them, except *langues d'oc,* have the distinction of being spoken literally at the edges of the country. The use of these languages is largely oral; only a small proportion of speakers have any idea how to read or write in them, so their vocabulary and grammar do not follow the times. The category of *langues d'oc* is the largest because it includes five varieties, such as Provençal (spoken by about a hundred thousand people, mostly in the interior along the Mediterranean coast between Avignon and Nice). Throughout the twentieth century, Provençal, Occitan, and other regional languages such as Breton and Alsatian have been much more influenced by French than they have influenced mainstream French.

Ironically, nineteenth-century writers reacted to academism by defying it and pushing French in new directions. After two centuries of language purism, literature and poetry had been stifled by conformism. The standards of the Academy had been elevated practically to the level of law. Tragedies had to be structured according to the classical dictates of unity of place, time and action. If they weren't, they were dismissed as simple melodramas. To be taken seriously, poems had to be written in the alexandrine form. Literary characters were expected to speak in *beau langage,* whether they were nobles or farmers. The French Academy even refused to recognize a new literary genre, the novel, as a legitimate art form (unlike poetry and drama, novels have no classical roots). Important novelists such as Alexandre Dumas and Émile Zola were never accepted by the Academy because they did not write poetry; the Academy went so far as to reject Zola's candidacy twenty-four times.

This stifling purism and conservatism ultimately fuelled a creative explosion, the Romantic movement, whose impact was more profound on France than on any other society, and is still being felt two centuries later. The French were late in embracing Romanticism. It had already begun in Germany and Britain by the late eighteenth century; refugees from the French Revolution had absorbed it during their exile, and they brought it back to France (the most famous among these were Madame de Staël and Alexis de Chateaubriand, whose writings were suffused with a novel sense of the self). Like the Germans and the British before them, French Romantics rejected seventeenth-century classicism and embraced all things natural and medieval—or at least pre-Classical. Romantics valued emotion over reason. Artistic creation became an expression of the self—a very new idea.

The development of French in the nineteenth century owes much to a series of larger-than-life personalities who were part of this movement. They were all driven by an obsession with furthering France's greatness in science, in industry and in art (more on this in Chapter 11). Among the writers, the figure of Victor Hugo stands tall. The son of a general in Napoleon's army, Hugo was only fourteen when he wrote in

his schoolbook that he would be "Chateaubriand or nothing."
He started his first literary journal at age seventeen and soon
made his mark with poems and a series of popular novels. He
wrote with an ease and freedom untypical of his predecessors.
At twenty-one Hugo earned himself a royal pension. His first
play, *Cromwell,* turned him into a celebrity. Its preface—in
which Hugo made a plea for what he called *le grotesque* (popular reality) and against the classical canon of unity of time,
place and action—was considered the manifesto of French
Romanticism. "All too often, the cage of unity contains a mere
skeleton," he wrote. As to the play itself, it was anything but
classical, with hundreds of characters and dozens of locations.

At about the same time Hugo began experimenting with
a new approach to prose, based on telling the story of less than
ideal characters—a poor bohemian girl, a deformed bell-ringer
and a lecherous archdeacon, the three pillars of *The Hunchback
of Notre Dame.* Few fans of the novel, which has inspired several successful films, know that Hugo wrote it to save the
famous Gothic cathedral of Notre Dame from demolition.
During the Revolution Notre Dame had been used as a salt-
petre plant. By the nineteenth century it had suffered so much
neglect that builders wanted to reuse its stones for bridge construction. Gothic art was then regarded as ugly and offensive,
so Hugo's choice of location was deliberate; it linked the
grotesque characters with the ugly art. The first three chapters
of the novel are a plea to preserve this monument of Gothic
architecture—in Hugo's words, a "gigantic book of stone," which
he, as a Romantic, found beautiful.

Victor Hugo entered the French Academy at a youthful
thirty-eight, as recompense for his poetry and theatrical
works, not for his novels. When the president, Prince Louis-
Napoleon, staged a coup in 1851 and proclaimed the Second
Empire, Hugo fled with his wife, children and mistress to the

Channel Island of Guernsey, sister Island of Jersey (discussed in chapter 1). While in exile he reinvented French poetry and produced another masterpiece, *Les Misérables,* which was immediately translated into a dozen languages (the English editions even kept the French title).

On the reverse side of our poster "A School before Jules Ferry" is a poster titled simply "Victor Hugo." Hugo, of course, is an icon of the French Republic. In the poster he is shown with his trademark snow-white beard, surrounded by a group of children. Because of his uncompromising political stance (he refused to return to France after Napoleon III's general amnesty to exiles) and because of his literary genius, he became a sort of grandfather of the French Republic—a curious fate, since he started out as a royalist. Yet, more than any other French writer, Hugo stands as the prototype of the militant intellectual so idealized in French culture. Hugo was so admired that half a million people paraded under his balcony on his eightieth birthday, including a band with 5,500 instruments! When he died in 1885 at the age of eighty-three, three million people came to pay their last respects at the Arc de Triomphe, where his body was laid.

In the history of the French language, Hugo is significant for more than his political activism, or even his literary genius. Hugo stood at the forefront of a movement of nineteenth-century novelists and playwrights who, in the name of realism, had their characters use popular language, including *argot* (slang). The roots of argot go back as far as those of standard French. In the fifteenth century, Argot was the name of a crime syndicate of brigands, thieves and killers who spoke together in *jargon* (a deformation of the Norman word *garg,* throat). Jargon was not a language so much as a system of words that criminals used so they couldn't be understood by anyone outside the group, in particular the bourgeois and aristocrats they robbed and the authorities who pursued them. By the seventeenth century the bourgeois referred to this criminal jargon as argot.

What is argot exactly? Semantically it is French, but argot borrows its vocabulary from regional and foreign languages and masks French words with suffixes. *Roupiller* (to slumber) is from Picardy; *zigouiller* (to kill) is from Poitiers; *pognon* (money) is from Lyon and *ringard* (corny) is from a northern dialect. *Loustic* (rascal) is from German, *gonzesse* (girl) is from Italian, *flouze* (cash) and *souk* (disorder) are from Arabic and *berge* (years of age) is Romany. Argot deforms standard French words with suffixes such as *-iergue, -uche, -oche* and *-igue,* which are the most common. So *vous* (you) in argot is *vousiergue,* and *moi* is *mézigue.*

Writers began using argot in the 1830s, around the time French authorities broke the crime syndicates that spoke it. In Hugo's novel, thieves living in the Paris sewers do not speak like Madame de Pompadour. Hugo shocked his contemporaries in 1830 when he had convicts in the novel *Dernier jour d'un condamné* (*Last Day of a Condemned Man*) speak argot. In his 1862 masterpiece *Les Misérables,* he wrote two detailed chapters—quite fun to read, but edited out of English editions—describing how the common and criminal elements of society expressed themselves. In adopting argot, Hugo proved that it was not only a legitimate form of French, but often a more expressive one.

By Hugo's time argot already had the double meaning of both criminal jargon and *bas langage* (low, impure French)—and it only underlines the elitist mentality of purism that a single term describes both. Hugo himself hesitates between the two meanings. But by the time Émile Zola published *The Drunkard* in 1876, all popular forms of speech were called *argotique.* Argot, still alive today, has long been the hammer and anvil of French lexical creation. Singer Edith Giovanna Gassion's stage name, Piaf, meant *sparrow* in the argot of Paris between the wars. Paris butchers later developed a jargon called *loucherbem*, which consisted of replacing the first letter of a word with an L and moving the initial letter to the end, then adding an *argotique* ending such as *-em, -oque* or *-igue*. *Loucherbem* is itself a *loucherbem* term for *boucher* (butcher). And the process remains a lively one: A term still widely used today is *loufoque* (zany) from *fou* (crazy). But the meaning of *argot* became somewhat diluted over the last century. It is generally used as a synonym for *French slang,* but many French trades, or *grandes écoles*, refer to their own specialized terminology as *argot de métier* (trade jargon).

It's strange to think that, by using *fautes* as a source of creativity, Hugo and his contemporaries would go on to enhance the prestige of French more than anyone before them (more on this in chapter 11). Paradoxically, though, their influence never made one dent in the *norme*. Throughout the nineteenth century the *norme*, and the idea of *le bon français*, remained as powerfully rooted in French education as ever, and education in turn was powerfully associated with the goal of teaching French.

As the century progressed and European countries entered the race to build colonial empires, the French, more than any other power, used education to try to consolidate their possessions. They taught French to local elites with the aim that they would support the colonial regime, ultimately hoping that education would assimilate Africans, Arabs, Polynesians and Asians to French culture. But, as they slowly realized, the methods that had been effective on French soil could not simply be grafted on to foreign populations.

Chapter 9 ~

TOOL FOR AN EMPIRE

TLEMCEN, ALGERIA, HAS ALWAYS been proud of its links to
Europe. Just east of the Moroccan border, the small city's
Spanish-style architecture, flowing fountains and leafy streets
give it a distinctly Western flavour. A university town with
about twenty-five thousand students, Tlemcen has a long and
vibrant history as one of North Africa's intellectual centres. Its
cultivated atmosphere, combined with attractions such as a
twelfth-century mosque and an ancient citadel, also made it a
popular tourist destination, at least until civil war broke out in
Algeria in the 1990s.

We visited Tlemcen in 2002 to attend a UNESCO-
sponsored conference on plurilingualism. The gathering, organized by a French organization called Le Monde Bilingue / The
Bilingual World, was the first international event to be held
in Algeria in a decade, and we were the first group of foreigners
Tlemcen had seen since the beginning of the civil war. Back
in France, our Algerian friends were alarmed by our plan to
attend the conference. Tourists had been kidnapped sporadi-
cally over the previous decade, and killings were still going on
in major cities.

A French colony for 130 years, Algeria still bears the scars of
civil war, the fallout from its violent war of independence from
France, which lasted from 1954 to 1962. As a result, the country
refuses to admit to its French heritage, at least officially. Unlike
many former French colonies, it did not make French one of
its official languages after independence.

The heritage of French colonialism is complex, and nowhere more so than where language is concerned. We met a young fundamentalist in Tlemcen who said he refused to speak the language of the colonizer and went as far as pretending he only spoke English (though he spoke it with a French accent). But the hostility towards France doesn't translate neatly into a rejection of French. Among the former colonies, Algeria actually has the highest proportion of French speakers, to the point that French is hardly even a second language there. Half the population speaks French fluently, eighty percent of Algerian newspapers and most of the TV channels are French, and nearly everyone has some understanding of it.

The fact is, despite how painful Algeria's colonial history was, the country is a striking example of how successful the French were in spreading their language during the second colonial push, which lasted roughly from 1830 to 1960. In many ways the second colonial era was the second great historical opportunity for French.

If French today is an official language in dozens of countries and territories and is widely used in Africa, the Indian Ocean, Indonesia, Polynesia, the Middle East, the Caribbean and even Latin America, it is because France and Belgium succeeded where other richer and more powerful countries failed. All European countries participated in colonialism, but France managed to carve itself out a vast empire, second only to Britain's. In the colonial heyday of the 1930s, the French flag floated over a good third of Africa, the larger part of Indochina, a section of India, a huge swath of the Pacific, islands in the Caribbean and a chunk of South America. France also expanded its sphere of influence to Egypt, Turkey, China, Palestine and beyond. Mexico was France's only large-scale colonial failure of the second wave, and even there it managed to attract the elites. Belgium's possessions

in central Africa—the Congo as well as Rwanda and Burundi—
added to the extension of a French language empire on which, in
a way, the sun still hasn't set.

Why and how did France and Belgium succeed where
Germany and the Netherlands failed, and where France had
failed a century earlier? Both France and Belgium had strategic
advantages such as direct access to the sea and proximity to
Africa. They were also highly motivated to build empires. By
the end of the nineteenth century France was falling behind its
neighbours demographically and Belgium had very few natural
resources left to fuel its economy. Both countries were looking
for ways to compensate for these weaknesses. In the second
colonial push, France adopted a more coherent approach than
it had in the first. It also had remnants of the first empire—for
example, Senegal and Pondicherry—that it was able to put to
use as bases for the second push.

Neither the French nor the Belgians were particularly
original in how they went about colonizing. Like every other
colonial power—including the United States and Russia—they
invoked a "mission to civilize" or some variant of that as justification for empire building. Historians still compare French
colonialism, which was based on the principle of assimilation,
to so-called British paternalism in order to show the relative
merits of either approach (depending on which side they're
on). In our opinion, this is nothing more or less than historical
revisionism. There was nothing better about the British "white
man's burden" than there was about the French "civilizing mission." They were the same thing: a pretext for dominating and
exploiting foreign peoples. All the European powers colonized
for their own ends. In 1885 Georges Clemenceau, France's leader
during the First World War and an outspoken opponent of
expansionism, nailed it when he said, "To speak of civilization
is to join hypocrisy to violence."

The French, like all colonial powers, performed some ambitious semantic pirouettes to try to hide the ugly face of the civilizing mission. They called the elites they created in their colonies *les évolués* (the evolved). The colonial administration developed a special status called *indigénat* (from *indigène*, native). The *indigènes* were given their own special justice system, as stated in the Code de l'indigénat, which authorized a new form of servitude, *le travail forcé* (forced labour), and so on. In Africa the broken French spoken by the *indigènes* was called *petit nègre*. Another racist term, more colloquial but still heard today, is *bougnoul*, a Wolof term that originally meant *black person*. The French used it pejoratively to refer to the *évolués* in Senegal, and today apply it to Arabs.

But the real difference in French colonial techniques was not the so-called civilizing mission, it was the way they went about it. For the French, the ultimate objective of colonization was cultural assimilation. They believed, or said they believed, that this could be achieved through mass education. More than any other colonial power, the French were explicit, if not adamant, about the importance of educating their colonial subjects and teaching them French. So the French language became a tool for empire building.

Of course, there was often a gap between the official discourse and reality. In Algeria, Senegal, Congo, Indochina and Lebanon, French and Belgian education policies were unevenly applied, with uneven results. In western Africa, particularly in Senegal, teaching began early in the nineteenth century, while in the Congo and central Africa there was virtually none until a century later. In some areas education was the work of the State, in others only missionaries were involved; in many, it was a combined effort. All in all, the French policies failed to educate the masses. But they succeeded in training an elite of so-called *évolués* who would act as colonial auxiliaries for the

French and take over after independence—this would become the trademark of French colonial techniques.

On the whole, France's effort to educate its colonial subjects does not explain how it succeeded in spreading the language so widely during the second colonial push. The main reason was that, as opposed to the first colonial push, the French this time sent settlers abroad. In the Pacific Ocean, where New Caledonia became a French colony in 1860, the French sent forty thousand convicts—four times the number of settlers and *engagés* they had sent to New France. Tunisia had attracted about 150,000 Europeans (mostly French and Italian) by 1906, still a considerable number. And the one million Europeans who had settled in Algeria by the 1930s were as numerous as all the settlers in all the other French colonies together. Not surprisingly, the second colonial push had a lot more impact on mainstream French than the first did.

Algeria was France's first colony, and the first African territory officially declared a colony by a European country. While many historians consider this the event that sparked the second colonial push, the French hadn't really set out to create a colony. For centuries, Algerian pirates had been in the habit of capturing European boats along the Mediterranean coast and selling their Christian crews as slaves. Between 1815 and 1824, British, American and Dutch fleets tried to put a stop to this practice by attacking Algerian fleets and bombarding Algiers, but it was the French who finally succeeded. Under King Charles X, France landed and seized Algiers in July 1830. The King's successor, Louis Philippe, then decided to turn Algeria into a colony, partly as an attempt to boost the legitimacy of the French monarchy and partly to spite England, which had taken the hotly disputed Egypt out of French hands in the first years of the century. The moment he took power, Louis

Philippe began laying siege to Oran and the rest of the Mediterranean coast. In 1833 France set up a colonial government in Algeria, the Gouvernement général des possessions françaises dans le nord de l'Afrique (General Government of the French Possessions in North Africa).

Then, for the first time in its colonial history, France got serious about sending settlers to a colony, partly because there were settlers anxious to go. France was late to enter the Industrial Revolution and was still largely a peasant country in the 1840s, but the population was expanding and land was becoming scarce. Landless farmers were seduced by promises of freely available rich farmland in North Africa, the legendary breadbasket of the Roman Empire. By 1850 there were twenty-five thousand European colonists in Algeria, mostly fishermen and peasants; half were French and the rest were Spanish, Italian, Maltese and Corsican. In the following decades unemployed Parisians and Alsatians poured into Algeria. By 1876 there were three hundred thousand Europeans in Algeria, half of them French. French winegrowers whose vines had been wiped out by the phylloxera epidemic in 1878 fled there looking for new land; Algeria was famous for its wines.

This contact between French soldiers and colonists and the Algerian *indigènes* brought a second wave of Arabicisms into French; the first dated back to the time of the Crusades (see chapter 1). But whereas then the French had borrowed scientific and technical terms from Arabic, the Arabicisms that slipped into the language in the nineteenth century were all popular expressions. Soldiers were the first to borrow from Arabic, using the word *barda* (from *bard'a*, packsaddle in the Algerian dialect) for their military kit. *Bled* (the country's interior) took on a pejorative sense in French, referring to an insignificant place. And the Algerian *tabib* (healer) became the soldier's *toubib* (still used in France for doctor). Other borrowings included *chouya* (a little bit), *maboul* (crackpot), *kif-kif* (the same) and *nouba* (party); all are used commonly in French even today, while others, including *casbah* and *raï,* spilled over into English. Dozens of other borrowings come from this period, many related to food, including the most famous, *couscous,* which is well on its way to becoming a national dish in France.

Almost from the beginning of the colony in Algeria, the French dreamed of replacing Arabic with French. French administrators declared French the colony's official language and set about looking for ways to get Algerians to learn it. One of the early plans was to pay children two francs a day plus a meal to attend French school. The scheme failed. In 1850 the government created a school for sons of tribal chiefs in Paris, but this also produced few results. The main obstacle was the fact that Algerians already had a tradition of education. Before the conquest, up to forty percent of Algerians learned to read and write by studying the Koran in Muslim schools, so few North Africans bought the argument that the French were bringing them "civilization." Meanwhile, the French settlers, who relied on exploiting undereducated *indigènes* as labour, were not too enthusiastic about applying the Paris education policies, which they considered too generous.

Nevertheless, the French persisted in their education objectives. In the 1850s the colonial government created "mixed" schools where students learned Arabic in the morning and French in the afternoon. By 1863 only a few thousand students were enrolled in them. From 1879 on, the French government began to create French *lycées, collèges* and schools of law and medicine in Algiers, and a full French school system was created in 1901. But the Muslim Algerians strongly resisted sending their children to the schools, and by 1914 only five percent of children attended French schools. The native inhabitants strongly opposed intermarriage as well, the other main means of assimilation.

Meanwhile, however, the French were assimilating almost all the other European settlers in Algeria. All the children of Europeans went to French schools, as did the Jewish population, both immigrant and indigenous. The overall result was that, by 1914, roughly a million inhabitants in a total population of 4.5 million spoke French as a mother tongue; three-quarters were Europeans, Algerian Jews and other assimilated foreigners, and one-quarter were Muslim *évolués*.

In spite of the failure of the school program, French made rapid progress, though for the least noble of reasons. With the help of the colonial government, European settlers had been able to take over the best of Algeria's agricultural lands, and they quickly transformed Algerian peasants into employees who had to speak the boss's language. The French government had declared Algeria part of France in 1848, with each French ministry responsible for its own affairs there, so French became the language of administration. It was also the language of military service. Many Muslims performed military duties because the French government made oblique promises to grant them citizenship in exchange for these "special duties." The overall result was that, by 1930, it was possible to go anywhere in Algeria without an interpreter.

The number of French settlers was considerably smaller in the rest of Africa, but there were so many colonies that it would be futile to try to give the details of how French progressed in each. The case of Senegal, however, is a good example.

What has gone down in history as the first French lesson in Africa took place in the town of Saint Louis, Senegal, in 1817. It was given by an equally legendary French instructor, Jean Dard, who was a visionary. When he arrived and opened a school that year, only a few thousand French people were living in Senegal. He began studying Senegal's most important local language, Wolof, and even went on to publish the first French-Wolof dictionary in 1826, which described the structure of the language.

Jean Dard developed a new approach for teaching French outside of France, called the "mutual method" or *méthode de traduction* (translation method). The approach was to teach children to read and write in their native language, Wolof, then to learn French by translating. It was a very modern and very effective method, and Dard was said to have achieved remarkable results with it. Unfortunately he had to return to France in 1820 for health reasons. He came back to Senegal in 1832, but died a year later.

Had Dard's methods taken root, the future of French in Africa might have been different. But his colleagues and successors favoured the "direct method," which consisted of teaching French from scratch to people who didn't even know how to read and write in their own language. Dard's method required teachers to learn Wolof, and that was too much work, so the French in Africa just used the same teaching methods they used on schoolchildren in France. In Senegal this meant banning Wolof from the schools. To do this, the French went as far as taking children away from their families and sending them to French schools in distant villages. The children were mystified, upset and alienated by the whole process.

Until the 1850s, when Britain stopped disputing France's dominion over the colony, there was no education policy to speak of in Senegal. That was when Senegal's first governor, General Louis de Faidherbe, put one in place. If Senegal is today the cultural capital of francophone Africa, it is no doubt as a result of his actions. Faidherbe was a modernizer. When he arrived in 1854 there were between twelve thousand and fifteen thousand French people living in the colony, but little economic activity. He transformed the economy of the colony by introducing peanut plantations (albeit based on forced labour). He developed the ports of Saint-Louis, Rufisque and Dakar, and trade tripled between 1854 and 1869. Faidherbe defined and put into practice a system to train an African colonial elite by creating the first school for sons of chiefs in 1857. Its mandate was to "train functionaries who would collaborate with France," including administrators, teachers and merchants. The schools later spread to Gorée, Dakar and Rufisque. Faidherbe also created a local infantry force, the famous *tirailleurs sénégalais* (though many of them came from Upper Volta, Guinea and Mali), who numbered 180,000 by 1914. It was an important means of Frenchification, as they had to speak to their officers in French.

Faidherbe's plan worked quite well, and the burgeoning Senegalese elite got the message that French was the key to social promotion. France tried to build on this momentum by using different measures. As Amadou Ly, professor of literature at Cheikh Anta Diop University, told us, "The Senegalese helped the French colonize other African countries. We were the auxiliaries of colonialism." In 1916 France extended citizenship to the residents of four colonial bases: Dakar, Rufisque, Saint Louis and Gorée. The people in these four towns were referred to as *les originaires* (natives), a status higher than *indigènes,* since they were French citizens. Starting in 1946, these four cities elected representatives to the National Assembly in Paris. During the colonial era, Dakar was the capital of French West Africa, and well into the first half of the twentieth century, colonial administrators came from all over western Africa to study at the École William Ponty, which trained colonial auxiliaries, administrators and even veterinarians. After the Second World War, France established scholarships to enable young Africans to pursue higher education in France. The first university in western Africa, the University of Dakar (now Université Cheikh Anta Diop), opened in 1950.

The results were less impressive among the rest of the Senegalese, few of whom learned French. In 1903 the French government passed a decree to put in place a system of secular primary education in its African colonies. The education system had three goals: to educate the masses, to establish French culture in Africa, and to train indigenous staff and assure the rise of an elite in the colonies. In 1912 there were 13,500 boys and 1,700 girls in French-language schools in West Africa. But the results in terms of language acquisition were weak. In 1925, across French West Africa, children still left school barely able to read or write. They learned only a few French words, often without understanding their meaning. After 1925 the French introduced village schools. The idea was to single out the children who had more aptitude for learning French, and send them on to regional schools. By 1945 the number enrolled had jumped to 94,400, but the numbers in French Equatorial Africa remained negligible.

The teaching of French never overcame some basic problems in Africa. First, the French simply never spent enough money on schools—a mere six percent of the colony's budget, at the most, was devoted to education. According to French colonial doctrine, colonies were supposed to be financially self-sufficient. In addition, there wasn't a lot of popular support for colonialism in France, so budgets were tight. Because of this mixture of colonial doctrine and financial considerations, the French didn't invest heavily in infrastructure, and that worked against education. France also continued to rely heavily on missionaries to teach French. The overall result was that, even at the peak of France colonial teaching efforts—just before the 1960s independence movement—no more than fifteen percent of African children went to a French school, and this was a threefold improvement over the rate from fifteen years earlier. Education rates were slightly higher in Algeria—up to twenty percent at the peak—and a bit higher in Tunisia and Indochina. And, as Professor Pascale Barthélémy of the University of Paris VII argues in an article on the question, "although France tripled the rate of schooling in French West Africa between 1945 and the end of the 1950s, only four in a hundred could continue in a secondary school."

Teaching methods were a major stumbling block. The French lacked qualified teachers throughout the colonial period. At one point they tried to put a teacher training school in place, but they never managed to develop a satisfactory method for teaching French as a second language. Not surprisingly, they never found a way to motivate Africans either. The objective was a steep one, considering that after 1791 it had taken the French ninety years to establish universal education in their own country. It is easy to imagine how disinclined young Africans were to learn a European language when their teachers insisted on using foreign references. In Senegal we met people old enough to remember textbooks that began with the famous phrase *"Nos ancêtres les Gaulois"* ("Our ancestors, the Gauls")!

Mass education in the colonies might have been more efficient had the French better understood, or at least better defined, their purpose. In France schools served to educate citizens by instilling the values of the Republic and teaching them skills to make them employable, and then singling out the best and brightest for elite education. But in the colonies, aside from training an elite of auxiliaries, it wasn't clear what the French were trying to achieve, or why they applied the same education scheme as in republican France to a population who had no rights or citizenship. As in Algeria, many French settlers in Africa objected to the idea of educating the *indigénat*—mass education is a dangerous thing to a dominant class that needs to keep natives in their place. The problem was that the settlers were the ones who were supposed to manage the program. So, in a way, the whole scheme was destined to fail.

The case of the Belgian Congo shows this problem in even more vivid terms. The Belgians were not interested in teaching French. They tended to educate students in local African languages and favoured technical training rather than providing a general education. They feared that if they created an elite, it would rise up one day and demand independence. By 1920 only ten percent of the schoolchildren in Belgian colonies were learning French. The teaching of French there, as in the colonies of France, was done through the ineffective "direct" method.

French made more progress in the Belgian colonies than Flemish did, primarily because it became the language of social promotion (as it was in Belgium). But French wouldn't have a large presence until after the Second World War, when the Belgians made a systematic effort to organize school systems. As a result of the Belgian preference for technical education, when it became independent, the newly formed country of Zaire (Belgian Congo) had only four native university graduates.

The most cost-efficient agents for teaching French were, by far, the missionaries. Decades, in some cases centuries, before European powers began to officially claim colonies, missionaries had been travelling to remote lands to establish their presence and convert pagans. Among the European powers, France was a leader in this work throughout the nineteenth century, sending missionaries to build schools and hospitals and teach French in French West Africa, Indochina and the Pacific islands. In fact, France sent more priests, nuns and monks into foreign missions in the nineteenth century than any other European country. In 1900, twenty-eight of the world's forty-four missionary societies were French; of the seventy thousand missionaries active in the world, fifty thousand were French.

In the nineteenth century, France's attitude towards the missionaries was in complete contradiction to the one it held towards religious organizations on the Continent. The Republic was radically antireligious, but it encouraged missionary work abroad. The French kicked the Jesuits out of France twice, in 1880 and 1901, but during the same period subsidized them heavily to continue their work abroad, particularly in Lebanon. The reason was simple: Even with the subsidies, missions cost less than public schools. As language teachers, missionaries got better results than regular teachers did because they tended to learn the local languages where they worked. Speaking the language of the people helped them convert local populations to Christianity, which was their primary goal. In effect, they applied Jean Dard's mutual method. In addition, teaching French was usually part of their civic mission. The French state supported them financially, and expected this service in return.

In the age of imperialism, with its project to "civilize," European rulers were very conscious of the role missionaries played as precursors of colonial expansion, and they monitored their efforts closely. Napoleon III encouraged Catholic missions in the Pacific islands in order to counteract Anglo-American colonial expansion. The missions played a crucial role in the Pacific Ocean, especially in Polynesia. Missionaries arrived in the Pacific islands of Wallis and Fortuna in the 1830s, fifty years before France laid claim to them. In the decades that followed, Catholic missions were established in Tonga and New Caledonia. The French missionaries were in a hurry, since Protestant English missionaries were already well-established in the Pacific, notably in Hawaii, Tahiti and New Zealand. By 1854 there were already 117 Catholic missionaries in the Polynesian islands, and soon French Protestant missionaries joined the fray—which is why France today still controls the largest section of the Pacific Ocean.

According to Professor Pascale Barthélémy, the total number of children in mission schools in all of Africa was almost equal to all those in government schools. In Africa, le Levant (the Middle East) and Indochina, missionaries ran thousands of schools. In the Ottoman Empire alone, one hundred thousand students were enrolled in French missionary schools by 1900. The Belgians relied almost entirely on missionaries. When he was private owner of the Congo basin, King Leopold II paid Catholic missionaries to go to Africa and open schools. The Belgian government maintained the same approach when it took over the country in 1908; Belgian Roman Catholic mission schools were given generous subsidies to continue their work. By 1920 some 185,000 children were studying in Catholic and Protestant missions, but fewer than 2,000 were in state schools.

Missionaries were not effective everywhere, though. European missionary presence in Indonesia began in the seventeenth century when the French tried, without success, to establish spice trading. The missionaries transcribed the Vietnamese language into the Latin alphabet (chapter 14 shows how this writing system would feed anti-French nationalism). But as in Algeria, the teaching of French faced several obstacles. Indochina had a strong history of Chinese education before the French arrived, and that made the Indochinese resistant to French schools. Also as in Algeria, the local population never bought the idea that the French were bringing "civilization." They already had civilization. The French implanted an education system in Indochina in 1919, but neither the missionaries nor the French state could overcome resistance.

Another problem in Indochina was that few French people ever migrated there. In 1937 there were thirty thousand French inhabitants in a population of twelve million, and half of them were soldiers. A great number of the rest were teachers and their families. The French writer Marguerite Duras was a daughter of one. Her famous novel *L'amant* (*The Lover*), which was made into an excellent film, tells the story of her torrid relationship with an *évolué* in the waning days of France's dominion over Indochina.

But the French language made surprising progress in Indochina. As in Algeria, indigenous merchants and functionaries picked it up and it quickly became a language of social promotion. Governor General Paul Doumer (1897–1902), considered the architect of French Indochina, reinforced an aggressive French administration. His policy pushed people to learn French so they could deal with the administration, though Doumer's actions later provoked resentment and fostered the rebellion that would lead to Indochina's independence movement. In the 1930s, one in ten Indochinese was bilingual; most were concentrated in the cities. Some famous francophone Indochinese people include Ho Chi Minh, Pol Pot and Norodom Sihanouk. A pidgin of French, Tay Boy, was used all over Indochina.

The situation of French in Syria, and more particularly Lebanon, was a mirror image of that in Indochina. In 1919 Greater Syria became a protectorate of France, rather than of Britain, largely because French had made so much progress there over the centuries. In a way, France's colonial expansion had started in Syria. The French presence dated back to the Crusades in the twelfth century, when Maronite Christians in today's Lebanon fought alongside Frankish Crusaders. In the sixteenth century King François I struck a deal with the Ottoman sultan, who made France the protector of Maronite Christians (and all Christians) living in the Ottoman Empire;

this is partly why the Greeks remain strong francophiles to this day. French missionaries began working in Syria in the seventeenth century, and in 1816 France forced the Ottoman Turks to set up an autonomous territory for the Maronites in Mount Lebanon, laying the groundwork for the creation of Lebanon in 1943.

Throughout the nineteenth century France increased its commercial relations with the area—the railway line between Jaffa and Jerusalem and the digging of the Suez Canal between 1854 and 1869 were among the most spectacular of those efforts. By mid-century, French was being taught along with English at the Collège Maronite Romain in a modern languages program. At the end of the nineteenth century a dozen French congregations taught seven thousand students in some fifty schools. With funding from the French government, in 1875 French Jesuit priests opened the Saint Joseph University in Beirut, where they ran schools of medicine, engineering and law before the French Protectorate was established.

When the Ottoman Empire collapsed at the end of the First World War, the area was placed under the military administration of the Allies. Because of language, France was an obvious candidate for getting the League of Nations mandate over Syria (which still included Lebanon). The mandate, directly inspired by the "civilizing" colonial doctrine of nineteenth-century Europe, was meant to prepare the area for eventual independence, though the process turned out to be rockier than expected. At the beginning of the 1930s, with independence in sight, Christians made up half the population of what is now Lebanon, but feared being overwhelmed by the Muslim population. So they convinced France to create a separate state of Lebanon that would give them control over Beirut, Tripoli, Sidon, Tyre and some areas in the south. France divided Syria into two states in 1943, reducing Syria's access to the

Mediterranean and sowing the seeds of future conflict between the countries.

The French presence in Lebanon led to a curious migration that has lasted to this day. Even before the protectorate, the Lebanese started to settle throughout the French colonial empire. In the colonies they were often sought as middlemen, in much the same way that the British Empire relied on Indian merchants. In Africa, in particular, Lebanese brought the settlers much-needed new blood. In Senegal at the time of independence they numbered more than seventy thousand, and in many colonies they greatly outnumbered the European settlers. The extent of this Lebanese diaspora was phenomenal—today Lebanese communities are spread across the planet. Famous members include the U.S. activist Ralph Nader, the Canadian René Angélil, manager and husband of pop singer Céline Dion, and Carlos Gosn, a Brazilian-born Lebanese who is now CEO of Renault-Nissan.

When we visited Senegal in May 2005, our hotel in central Dakar was directly across the street from the Mission Libanaise (Lebanese Mission). To get a better understanding of the community, we met with Samir Jarmarche, an energetic businessman and head of the local Lebanese cultural organization. Jarmarche showed us his scrapbook of pictures of his family, who were part of the second wave of Lebanese immigrants to Senegal. His father was actually on his way to America in the 1920s when, as Jarmarche put it, "fortunately or unfortunately the boat stopped in Dakar, he met some people from his village and ended up staying in Senegal."

The Lebanese had first come to Senegal in the 1880s, when they were fleeing the Ottoman Empire. In Senegal, as in all the French colonies, they ran textile and furniture factories, real estate and grocery businesses. They also reinforced the "French" presence in the country's interior by operating peanut factories and depots where the French rarely went. The most successful opened businesses in other parts of French West Africa, and their families are spread today over the entire area. In fact, Lebanese belong to the economic elite of every African country where they are established. The richest of the Lebanese Senegalese, the Shararah family, run businesses in every country of former French West Africa.

In 1948 Senegal's Lebanese community opened a Lebanese mission in Dakar to school children in French and Arabic and to maintain their religion, the Maronite faith. The mission became the backbone of the community. Since Senegalese independence, however, the Lebanese population has dropped from seventy thousand to twenty thousand. Although most Senegal-born Lebanese speak Wolof and Arabic, relations between the Lebanese and the Senegalese are not always harmonious. The Lebanese continue to educate their children in French and rarely intermarry with the Senegalese. The Senegalese are critical of this, and hotly contest the huge role the Lebanese still play in Senegal's economy. But the complex heritage of French colonialism has given the Lebanese a triple identity that will probably last for many decades to come. As Mr. Jarmarche told us, "I am French, I am Lebanese and I am Senegalese, and this is my home."

While the French never came close to achieving their goal of assimilation during the second colonial push, they did manage to create a solid French-speaking base in all of their colonies. In a few areas, like Syria, newly independent states quickly adopted aggressive anti-French policies that would virtually wipe this base out. But, ironically, in most of the colonies French progressed more after independence than it had before.

In the meantime, French speakers in France's first colonial empire in North America were facing aggressive assimilation efforts by British, Canadian and American authorities. Against all odds, the people of this dynamic French-speaking Lost World found ways to survive.

Chapter 10 ~

LOST WORLDS

ON MAY 18, 1942, President Franklin Roosevelt of the United States wrote to Canadian Prime Minister William Lyon Mackenzie King. It was the darkest moment of the Second World War, when Nazi Germany and Japan seemed unstoppable and the world was ablaze. But Roosevelt had another problem on his mind. Three weeks earlier, Canada had conducted a national referendum on conscription. Although a majority of Canadians had said yes, seventy percent of French Canadians refused to be conscripted for overseas service. Riots even broke out in Montreal over the question.

The White House was worried that this controversy would be detrimental to the Canadian war effort. In his letter to the Canadian prime minister, Roosevelt bragged that French Canadians who had migrated to New England were finally converting to "Anglo-Saxon ways" and speaking English in their homes. He proposed that Canada and the U.S. join forces and do "some sort of planning . . . perhaps unwritten" to assimilate the remaining French speakers in Canada.

It's surprising to find that Roosevelt was grappling with the issue of French Canadians while there was a war going on. Yet the fact was, two centuries after France's defeat and withdrawal from the continent, and despite overwhelming odds, French remained an American language. Like Roosevelt, many people wondered why. And like Roosevelt, many people still wanted to see French in North America disappear as a native language .

The story of French in America was very different from that in the rest of the world. Linguistically, it was the first time that any European language had been completely cut off from its origins and evolved separately from the source of their language. Since 1763, French Canadians lived in a kind of linguistic Lost World. Contact between Canada and France was limited to a few priests who emigrated, a few books that made their way over, and a few ships that docked in Quebec— the first French ship to drop anchor in the port of Quebec City, *La Capricieuse,* arrived in 1855, ninety-two years after the end of the French regime.

In Canada, various attempts to assimilate francophones had not only backfired, they had created two distinct French-speaking peoples: the French Canadians and the Acadians. Over the centuries both groups developed a quasi-tribal sense of identity so powerful they refused to let go of their language— at any price.

When France still had a presence on the American continent, before 1763, its two main colonies were Quebec and Acadia. Today, the native francophones of America all belong to one of these two related but distinct trunks, some of whose branches have become intertwined over the centuries. The French Canadians, based in Quebec, are the largest group. Today six million francophones live in Quebec; they call themselves Québécois, an appellation used only since the 1960s. These French Canadians spawned many groups, including today's half-million Franco-Ontarians, a hundred thousand French Canadians in the Canadian West, and two hundred thousand Franco-Americans, mostly concentrated in Maine, New Hampshire and Rhode Island.

The Acadians are an entirely different group. Early French settlers in what is today the province of Nova Scotia, they numbered ten thousand when France lost the colony to

Britain in 1713. Forty years later the British deported half of them—to Britain, its own American colonies and elsewhere. The other half slipped through British hands and fled, mostly to present-day New Brunswick, where three hundred thousand Acadians now make up a third of the population. Others went to Louisiana, where they were known as Cadiens—later, Cajuns. Today their descendants number about two hundred thousand. Acadians in New England became American citizens and, over the centuries, mixed with French Canadians who had also migrated to New England, so no one knows their real numbers today. But the violent attempt to wipe the Acadians out forged a strong, distinct identity that has lasted until this day, even among those who no longer speak French, much like most of the world's Irish or Scots who long ago forgot Gaelic.

The history of the Acadians is full of ironies. In the seventeenth century these industrious French colonists transformed thousands of acres of tidal marshlands in the northern hump of present-day Nova Scotia into some of North America's richest farmlands. The area they occupied was much disputed between the English and the French, and it changed flags a dozen times before the Treaty of Utrecht ceded Acadia to the British, once and for all, in 1713. For the next forty years the Acadians remained neutral and prospered. But in 1748 the British started to get nervous; they feared the Acadians would side against them in the ongoing colonial struggle with France. The solution, they thought, was to get rid of them and free up the rich farmland for British settlers.

In 1755 the British began the operation Acadians still remember as Le Grand Dérangement (the great upheaval). Soldiers began rounding up the Acadian settlers. Families were broken up, houses were burned, those who resisted were shot and the rest—ten thousand in total—were packed into boats and scattered among the Thirteen Colonies or shipped to Britain, France and even the Falkland Islands. Some boats sank, and those who survived drowning and sickness arrived dirty, dispossessed, malnourished and often separated from their families.

While the move did free land for English settlers, it hardly erased the Acadians from the continent. Thousands of them slipped through British hands and founded a New Acadia in what is now New Brunswick. The Acadians who were deported— whether to other British colonies or abroad—resisted all attempts to assimilate them. Most of the deportees in the thirteen British colonies trekked back to Quebec, or to other safe havens such as New Brunswick and Louisiana.

Far from eradicating the Acadians, Le Grand Dérangement became the founding moment of Acadian identity—and it remains so to this day, even though Acadians are spread all over the North American continent and many have long since been assimilated. We witnessed the power of Acadian identity when we attended the third World Acadian Congress in the summer of 2004. The event was held in Nova Scotia, where sixteen thousand Acadians still live. After touring the francophone villages of Nova Scotia's French shore, we arrived in Grand Pré, the spiritual heartland of Acadia, where the deportation is said to have started. There we attended the closing ceremony of the conference, the *grand messe,* an outdoor Mass attended by eight thousand people, including dignitaries such as the prime minister of Canada, the premiers of Nova Scotia and New Brunswick and the governor of Louisiana—the latter two, Acadians. Licence plates showed that the revellers had driven from as far away as New York, Pennsylvania and Louisiana to be at the event. Thousands sat in the blazing heat under red-white-and-blue umbrellas (the colours of the Acadian flag) and bowed their heads while Acadian priests and bishops performed the Mass in French.

On an earlier trip to Louisiana, we had noticed that the local descendants of Acadians were much more interested in Nova Scotia, where only several thousand speak French, than Quebec, where millions speak French, or even New Brunswick, which is the real heart of Acadia today. At Grand Pré we understood why: Cajun identity is based much more on the historical moment of the deportation than it is on modern affinities with Quebeckers and Acadians living in New Brunswick.

Before the Grand Mass, Acadians had been flocking to Grand Pré all summer to gaze at the statue of a buxom eighteenth-century peasant girl standing in the fields near the town's church. The girl, Évangeline Bellefeuille, never actually existed—she was a literary creation of the American poet Henry Wadsworth Longfellow, of Portland, Massachusetts. Longfellow was not Acadian himself, but when he heard the legend of a pair of lovers who had been separated by the deportation, he developed a fascination with Acadian history and decided to turn the story into an epic poem, *Evangeline*. The story begins when the British tear the heroine's fiancé from her arms during their engagement party. After Evangeline is shipped away, she spends her entire life seeking Gabriel, finally finding him on his deathbed in Delaware. Published in 1847, the poem was immensely successful. It was translated into French in 1865, and is considered one of the factors that contributed to the Acadian *réveil* (awakening) of the nineteenth century.

From 1755 until the middle of the next century, Acadians survived by keeping a low profile. As Roman Catholics they were deprived of the right to vote in New Brunswick until 1830. But by the 1850s they had started to open their own colleges and found their own newspapers. In 1881 they even organized a *convention nationale* (national convention), which assembled five thousand people at St. Joseph College in Memramcook, New Brunswick. As their patron saint they chose the Virgin Mary. By

1884 they had an anthem, "Ave Maris Stella" ("Hail, Star of Mary"), and had designed the Acadian flag, a French tricolour with the star of Mary in papal gold in the upper left corner. The convention sparked the Acadian *réveil* and was followed by at least a dozen similar events held every decade or so after that. Until the 1960s these symbols were really the only things the Acadians had to unite them as a community, aside from the Church and the French language.

The most famous Acadian deportees are the three thousand who settled in Louisiana in the 1780s (invited by Spain, as we explain in Chapter 4). Among the various groups of francophones who settled in Louisiana in the eighteenth and nineteenth centuries, the Acadians were the ones who survived assimilation the best. The explanation for this goes back to the time of the Louisiana Purchase of 1803, when the American government bought Greater Louisiana from France for fifteen million dollars. At the time forty-three thousand inhabitants were living in what would become the American state of Louisiana, ninety percent of whom spoke French. They belonged to three groups: the Cadiens; the original French settlers of Louisiana, who had already mixed with the Spanish, Natives and black slaves living there; and finally, ten thousand refugees from Saint-Domingue, mostly Creole planters and free people of colour. The main difference between the groups, aside from background, was that the Acadians did not mix with the others. They had settled far from New Orleans, on the west bank of the Mississippi around the town of Vermilionville (now Lafayette), where they prospered on family farms of their own.

By 1879 eighty percent of the Creole planters had been assimilated to English, but more than half of the state's population still spoke French. The Cadiens were isolated from the rest of the state by the enormous Atchafalaya Swamp, and they remained untouched by changes–they still called Americans *les Anglais*. However, the Cadiens did assimilate the Irish, Natives, blacks and Germans who managed to cross the swamp. It was this blend that created the unique Cajun culture with its crawfish and barbecued shrimp dishes, two-step dancing, fiddle music and zydeco (a mispronunciation of the French *les haricots*, beans; more on this in chapter 14).

Why did these Acadians survive? Until the American Civil War, the French-speaking Louisianais deftly used whatever institutions were available to them to preserve their language and resist assimilation. Although the state constitution of 1812 decreed that laws had to be passed in the language of the American Constitution, the legislature was French-dominated. So it continued to vote laws in French anyway, for the next fifty years. State law used the French Civil Code, in French, and a penal code in French was created in 1825; most judicial proceedings took place in French. The word *Dixie*, an important term for the Old South, is a deformation of the number *dix* (ten) that appeared on the back of Louisiana banknotes.

Culturally speaking, the French Canadians, who were based in the valley of the St. Lawrence River–today's province of Quebec–were always better off than either the Acadians or the Louisiana Cajuns. They were never deported, and were five times more numerous than Acadians from the outset. One of their best tools against assimilation was a fantastic birth rate–for nearly a century it enabled them to outpace British immigration to Canada. By 1830 the original fifty thousand Canadiens had multiplied tenfold, to number half a million.

Perhaps because of their numbers, the French Canadians were always more politically assertive than either the Acadians or the Cajuns. Through political manoeuvres they forced the

British authorities to keep certain French institutions, and even to grant Quebec its own parliament in 1791, which French Canadians have dominated ever since. By 1867 French Canadians made up only a third of Canada's total population, but they still constituted a large majority in the province of Quebec. The Canadian constitution, the *British North America Act,* which was written that year, was the high-water mark of French-Canadian assertiveness. It united the five colonies of British North America and created an independent Canada. French Canadians had made sure that Canada became a federation of former colonies rather than a unitary state, so French speakers would have some clout in Canadian politics. The Act gave formal status to the French language—for the first time in Canada's history. It made the use of both French and English mandatory in Parliament and before the courts, both at the federal level and in the province of Quebec. This was hailed as a political victory, and it created much hope, especially after the federal government safeguarded the rights of French speakers in the newly created province of Manitoba in 1870. However, French Canadians quickly saw that the federal government and English Canadians had no intention of respecting either the spirit or the letter of the law. French Canadians would spend the next hundred years trying to get English Canada to respect its side of the deal.

Throughout their history French Canadians' willingness to rock the boat has always distinguished them from Acadians and Cajuns. The most violent episode was the 1837 revolt that cost hundreds of lives and was a major setback for the French-Canadian leadership. Rebelliousness is not exclusive to Quebeckers. In the 1870s a mixed-blood people in Manitoba, descendants of Indians and French Canadians known as the Métis, carried out a particularly violent revolt. At the time some ten thousand Métis were living in western Canada, centred around the French parish of St. Boniface in present-day Winnipeg. They were an industrious lot of farmers and hunters, all French-speaking. The end of the 1860s had brought a massive influx of Irish Protestants who were rabidly anti-Catholic and anti-French, and even went so far as to reject the French system of land allotment in strips along rivers.

Louis Riel, a Métis who had been schooled in Montreal as a priest, led his people in a revolt against the Irish immigrants. His action forced the federal government to promise that the rights of the French-speaking Métis would be guaranteed in the newly formed province of Manitoba—it was a breakthrough for the rights of French speakers west of Quebec. But after a second Métis uprising in 1885, Riel was captured and hanged. Five years later a new provincial act declared English to be Manitoba's only official language. This flagrantly contradicted the *Manitoba Act,* and as the federal government did nothing to enforce its own law, it became clear that French speakers living west of the Ottawa River would enjoy no constitutional protection.

Another example of French Canadians' assertiveness was, of course, their decision to take to the streets over the question of conscription. The anti-conscription riots Roosevelt refers to in his letter to King (there were also riots over conscription in 1917) created anti-French resentment all over Canada. Although French Canadians had many reasons for refusing to fight overseas, the main one was that, in seventy-five years of Canadian history, the Canadian Army had not found time to create a French-speaking chain of command to accommodate soldiers from the other founding nation. The message was: It's not our war if we can't fight it in French. The riots were a radical move, but they did attract attention. It was at that moment that radical French Canadians, especially those in Quebec, began to consider the idea of separation from

Canada, though they remained a very small minority until
the 1960s.

Political wheeling and dealing and protests were two ways in
which both Acadians and French Canadians resisted assimilation, but there were others, from the militancy of the Catholic
Church to a strong emphasis on *la vie associative* (community
life, but one that extends beyond local communities) to their
extraordinary birth rate.

Since 1763 French Canadians and Acadians have multiplied a hundred times, to about 7.5 million. That figure
excludes another 4.5 million descendants who have assimilated
into English in Canada and the U.S. (most people in North
America with the family name White are actually descendants
of Leblancs; one of the most famous *assimilées* is the singer
Madonna, whose mother was a third-generation Franco-
American from the Fortin family). Until the 1960s, French
Canadians held their ground demographically thanks to their
birth rate. They even colonized—hundreds of thousands left
to settle in Ontario and the western Canadian provinces, and
one million settled in the states of New England.

The apparently bottomless human resources of the St.
Lawrence River valley spawned a smaller subgroup of French
Canadians who pursued exploration of Greater Louisiana and
later the American Midwest, and whose influence lasted well
into the middle of the nineteenth century. Most of the early
legends of the American frontier were in fact created by French-
Canadian *coureurs des bois*, *voyageurs* (boatmen), merchants,
muleteers and missionaries. Without them, Meriwether Lewis
and William Clark would have had a considerably harder time
making their 1804–5 trek across the continent.

In spite of their accomplishments, French-Canadian
frontiersmen remain a mere footnote in American history.

Travelling down the Mississippi on our way to Louisiana, we were stunned to see that the museum under the Gateway Arch in St. Louis, Missouri, hardly mentions them. To be fair, the low profile of the *coureurs des bois* can be at least partially explained by prejudice towards them as illiterates who had married Indian women or were so-called "half-bloods" themselves. On the other hand, they were the first settlers of New Mexico; they also found the passage for a train route across the Rockies, discovered gold in California and befriended other legends of the American West. Their society, centred on present-day Missouri, remained predominantly French until the 1840s, after which English-speaking Americans overwhelmed and assimilated them.

Another reason that French Canadians and Acadians survived was that they discouraged intermarriage, especially with English speakers. Roosevelt himself pointed out this "problem" in his correspondence with King. French Canadians knew that intermarriage would spell the end of French in Canada, as it did in the American West in the nineteenth century and in New England and Louisiana by the Second World War. Interestingly, though, they did practise it selectively. In situations where they felt they could assimilate English speakers, they actually encouraged it. Some important Quebec political families, such as the Johnsons and the Ryans, who were both originally Irish, became French-speaking this way. Canadian prime ministers Pierre Elliott Trudeau and Brian Mulroney, Quebec premier Jean Charest and New Brunswick premier Bernard Lord were products of such intermarriages.

Their abundant birth rate and tendency to avoid disadvantageous intermarriage helped create a quasi-tribal identity among French Canadians and Acadians. One of the most striking features of French Canadians and Acadians (and their descendants, even the ones who are assimilated) is their fascination with

genealogy. Almost all old-stock French Canadians and
Acadians know the first name of their ancestor who first set
foot on the continent, which is impressive, since many arrived
in the seventeenth century. The explanation is simple: The
French companies that brought the settlers kept thorough
records of the settlers' names, and later, Catholic parishes kept
their records in good order. During the World Acadian
Congress, Acadian visitors drove from all over North America
to Moncton, New Brunswick, to consult the exhaustive
genealogical files stored at the University of Moncton's Centre
for Acadian Studies. Julie was stunned to discover the existence
of a *Dictionnaire biographique des ancêtres québécois* (*Biographical
Dictionary of Quebec Ancestry*) when we visited the Centre.

As far as the French Canadians' remarkable birth rate
was concerned, there was nothing spontaneous about it.
French Canadians' and Acadians' sturdiest and most resilient
institution, the Catholic Church, held up as models families
of ten, fifteen or even eighteen children. The Church was the
central pillar of French-Canadian society from 1763 up until
the 1960s. The clergy opened schools and ran them either
directly or through religious orders. In the second half of the
nineteenth century the Church sent missionaries and settlers
west to Manitoba and Alberta and established a network of
French-language schools, colleges, convents, hospices, hospitals and parishes throughout the country—the first colleges in
New Brunswick were started by Quebec and French congregations. The Church also ran hospitals; in fact, there were few
aspects of daily life that it did not manage.

In the extensive notes that Alexis de Tocqueville took
while he was researching *Democracy in America,* he described
the French-Canadian clergy as better educated and better
mannered than the clergy of France. When their parishioners
were in conflict with the English authorities, he noted, the

clergy defended the parishioners. Tocqueville had touched on an important political difference between Canada and France: The French-Canadian clergy were in favour of democratic representation and institutions, while the French clergy were not only conservative but also predominantly opposed to democratic institutions. Despite their militancy, though, the Canadian clergy never led revolts. When political tensions rose, they tended to side with the authorities and oppose open rebellion.

While the clergy promoted the rights of French Canadians, Church policies were not always beneficial to them. A century of religious nationalism produced countless mottos such as "*la langue, gardienne de la foi*" ("language, keeper of the faith") or "*Qui perd sa langue perd sa foi*" ("He who loses his language loses his faith"). But when the interests of faith and language collided, faith always came out on top. Where everything besides language was considered, the Catholic Church was conservative to the point of being reactionary, and it did all it could to shelter French-Canadian souls from what it considered the deleterious influences of modern life. The result was that the Catholic clergy in Quebec actually forbade the reading and viewing of France's most cutting-edge writers and cinema, and preached against city life, industry and even money in general, which were considered Protestant and therefore immoral. In the long run this policy had the effect of isolating French Canadians from the French mainstream even more, and it kept them shockingly out of touch with modern realities and progress (more on the consequences of this in chapter 15).

To resist assimilation, French Canadians and Acadians developed diverse, sometimes wacky forms of *la vie associative,* from language conferences and cultural associations to secret societies. The first association was created at a banquet held in Montreal on June 24, 1834, St. John the Baptist Day (and because the banquets continued to be organized on that day, John the Baptist went on to become the patron saint of French Canadians), and led to the founding of the Société St-Jean Baptiste (St. John the Baptist Society), whose central mandate was to defend the rights of French Canadians. Dozens of other associations were formed in French-Canadian communities in Quebec and elsewhere in the decades that followed. The movement spawned a wide array of symbols, some of which, such as the maple leaf and the beaver, went on to become Canadian emblems. The Société St-Jean Baptiste even devised the anthem, "O Canada," that eventually replaced "God Save the Queen" as Canada's national anthem in 1980. Their flag—blue with a white cross and four fleurs-de-lys— became the flag of the province of Quebec in 1944 and the official symbol of all French Canadians. It hung in schools in Ontario, Manitoba and even Manchester, New Hampshire, and Woonsocket, Rhode Island, until it became exclusively the symbol of the Quebec independence movement in the 1960s.

Some of the most flamboyant instances of French-Canadian activism were the *conventions nationales* (national conferences), a custom started in Manchester, New Hampshire, in 1865. In 1874 Montrealers followed up on the idea by organizing the first congress open to all French Canadians; it was attended by eighteen thousand Franco-Americans, who arrived in 250 train cars. Delegates came from across North America, and even as far as France and Haiti. The main event was a three-hour *défilé* (parade) featuring thirty-one brass bands, twelve floats, a regiment of French-Canadian Zouaves (papal soldiers), and representatives of professional and trade associations and the clergy. Even the premier of Quebec paraded. This first *convention nationale* impressed the Acadians so much that they organized one of their own in 1881.

In the twentieth century the high points of French-language activism came during three French-language conventions in Quebec City in 1912, 1937 and 1952, organized by the Société du parler français au Canada. These events, at once religious, patriotic, tourist and academic, attracted delegates from the United States and Europe, including a representative of the French Academy. They always culminated in some kind of declaration to save French in North America. The 1912 *congrès* ended with members taking an oath to the French language. In 1937 the Quebec deacon and arch-activist Lionel Groulx called for the creation of a French state *within* Canada. It was the first time in Canada that the word *nation* was used to refer not just to a language group but also to an organized political body; Quebec nationalists would begin to aspire to political separation twenty-five years later.

One of the craziest schemes to resist assimilation took place in Louisiana, where Cajun Senator Dudley Leblanc tried to reverse the trend of Cajuns intermarrying with Americans by importing his own version of the *filles du roy,* the group of nubile orphans the King of France had sent to Quebec in 1660 to boost the population of the colony. Dud Leblanc—known among Cajuns as Coozan Dud (Cajun for *cousin*)—was a colourful businessman who had made his fortune in the 1940s selling Hadacol, a tonic that was supposed to be beneficial for people suffering from diabetes, cancer, heart problems, epilepsy and tuberculosis (and even more). Leblanc saw that intermarriage had resulted in few children being raised in French in Louisiana. So he came up with a scheme to import Acadian women from Canada to be brides for Cajun men, giving the old *filles-du-roy* scheme a modern twist by portraying it as a kind of cultural exchange.

We had heard the *filles d'Acadie* anecdote when we were in Louisiana, but had brushed it aside as myth until we came face to face with one of the former "*filles*" (now a grown woman) at the World Acadian Congress. A professor at the University of Moncton (who preferred not to be named), she told us it had been easy to sucker her into this "exchange" because, like every educated girl in the 1960s, she was looking for a way out of New Brunswick. Twenty-two girls went on the trip. She backed out shortly after she got to Louisiana when she sensed something shady about the whole operation, and went to study in France instead. The scheme never worked.

Historically, North Americans have tended to see the assimilation of French speakers as inevitable, if not natural, given their numeric weakness in the ocean of English speakers that has flooded most of the continent. But there was nothing natural or inevitable about it. The deportation of the Acadians and the anti-Métis repression in the Canadian West were only the most violent attempts to erase native French speakers from the continent. In Canada as well as the United States, francophones faced a barrage of semi-official and official assimilation policies, both tacit and overt.

In Louisiana the Yankees stripped francophones of their linguistic rights almost overnight. Because France had sided with the Confederates and with Louisiana in the Civil War, the Northern occupation government adopted starkly anti-French measures. Louisiana's constitution of 1864 removed any clauses that favoured French, whether in the legislature, in law or in education. In 1927 Louisiana outright prohibited education in French. The state even hired teachers from out of state to make sure they couldn't understand French, so they wouldn't respond to it. Any Cajun schooled before the war recalls stories of children wetting their pants because they didn't know how to ask to be excused to go to the toilet in English— and they weren't allowed to do so in French. Intermarriage was

one problem, but historians agree that the removal in 1864 of
the institutional framework protecting French spelled the disappearance of French in Louisiana.

Louisiana was not an isolated case. Nova Scotia forbade
teaching in French as early as 1864. New Brunswick did the
same in 1871, followed by Manitoba and Saskatchewan in 1890
and Ontario in 1912. Many French Canadians and Acadians
have a retired teacher in their family who remembers desks
with false bottoms where students could hide their French
books from the school inspectors. Teachers were not even
allowed to teach French in French: The famed Acadian writer
Antonine Maillet, who won the Prix Goncourt in 1979 for her
novel *Pélagie-la-Charrette,* learned French from a French grammar book written in English.

In Canada, the *British North America Act* of 1867 safeguarded the rights of French speakers in Quebec and in federal
institutions, but English was clearly more equal than French.
Until the 1960s the federal government did absolutely nothing
to defend the rights of francophones outside Quebec
(although, ironically, Quebec had a constitutional obligation
to protect the rights of its own anglophone minority). The
federal government simply did not apply its own laws or the
country's constitution; for example, when Manitoba denied
constitutional guarantees to its French community in 1890,
Ottawa did nothing. It was only because French Canadians
lobbied to have French words on Canadian stamps commem-
orating the fiftieth anniversary of the Act in 1927 that the federal government eventually agreed to do so. French didn't
appear on Canada's currency until 1936, and the lack of
French in the Canadian military was still a problem in the
Second World War.

On the whole, the federal government's stance only reinforced the already strong link between French and the Catholic

Church. The constitution guarantees confessional schools, which means that provinces can prohibit French schools, but not Catholic ones. By running their schools in French, the Catholic clergy became the saviours of the language. However, in New England and Louisiana the clergy decided it was more important to convert Protestants than to shelter the French-speaking community. They appointed English-speaking bishops and Irish priests, some of whom were starkly anti-French. This strategy was also used in every Canadian province west of Quebec. In Ontario, in the first quarter of the twentieth century, Irish Catholics were adamant about keeping French Canadians "in their place," and Bishop Michael Fallon, who led them, did all he could to bar bilingual Catholic schools. Franco-Ontarians, who form the largest group outside of Quebec, protested so vehemently that the clergy reversed their strategy. Wherever these practices were accepted without protest, French communities lost their parish and, with it, their most solid institution. In Louisiana the last Mass in French was sung in 1940.

Other powerful groups also worked against French. In the Canadian West, for instance, the Ku Klux Klan was openly anti-French and anti-Catholic and allied itself repeatedly with conservative parties to push for bans on teaching French. The Klan was also active against francophones in Maine.

Throughout the nineteenth century, French was still the dominant international language and the language of elites everywhere—even Roosevelt spoke French. But while this prestige helped bolster the place of French in Europe and even the teaching of French as a second language in America, it did nothing to help local francophone populations who were under siege by English-speaking elites. McGill University linguist Chantal Bouchard described this process in detail:

English Canadians and Americans developed a clear distinction between Parisian French and French Canadian "patois." The latter was totally discredited, barely considered a real language. Job offers for French teaching positions in American universities often stated, "French Canadians need not apply."

One of the first reports of this linguistic prejudice dates back to the 1850s and comes from a Frenchman, Emmanuel Blain de Saint-Aubin. He had been hired to teach the children of a rich English-speaking Montreal family, the Monks. The mother had specifically hired a Frenchman to teach her kids so they would never speak "awful French-Canadian patois," as she put it. Blain himself did not share her prejudice, but he did notice that the notion of a French-Canadian patois was firmly rooted among the Anglo-American elite.

At this point there were dialectal differences between the French spoken in Quebec and that spoken in France, but they weren't as huge as the Anglo-American and Anglo-Canadian elites pretended. In 1830 Alexis de Tocqueville, who toured Quebec for two weeks during his research for *Democracy in America,* had few comments to make about the language spoken there. One amusing anecdote he recounted described a time when he was travelling in the interior of Illinois guided by a Native man; he was surprised to hear the man speaking French with a Norman accent.

The term *patois* is far from neutral—and it's an exaggeration. In contrast to the Caribbean colonies, where slaves developed a French-based Creole, the French spoken in North America never definitively broke away from the mainstream. Today French Canadians and Acadians speak the most distinctive variety of French in the French-speaking world, not just because of its accent, but also because of its great variety of idiosyncratic expressions. But the difference between Parisian and Canadian French is no greater than that between British English and the

English spoken in Texas. There are dialectal differences, but never so extreme as to make them mutually unintelligible.

The "French-Canadian patois" label was in fact a political tool used to hasten the assimilation of francophones. It stripped French Canadians of the status and prestige they might have been able to take advantage of as speakers of the main international language of the time, and gutted francophones' confidence in front of their English bosses (with no small thanks to the Catholic Church, urban francophones had become a proletariat, while the English-speaking elite owned most of the economy).

The same prejudice against Quebec French persists to this day. When we give lectures to teachers of French, Julie draws more praise for her French than Jean-Benoît does (she has a lighter Quebec accent and picked up an international style of French during our three years in France, which she uses on formal occasions and for public speaking). Sometimes the praise she receives is meant as encouragement, or admiration for the fact that she mastered French only as an adult. In almost every case her French is compared to that of Jean-Benoît, whom many teachers claim not to understand. Strangely, their inability to understand Jean-Benoît is never considered a handicap on their part—it just seems to go without saying that there is something wrong with Quebec French. The comment is absurd, not to mention puzzling, since Jean-Benoît has considerably better mastery of the language than does Julie. The reality is that, although they mean well, these teachers have absorbed a centuries-old prejudice that was designed to put an end to French Canadians.

Although there is no (legitimate) reason to consider Canadian French inferior, the patois label is rooted in real linguistic differences. Throughout the nineteenth century, dialectal differences between North American and European French increased. At the start of the twentieth century these were more marked than ever, to the point that even the French-Canadian elite became alarmed. The situation was, again, the result of French Canadians' isolation. During the French regime in Canada, French Canadians were reputed to speak better French than most people from France (we explain this in chapter 4).

Dialectal differences had begun to develop as soon as the British took over. But at first it was not the Canadiens' French that changed, it was the French spoken in France. Alexis de Tocqueville remarked repeatedly that New France was in fact an Old France—both in speech and in mores. Canadiens maintained the old aristocratic pronunciation of vowels in *oi*—for example, *moi* (me), *toi* (you), *poil* (hair)—as *mwé, twé* and *pwèl*. To this day some old-stock francophones in North America use pronunciations and vocabulary that date back to the French regime. The Canadiens retained the long vowel, which has all but disappeared in Paris. For words like *bête* (beast), *être* (to be) and *arrêter* (to stop), Quebeckers draw out the first vowel, whereas the French keep it short. Quebeckers have also maintained diphthongs, which evolved on their own; a verb such as *faire* (to do, to make) is pronounced *fair* in France, while Quebeckers introduce an extra vowel (almost an extra syllable) and pronounce it as *fah-air*. Quebeckers pronounce *pâte* (dough) as *pawt* rather than *pat,* and *fort* (strong) as *fawr* rather than *fore.*

North American French has also maintained old consonantal sounds such as *dj, tch, dz* and *ts,* which have disappeared in standard French. A phrase like *tu dis* (you say) often comes out as *tsu dzis,* with a strong sibilance after the consonants. We noticed this feature in the French spoken in Guadeloupe as well, though Acadians have very little of it. Some of Jean-Benoît's uncles, construction workers raised in the rural Beauce area of Quebec, speak a version of Quebec French that has held on to the *tch* and the *dj*. A verb like *tiens* (take) is pronounced *tchien* or even *quiens*, and a verb like *marier* (to wed) is pronounced *mard-jer*. This type of pronunciation is still common in some parts of France, including central Auvergne. Quebeckers also roll the R as it used to be rolled in the *ancien regime*.

Some features of French-Canadian word composition, grammar and syntax are also typically seventeenth century. Jean-Benoît's grandfather used to say *formage* despite the French Academy's decision that *fromage* was the proper term. In Acadia, French speakers often conjugate verbs in an archaic style, saying *je chantons* rather than *je chante*. French Canadians also commonly use expressions like *mais que* instead of *quand* (when), or *être après* instead of *être en train de* (to be in the process of doing something).

Over the centuries Acadians and French Canadians also developed their own regional vocabularies. Acadians tend to say *éparer* (to lay out, as laundry to dry) instead of *étendre*, while Quebeckers say *garrocher* (to throw) instead of *lancer*. Each also developed special terms to suit their circumstances, like the Quebec term *poudrerie* (powdered snow). Having missed the French Revolution, and being sheltered from France's most extreme post-revolutionary anti-clericalism, French speakers in America maintained a lively tradition of religious profanity that originated in sometimes obscure religious tools or practices. This is one of the most original features of their language, and is instantly recognizable.

The characteristics described above are rarely all found in a single speaker, and the general manner of speaking in urban Quebec today is a lot more polished than it was fifty years ago. The norm being the norm, most educated French Canadians and Acadians can easily drop dialectal differences from their speech, which they tend to do in public speaking and in writing. (Though different in some ways, French writing in Canada is as normative as it is in France, and it conforms to the same norms.) How pronounced these features are in speaking often depends on class, education and whether the person has an urban or rural background. There is no real formula to describe how much or how little Quebecker speaks with the traditional Quebec accent—or accents, since there are many regional variations. Jean-Benoît is educated, urban and bourgeois, but speaks with a strong Quebec accent, no matter to whom he's talking. But even if some versions of modern Quebec French are more polished, major dialectal variations still remain. They are particularly noticeable in the speech of children, who are not yet conscious of "correctness."

Anglicisms are another feature of French in America. Historically, the French and Quebeckers have had very different relationships with English. While the French have to deal with the relatively recent influence of English as a global language, French Canadians and Acadians have been dealing with the imposing local presence of English for centuries. This has resulted in many borrowings, such as *poutine*, the name of a Quebec dish of French fries and cheddar cheese curds with brown gravy. An English listener is always surprised to learn that *poutine* is a corruption of the English *pudding*, itself a deformation of the French word *boudin* (a type of blood sausage).

But anglicisms play completely different roles in European and Quebec French. In France they convey a certain chic. In Quebec, anglicisms are a clear marker of class and education, and are usually considered a sign of ignorance. But even if French Canadians have borrowed many words from English, these have hardly affected the phonetics of the French they speak. Borrowings, in fact, rarely affect phonetics or grammar, the skeleton of any language.

However, borrowings became so intense at the start of the nineteenth century, particularly in the cities, that they affected the structure of the French spoken in America. In Louisiana, in New England and in some communities of the Canadian West, many native francophones lost their capacity to conjugate verbs. For example, an anglicism such as *"Il faut watcher son français,"* (you need to watch your French), inelegant as it is, is still structurally French. But *"Il faut watch son français"* (which we heard in Acadia) shows that the speaker hasn't mastered the basic system of verb conjugation in French. Today, if you have to go through a Canadian call centre (outside of Quebec), you will regularly hear recorded messages saying they will *"répondre votre appel"* (a calque of "answer your call") and *"accéder votre dossier"* (from the English "access your file")—proper French calls for the preposition *à* after the verbs in this context.

Those kinds of anglicisms, which are extremely rare in Europe among native speakers of French, are heard much more frequently in North America, and even more so outside of Quebec. They are often a clear indicator of imminent assimilation. Even as early as the beginning of the nineteenth century, French-Canadian newspapers were blowing the whistle on anglicisms and bad French, trying to stop the process of anglicization. Their efforts had varying degrees of success. In the twentieth century, Quebeckers would come to realize that these anglicisms were the result of a power relationship—English bosses often forced them to speak in English even among themselves (more on this in chapters 15 and 18).

But power relations do not explain everything: Other anglicisms show how technology plays a role in disseminating language. At the start of the nineteenth century, Canadian turbines and locomotives came not from France or Belgium but from England and the United States. The result: The vocabulary of construction workers and mechanics in Quebec is a study in anglicisms. Many Quebec mechanics speak of *le muffleur, le bumpeur* or *le wipeur,* whereas his French colleague says *silencieux, pare-chocs* and *essuie-glace.* The difference, of course, is that the instruction manual for a Ford, Chrysler or GM car used to come in English only, unlike those for Peugeots, Citroëns and Renaults. Technology-based anglicisms are one of the main forms of variances in North American French, and they show that technology is a vehicle of culture.

Of course, these technology-based anglicisms also highlight how much French Canadians and Acadians had been missing out on the important technical and intellectual developments that were taking place in France in the nineteenth century. Even while France was being outpaced by competing nations, Paris was still at the cutting edge of modernity. French culture, scientific and technological advances attracted millions of tourists, earned the admiration of the world and made the whole world hungry for French.

Part Three ~

ADAPTATION

Chapter 11

THE POWER OF ATTRACTION

MOST TEACHERS OF FRENCH we met and interviewed during the research for this book confirmed to us, with regret in their voices, that French was indeed waging an uphill battle against English in the war of second-language studies. Naturally we were curious to find out what kept them and their students so enthusiastic about French. The teachers cited a wide variety of motivations, ranging from extremely practical reasons to a kind of generalized idealization of the language. But one striking theme shone through in almost all their answers: People learn French to get access to French culture—or a certain idea of it—whether it's France's lively literary and artistic scene, French cuisine, French intellectuals, French films or just the French way of life.

In the history of any international language, there are two reasons why it spreads: It is either forced on people or people are interested in learning it. The global growth in French speakers in the nineteenth century owed a lot to French colonialism. Yet during the same century, the language continued to gain speakers outside of France's colonial empire, in places as diverse as Argentina, the U.S. and Germany. The reason? People wanted to speak French because it gave them access to what was modern, sophisticated and state-of-the-art.

This chapter, admittedly, is not as much about the French language as it is about how French gained its mass appeal. Few people studying French today realize to what extent their motivations are rooted in nineteenth-century developments in

France. In that century French went from being an elite language to a being language with mass appeal. It became definitively associated with luxury products, artistic innovation, tourism, cuisine and sophistication in just about every field, as well as scientific and technical progress. At the same time, French continued to develop the double personality it had gained during the Revolution-and-Empire period, and became even more strongly associated with universal values and human rights.

Nineteenth-century France was an amazing centre of creativity and innovation, and its tremendous artistic, scientific and intellectual production boosted the prestige of French across the planet. From Europe to South America and beyond, people knew French would give them access to the cutting edge of almost everything, and they wanted it. It was in this century that the French began speaking of the *rayonnement* of their language—a difficult term to translate, meaning a mixture of influence, spread and appeal. The French would later build on that appeal to construct widespread networks of associations and organizations that promoted French—many of which are still in place today (as we explain in Chapter 12).

The source of France's early mass appeal is very little documented. One of the rare books on the topic is Harvey Levenstein's *Seductive Journey,* which recounts the history of American tourism in France from Jefferson to the Depression. As Levenstein explains, tourism in eighteenth-century Paris consisted mostly of small-scale travel for personal cultivation. It became increasingly recreational over the next century as the number of travellers grew. The development of steam power enabled people to get to France by land and by sea faster than ever before. As many as a quarter of a million Americans visited the country each year before the First World War, and the number of English and German visitors was much larger.

French was still the language of high-level politics and diplomacy in Europe, and this status, unchallenged until 1919, inspired considerable interest in France. But the nation was also considered a window to the future. The thirst for novelty and progress attracted unprecedented numbers of visitors to the four world's fairs that France hosted in the nineteenth century. Between the fair of 1855 and that of 1867, attendance tripled from five million to fifteen million people. In 1889 it more than doubled to thirty-two million, and in 1900 it reached fifty million—considered a good turnout for international exhibitions even today.

The Anglo-American elites, couldn't get enough of France, to which they began travelling en masse. By the 1880s the community of American and British expatriates was big enough to support Paris's first English-language paper, the *Paris Herald,* created in 1887. And Paris's influence shone as far as the American West, where people went to saloons (a corruption of *salon*) and enjoyed lively French operettas by the likes of Offenbach—and the French cancan.

The reasons for this interest in Paris were complex. For a long time Paris had been a mandatory stop on the grand tour, as the British called their cultural pilgrimages across Europe (the source of the term *tourism*). Nineteenth-century developments in arts, tastes, science and industry made Paris even more tantalizing. French taste in food and design set the standard for the world's elite. Luxury items from the realms of fashion, perfume, wine and cuisine, already a French forte, acquired even more renown. Demand for these goods led an ambitious French merchant, Aristide Boucicaut, to buy the Paris store Au Bon Marché in 1852 and turn it into the first of the *grands magasins* (department stores), an idea that soon made its way abroad, notably to New York City.

Everyone looked towards France for the latest developments in everything. To keep the public informed and to transmit information to the capitals of Europe, a translator, Charles Émile Havas, created Agence Havas, the world's first news agency, in 1841; one of his employees, Julius Reuters, started his own telegraph wire service in London in 1851. A Russian Jewish refugee in Paris, Eliezer Ben Yehuda, was so impressed with the French daily *Figaro* that he decided to recreate and modernize the Hebrew language so it could be used for modern communications (more on this in Chapter 17).

The popularity of French cuisine grew in step with the development of tourism. Even today, the French word *cuisine* is the universal synonym of gastronomy in every language, and *cuisine* is cited as one of the best reasons for learning French. France was already famous for food before the Revolution, although most people today would be surprised by a French meal of the time. Dishes were prepared a couple of *days* in advance and laid out in serving dishes on the table—individual servings became popular only in the nineteenth century, under the influence of Russian-style service.

Things started to change with the development of the restaurant at the end of the eighteenth century. The term *restaurant* originates from a shop near the Louvre Palace in Paris that in the 1760s served a meat-based broth known as a *bouillon restaurant* (restoring broth). The term gave birth to the idea of a *restaurateur,* the person who owned the establishment. But the big shift came with the Revolution. Prior to that, most chefs cooked for bourgeois or aristocratic families and their numerous guests. When their bosses fled abroad to avoid jail or the guillotine during the Revolution, these chefs and *maîtres d'hôtel* found themselves out of work, so they started opening their own establishments. The number of restaurants in Paris had multiplied sixfold by 1810. By 1830 there were more than three thousand restaurants in Paris, of varying quality—some already of a high standard. The word *restaurant* entered the dictionary of the French Academy in 1835. Since not everyone in France could afford to eat at the expensive table of a great chef like Auguste Escoffier, *brasseries, bistrots* and *cafés* began to multiply in order to cater to different clienteles.

Haute cuisine, already a big draw by the nineteenth century, became a tourist magnet, especially for wealthier Americans visiting France (middle-class tourists tended to stick to modest hotel restaurants); this was when the word *menu* appeared in the U.S. At the same time, the British took to drinking claret, as they called Bordeaux. The French fed the new demand for high-end products, developing brands such as Lu cookies and Schweppes sparkling water. Near the end of the century they developed the system of *appellation d'origine* (label of origin) to classify French wine—and later extended the appellation concept to other produce such as Roquefort cheese, onions, lentils and meats. Escoffier and Swiss hotel owner César Ritz began a policy of exporting French cooking by placing French chefs—about two thousand in all—in hotels and restaurants across the world. French became essential for any chef with ambition, and remains so today, which is why people still speak of *entrées, hors d'oeuvres, casseroles, vinaigrettes* and *meringue,* to name but a few French gastronomic terms used in English.

Grave political upheavals shook France over the nineteenth century, although they did little to damage France's attractiveness. Between 1830 and 1871 the French changed regimes no fewer than four times, each time violently. Paris was partially destroyed during the Prussian siege of 1870 and during the Commune uprising of 1871, but the tourists kept coming anyway. Not even the catastrophic invasion of phylloxera, an American parasite that almost wiped out the French wine industry, was enough to kill interest in French cuisine and winemaking.

Curiously, while the French language came to be associated more and more with elite culture and tastes, it also became the language of human rights. It remained the language of the European elite throughout the nineteenth century despite the competing influence of English and German. But the Revolution of 1848, an insurrection that ended the rule of King Louis-Philippe and ushered in the Second Republic, spread anti-monarchical rebellion to all the European capitals except London, associating French once again with progressive, reformist circles, as in the early years of the French Revolution. The association of French with anti-conservative politics got even more impetus from the rise of great French literary stars such as Victor Hugo, Alexandre Dumas and Alphonse de Lamartine—all reformist thinkers who played a role in the Revolution of 1848. It is something of a semantic miracle that French kept its elitist reputation while surfing the wave of democratization. One of the keys to this double identity probably came from the development in France during this century of the outspoken public intellectual. Even today France manages to be an aggressive player in the globalization movement while articulating a coherent anti-capitalist, pro-socialist discourse on the international stage.

Strangely, although France experienced political upheavals throughout the century, it also benefited from a period of peace in Europe that lasted from the 1815 Treaty of Vienna to the beginning of the First World War (even the 1870 Franco-Prussian War failed to drag in other powers). In France this unleashed creative energies that had been suppressed for at least a generation, which in turn reinforced the importance and prestige of French in the world. The progress of French in France through education (recounted in chapter 8) was critical. It created a bigger domestic market for the consumption of culture, but also dramatically increased the number of French-speaking potential artists, writers and scientists whose success would feed the demand for French.

Nowhere was this more obvious than in literature and the visual arts. There is much debate over the actual definition of Romanticism, but its central tenet—the expression of an enhanced sense of self and feelings of revolt—impelled France's literary ideals for most of the century and beyond, spawning generations of literary masters (until the 1970s the French won a fifth of all Nobel prizes in literature). Even after the First World War, a generation of young American writers—Ernest Hemingway, John Dos Passos and F. Scott Fitzgerald among them—flocked to Paris for inspiration. Hemingway's autobiographical *A Moveable Feast* shows how a young American hoped to learn from the French capital even when he didn't write in French.

The figure of Victor Hugo (described in chapter 8) stands tall in this century, but he was not alone. A dozen other French authors could have made a solid claim of having surpassed him in literary production, although none could claim equal status as a public figure. Whereas the previous century had been characterized by a generation of philosophes whose artistic output was rather thin, the nineteenth century produced a score of great writers who made significant contributions to world literature—some of whom became famous internationally in their lifetime. While Alexandre Dumas invented the popular historical novel, Honoré de Balzac invented the novel series. In a space of twenty years, between 1827 and 1848, Balzac wrote the ninety novels that composed his *Human Comedy*. Gustave Flaubert (1821–80) and Émile Zola (1840–1902) invented literary realism; Zola, the founder of naturalism, brought literary craft to social inquiry. Their friends the Goncourt brothers developed a parallel academy to compete with the French Academy, and their literary prize, the Prix Goncourt, is today considered pre-eminent. Zola and Flaubert were so widely read during their lives that they became familiar names in capitals all over Europe and beyond. When Zola was tried for accusing a number of

French officers of forgery in the famous Dreyfus affair, thousands of people demonstrated in London and New York to support him.

The most widely translated of all nineteenth-century French authors was Jules Verne (1828–1905). Verne invented the genre that would come to be known as science fiction, and he still ranks high on the list of the world's most read authors, even in English. He came from a bourgeois family and was expected to become a lawyer, but instead he dreamed of travel (he had his own yacht) and began to write adventure novels. As his career progressed, Verne became more and more interested in scientific speculation—one of his famous emulators was H. G. Wells. He created characters such as Phileas Fogg, who travelled *Around the World in Eighty Days*; Captain Nemo, who sailed *20,000 Leagues under the Sea*; Professor Hardwigg, who made a *Journey to the Centre of the Earth*; Impey Barbicane, who flew *From the Earth to the Moon*; and other "Extraordinary Adventures," like the *Mutineers of the Bounty.* Like Dumas, Verne eventually became a favourite of the film industry (in Verne's case, of Walt Disney).

Much as in literature, the spirit of exploration was strong in the visual arts in France, especially after 1850. In the spring of 2002 Jean-Benoît had lunch in the lovely town of Barbizon, southwest of Paris, on the edge of the beautiful Fontainebleau Forest. He was a guest of the late author Jacques Meunier, a travel writer and native of Barbizon. After a wonderful meal in a hidden garden off the town's main street, Jacques took Jean-Benoît through a door in his backyard that led straight to a small museum located in the workshop of Jean-François Millet, one of the most famous members of a school of landscape artists called the *école de Barbizon*.

Although Millet's paintings now seem conventional, they were groundbreaking, partly for their technique and partly for their choice of topics. At the time, France's Academy of Fine Arts condoned only mythical or grandiose subjects. Millet chose to depict peasant life in all its simplicity. The Barbizon school's most famous member was Théodore Rousseau. Although none of these painters was revolutionary, they did foster a nonconformist approach that influenced a generation of artists who rose to prominence in the last third of the century: the French Impressionists, whose paintings still fetch the highest price in art auctions.

Impressionism started with Édouard Manet, who was himself strongly influenced by the British painter William Turner. Manet's Impressionist revolution, which the Academy of Fine Arts rejected for half a century, brought forth a series of creative artists: Cézanne, Monet, Renoir, Gauguin. Since a command of French was not a requirement for belonging to their movement, nineteenth-century painters were much more open to outsiders than writers were. Foreign artists began to flock to France—from Van Gogh and Picasso to Dali and Chagall. These artists, whose works would enrich the collections of American connoisseurs and museums such as the Guggenheim, completely revolutionized visual art, making Paris its world centre for nearly a century. Generations of artists from other countries still flock to Paris and France to recapture the ideas and the feeling of discovery created there in the nineteenth century. Since the Second World War Paris has lost some of its edge in the visual arts, but it remains an important centre of creativity.

The power of Paris's appeal was not limited to art, culture and food. France was also a land of modernity in science, technology and industry. The city itself was one of the first examples of comprehensive urban planning. Although tourists even then went to France seeking history and culture, the city of Paris was modern by European standards. Napoleon had been a great builder, but his nephew Napoleon III surpassed him. He ordered the prefect of the city, Georges Eugène Haussmann, to rebuild Paris almost completely, to create gardens, lay out its great avenues, add sewers and water reservoirs and more (partly to destroy the old Parisian neighbourhoods, which were known as revolutionary hotbeds). Today's Paris is largely a result of Haussmann's work, which touched almost every neighbour-hood, with the exception of Île St-Louis and Île de la Cité. The problem of sanitation was critical at the time, and in 1884 another prefect of Paris, Eugène Poubelle, ordered citizens to store garbage in metal containers—little did he know that his name, *poubelle,* would become the usual term for a garbage can.

The very symbol of Paris, the Eiffel Tower, was one of the great technological achievements of the century. Its builder, Gustave Eiffel (1832–1923), is himself the prototype of the spirit that animated the people in this century of creativity. Eiffel, who had already built the tallest suspended bridges of the time, intended his three-hundred-metre tower to be a show-case for the Paris World's Fair of 1889 and to demonstrate the strength of metal structures. Its construction required dozens of innovations to overcome technical obstacles—Otis, the young American elevator company Eiffel hired, had to come up with an elevator design that could carry people more than eight floors at a time. Although it has long since been surpassed in height, the Eiffel Tower was a technical tour de force. It was almost twice as high as the Washington Monument, the next tallest structure, but took only two years to build (compared to thirty-seven) and was one-fifteenth the weight. Two million people flocked to Eiffel's tower in 1889 and bought an expen-sive ticket to ride its elevator—one franc for the first storey, two francs for the second and three for the ride to the top. Eiffel had himself footed most of the tower's cost—7.8 million gold francs—but he recouped his expenses in the second year of operation. He later installed the world's first aerodynamics laboratory in the tower, where he tested wing shapes.

Innovations and inventions in the nineteenth century made Paris a window of discovery. Although the French were late to enter the age of steam, they were at the vanguard of the next stage in the Industrial Revolution: the search for an internal combustion engine. Its obvious application would be to propel self-moving autonomous carriages (automobiles) and heavier-than-air flying machines (airplanes).

Automobile technology in fact had many fathers—German, English and French. The German Benz created the first light motor and the first automobile. But Louis Renault designed the first automobile that did not look like a horse-drawn carriage, as well as a number of other critical pieces of equipment, while Édouard Michelin was the first to put tires on cars, in 1897. More than the Germans or the British, the French were passionate about the automobile, and it soon became a craze. Many foreigners saw their first automobile in the streets of Paris. Between 1898 and 1902, automobile makers and the media organized dozens of ambitious car races, the most spectacular of which was the Paris–Peking race. Hundreds of cars were at the starting line of some of these races, and they were often fatal; twelve people died in the Paris–Madrid race of 1902.

The French were also at the forefront of aviation. In 1805, twenty years after the Montgolfier brothers developed the first hot-air balloon, the physicist Louis Joseph Gay-Lussac climbed to the record height of seven thousand metres (twenty-three thousand feet) in a hot-air balloon to study the composition of the atmosphere. Clément Ader is credited with the first takeoff on board an air contraption, which was propelled by steam, in 1890. Although the Wright brothers succeeded with the first controlled flight in 1903, they owe their breakthrough to the contribution of little-known French engineer

Octave Chanute, who emigrated to the U.S. and gave them access to critical knowledge in the field, mostly from France. The Wrights' invention raised little commercial interest in the U.S., and they had to come to France to find interested crowds, industrialists and buyers. It didn't take long for French inventors and aviators to improve on the Wright design, and Louis Blériot flew across the Channel in 1909. Others, including brothers Henri and Eugène Farman, started their own aircraft firms, building the first assembly lines for biplanes.

Cinematography, another cutting-edge technology of the time, was developed in France. While Thomas Edison had invented a personal viewer for moving images, it was the Lyon chemist and industrialist Louis Lumière (1864–1948) who figured out how to project reels of film onto a screen. The Lumière family argued over the name of their new invention, toying with the name *domitor,* until they settled on *cinématographe.* Their patriarch, Antoine, a commercial visionary, began showcasing films in Paris. On the first day, December 28, 1895, in the basement of the Grand Café near the Opera, the show attracted thirty-three people. A few weeks later three thousand had attended. The new invention soon swept the planet. By 1897 there had been eight hundred thousand Lumière shows across the world—with images showcasing Paris. A circus organizer, Georges Méliès, made the first motion picture in 1902, from a Jules Verne novel, *From the Earth to the Moon,* and created the first film studio. In the 1930s the unassuming Louis Lumière remarked dryly, "They say I invented cinema." He was reputedly much more interested in photography, and had invented the colour print in the meantime.

At the start of the twentieth century the scientific climate in Paris was exuberant. Some inventions made waves even though they didn't have the popular appeal of cars and movies. In the 1880s Louis Pasteur discovered a cure for rabies—

and invented modern biology. He also developed a process to kill the micro-organisms responsible for fermentation, which came to be known as pasteurization. At the turn of the millennium a Polish scientist, Marie Sklodowska, and her French husband, Pierre Curie, became the first to understand radioactivity. Marie Curie earned not one but two Nobel prizes—for physics in 1903 and for chemistry in 1911—before inventing the mobile radiology unit during the First World War. (It was partly as a result of the couple's work that France remained in the lead in atomic research until the 1940s.)

The Curies' curium (an artificial element), Pasteur's pasteurization and Poubelle's *poubelle* were not the only cases of people's surnames being used to name discoveries and inventions in this period. The new writing system for the blind, Braille, was named after its inventor, Louis Braille. Louis Godillot's army shoes became known as *godillots*, which then became the deprecatory *godasses* (a term of which M. Godillot's heirs are certainly not proud). However, inventors and researchers generally preferred making up new words from Greek or Latin components, such as *autoclave, bathyscaphe, capillarité* (capillary action), *galvanoplastie* (electroplating) and *inoxydable* (stainless steel). The other main source of new terms was borrowings from foreign languages, such as *caoutchouc* (rubber, from Spanish). People also borrowed freely from English for scientific and technical vocabulary and words for daily life. It was in this century that two ancient gallicisms from English, *gentleman* and *toast*, re-entered French. Other terms such as *packet boat* and *riding coat* were frenchified into *paquebot* and *redingote*.

The Industrial Revolution profoundly changed class relations in France, as everywhere, and the French had to invent new vocabulary for this phenomenon as well. *Communiste,* a word invented in the previous century, became popular in 1840, as did *socialiste*. Workers organized into *syndicat*s (unions), which produced *syndicaliser* (to unionize) and *syndiqués* (unionized workers). To go on strike became *faire la grève*. *Grève* means *beach*—the first strikers in France gathered on the edge of the Seine River at Place de Grèves, which is right in front of Paris's city hall.

During this period the French earned an international reputation for grand schemes of all sorts. In the 1880s the French sculptor Frédéric Bartholdi proposed that France offer its sister republic, the United States of America, a great gift to celebrate its centennial. He designed a gigantic thirty-three-metre statue titled *La Liberté éclairant le monde* (*Liberty Enlightening the World*). Though rather academic in its design, the Statue of Liberty was the tallest statue of its time. Bartholdi even took a boat to New York City to choose the island where it would stand.

But other schemes did more to directly spread the influence of French. The French had invented the metric system during the Revolution, but during the second half of the nineteenth century it spread to become an international system, thanks to a campaign by French diplomats, scientists and industrialists to convince other countries to adopt it. The campaign succeeded because the need was there: Commerce and science in Europe were handicapped by different national standards in weights and measurements, which might involve fractions and proportions based on eight, twelve or sixteen, making international calculations extremely difficult. By 1875 some forty countries had joined the International Bureau of Weights and Measurements. Today most of the world uses the metric system to some extent. The United States adopted the metric system in 1866, but it remains one of the rare countries—along with Liberia and Myanmar (Burma)—that still use the old imperial system in day-to-day life. However, it is a little-known secret that even American standards like pounds and miles are defined in terms of the metre as established in Paris; for example, the official length of the foot is 0.3048 metres.

The most grandiose of nineteenth-century French schemes was Ferdinand de Lesseps' (1805–94) idea of digging a canal across the Isthmus of Suways (the French called it Suez) between the Mediterranean and Red seas. Lesseps did not come up with the idea on his own; it was one of the many projects that had motivated Napoleon's Egyptian expedition of 1798. But Lesseps' idea of a trench 163 kilometre long and 30 metres wide to link three lakes across the desert, was ultimately the one that was applied.

It took Lesseps as much time to convince people his plan was feasible as it did to actually dig the canal. The British in particular were extremely critical of the scheme. They didn't want France meddling in their naval domain, and they rightly saw the canal as a move to further French foreign interests by building a base for colonial expansion (which we discussed in chapter 10). In 1854 Lesseps, who spoke fluent Arabic, convinced the khedive of Egypt, who was a personal friend, to adopt the project. Then he spent the better part of the next fifteen years convincing shareholders to finance it.

Although this massive project was threatened with bankruptcy several times, it was a truly international enterprise—even the British public bought shares. When the canal finally opened in 1869, it was an immediate success, carrying fourteen percent of international sea traffic. The canal's international convention of neutrality was respected until 1948. As an ultimate tribute to Lesseps' idea, the British took a controlling share by buying back the khedive's Suez Canal shares in 1875. But it was through this scheme that the giant French multinational Suez was created, allowing the French to make their mark in massive engineering projects, a field in which they remain world leaders today.

The Suez Canal also had the desired effect of raising the profile of French in the Middle East. From this date on, French was an important language among the Egyptian bourgeoisie and elite, even after Egypt became a British protectorate in 1914. So, not only did Lesseps embody the spirit of progress of nineteenth-century France, but his idea raised the profile of French everywhere, and in particular within the crumbling Ottoman Empire.

In the meantime, France—or, more properly speaking, the French—would put the incredible influence of their culture to use in deliberately spreading the French language in an entirely original way. French elites knew that geopolitically France was slipping, despite the achievements of the century. They decided to use the French language to compensate for this growing weakness. Between the 1860s and the Second World War, the French built a multi-tiered system of language associations, cultural centres and schools that would not only reinforce French where it was already present—in Europe, the Middle East and North America—but also carry it across the globe. This massive system was part of a new initiative called cultural diplomacy. And it succeeded largely because so many people across the planet already wanted to learn French.

Chapter 12 ~

THE INVENTION OF CULTURAL DIPLOMACY

IN THE SUMMER OF 2003, Julie spent two weeks in Lesotho, a tiny mountain enclave in the middle of South Africa. She was there to watch a friend conduct workshops aimed at reinforcing democracy at the local level. African democracy may sound like an oxymoron, but in fact Lesotho, with its population of two million, gained independence peacefully in 1966 and has a growing reputation as one of the few functioning democracies on the continent.

French missionaries were present in Lesotho in the early nineteenth century; they supported Lesotho's king against attacks from neighbouring Boers, and they transcribed the language, Sesotho, into Roman letters. However, in 1868 Lesotho became a British protectorate. As a consequence, today English is the second language taught from the early years in Lesotho's primary schools—and evidently with much success. Julie met teenage girls in the countryside who could carry on long conversations in fluent English.

Surprisingly, though, the French presence remains. Strolling through downtown Maseru, the country's capital, Julie discovered that Lesotho's single public library is, in fact, an Alliance française. A British couple donated the century-old sandstone building to the city in 1946 with instructions to turn it into a public library. When the library foundered in 1982, the Alliance française took it over and turned it into a combination city library, video rental store and language school. When Julie strolled in to take a peek, she saw that roughly half the shelves were stocked with English books and videos, while the other half had a good selection of French literature and films, encyclopedias, magazines and even some classic French comic-book series such as *Astérix* and *Tintin*.

There was more. The director of Maseru's Alliance française informed Julie that the French language school was actually rather busy. At the time of her visit some 250 students were enrolled in French classes. Julie asked the director what could possibly motivate people in this isolated, poverty-stricken former British colony to pay for French lessons. He quickly replied, "French is an African language." The students, he explained, were mostly lawyers, doctors and members of the military. Over half the fifty-seven countries in Africa and around the Indian Ocean use French, many as an official language, and French is an official language of the Organization for African Unity. So upwardly mobile professionals in Africa need French to pursue an international career on the continent.

Maseru's is one of 1,074 Alliances françaises now operating in 136 countries. The language schools, together with some thousand institutions that teach French abroad, form the backbone of an extensive international system of French cultural promotion established in the late nineteenth and early twentieth centuries. The system, which came to be known as cultural diplomacy, marked a new stage in the history of language. For the first time the French realized that foreign demand for their language had to be cultivated and maintained. Almost spontaneously, individuals took on the task. Like missionaries, French men and women set out of their own accord to spread French language and culture, like a religion. The French government didn't play an important role in the movement until forty years after it started.

The actual origins of the movement are not widely known. The Alliance française is such a well-known brand that even well-informed people tend to think it was the first French association to start opening language schools abroad, and is the only one that operates them now. In fact, twenty-three years before the foundation of the Alliance française in 1883, a group of eighteen French Jews founded the Alliance israélite universelle (Universal Israelite Alliance), which wanted to spread French for different reasons. This organization was the brainchild of a lawyer, Adolphe Crémieux, and seventeen doctors, teachers, lawyers and journalists, all fervent believers in the ideals and principles of the French Revolution. In the middle of the nineteenth century, when only a tenth of the world's Jewish population enjoyed basic civil rights and most Jews lived in abject poverty, French Jews were allowed to vote, own property, live where they wanted, practise liberal professions and enter politics—rights they had enjoyed since 1791. Many French Jews had risen to become influential figures in the country. Crémieux himself, when he became minister of justice ten years later, would pass a law granting full citizenship to Algerian Jews in 1870. In short, although French Jews were still subject to unofficial persecution, they were considerably better off than the vast majority of Jews in the world. The founders of the Alliance israélite universelle aimed to help poor Jews by creating an educated Jewish middle class, specifically in Eastern Europe, North Africa and the Middle East.

But Crémieux and the AIU's founders did not believe that the situation of Jews would be improved by mass migration to France. They wanted to bring modernity to existing Jewish populations so they could integrate into the societies where they lived. Their first tactic was to attempt to influence the French government to put pressure on other European governments to grant rights to Jews. Within several years, however,

they decided that the best way to bring modernity to Jews was
to educate them. Crémieux and his followers were modernists
who were convinced that the traditional teachings of Hebrew
schools would do nothing to improve the condition of Jews.
They aimed to create French language schools whose graduates
would go on to work in the banks and civil administrations of
the countries where they lived.

The AIU's first target country was Russia. When the
Russian czar objected to the project, the association redirected
its efforts towards Sephardic Jews living in Morocco, who were
not as poor as Jews in Europe but more cut off from modernity.
The AIU established its first French school in Tétouan,
Morocco, in 1862, followed by a school in Tangier in 1865. The
association created a teacher training school, the École normale israélite orientale, in Paris in 1867 to train teachers who
would return to their countries of origin. The schools were
strictly secular, and not always well accepted by the local
Jewish leadership. Yet they soon spread to North Africa,
Turkey and Europe; fourteen had been opened by 1870, and by
1900 there were a hundred schools with twenty-six thousand
students. Those numbers had doubled again by 1914.

Crémieux and his successor, Narcisse Leven, did not glorify
the French language itself so much as embrace its potential as a
tool. Over the decades, however, the AIU's success drew the
attention of the cultural leaders in France, especially in diplomatic circles. Despite the fact that the world's elites still gravi-
tated towards French as both a prestigious and an important
international language, France's rank on the world stage was
slipping rather quickly by that time. The efforts of the Alliance
israélite universelle showed that by exporting French culture,
secular, missionary-like activists could create a new sphere of
influence for France that went beyond foreign policy, instead
reaching out directly to individual sensibilities.

Inspired by the model of the AIU, a group of members of the Société historique Saint-Simon met in Paris in 1883 and founded the Alliance française. One of these founders, Paul Cambon, who was French ambassador to the protectorate of Tunisia, had been impressed by the results of Catholic religious schools and the local AIU organization there, although the goal of the Allliance française founders was as much humanitarian as propagandist. The AF decided to create a network of "support committees" in France and abroad that would raise money to open and manage language schools, organize lecture tours and provide a forum for French personalities travelling abroad. However, the eight founding members realized immediately that, as a rather anonymous group of diplomats and civil servants, they didn't have the clout to get such a movement off the ground. So they decided to rally influential figures such as the former governor of Senegal, General Louis de Faidherbe, Suez Canal–digger Ferdinand de Lesseps and the famed microbiologist Louis Pasteur to their cause.

Like the AIU, the Alliance française was immediately successful because the demand for French at the time was very high, and because abroad it relied on local committees that operated without interference from Paris (still the basic organizational structure today). In the first three years after its creation, the AF had twelve thousand students. As a result of local initiatives, many of these founding committees morphed into schools, and by 1900, 250 schools were operating in Europe, Asia, Africa and Latin America. The first North American school opened in Montreal in 1902, followed by Toronto in 1903, then Winnipeg and Kingston. In the United States the first schools opened in the early 1900s in Boston, Baltimore, Lafayette, Detroit, Providence and Philadelphia. Support committees were formed in the first decades of the twentieth century in Argentina, Mexico, Chile, Colombia,

Paraguay and Peru, and quickly became popular. The biggest Alliance française school during the 1920s was in Buenos Aires; in 1924 it had ten thousand members and offered eighty-one different language courses.

At the World's Fair in Paris in 1900 the Alliance française ran one of the most popular pavilions. The exhibit featured a model classroom decorated with maps of France's colonies and with students' written exercises pinned to the walls. From May to November visitors flocked there from all over the world to watch *La leçon de français*: a teacher delivering a French lesson to a group of men, women and children from as far away as Madagascar, Indonesia, Senegal and Norway. The Alliance française had asked foreign governments to send a class for the event but few could afford it, so it borrowed foreign students from Paris's Berlitz language school for the duration of the Fair. This slight misrepresentation didn't detract from the exhibit's appeal; the World's Fair organizers awarded the Alliance française pavilion a gold medal.

Meanwhile, other projects to promote French in the world quickly sprang up on the AF's heels. French universities in Grenoble and Toulouse struck up partnerships with universities in Prague, Milan and Barcelona to organize conferences and courses on French language and culture. Within several years these "feelers" from the French universities had developed into establishments known as cultural centres or institutes. The idea was not to compete with the Alliances françaises but to complement them by offering information and documentation on France and French culture, organizing colloquiums and events, and inviting French artists. This initiative also caught on quickly and the cultural centres flourished, especially in areas where the Alliances françaises weren't strong, such as in Europe outside of France. Cultural centres opened in Florence in 1908, in London in 1910, in Lisbon in 1928 and in Stockholm in 1937. By the end of the 1930s most of them were independent from the universities where they had started. There are now 153 *centres culturels* or *instituts français,* but unlike the Alliances françaises, they belong to the French government, whereas the Alliance remains a private organization.

The Mission laïque française (French secular mission) was created in 1902 by a group of French teachers and university professors who shared an almost evangelical desire to spread the French language and culture throughout the world. They chose the term *laïque* to distinguish themselves from the Catholic and Protestant missions, which were still very active, especially in the French colonies and the Middle East (as discussed in chapter 9). The program of the Mission laïque was to train teachers and to refine teaching methods so that teachers could overcome cultural differences; the ultimate goal, of course, was to open more French schools outside of France.

In 1905 the Mission laïque began publishing the magazine *Revue de l'enseignement colonial* (*Colonial Teaching Review*), later renamed *Revue de l'enseignement français hors de France* (*Review of French Teaching Outside of France*). The organization opened schools in Greece in 1906 and in Beirut, Cairo and Alexandria in 1909. In 1902, in Paris, the agency opened the École normale Jules Ferry, a college for training language instructors to deal with cultural difference and adapt teaching techniques to foreign cultures and languages. Until the beginning of the twentieth century, the development of French cultural diplomacy remained the work of private associations, but in 1906 the Mission laïque benefited from the first subsidies from the French government. The government was beginning to understand the political potential of cultural diplomacy. During the 1920s the Mission laïque opened more schools in the Middle East, Russia and Japan.

A third scheme to spread French had been in the making for two centuries by this time: foreign *collèges* and *lycées,* the oldest of which was the Collège français of Berlin, founded in 1689 by French Huguenots. However, the schools did not really form a network. Most of them were ad hoc creations of French expatriates who later opened them to non-French students—such as the *lycée* of Frankfurt, created in 1949 for children of the staff of the French consulate, but later opened to any locals who wanted their offspring educated in French. The history of this network prior to 1990 is sketchy because the schools were not organized as a common body; some of them operated under the aegis of France's ministry of foreign affairs and others were run by the ministry of education; most were local organizations with some form of support from the French government. In 1990 France put them all under the authority of a single entity, the Agence pour l'enseignement du français à l'étranger (Agency for French Teaching Abroad).

There are now more than 430 French *collèges* and *lycées* in 125 countries, schooling 235,000 children, a third of them French. A quarter of the schools are in the United States, Morocco, Lebanon and Spain combined. The largest *lycée* is that of Madrid, with 3,700 students; the average has six hundred. Everywhere these colleges benefit from a reputation for offering high-end education—in Morocco the demand is so strong that kindergarten candidates have to take an admissions exam. Most of the schools are autonomous; only seventy-nine are directly managed by the Agence. The rest are run by locals, although programs have to conform to French education standards, and all or most of the teachers are of French origin. Famous former students of these *lycées* include former U.N. Secretary-General Boutros Boutros-Ghali; the president of Latvia, Vaira Vike-Freiberga; the architect Ricardo Bofill; and actor Robin Williams (who gives interviews in French).

France's network of cultural diplomacy was nearly destroyed by the two world wars. The Alliance française, being entirely private, suffered badly from the First World War, particularly inside France, where many schools could not afford to operate after the war. In 1920 the Alliance opened the École pour étrangers (School for Foreigners) in Paris. Meanwhile the popularity of the schools was still growing where the war had not had much effect, especially in Latin America. By 1939 the AIU had doubled its enrolment to forty thousand students.

The Second World War was another setback for all the associations in the system. France's Vichy government, which was strongly pro-Catholic, shut down the Mission laïque during the war. The occupying Germans were determined to get rid of an association devoted to the expansion of French civilization, so in 1940 they closed the Paris office of the Alliance française on Boulevard Raspail and removed the association's archives (the archives were thought to have been lost until they resurfaced in 2001, in twenty-three boxes among Soviet archives). During the war the Alliance relocated its head office to London, and Charles de Gaulle, leader of the Free French, was named honorary president. Meanwhile, though, the number of students across the world fell drastically.

But the Second World War turned out to be pivotal, and gave French cultural diplomacy new life. In 1945, when France was just emerging from the humiliating German occupation, France's ministry of foreign affairs began looking for ways to resuscitate the country's damaged morale and reassert its global presence. Language became its new tool. The network already existed, and the government believed it could use language and cultural promotion to prove to the world that French language and culture were still vital and important. For the first time the French government created a body to coordinate the different associations already in place: the

Délégation générale des relations culturelles et des oeuvres françaises à l'étranger (Directorate General of French Foreign Cultural Relations).

Although the Alliance française had been hard hit by the Second World War, it rebounded swiftly in this new environment: By 1949 there were AF schools in 650 cities in France, Europe, Africa, Asia and the Pacific, North America and Latin America. By 1950 the Alliance had quadrupled its postwar figures, with a total of fifty-five thousand students; by 1967 that number had again quadrupled to two hundred thousand students. More than ever, Latin America became the AF's stronghold. The schools were extremely popular in Argentina, Brazil and Mexico, countries with some of the biggest schools in the AF network to this day. In 1967 the Alliance expanded inside France, renovated its office on Boulevard Raspail and built the seven-storey Centre Georges Duhamel to house the expanding activities of the École internationale de langue et de civilisation françaises (International School of French Language and Civilization). Founded in 1952, the school had students from 187 nationalities in teacher training and language classes by 1970.

After 1945 the *centres culturels* and *instituts culturels,* already strong in Europe, actively boosted their efforts in areas where the Alliance française was least present, notably in Germany (to this day Germany has more French cultural centres than any other country). In the 1960s the Mission laïque was also given a new vocation: to open schools for the children of managers of French companies running projects abroad. These *écoles d'entreprises* (company schools) were staffed by teachers certified by the French national education system. The first one opened in Calgary, Alberta, in the 1960s for children of French managers of the oil company Elf Aquitaine. The Mission laïque continued to open new company schools throughout the 1970s, and by 1985 was operating fifty-seven schools with 2,500 students. Today thirty of the Mission's fifty-four schools are company schools. They span the globe from the École MLF–Aventis Pasteur (a pharmaceutical company) in Allentown, Pennsylvania, to the École MLF–Peugeot Citroën in Kaduna, Nigeria. In all, they school twenty thousand children, twenty percent of whom are not French.

The schools of the Alliance israélite universelle flourished during the 1920s and 1930s, but lost much of their clientele during the war as the Nazis systematically destroyed Europe's Jewish population. By the end of the war the organization had also lost its raison d'être; the dream of creating a Jewish middle class had to some extent been achieved. With massive emigration to Palestine and the Americas after 1946, the AIU shifted its focus and energy to the state of Israel, where it opened schools that would downplay French culture and reinforce Jewish religious education, which was not stressed in Israel's new secular school system. In 1949 the AIU opened *lycées* in Jerusalem, Haifa and Tel Aviv, where most AIU students are concentrated to this day.

From the inception of the Alliance israélite universelle in 1860 to the creation of the Délégation générale des relations culturelles in 1945, it had taken the French government nearly a century to wake up to the tremendous potential these private initiatives represented. Since then the government has fully co-opted the entire network, to the extent that today no country in the world is as actively engaged in cultural diplomacy as France.

In a world of instantaneous global communications, the idea that a country's reputation depends on its ability to represent itself through artistic and educational programs has become familiar. In his book *Soft Power*, which explores the phenomenon of cultural diplomacy, Joseph Nye argues that diplomats today achieve as much by capitalizing on the attractions of their country as they do by using coercion or offering financial aid. Most nations—especially the large ones—have systems of cultural diplomacy in place, which the Americans also call "public diplomacy." The United States practises cultural diplomacy through the American Cultural Exchange and Fulbright programs. Britain has 151 British Councils. Germany runs 128 Goethe Institutes. Spain has 58 Institutos Cervantes. These institutions are important tools of foreign policy. But Nye acknowledges that France is still exceptional in the field, spending close to a billion dollars a year to spread its civilization around the world—at least as much as the U.S. spends on "public diplomacy," and much more per capita than the U.S. spends on overseas development projects. The budget for France's cultural centres is considerably inferior to that of the British Council, but France compensates by pulling its Alliances françaises, Missions laïques, *collèges* and *lycées* into the effort.

France also has a type of individual outreach program. When Julie went to Lesotho she was accompanying Edy Kaufman, an Israeli professor of Argentine origin who is himself a product of France's cultural diplomacy. In the 1960s he was president of the National Union of Israeli Students when he was asked to apply for a scholarship to do his PhD in France. Edy's French was sketchy at the time, to put it mildly, but the French were interested in candidates they thought would go on to have a political career—this was one of the main criteria for selection. Edy ended up spending two years in Paris, wishing he could join in the May 1968 riots (he risked losing his student visa if he got caught protesting). In the end he turned out not to be an Israeli leader but rather a researcher and director of a peace institute at the Hebrew University in Jerusalem. Of course he was not the only intellectual the French government bet on—there were thousands like him, including Samir Kader, an Iraqi who did his university studies in France and Geneva and later became editor-in-chief of the Qatari TV broadcaster Aljazeera.

Language is still the linchpin of France's cultural diplomacy effort. In 1999 the French government created the organization Edufrance to bring more foreign students to France. There are 250,000 foreign students in France, compared to 600,000 in the U.S., a considerable number when you compare the size of the countries. France distributes twenty thousand scholarships to foreign students and supports 26 research centres and 176 archaeological missions abroad. In addition to direct education initiatives, France sponsors a host of cultural, media and artistic organizations that either use or promote French abroad. The Association française d'action artistique helps French artists exhibit and perform in foreign countries while welcoming foreign artists to France. The French embassy in the United States recently created French American Culture Services and Education Aid (FACSEA) to promote French films on the campuses of American universities. Since 1949 Unifrance has promoted French cinema in fifty-five countries—which is why foreign sales of French films are equivalent to sales at home, a performance matched by no other country except the U.S. France's international radio network RFI has forty-five million listeners. France distributes a million books and pays for six hundred translations per year, and the French government has been an important funder of cinema in the developing world since 1985. And that's not counting the efforts of the French ministries of education and research, which each run their own exchange programs. In 2004 France's 270 embassies, consulates and foreign representatives participated in the organization of ten thousand cultural events across the world—814 in Germany alone—including the Sounds French festival in New York, the May in France festival in Hong Kong, Printemps Français (French Spring) in Manila and

France Dances in Japan. And to top that off, France spends 6.4 billion euros on foreign aid, three times more per capita than the U.S. does. These initiatives don't even include the efforts of the Francophonie and other French-speaking countries such as Belgium, Switzerland and Canada.

The cultural diplomacy activities of Switzerland and Belgium are not as impressive as they could be, largely because language has always been a contentious issue in these countries. In Switzerland the federal government has a hands-off approach to the issue and leaves it up to the initiative of lesser jurisdictions, but Swiss cantons do not have enough resources. Nonetheless, cultural diplomacy is one of the functions of the Swiss arts council, Pro Helvetia, which runs five cultural centres (in Paris, New York, Rome, Milan and Venice), eight bureaus (in Eastern Europe) and three liaison offices (in Cairo, Capetown and Warsaw). As for the *communauté française de Belgique* (French community of Belgium), it has been wrestling with chronic unemployment and severe restructuring of its economy since the 1960s, which has left it poorer than the Flemish half of the country—a major reversal of fortune. The *communauté* is not doing as much as it wishes it were, but it does manage to achieve a fair bit through the Francophonie (discussed in chapter 16). Outside of France, Canada and Quebec are the most openly active, because both levels of government are actually competing for recognition and prestige abroad (Quebec has its own network of overseas bureaus and delegations). For instance, each supports its network of Canadian or Quebec studies; the International Association of Quebec Studies has an assortment of 2,600 experts in fifty fields of research in sixty-five countries.

France's cultural diplomacy is so effective that the French language continues to be attractive even where France isn't. We visited one of the seven AIU schools in Israel, the École

Edmond-Maurice-Edmond de Rothschild, located in a com-
fortable neighbourhood of Tel Aviv. Known simply as the
Alliance, it is one of the best-functioning schools of the AIU
network. Many students who arrive here as young adolescents
speak Hebrew and either English or French. They spend seven
hours a week learning French—which is mandatory—as their
second foreign language. When they graduate, they can carry
on a conversation in French.

Although it is a little-known fact, Israel is the home of a
large French-speaking minority; seven hundred thousand francophones live there (ten percent of the population), many
from North Africa, but also sixty thousand French immigrants
living in Jerusalem. France lost popularity in Israel when it
supported the Palestinians in the 1967 war, and its reputation
among Israelis has been declining since, particularly in recent
years, as tensions between the large Arab and Jewish populations in France have led to attacks on Jewish cemeteries, syna-
gogues and even businesses. Yet France is still the number-one
tourist destination for Israelis, and French tourists make up the
largest group of visitors to Israel—even larger than the number
of Americans. French is not a very popular second-language
choice in Israeli schools, partly because of tense relations with
France, and partly because most students choose Arabic as
their first foreign language after English.

So what compels Israeli students to attend a French *lycée*
(or their parents to send them)? French culture still has such a
good reputation that Israeli parents continue to want their
children to get a French education. As Colette Bitton, a
teacher at the École Edmond-Maurice-Edmond de Rothschild,
explained to us, the Alliance schools have a reputation for providing a "classic" education as opposed to the down-to-earth
approach of the Israeli school system. The school is public—
and free—but it happens to be located in a upper-middle-class

neighbourhood, so it is attended by better-than-average students. As Jacques Wahl, director of the AIU in Paris, told us, "Parents send their children to study at the AIU schools not *because* of French, but *in spite of* French."

Practically speaking, even in Israel, learning French has its advantages. Many students of the École Edmond-Maurice-Edmond de Rothschild find good summer work as tour guides and interpreters for French tourists. In 2002 the Tel Aviv Chamber of Commerce deliberately sought to hire students from French *lycées* for summer jobs in tourism. They were given special training to master the vocabulary of hotels and restaurants. Many of the *lycée* students also go on to do university studies in France.

The popularity of the 1,074 Alliances françaises spread across the planet defies conventional logic; in spite of the rapidly growing appeal of English, the Alliance française is still expanding. In some countries, such as Brazil, attendance is growing because French programs in schools are being cut (Alain Marquer, director of foreign development at the Alliance française in Paris, told us that some AF schools are catering more to children and teenagers, and overall attendance has been growing five percent a year since the mid-1990s). In India, demand has exploded in the last ten years because of the country's growing interest in foreign trade. "In New Delhi, we turn away two hundred to three hundred people *a day*," says Marquer. The organizations operate differently, not only from country to country, but also from one local organization to another, adapting to local conditions and cultural differences wherever they spring up. In Madagascar the Alliance française is under contract to train French teachers for the public school system. In Lesotho it offers courses in Sesotho, the national language, for the few foreign aid workers and diplomats who still make it there (the British Council closed its office in 1998 but the Alliance is sticking it out). Some Alliances, such as San Francisco's, even offer English courses for French nationals. The teaching of local languages in addition to French distinguishes the Alliance from other international language networks.

To this day Alliance française schools remain mostly a product of local initiatives, as they were intended to be from the start. The French government supports the organization with subsidies and by lending personnel–perks that are available to small countries that can't afford them, such as Lesotho, but also to high-profile showcase organizations such as the Alliance française of Miami. The Alliance school in Miami has three thousand students and enough resources to build a $1.5 million new facility, which it opened in the spring of 2005. The largest Alliance française in the United States is in New York City, with an impressive staff of sixty teachers, seven thousand students and a library of thirty-five thousand books. Some of the Alliances are run by directors who are on the payroll of the French foreign affairs ministry.

In the fall of 2004 the Délégation générale de l'Alliance française, the umbrella organization for American Alliances, in Washington D.C., organized a book tour for us to speak at twelve local Alliances in the eastern United States. It is almost impossible to generalize about the American Alliances, beyond the fact that many members are French teachers. Some local Alliances, for example Miami and Boston, are large, professional language schools and cultural organizations. On the other hand, the Providence, Rhode Island, school is housed in the basement of a church. Like the one in Lubbock, Texas, a number of U.S. Alliances offer no language classes, but are just French clubs where members meet regularly to practise their French or discuss French affairs. Or, as in Norfolk, Virginia, Alliances serve as networks for French teachers.

The American Alliances demonstrate how French cultural diplomacy has retained its power. Interestingly, though, this power is not necessarily tied to France anymore. Some Alliances, particularly the older, more established ones, have a strong bias towards "French from France." Members of these groups consider France to be the definitive and exclusive source of French culture; they usually had difficulty (or said they had difficulty) understanding Jean-Benoît's Quebec French. But many of the newer Alliances have adopted a broader franco-phone philosophy that is, in fact, more in line with the present orientation of the overall organization. The members of these Alliances know a lot about Quebec and Canada, are interested in the rest of the francophonie, and in terms of culture and dialects tend to place all francophone countries on equal footing. The Alliance in Lubbock, Texas, was particularly attuned to French-Canadian culture: It was run by an Algerian who could cite Quebec authors and singers by heart. He also knew a great deal about African literature.

So has French cultural diplomacy begun working to the advantage of other French-speaking countries? There is no doubt that France has been very successful in cultural diplomacy and in projecting "soft power" by promoting its language and culture across five continents for the last century and a half. The surprising result seems to be that the French language today is more popular than France itself.

Chapter 13 ~

A NEW PLAYING FIELD

AT THE SAME TIME the French were busy establishing a system of cultural diplomacy all over the planet, geopolitics was not working to the advantage of the French language. Between 1850 and 1945 France declined as a European power in contrast to Germany and Britain, which were steadily climbing. The world wars were devasting both to French morale and to France's international reputation, and logically should have spelled the end of French as an international language.

But exactly the opposite happened. At the beginning of the twenty-first century French has a unique position among international languages. French ranks only ninth in the number of speakers today, well below international languages such as English, Spanish, Arabic, Portuguese and Russian. But it has official status in more countries than any other language besides English. Two G8 countries are French-speaking; two francophone cities, Brussels and Geneva, are important centres of internationalism. Francophone countries have even gone on to create their own version of the British Commonwealth, the Francophonie, which has fifty-three member countries (see table 6 in Appendix).

What happened? In a nutshell, the world changed, and French adapted to it rather nimbly. The same events that brought about the collapse of France as a world power in the first half of the twentieth century ushered in a new world order where language became a source of shared identity that transcended geographic borders—and would soon become a tool that nations would use to further their influence. Partly because of the work France had already done in spreading its language across the globe, partly because of the creation of new French-speaking states after Napoleon's defeat a century earlier, and partly as a result of post-war decolonization, French was able to take on a surprisingly forceful role in this new internationalism.

The clouds were already gathering by 1850. Until the eighteenth century French had benefited from being the language of Europe's largest country and strongest continental power. The next biggest competitors, German and Italian, were spoken in hundreds of city states, principalities, duchies and bishoprics. This lack of unity favoured the language of the continent's biggest nation, France, especially in the courts and among the urban elites. Then, in the nineteenth century, the Germans and Italians created unified countries, and French lost two of its main "markets." French intellectual, industrial and technical supremacy was now challenged by equally good, often better, production in other languages. As British commerce, German science, American industry and Soviet ideology established their influence, the cultural lustre of French faded. France compensated by pursuing influence in other regions (namely Romania), but the glory days when French did not need to share the field were clearly over.

During the same period France's population growth slowed. By 1914 there were only forty million French people—a small increase from the twenty-eight million at the time of the Revolution. The British population had tripled to forty-three million by this time and the German to sixty-seven million. The populations of Russia and the United States, meanwhile, were close to 125 million and 100 million respectively. With stunning foresight, Alexis de Tocqueville had predicted in his book

Democracy in America–published in 1835–that America and Russia would one day share dominion over the world. By 1919 this was already happening.

The French, however, had developed ingenious strategies to compensate for geopolitical and demographic stagnation. Seizing their second chance after the failure of their first colonial push, they carved out a new empire in Africa and Asia that would be second only to Britain's. They began granting automatic citizenship to people born in France, a policy that made France the most welcoming country in Europe, and a country of immigration rather than emigration. France also sought to strengthen its position by building alliances, first with Britain, but also with Russia; Paris's majestic Pont Alexandre III (Alexander III bridge), dedicated to Czar Alexander, is testimony to this new approach.

But France went to war against Germany three times in three generations, in 1870, 1914–18 and 1939–45, and each conflict hit the French worse than the previous one. The human and material cost of the First World War damaged not only France's economy, but also Belgium's–most of the fighting took place precisely where Belgium's industrial base was located. On paper France was better off than Belgium; it had withstood the German assault and won. But it was a pyrrhic victory, more crippling to the victor than to the defeated. The country had lost 1.3 million soldiers in battle, and as many more were maimed or permanently injured. The civilian population had endured four years of privation, with two hundred thousand killed in warfare and another half million by the Spanish flu epidemic of 1918. German reparations didn't cover the cost of reconstruction and France got little assistance from its former allies; the Americans, who had sworn to protect the French against Germany, refused to ratify the Treaty of Versailles. So France had to rearm itself alone, against an enemy that was twice as big.

The war seriously undermined French capitalism, which had been a dynamic force up until then. Investment had been reduced in all economic sectors that were not necessary to the war effort, inflation soared and France lost much of its edge in the two high-tech industries of the time: aviation and cinema. France remained an important manufacturer of airplanes, but soon lost its status as leader to the Americans (a situation that might have come about whether or not there had been a war). The effect on cinema was even more devastating. French film production (except for propaganda) ground to a halt during the First World War, and after the war the Americans flooded the Continent with cheap silent productions that appealed to speakers of all languages.

The Russian Revolution of 1917 also took a heavy toll on France's financial sector. One of France's great diplomatic successes of the *belle époque* (1890 to 1914) had been to strike up an alliance with Russia in order to contain Germany. As part of the deal France had promised to invest heavily in the Russian economy. The French populace gambled millions of francs in high-return, high-risk loans to Russian industry, loans that the French government encouraged and the Czar guaranteed. Everything seemed rock-solid until the Bolsheviks destroyed the Czar's regime and refused to honour debts incurred to the bourgeois capitalists of France. Overnight, half a century of French savings vanished. France gained tens of thousands of White Russian (anti-Bolshevik) refugees out of the deal—the French Academy's present *secrétaire perpétuel* is a descendant of one such family—but it was little compensation for the destruction of so much French capital. (This is the main reason why, to this day, the French are touchy about investing in the stock market.)

France and Belgium had barely recovered from the First World War when the same scenario repeated itself in 1939. And this time the consequences for French were even worse. Both countries were temporarily wiped off the international political scene, and their empires began to fall apart. As France tried to deal with the aftermath of German occupation, the legacy of Nazi collaboration, and its own active participation in the Holocaust, its reputation plummeted. Tales of the French Resistance salvaged some of France's national pride, but the country's reputation would suffer again during the messy post-war decolonization of Vietnam and Algeria.

In the middle of all this French lost its status as Europe's only diplomatic language. After the First World War, France's Georges Clemenceau, Britain's David Lloyd George and the United States' Woodrow Wilson met in Paris in 1919 to discuss the conditions they would impose on Germany and how they could create a peace that would last. Hundreds of representatives from other countries and would-be nations spent six months hammering out a peace settlement. The resulting Treaty of Versailles divided up the possessions of the three defeated empires (Germany, Austria-Hungary and the Ottoman Empire) between France, Britain and Belgium. Syria and Lebanon went to France and Burundi and Rwanda went to Belgium. It was the last treaty in which nations bartered entire populations.

The treaty was a radical break from the past; at the request of Prime Minister Lloyd George and President Wilson, it was negotiated and written in both French and English. Wilson could not speak French and Lloyd George was a rare case of a British prime minister who hardly could either. Georges Clemenceau, who had been a diplomat in Britain and was married to an American, was the only one who could accommodate the others, so he agreed. For the first time since the Treaty of Rastatt in 1714, French was not the exclusive language of high diplomacy in Europe. The issue sparked outrage in

France, but there was no turning back. English had begun its steady ascent as the new international language of diplomacy.

French also lost out in the creation of a new international body. The Treaty of Versailles created the League of Nations, based in Geneva, which would serve as the prototype of the United Nations and the foundation of a new world order based on international institutions. In this new body French had to share official status with English. But a mere twenty-six years later, when the international community replaced the failed League of Nations with the United Nations, French barely made it as one of the five official languages along with English, Chinese, Russian and Spanish—and that was thanks to France's permanent seat on the Security Council. Only English had official status as the working language of the Secretariat General. French was voted a working language in 1946, but some U.N.-related organizations created prior to this, such as UNESCO and FAO, would be known only by their English acronyms.

Perspectives were bleak, yet the French language would prove to have uncommon fortitude in adapting to the new international context that was taking shape. French did not go down the road of Russian, which became an important international language almost overnight as a result of the Communist revolution of 1917 and the U.S.S.R.'s superpower status after 1945. The Russian language, which was taught in all Western and Third World universities during this period, was sent back to its original turf when the Berlin Wall collapsed in 1989. In Paris, the Algerian who ran our photocopy shop was a former professor of Russian—eighty percent of them had had to recycle themselves practically overnight. Unlike Russian, French was not the language of an ideology.

But more important, the same forces that brought the collapse of France as a world power in the first half of the twentieth century–European nationalism, imperial destruction, decolonization–actually helped French rebound in the second half of the century.

The seeds of this rebound had been planted a century earlier, at the Congress of Vienna in 1815. It was here that European countries recognized for the first time that the constant use of brute force to solve quarrels was unproductive and cost more than it achieved. They attempted to create informal mechanisms to settle disputes and avoid war by establishing a level playing field between nations. The founding principle of the new game was that might was not right. Throughout the nineteenth century imperial powers took concrete steps to achieve this goal, including the creation of the International Committee of the Red Cross in 1863, followed by a series of new organizations based in Geneva (the International Telegraphic Union of 1865, the Universal Postal Union of 1874, the International Bureau of Weights and Measures in 1875). All of these bodies were designed to eliminate topics of dissent between states and settle problems before they led to war. Many operated in French; in fact, French is still the working language of the Universal Postal Union. In the case of the International Olympic Committee, founded in 1896, when discrepancies arise between French and English versions of written materials, the French version prevails even today.

At the beginning of the twentieth century, European powers went a step further and created the first arbitration court (though it failed to prevent the First World War). The 1919 League of Nations was the first real attempt to create a permanent multilateral institution, although it was flawed and did not prevent the outbreak of a second world war. One of its biggest limitations was that the Americans, whose idea it had been in the first place, refused to join. The creation of the United Nations and its various agencies and institutions in

1945 reached a new height in this type of international law: It gave each member country an equal vote no matter how great its wealth or power. In this new world order no country was too small to have a voice. Even failed states such as Haiti sat as equals next to developed countries—though other institutions, such as the powerful executive body, the U.N. Security Council, still gave special privileges to the mighty. French would benefit more than any other language except English from this new context.

The United Nations was created through discussions between the U.S. and Great Britain, in conjunction with the Soviet Union and China, all of whom became members of the Security Council. France was still occupied at the time of the original discussions, between 1942 and 1944, so it was not considered for membership. It was included on the Security Council in 1945 thanks to lobbying by Britain (Churchill was feeling rather small, all alone between the U.S., the U.S.S.R. and China). At the official creation of the U.N. in 1945, the fifty member countries chose to have five official languages— English, French, Russian, Spanish and Chinese—but English was the only working language of the Secretariat General. In practice this meant that members had to be able to express themselves in one of the five official languages, but all had to understand English.

Then, in January 1946, French was voted unanimously as the second working language of the Secretariat General. By then many countries felt that having English as the only working language gave the United States too much of an edge. As Joseph Nye puts it in *Soft Power*, it was already clear that institutions such as the International Monetary Fund and the United Nations reflected the liberal and democratic values of the American system. So French, representing the same values but from a different tradition, provided a counterweight. The fact that it received unanimous endorsement a mere six months after barely making it as an official language showed that French still carried a lot of weight. There were also practical reasons for adopting French, according to Pierre Gerbet, author of *Le rêve d'un ordre mondial, de la SDN à l'ONU* (*The Dream of a World Order, from the LN* [League of Nations] *to the UN*. He explains that the early U.N. suffered from an "Anglo-Saxon" spirit that favoured vagueness and flexibility as means to reach unanimity. Working in French and English, diplomats had to clarify their ideas, because the spirit of French favours precise definitions.

A case in point is the U.N.'s famous article 242 of November 1967, voted in the wake of the Six Day War between Israel and Egypt, Syria and Jordan. Because of peculiarities of grammar, the French and English versions do not say the same thing. As a result of the ambiguity of English grammar, the English version is open to interpretation. It calls for the "withdrawal of Israeli armed forces *from territories occupied* in the recent conflict." This could mean any or all occupied territories. The French version is more specific and demands "*le retrait (. . .) des territoires occupés*"—meaning all.

French went on to become a working language of most U.N. entities, agencies, institutions and operations, from the Human Rights Commission to UNESCO and the International Labour bureau. French is also a working language of independent agencies such as the OECD, INTERPOL and Intelsat, as well as hundreds of non-governmental organizations such as the International Red Cross, the Union of International Organization and Doctors without Borders. While there is no definitive list of organizations that use French as an official language, there is no doubt that the use of French at the U.N. is declining (more on this in chapter 16). Still, U.N. statistics on the number of documents produced in French and the number of people learning French at the U.N. show that French is still a strong second language after English, and still in a class of its own with respect to other U.N. official languages. According to professor Richard Shyrock, of Virginia Polytechnic Institute and State University, a recent listing of international jobs distributed by the U.S. State Department stated that 204 required or preferred French, 71 a U.N. language (one being French), 53 Spanish, 19 Arabic and so on.

The reason French rebounded so strongly on the world stage was that language played a paramount role in the new world order. Language is so strongly associated with our modern idea of nations that we forget that there was a time before the French Revolution when it was hardly a consideration in either domestic or foreign affairs. The treaties of 1713 and 1759, which granted the colonies of Acadia and New France to Britain, never mentioned language. In the seventeenth century the French-speaking people of Jura and Franche-Comté, near Switzerland, were annexed by France against their will. They wanted out of France, even though they spoke a closely related Romance language. At the same time, the Germanic-speaking Alsatians wanted *in*. Even when Napoleon was at the height of his imperial expansion in Europe, and France had formally annexed parts of Italy, Germany and the Netherlands, language was rarely an issue—France itself was barely French-speaking at the time.

In 1707 the English officially united Scotland and England under the umbrella name of Great Britain in an attempt to merge the two peoples into a common British identity—though *British* means *English* more than anything else. At the time of Revolution-and-Empire, the French successfully imposed the idea that France and the French language were one. And although it took them another century to actually disseminate French throughout the population, few French citizens would have challenged the idea that France was French, even by 1815. In fact, language really only came to be associated with nations in the nineteenth century, when it became a basis for unifying the German-speaking and Italian-speaking principalities, city states, bishoprics and duchies. That's why in 1835 Tocqueville wrote in *Democracy in America*, "Language is perhaps the strongest and most enduring link which unites men."

What was true of nations in the nineteenth century would be true on the international stage of the twentieth century: Language became an organizing principle of a new form of internationalism. The German chancellor Otto von Bismarck is famous for having said that the great event of the nineteenth century was that the United States spoke English. He foresaw that the link created by a common language would, in the long run, determine international affairs. The idea was also becoming clear to French speakers, as their efforts in cultural diplomacy demonstrated.

Language came to belong neither to the classical sphere of geopolitics (where armies, food, energy, resources, supplies and logistics account for influence) nor to the economic sphere (where industry, capital flow, workforce and patents are paramount). Rather, like religion and ideology, it belongs to what we call a geocultural sphere. This sphere is seldom talked about, but it is not new. The Soviet empire, though a geopolitical behemoth, was held up by the geocultural sphere—ideology— and brought down partly thanks to religion, the result of the Papacy's destabilization efforts among Polish Catholics, who eventually defied the Soviets.

Like religion and ideology, language is a source of identity that transcends national borders, has its own symbols and creates affinities between citizens of different countries. Of course, like religion and ideology, language can contribute to (or detract from) a country's influence in traditional spheres such as diplomacy. Japan is the world's second economic power, yet its language (like its religion) has little influence, making Japan's overall influence in the world weaker. While oil gives Saudi Arabia some geopolitical clout, religion and language give it as much influence (the country remains an economic dwarf). An extreme example is the Vatican, which has geocultural clout but nothing else. Consider Belgium: Most of its influence comes from the fact that two of its native tongues, Dutch and French, are international languages, and the latter draws on a large international club. The cases of Canada and Quebec are also interesting. As a province, Quebec has more geocultural clout than it has geopolitical or economic influence on the world stage, because it draws on the international influence of French. And Canada's influence owes a lot to the fact that it is part of two important geocultural spheres: English and French.

It is the Anglo-American experience that best illustrates how language became a factor in creating and solidifying transnational identities. Starting in the late eighteenth century, the British and the Americans led the way in developing their geocultural sphere. Much in the way the French developed cultural diplomacy to compensate for their geopolitical weaknesses in the nineteenth century, the British, after their defeat in the American Revolution, quite spontaneously sought what came to be called a "special relationship" with the United States.

Right from the 1780s, cultural affinity justified numerous trade agreements, accords and treaties between Britain and the United States. The United States' support of Britain against Nazi Germany (when the U.S. was still officially neutral) was justified on that basis. Churchill was especially sensitive to linguistic affinities, an idea he developed in his 1956–58 volumes

A History of the English-Speaking Peoples. With the same logic, during the interwar period Britain sought to unite its former colonies Canada, Australia, New Zealand and South Africa as a Commonwealth of Nations. The British and the Americans quickly saw there was a lot to gain by linking language, culture and industrial interests in the right way. In *Soft Power*, Joseph Nye makes a good case that the penetration of American films helped sell not only more baseball caps and cars, but also values and ideas about the American way of life—all of which produced a remarkable reservoir of goodwill towards the U.S. In essence, the Anglo-Americans had the same goal as France did in pushing cultural diplomacy. But they had two advantages over the French: The combined populations of the U.S. and the U.K. were much bigger than those of France and Belgium. And compared to France and Belgium, Britain and the United States had sustained relatively little damage during the Second World War. The Anglo-Americans also got reinforcement from four other English-speaking nations: Australia, New Zealand, South Africa and Canada—the last of which did not care much about French until the 1960s. It would not take long for the Anglo-Americans to push their edge a little further and spread the idea that the English language was not merely useful, but necessary.

English is not the subject of this book. However, it is impossible to understand the attitudes and actions of francophones in international institutions and forums today—which are both offensive and defensive, as we explain in coming chapters—without understanding some of the reasons English got where it is. Since the Second World War, American and British diplomats, businesses, universities and associations of all kinds have led a very systematic and competent, if not always concerted, lobby to promote English across the planet. While it would be an exaggeration to speak of a huge coordinated English conspiracy, it would be false to pretend that the present ascendancy of English happened naturally. There was nothing natural about it. Americans, and to a lesser extent the British, used the English language as a tool of power through a number of explicit or tacit policies on the part of government, but also through the official and unofficial actions of decision-makers in corporations and different associations.

The role of diplomats was paramount from the beginning of this period. In 1946 they imposed the removal of quotas on American cinema as one of the conditions for American aid to France. As far as the Americans were concerned, culture and language had clearly become strategic on the world stage. Shortly after the 1945 creation of the International Civil Aviation Organization, which more than forty countries joined, the dominant Americans succeeded in making English the universal language of all airports. Meanwhile there was a new development at the U.N. While French and English were the organization's official working languages, jobs for senior and middle management began to be posted in English only, and more and more of them required fluency in English, with no mention of French. And any criticism of this practice was dismissed as irrelevant or as an annoyance.

Scientists also played a part in spreading the influence of English, and pretty much on their own. In their book *Alerte francophone,* former French diplomats Alfred Gilder and Albert Salon point out that the Anglo-American Conference of 1961 produced a confidential report to the British Council that recommended the use of only one language (English) in the field of scientific communication. Starting in 1967, most American universities suppressed the mandatory foreign language tests for PhD candidates. During the same decade, American, British and Dutch scientific publications began refusing papers that had been published in any other language than English. They also developed systems for measuring scientists' influence, such as the *Science Citation Index*. Such reference systems, which are regarded as objective, count the number of times scientists are quoted by other scientists—in English-language publications. All these self-reinforcing mechanisms managed to produce a belief that no science is being done in any other language, even among people who speak other languages. And that belief is stronger than ever today.

Business people also played their role in pushing English. The development of British and American business is one of the most remarkable phenomena of the last two centuries. Ideology, pragmatism, naval domination and dynamism (and luck) have helped create a universal impression that English is the exclusive language of business. Much like the U.S. Army, which refuses to negotiate in any other language than English no matter where it is, Anglo-American business people have become notorious for expecting meetings to happen in English no matter where they are. At the turn of the twenty-first century this has taken a new angle, as international law firms have begun denigrating French Civil Code–based legal systems (nearly half the countries of the world use the Civil Code rather than English-based common law) by claiming that they are ineffectual for business. The real problem is that they refer to legal practice, texts and jurisprudence in French, or any language other than English.

We are not blaming the British or the Americans for understanding that they can promote their interests through the geocultural sphere, and we are by no means arguing that there is a grand conspiracy going on among Anglo-American interests. But it is important to underline that there was nothing inevitable or natural about the spread of English. A multiplicity of agents have been working for decades to further English with the goal of increasing Anglo-American power and spreading their influence. The result? Anglophones are convinced, and have convinced others, that English is the world's only language of diplomacy, science and business, when in fact it is the language of some institutions, of scientific journals and of business papers. The confusion, self-serving as it is, has created an illusion that other languages are mere obstacles that have to be overcome in the name of making international affairs function smoothly.

Chapters 16, 18 and 19 discuss what francophones have done and are doing to counteract this tendency, sometimes successfully, sometimes not. But we wish to be clear on one point: Injured national pride is not what motivates French, Belgian, Canadian, Algerian and Senegalese diplomats to argue for the use of French in international forums. It is an issue of power, plain and simple. Everyone knows that when it comes to language, not all speakers are equal: Those speaking their mother tongue almost always have an edge over foreigners who learned the language at school. In any negotiations, discussions or arguments, whether between diplomats, business people or scientists, the choice of language amounts to deciding who will have to fight uphill and who will fight downhill. Diplomats constantly try to keep the playing field slanted their way when they have the upper hand, or to level it when they are at a disadvantage. This was why French became an official language of the League of Nations in 1919, why it was reintroduced as a working language of the U.N. in 1946 and why francophones are still fighting hard to maintain French in diplomatic circles.

On the playing field of geocultural influence, francophones, like anglophones, enjoyed the advantage of being early starters and setting many of the first rules of the game. One reason French remains an important international language is that, like Britain, France understood quite early how culture and language can be a source of power. In other words, while the Americans and the British were lobbying to impose their language on the new playing field, francophones were not exactly sitting on their hands.

In a speech from the 1960s, France's minister of culture André Malraux spoke of language as "*une nouvelle république de l'esprit*" ("a new republic of the mind"). A decade earlier, Albert Camus had written, "*Ma patrie, c'est la langue française*" ("My country is the French language"). Linguistic patriotism is not unique to francophones, but it is one reason the French, and by extension all francophones, have functioned well in this new world order, playing the geocultural game skilfully, even shrewdly.

By 1945 France had already built a strong framework of cultural diplomacy. That was immediately put to work when language became a major factor in the battle for geocultural influence. So France was particularly well placed to exploit the international status its language had gained through international institutions. Other factors gave French a geocultural influence disproportionate to its actual number of speakers, chiefly France's dynamism in industry, science and cultural creation of all sorts.

During the period between 1945 and 1975, known in France as *les Trente Glorieuses* (the thirty glorious years), the French economy boomed and France transformed itself from a predominantly agrarian society to a post-industrial consumer society (some joke that France skipped the twentieth century and went directly from the nineteenth to the twenty-first). France modernized its telecommunications sector and created Minitel, the first national information network, which was based on teletext. The terms *fournisseur de service* (service provider) and *autoroute de l'information* (information highway) went on, via English and the Internet, to become part of the standard vocabulary of information technology, transposed into almost any language. At the same time, France became the world's fourth nuclear power and developed successful programs for high-speed trains, civil nuclear energy and space launchers. It is now the world's fourth-biggest car producer and the number-three arms dealer. Fibre optics, HDTV and smart cards are all French inventions. Through all of this, France maintained a very productive agricultural sector that made it a giant in agribusiness. It also developed a gigantic modern tourism industry, to serve first its own nationals, then foreigners.

Understanding the importance of international communication and media, Charles de Gaulle nationalized the world's oldest wire service, Havas, to create Agence France-Presse, which is still the world's third-biggest news agency, after Reuters and Associated Press. Its 117 offices produce three million words a day in six languages (French, English, German, Spanish, Arabic and Portuguese). Although French has nowhere near the influence in the field that English does, it clearly has a niche of its own. A newspaper such as *Le Monde* is a recognizable franchise everywhere, and TV5, the international francophone television network, enjoys an audience that makes it the world's number-three network after CNN and MTV. Other French media have also built international franchises—such as *Paris Match* and, more famously, *Elle,* now produced in thirty-seven foreign editions. In the Big Ten global advertising companies, French-language Publicis ranks fifth. And in the wider field of communication (including public relations), Publicis and Havas hold fourth and sixth place.

Even after the nineteenth century, Paris continued to enjoy high status in its artistic and cultural output. Although it no longer sets the standard in literature and visual arts, with its seventy thousand painters, France has lost none of its critical mass in the field. Antoine de Saint-Exupéry's *Little Prince*, which sold 75 million copies, is the novel that was translated in the most languages, over 160. Artists such as Jean Cocteau,

musicians Edith Piaf and Erik Satie and writers such as Jean-
Paul Sartre and Simone de Beauvoir managed to forge an
almost mythical association between the French language and
cutting-edge artistic innovation. The French intellectual class
continued to be at the forefront of scholarly experimentation,
and remained influential in spite of a long flirtation with
Stalinism. The French produced a new literary genre, the *nouveau roman* (new novel), which sought to reinvent the mode of
narration. Aside from a few fans in Italy, it never seduced anyone outside France, but it did contribute to the mystique of
French in intellectual circles throughout the world.

Throughout the period, France also remained an important
force in cinema. Because the industry was never touched by a
McCarthy-style anti-communist witch hunt, and because it
resisted the onslaught of U.S. blockbusters, French films and
France's star system have continued to generate international
appeal. Paris intellectuals such as Foucault, Derrida and Ricoeur
are the darlings of American liberal arts colleges. France has
become one of the main centres of world-beat music, and
continues to harbour many immigrants and intellectuals who
contribute to its artistic production. To this day a great number of non-English novels first come to the attention of the
English market after they have been translated into French.

Decolonization also worked to the advantage of French,
though it could have worked against it, as in the case of Dutch.
In 1945 the Netherlands had one huge colony, Indonesia. The
Dutch fought an extremely violent decolonization war, no less
brutal than the ones France fought in Indochina and Algeria.
After independence the Indonesian elite abandoned Dutch, and
the Dutch language lost a country that would become the
world's fourth most populated. This is why, even today, Dutch
is regarded as a "small" language, even if it is in reality "mid-
size" (it is spoken by 21 million people in the Netherlands,

Belgium and Suriname, which places Dutch well within the top one hundred of the world's six thousand languages, although clearly in a different league from English and French). In comparison, most of France's former colonies chose French as an official language or kept French as the language of administration after independence. So, in spite of the fact that the French were never as successful as the British and Americans in expanding their language through the geocultural sphere, the number of countries that had French as an official language, a national language or a language of administration had multiplied sixfold by the 1970s to reach thirty. And this excludes Algeria, where the proportion of fluent speakers is well above fifty percent even though French has no official status there at all. This phenomenon was significant in the new international system that created institutions that afforded every country a vote, no matter how small they were. (For more details, refer to the tables in the Appendix.)

The fact is, despite the way French benefited from the new world order, numbers still count for something. Had French been confined to its original domain, it might have gone the way of German or Dutch. No matter how one looks at it, the reason French has remained an important international language is that more people than ever have added their voice to the concert of French. What is really surprising is that French grew stronger in nine out of ten former colonies of France and in all the former colonies of Belgium after their independence than it had been before. It is one of the enigmas of decolonization that still puzzles people to this day.

Chapter 14 ~

CHOOSING FRENCH

WE MET IBRAHIMA KOUYATÉ because the Lonely Planet guidebook to Senegal recommended him as the best nature guide in Niokola-Koba National Park, the country's famous wildlife reserve. While he was indeed an excellent guide, his story also gave us a first-hand illustration of the power of French in poor African countries. Ibrahima's parents' land was expropriated in 1954 when the French turned the area into a national park. Ibrahima, the youngest of five brothers, grew up in Dar es Salam, the village located at the entrance of the park. As a child he spent hours exploring the park, and from this early passion for wildlife he developed an almost encyclopedic knowledge of the park's flora and fauna. So his decision to become a park guide came naturally.

But as we learned during the three days we spent with him, passion wouldn't have been enough to secure Ibrahima's future in his chosen profession. To become a certified park guide he had to pass a written exam in French. The problem was that Ibrahima, who grew up speaking Mandingo, went to school for only three years. His mother died giving birth to him; his father, who suffered from leprosy, pulled him out of school early and sent him to work as a shepherd. Ibrahima was orphaned at age twelve, so he had practically no chance to learn French.

We couldn't believe the story when we heard him tell it—in excellent French. He evidently wrote well enough in French to send a thank-you note to Lonely Planet for praising him

295

in their guide. "I was inclined towards French," he told us, a rather vague explanation for his remarkable success in mastering the language. Later, Ibrahima elaborated: After his father's death he had sought out every opportunity he could to expand his French vocabulary and learn to read and write, even visiting the library in the next village. Over the years he also used his continual exposure to Europeans visiting the park to polish his French.

Before we left the park, Ibrahima asked us if we could send him back books about African wildlife from Canada. We offered to include a French–English dictionary in the package, thinking that such an ambitious fellow would see learning English as the logical next step in his career development (Lonely Planet recommended Ibrahima even though he didn't speak English). Ibrahima told us he would like that very much, but we could see he was being polite. For most Senegalese, particularly those who, like him, live in the countryside, the advantages of speaking English are still pretty remote. French remains Senegal's language of social promotion, and just learning it opens a world of possibilities. Before learning English, Ibrahima wanted to get his driver's licence so he could pick up tourists in Dakar and tour them through the park without hiring a driver. That alone would multiply his business and profits by ten.

Like the majority of Senegalese, Ibrahima had not even been born at the time of independence from France in 1960. Yet, like him, millions of young Africans born after independence want to learn French. That's because, in most former French and Belgian colonies, French progressed more after decolonization than it had during the colonial period. The only exceptions were Syria and Indochina.

The French and Belgian empires, like the British, began to disintegrate during the Second World War. The French protectorates of Lebanon and Syria became formally independent in 1941. Tunisia and Morocco followed in 1943. Wars of independence started in Indochina in 1945, and in Algeria in 1954. In the Belgian Congo, as well as Rwanda and Burundi, the cracks in the empire didn't start to show until the 1950s, but by 1960 most of France's colonies in sub-Saharan Africa, and all of Belgium's, had become independent.

Most former French or Belgian colonies in sub-Saharan Africa kept French as one of their official languages. Countries such as Ivory Coast, Senegal and the Democratic Republic of Congo (former Zaire) made French an official language along with some of their national languages. Some countries made French their only official language. In others, such as Madagascar and all the countries in North Africa, French remained the de facto language of administration and education in spite of official policies to eliminate it.

In the spring of 2004 we met Abdou Diouf—now secretary-general of the Francophonie, and president of Senegal from 1981 to 2000—at his office in Paris. At the time of Senegal's independence he was a young politician and protégé of the country's first president, Léopold Sédar Senghor. Diouf had watched Senegal's independence unfold from a front-row seat, so we thought he was in a good position to explain why Senegal kept the French language even though they kicked out the French. His answer was simpler than we expected: "French was forced on us during colonialism, but then we chose it." Newly independent countries had a number of reasons for holding on to French, depending on their situation. In most African countries, ethnic groups speak a very wide array of languages (as many as 250 in Cameroon). Today 750 African languages are spoken in the thirty French-speaking countries in Africa. At the time of independence French was a neutral language that didn't privilege one ethnic group over another.

The decision to keep French was also the product of a class struggle. The former *évolués,* who spoke the best French, took the reigns of power after independence, especially in Africa. Keeping French as an administrative language helped them maintain their grip on domestic affairs. The exceptions were in North Africa and Madagascar, where the political groups who came to power after independence quickly moved to erase French, mainly through campaigns to Arabicize (in the Maghreb region of North Africa) or "Malgachize," in the case of Madagascar. Even here, though, French-speaking elites resisted so staunchly that the presence of French remained strong.

French also remained the language of education in almost all the newly independent countries, mostly because putting a new education system in place was a costly endeavour that few could afford. At any rate, in Africa most native languages lacked words to describe modern realities, and many had neither a full dictionary nor a complete grammar system. Berber, one of the few native groups of North Africa that survived the onslaught of Islam and Arabicization that started in the seventh century CE, speak their language, Tamazight, in half a dozen dialectal varieties across the region, few of which are written. Even in Algeria, where Tamazight has gained official status, few agree on a standard. So teaching in French (or Arabic) was more convenient, and schooling in French was also a guarantee of quality. Zaire, a former Belgian colony, rejected Flemish and switched its new education system to French standards. According to French lexicologist Jacqueline Picoche, Zaire's President Mobutu (in power 1965–97) went as far as fining civil servants who used the Belgian terms *septante* and *nonante* for *seventy* and *ninety* instead of the French *soixante-dix* and *quatre-vingt-dix.*

Finally, French gave newly independent countries access to science, technology and industry, and not only from France. In countries such as Gabon, Rwanda, Algeria and Senegal,

French quickly made it possible to reach beyond the former colonial power and develop commercial and intellectual relations with a francophone universe that included Quebeckers, Acadians and the Swiss.

France and Belgium, of course, made deliberate efforts to ensure that the newly independent Nations would keep French. With decolonization on the horizon, both countries made last-ditch attempts to boost their influence in their colonies by investing heavily in infrastructure and industry. When de Gaulle took power in France in 1958 he invested billions of francs to build infrastructure for oil production, ports and other industries in Algeria, including a nuclear testing site in the south, even though the country was in the middle of a violent war of independence. De Gaulle had seen the writing on the wall for some time, but he believed that even if French investments failed to convince the colonies to remain French, investment would help maintain links after independence. This effort buttressed the presence of French and Belgian industry, technology and capital in Africa at a critical juncture. After independence, when France no longer had colonial representatives in its former colonies, it sent forty-five thousand *coopérants* (equivalent to the Peace Corps) as teachers, professors, military advisors and administrators, all of whom were on the payroll of French ministries or multinational corporations.

Before decolonization the French had also attempted to unite their colonies in a short-lived federation called the Union française, which included France. The Union, created in 1946, was motivated partly by the desire to hang on to France's colonies and partly out of recognition that its colonies had allowed France to remain a world power. It was a federative system in which former colonial elites became French citizens. The plan was never fully put into practice and anyway came too late to hold the empire together. But in 1946 colonies started sending representatives to the French parliament. Soon-to-be-famous writers Aimé Césaire and Léopold Sédar Senghor became members of France's National Assembly for Martinique and Senegal respectively. In 1956–59 Félix Houphouët-Boigny became the first African to hold cabinet positions in successive French governments; he went on to become the first president of Ivory Coast in 1960.

But the Union française simply could not withstand the rising independence movement in Africa. In 1958 de Gaulle offered the African colonies the choice of remaining part of France or becoming independent. Initially all the colonies except Guinea chose full association with France. But independence fever was rising sharply. By the end of 1960 all of them (except Algeria) had chosen independence. In sub-Saharan Africa the former French colonies almost created their own French-African federation, but this project also fell victim to rising nationalism. Some parts of the former empire—French Guiana, Guadeloupe and Martinique in the Caribbean, and Réunion in the Indian Ocean—had opted to remain part of France. They became either overseas territories or overseas Départments, fully integrated into France in the same way that Alaska and Hawaii are part of the U.S. In the Pacific, Polynesia and New Caledonia have retained some theoretical autonomy, but their status more resembles membership in a French federation.

France and Belgium also used education to try to hold their empires together. Starting after the Second World War, they invested billions of francs to put in place universal public education systems, and even built universities in their colonies—the University of Dakar was opened in 1950. Belgian efforts were never as coherent as those of the French, partly because Belgium had to deal with its own ongoing quarrel between francophones and Flemish speakers. Still, Belgian missionaries continued to be so effective at teaching French that former Belgian colonies had the reputation of being more francophone than the French colonies. The world's second-largest francophone city is not Montreal, Dakar or Algiers, as most people would assume, but Kinshasa, capital of the former Zaire.

The figure of Léopold Sédar Senghor (1906–2001), president of Senegal from 1960 to 1981, stands tall in the history of French. Senghor was literally a product of two worlds. He worked all his life to tie Africa's destiny to the French language, and vice versa. Senghor was a Serere, a member of an ethnic group that makes up fifteen percent of Senegal's population. His father, a Christian who had retained the animist custom of polygamy (Léopold had forty brothers and sisters), placed his son in a missionary school at age seven to learn Wolof and French. A brilliant student, Senghor completed secondary school in Dakar and was admitted to the Sorbonne in Paris, where he arrived in the 1920s. His classmates there included future French president Georges Pompidou (ruled 1969–74).

In Paris Senghor befriended fellow poets from African colonies—most notably the Martinique poet Aimé Césaire (born 1913). He went on to play a key role in the cultural renaissance of sub-Saharan Africa that started in Paris in the 1920s. The climate of intellectual and (relative) racial freedom in Paris in the first quarter of the twentieth century had drawn many black American authors of the Harlem Renaissance to Paris. They in turn inspired African intellectuals and future African leaders and intellectuals such as Senghor and Césaire. The encounter between American and African blacks sparked a transformation of African language, poetry and politics. As Amadou Ly, a literature professor at the Sheikh Anta Diop University in Dakar, explained to us, "Prior to that, the literature produced in Africa was a translation of colonial ideology."

During the 1920s and '30s, Senghor and Césaire formulated the concept of *négritude,* an affirmation of black cultural expression that celebrated African culture for its own sake. *Négritude* later became the ideological basis of Senghor's effort to federate French sub-Saharan Africa. Yet, while he promoted *négritude,* Senghor never renounced his French heritage. In fact, he remained convinced all his life that the future of Senegal lay in cultural *métissage* (literally, cross-breeding) with France. In Senghor's mind there was no rejecting the influence of French culture in Africa, even after independence. Throughout his life he famously refused to *vitupérer contre* (inveigh against) the former colonial power, and much of the beautiful poetry he wrote was inspired by the notion of *métissage.* Along with other African leaders, Senghor resurrected the concept of *francophonie* (the term had been coined in the nineteenth century) and used it to lobby for the creation of a union of French-speaking countries, what would become the Francophonie. Forty years later, Senghor's concept of *métissage* continues to inspire very active cultural, political and economic exchange within the French-speaking world (which we discuss in chapters 16 and 19).

The Senegalese have the reputation of speaking the "purest" French in Africa. The claim is impossible to substantiate, and the Gabonese and Beninese say the same thing about their French. But one thing is certain: During his life, Senghor worked tirelessly to boost the status and quality of French in Senegal. When he took power in 1960 he knew he couldn't make Wolof the official language, as the speakers of Pulaar, Serere, Dioula, Mandingo and Soninke would have objected. Instead, he gave all six the status of "national languages" and made French Senegal's official language. French was an obvious choice as a neutral language, all the more so since people such as Senghor, Diouf and the former *évolués* who were now running Senegal spoke and wrote it beautifully.

Culture and cultural development were outstanding themes while Senghor was leading his country through its first two decades after independence. Throughout the period he pursued his career as a writer and poet, and remained a fervent admirer of and contributor to French culture and, especially, the French language. His poetry won him a seat in the French Academy in 1983. A former teacher, Senghor became legendary for inviting journalists to the presidential palace to correct their written mistakes in French, and even to give them grammar lessons. He was famous for scolding Senegalese journalists with the phrase "*Ar-ti-cu-lez s'il-vous-plaît*" ("Please ar-ti-cu-late").

France today retains an exceedingly strong economic hold on Senegal: Many schoolteachers, journalists and business leaders we met there remarked bitterly that the French still "own" Senegal. There is definitely resentment towards the French, but at the same time the Senegalese elite and urban middle class remain strongly attached to the French language, complaining just as bitterly about the fact that in recent years France has made it hard for them to visit and exchange with French colleagues in their fields. Although Senegal has suffered from abortive education reforms and a chronic lack of qualified teachers, in the last four decades French has still been spreading. More and more people outside of the cities are hearing French and picking up the basics of the language, thanks to the spread of radio. About ten percent of Senegalese master French, but another twenty percent are said to have a functional understanding of it; these proportions are higher in the cities and lower in the countryside. We didn't meet many taxi drivers in Dakar who couldn't communicate to some degree in French, though of course the language of everyday affairs in Senegal is Wolof (although only forty-three percent of the population are Wolof, more than eighty percent of the population use the language in daily exchanges).

In linguistic terms, Ivory Coast is a striking contrast to Senegal. Whereas thirty percent of Senegalese are considered to have a decent command of French, the proportion in Ivory Coast is seventy percent. The country has a significantly higher population than Senegal (sixteen million compared to ten million), but the main difference is that, unlike Senegal, Ivory Coast was never dominated by one African language, like Wolof. Ivory Coast has twenty major ethnic groups who speak different languages, including Dioula, the common language of trade in West Africa. Unlike Senghor, Ivory Coast's first president, Félix Houphouët-Boigny, was never a proponent of *négritude*. He was interested in making economic progress and maintained strong connections with France to that end. In the first fifteen years after independence, Ivory Coast became the economic miracle of West Africa, with rapid economic growth due notably to exports of coffee and cocoa. The country also became a magnet for migrant labour from neighbouring countries such as Mali, Guinea and Burkina Faso, and for foreign investors, notably from Lebanon but also from China.

As a consequence, in Ivory Coast French became a language of communication within an extremely diverse population—it was not just the language of the elite. Ivorians are known to speak their own brand of French, *français populaire ivoirien*. In addition, Dioula melded with French to create a widely spoken dialect called Moussa. Young Ivorians later transformed Moussa into an artificial slang called Nouchi. Nouchi is grammatically based on French, but incorporates words from other languages that have landed on Ivorian soil— Arabic, Chinese, English and more. This slang, in turn, has developed into another, competing jargon called Zouglou. Linguist Robert Chaudenson, a Creole specialist, provides a good example of how the language works with the sentence "*Même moro côco moyen tomber.*" Literally, it reads "Even *moro coco* meaning to fall," but it means "Even if you only have a five-franc coin on you, there's going to be a sucker who'll ask for it."

Only a very small minority in former French colonies speak French as a mother tongue. Most learn it in school or later as adults, and among those, an even smaller minority master written French. As a consequence, there are important regional variations in the French spoken in different countries, and the influence of local languages is considerable, even within single countries. African francophones use the resources of French differently, and with much less constraint, than northern, native speakers, who are fully schooled in French and heavily influenced by the concept of the *norme*. In Mauritius, where the influence of English is important, the locals speak of *contracteur* (contractor) and *laboureur* (labourer), words that exist in standard French but with different meanings (*constrictive* and *plowman,* respectively). From the words *doigt* (finger), *cadeau* (gift) and *grève* (labour strike), Africans invent the verbs *doigter, cadeauter* and *grever.* A Congolese may speak of his girlfriend as a *blonde* and of his mistress as *deuxième bureau* (second office). From North Africa, words like *kiffer* (to get pleasure out of something) and *tchatcher* (to speak) have entered mainstream French, as well as *caillasse,* a regionalism for *caillou* (stone) that was extended into *caillasser* (to throw stones at). *Caillasser* entered the mainstream French political vocabulary, where it has the sense of opponents throwing things (eggs, stones, tomatoes) at a politician. Africans also express nuances that don't exist in standard French: *père* (father) is a white missionary, whereas *abbé* is a local priest.

The variations of French found throughout France's former colonial empire are striking. In Martinique and Guadeloupe the Continental French are called *métropolitains* (from *métropole*); in the same spirit, locals who move to France are called *négropolitains.* Someone who is timid is said to be a *crabe* (crab). In Africa, a writing mistake is a *chameau* (camel), which is made into the verb *chameauser* (to make such mistakes). In Ivory Coast, putting a curse on someone is called *grigriser* (from *gris-gris,* a spell or charm), while the Senegalese call this *marabouter* (from *marabout,* a religious leader). Of course, from a purist stand-point, many usages in popular African French are technically mistakes. Verbs are often used with a form of the auxiliary *avoir* rather than *être,* or the wrong verb ending; for example, *fuir* (to run away, in standard French) is sometimes pronounced *fuyer* and *plaindre* (to complain) becomes *plaigner.* Genders of nouns are often reversed. These variations are not surprising where a large chunk of the population communicates in a second lan-guage. But interestingly, Africans may be at the vanguard of an important linguistic shift, as most francophones are now gener-alizing the use of the *-er* infinitive ending for new verbs (this is discussed in more detail in chapter 17).

There are very few instances in African countries of French creolizing the way it did in the slave colonies two cen-turies earlier (that is, evolving far enough from the semantics and phonetics of French to create a new language). The main reason is that French-speaking elites in Africa cling to the *norme* and continue to impose it through the school system and the media, especially radio. Their mastery of French is often nearly perfect, and they purposefully project themselves as a model for others. In addition, the practice of African mother tongues is strong and this daily use means that the population doesn't need Creoles the way slaves in the New World did.

Nonetheless, regionalisms have begun to spawn their own national literatures. The founder of this movement was Amadou Kourouma (1927–2003), a writer from the Ivory Coast also known as "the black Voltaire." He belonged to a generation of writers, post-Senghor, who became disillusioned with the results of independence and expressed this through their writing.

Kourouma's first novel, *Les soleils des indépendances,* is written in French but the syntax is heavily influenced by that of his mother tongue, Malinké. The title itself is a regionalism: *Soleil* in Ivory Coast means an era, not just *sun.* To speakers of standard French, Kourouma's writing can seem unsettling, or even unruly. In the 1960s two dozen French publishers turned Kourouma's novel down before a Quebec house decided to publish him. It went on to become a classic of francophone literature.

It's no accident that this type of writing came from the pen of an Ivorian writer. Linguists debate whether a process of creolization is actually underway in Ivory Coast, as well as in former Zaire. But everyone agrees that local variations of French run most deeply in these two countries. More and more contemporary African writers share the view expressed in 1976 by Congolese poet Gérard-Félix Tchicaya U Tam'si: "*Il y a que la langue française me colonise et que je la colonise à mon tour*" ("It so happens that the French language is colonizing me and that I am colonizing it in turn").

There are many more Arabicisms in mainstream French than Africanisms. That's because the largest concentrations of French speakers in the former colonial empire, in both density and numbers, are in North Africa. Their presence is significant; since independence two million Algerians have emigrated to France. As a result, terms such as *clebs* (dog), *smala* (tribe, following), *caïd* (big shot, mafia boss), *flouze* (dough, cash), *baroud* (ultimate battle), *fissa* (quick), *souk* (market, disorder), *caoua* (coffee) and *bakchich* (baksheesh) are now common in colloquial French in France and elsewhere.

In many ways this is a surprising phenomenon, because, unlike sub-Sarahan countries, Tunisia, Morocco and especially Algeria did all they could to erase French from their country after independence. To Algerians, language was an important tool for exorcising 130 years of colonial occupation and a violent eight-year war of independence, which lasted from 1954 to 1962 and cost the lives of two hundred thousand to six hundred thousand Arabs and twenty-five thousand to fifty thousand Europeans. At the time of independence, only one in ten Algerians had fully mastered French. Immediately following independence Algeria embarked on a strict Arabicization program, introducing teaching in Arabic in primary schools by the late 1960s. This was later extended to secondary schools, and the first high-school graduates of Arabic programs appeared in 1989. Because most Algerians during the colonial era had been schooled either in French or not at all, Algeria had to import thousands of Arabic-speaking teachers from Egypt and Syria.

Yet these efforts were only partially successful at best, partly because university professors and civil servants rejected the program. On one hand, Arabic threatened their status. On the other hand, they foresaw the difficulties Algeria would have in finding enough university-level Arabic-speaking professors of as high quality as the French-speaking professors it already had. Furthermore, many of the Egyptian and Syrian teachers Algeria imported turned out to be Islamic fundamentalists, dubbed *les barbus* (bearded men). While the Arabicization program wasn't entirely to blame, it was tensions between fundamentalists and modernists that led to the outbreak of Algeria's civil war in 1992. The war cost a hundred thousand lives, lasted eleven years (some say it is not really over yet), cut Algeria off from most Western powers and produced chronic unemployment. But it also took a toll on the Arabicization campaign of Algerian Islamists, who were discredited in the eyes of both the government and many Algerians. Algeria today ranks as the most francophone among France's former colonies—as our personal experience showed, even more francophone on the whole than Canada.

Today most Algerians have a more open attitude towards French than their country's official policies suggest. More than half of Algeria's thirty million inhabitants speak at least some French—a widely accepted estimate, though there are no reliable statistics on language use in Algeria. Arabic is the principal language of everyday communications and of government, but French is the language of social promotion and of science. In the media, eighty percent of newspapers and an even greater percentage of the total readership use French. The Algerian journalists who covered the conference with us in Tlemcen took their notes in French rather than Arabic. Most of the media, industry, most of the publicity and a large proportion of brands are French or in French. In 1997 the government required all laws to be decreed in Arabic, but in 2002 they were still being voted on in French and then translated. When asked, only ten percent of high school graduates of Arabic programs say they want to go on to study in university in Arabic. Although the country has never officially been part of the Francophonie, it never forbade its universities to be part of the Agence universitaire francophone, the international agency that networks francophone universities.

Since the end of the civil war, the Algerian government has gradually become more tolerant of French in its official discourse. It is even toying with the idea of joining the Francophonie (the subject of chapter 16). Algeria recently reintroduced French classes at the secondary and primary levels, and French is now mandatory from the second year of primary school. In effect, Algeria is moving towards a language policy that better reflects the linguistic reality of the country, similar to the approach of its two neighbours, the former French protectorates of Tunisia and Morocco.

French was never as contentious an issue in the latter two countries as it was in Algeria. For one thing, neither society ever had to deal with as huge a class of European settlers as Algeria did. And neither had a war of independence (both became independent peacefully in 1956). French is not an official language of either country, but there is nothing close to the kind of hostility towards French that there is in Algeria. A third of Moroccans and half of Tunisians are regarded as functionally francophone. Both countries have an open, tolerant, rather pragmatic attitude towards French, which they consider the language of the "modern world." Technology, engineering, science and medicine are all taught in French.

National languages also played a role in shaping Moroccan and Tunisian attitudes towards French. Besides the fact that Morocco never travelled a violent road to independence, it has the highest proportion of ethnic Berbers in North Africa—fifty to sixty percent of the population, compared to twenty to thirty percent in Algeria (these are estimates). The Berber presence had a surprising impact on how French is perceived. Tamazight (the Berber tongue) is still used as the principal language of daily life in Morocco, and a sort of Berber renaissance underway at the moment is making efforts to revive and encourage its use as a written language. Historically the Berber majority in Morocco consider Arabic, not French, the language of the colonizer (Morocco started being Islamized in the seventh century). When the French arrived, the Berbers to some extent saw them as liberators from Arabic oppression. Indeed, it was the French who, in the early twentieth century, established the first institute to study Tamazight and Berber culture. On the whole, Berbers consider the French "on their side," and the French language is neutral ground between Morocco's native languages and Arabic, the language of religion.

Syria is the only former French protectorate that really succeeded with post-independence Arabicization. In 1963 the Baath regime embarked on an aggressive campaign to make Arabic the language of education, administration and everyday use. This campaign worked, partly because in 1941 the French had partitioned Greater Syria to create Lebanon, slicing off the most francophone (and Christian) part of the country. In 1943 there were 134,000 students of French in Lebanon and 104,000 in Syria, though the latter country is four times more populous. Now the number of francophones in Syria has fallen to fifteen thousand, but 294,000 children learn French in school.

In Lebanon the status of French was as ambiguous as it was in Tunisia and Morocco; Arabic was (and still is) the only official language. But French was sheltered in the newly independent country because Lebanon's constitution ensures total freedom of language in teaching (and still does). Today French is still Lebanon's first second language. Almost forty percent of Lebanese are considered francophone (according to the criteria of the Organisation internationale de la Francophonie) and another fifteen percent "partial Francophones." Some seventy percent of Lebanon's secondary schools use French as the second language of instruction, compared to thirty percent that use English.

Lebanon's school system is the main reason that French survived. When children start elementary school they are taught in Arabic, but they begin learning a second language almost immediately. Schools teach one second language, either English or French, but not both. In French schools math and science are taught in French, while history and literature are taught in Arabic. As students advance to secondary school and university, they are taught progressively more in their second language: In French schools, math, physics, chemistry and biology are taught in French, while history and literature, in most cases, are taught in Arabic. The education system is modelled on the French system, from primary school through university (a hangover of the protectorate). Lebanon also has

three French-language universities—Libanaise, Saint-Joseph and
Saint-Esprit—with a total of forty thousand francophone students. Lebanon has maintained strong cultural connections with
France through scholarships and university exchanges. There are
roughly fifty French-language publishing houses in the country,
and literally thousands of French cultural centres, institutes
and teaching bodies.

Roughly ninety percent of Lebanon's Christians still
speak French as their principal second language, whereas
Muslims tend to favour English (but in a lesser proportion).
Traditionally the Christians' links to France and French culture
have always been strong. We met Fady Zein, the Lebanese consul in Montreal, to discuss the situation. A passionate francophile, Zein talked about how much French-speaking Lebanese
revere France, which has always supported them diplomatically,
militarily and economically. "We consider France our beloved
mother," he said. Even Zein's Arabic was punctuated with
French words such as *ça va, merci* and *d'accord.*

Besides Syria, Indochina (now Vietman, Laos and
Cambodia) is the only other former colony where French
regressed after independence. With their language policy
there, the French very early planted the seeds that would lead
to the loss of their colony. The seventeenth-century French
missionary Alexandre de Rhodes was the first to transcribe the
Annamite (later called Vietnamese) language from ideograms
into Latin characters. Later French colonizers used this language, known as Quôc Ngu, in their attempt to introduce so-
called "civilization." They succeeded in displacing the influence
of Chinese, but it was the Quôc Ngu language, not French, than
benefited most from their efforts. Quôc Ngu gained popularity
among the growing class of Indochinese intellectuals in the
1920s. By the late 1930s books, as well as hundreds of different
periodicals, newsletters and bulletins, were being published in

Quốc Ngu. This literary renaissance spawned a nationalist movement that became increasingly critical of the French colonial system. By the 1930s the movement had grown into a full-fledged protest against the colonial government.

The key figure of the period was Nguyen Tat Thanh (1890–1969), much better known as Ho Chi Minh ("he who brings light"). Ho Chi Minh studied at the French *lycée* of Hué and moved to Paris in 1917, where he worked at a number of odd jobs. In 1919 he attended the Paris peace negotiations as a cook's assistant in the kitchen of the hotel that hosted the conference, and filed a petition asking for independence for his country. He organized groups of Vietnamese workers in France and joined the French Communist Party in 1920. In 1946 he declared Vietnam's independence, sparking a bloody war of liberation with the French that later led to a civil war, which in turn would draw in the United States and China. It is still remarkable to consider how the Vietnamese forced a humiliating retreat on both the French and the Americans.

During the colonial period, French schools in Indochina were not very successful. As in Algeria, French spread almost exclusively through trade and commerce and because it was a language of social promotion. It was mostly spoken in the cities. After independence, when Vietnamese became the official language used in business, administration, education and the media, French began to decline. The virtual occupation of the country by the Americans in the 1960s and the growing influence of China to the north spelled the end of French. As in Louisiana, some older people still speak it today, but many people believe it will die out with the last generation that lived under colonialism.

Cambodia was a different story: French stood a better chance of outlasting colonialism there. This kingdom had been relatively accepting of French colonial power and remained part of the Union française until 1955. But the seeds of the future Communist revolution, which would reach its peak in the mid-1970s, were already growing. Pol Pot (1928–98) was a prime example of a former *évolué* who had been schooled in France, but he would literally wipe out all the French speakers in Cambodia. The Khmer Rouge closed schools and monasteries, abolished private property and emptied the cities. Between 1975 and 1979 they killed about fifteen percent of the population—about two million people—mostly from the bourgeoisie and middle class, among whom were ninety percent of the French-speaking elite.

Still, the proportion of francophones in Cambodia is equal to that in Vietnam. According to statistics, 0.6 percent of Vietnamese speak French, compared to 0.5 percent of Cambodians and 0.2 percent of Laotians. The new king of Cambodia, Norodom Sihamoni, speaks perfect French, and in Laos, government forms are in both Laotian and French. French is said to have disappeared as a principal language in Vietnam. But some 163,000 Vietnamese are studying French right now, a number that compares favourably to the seventy thousand who attended French school during colonial times. In Thailand, which was not a French colony, fifty thousand people are learning French in order to emulate the strongly francophile royal family. The picture is the same in Cambodia, where the royal family is still very francophone. Interest in French has recently picked up again in the region as a result of the efforts of the Agence universitaire de la francophonie, and since the 1997 Francophonie summit in Hanoi, which Vietnam insisted in hosting (more on the Francophonie in chapter 16). So the story of French is not over yet there.

Statistics on French-language users (and for all other languages) have to be considered with care. While we were travelling to research this book, we came to the conclusion that the statististics didn't always correspond to the actual state of French in a country—or of English, for that matter. Part of the problem is the difficulty in defining a francophone. Does the term apply only to those who speak French as a mother tongue? Or does it apply to second-language speakers who master oral French? Does one need to be able to write it? And where do French students fit in?

We became particularly sceptical about statistics when we visited Algeria and Senegal. Although only ten percent of Senegalese are officially regarded as fully francophone, and another twenty percent as partially francophone, it was rare to meet anyone in a city who didn't have a functional understanding of French. Even in the countryside, most people we met had at least a veneer of French, picked up through a few years of school or from the radio. The picture was roughly the same in Algeria, although the proportions and numbers of francophones are much greater. Fluency is a question of degree, and no statistics clearly account for that.

During our travels we tried to get an idea of how much English was displacing French in France's former colonies. This led us to understand a curious phenomenon. History has led many Americans, British, French, Spanish and Arab speakers to believe that languages are somehow a zero-sum game, that the gains of one language necessarily come at the expense of another. This point of view is widespread among journalists, business people and even diplomats. Yet from what we saw, nothing could be further from the truth. Most Algerians, Senegalese, Indians and Polynesians are at least bilingual (not surprisingly, since only ten countries in the world, and very small ones at that, are classified as strictly monolingual). The progress of French in Algeria and Senegal has made no impression on Arabic or Wolof. By the same token, the progress of

French in some former British African colonies (French is now an official second language in Nigeria, for instance) has not affected the status of English there. And of course, in countries where French second-language teaching is the most extensive— Britain, the United States, Canada and Australia—few, if any, have lost their English.

Despite widespread belief to the contrary, English is not really threatening the status of French in France's former colonies. In most cases the threat to French is coming from declining education systems. This is true in almost all developing countries, but especially in Africa (more on this in chapters 16 and 19)—and for that matter it represents a threat to English as well as French. As a result of failed investment, austerity measures and plain mismanagement, investment in education in Africa has been declining since independence. So, not surprisingly, few sub-Saharan countries can afford to teach new foreign languages, whether English or any other. In Atlanta, at the conference of the International Federation of Teachers of French, we met many African French teachers who deplored the fact that they didn't have teaching materials adapted to African realities. "We still have teaching books with stories that talk about French castles and snow," says Congolese professor Désiré K.Wa Kabwe-Segatti, who teaches French at a university in South Africa. "Kids in the francophone Congo don't know what snow is!" And the fact is, introducing English into the schools is a luxury few African countries can afford.

While we were in Senegal, the question of English frequently came up. Over the past ten years there has been something of a *rapprochement* between Senegal and the United States. Making a departure from his predecessors' ways, Senegal's president Abdoulaye Wade has actively sought to steer his country away from France's influence and into the diplomatic orbit of the U.S. To gain George Bush's favour, Wade went as far as hosting a conference on terrorism in Dakar in 2002. Among the Senegalese elite there is much speculation about how this political realignment will affect French. One of Senegal's star journalists, and a respected political analyst, Abdou Latif Coulibayi is the author of half a dozen books on the Senegalese political landscape and the owner of the country's most influential private radio station, Sud FM. He assured us that the Senegalese elite have nothing to fear from English. "The Senegalese elite are keen on learning English," he told us. "But by the time students discover English, they are already francophones. Not even the United States can erase the effects of three centuries of French presence in Senegal."

While French remains largely a language of the elite, many Africans don't think of it as a foreign language. At the cinema near our hotel in Dakar, Senegalese were going to see American films, but dubbed in French, not Wolof (the same is true in Algiers, Beirut, Yaoundé, Abidjan and Libreville). Though few children make it through the school system, most get some schooling and experience of French culture. The media expose them to French cultural references—radio is important everywhere. Since French is the language of everything from banking to industry and government, even poorly schooled children have good reasons for learning it—the life of our tour guide Ibrahima Kouyaté shows this well. As Coulibayi told us, "Links are so strong with France, francophones and French that it would take a strong, concerted and uncontested government policy to make even a small change here. I simply don't see it happening at present."

In Lebanon, however, English is definitely on the rise. Historically, Lebanese Muslims have tended to speak English and pursue university studies at the American University in Muslim West Beirut. English is slowly taking over as the language of science, and increasingly as the language of business

among both Muslims and Christians, and this trend will continue. But for the moment French is still firmly established as
the language of intellectual life; Arabic remains the language
of culture and communication. As Fady Zein, the Lebanese
consul in Montreal, told us, "So far, English is advancing, but
not really hurting French."

As in Lebanon, English is making progress in Morocco,
but again not really at the expense of French. Mohammed
Guerrsel, a Moroccan linguist at the Université du Québec à
Montreal who returns to Morocco regularly, told us he has
noticed a definite increase in English in the past decade, particularly in advertising (we have noticed the same in France over
the past six years). But he doesn't feel it's threatening the status
of French. "For English to overtake French, the Moroccans
would have to make a conscious effort, and for most people,
switching to English and dropping French is just not worth
the trouble," he explained. "In the end, decision-makers
always do things gradually, so they won't do anything radical to
change the status of French. French is free. As an international
language, it still does the job."

Chapter 15

ROCKING THE BOAT

AFTER THE LONG WINTER, the temperature in Quebec rises quickly in March as the days get longer and the National Hockey League begins its playoff season. Hockey has been an obsession of French Canadians since Radio-Canada started broadcasting Montreal Canadiens games in the 1940s. The hockey hero of the time—and for all time—was Maurice Richard, baptised Le Rocket in Quebec Frenglish. Quebeckers revered him for beating off his English opponents and reversing the odds of the game seconds before it ended. When the game wasn't going his way, Richard would drop his gloves and hammer *les maudits Anglais* (the damned English) with his bare hands. This gumption made Richard virtually a cult figure. He could have become premier of Quebec if he had wanted to.

Without knowing it, Richard was the catalyst for a rage growing among French Canadians in the 1950s. When he was disqualified from the Stanley Cup playoffs for punching a referee in 1955, the National Hockey League's decision provoked a riot, as hockey fans ransacked Montreal's St. Catherine Street on St. Patrick's Day. Though he was a rather humble fellow who never fully understood the symbolic burden that Quebeckers had loaded on his shoulders, Maurice Richard was in many ways the Cassius Clay of French Canadians. The Stanley Cup riot, the first major incident of French Canada's political awakening, took place when black Americans and colonial Africans were demanding emancipation and looking for ways to gain power and affirm their rights. In Quebec the movement gained momentum in the 1960s and early 1970s, when the Front de libération du Québec (FLQ) launched a terrorism campaign of bombing and kidnapping. (Some Quebec revolutionaries also nurtured friendships among the Black Panthers, and a few were even questioned regarding an attempt to bomb the Statue of Liberty, and other terrorist activities.)

The link with the cause of ethnic minorities and anti-colonial discourse was a powerful one. One prominent FLQ sympathizer (and terrorist), Pierre Vallières, wrote a book called *Les nègres blancs d'Amérique* (*White Niggers of America*). The title pretty much encapsulated the feelings growing among Quebeckers at the time. In 1968 Quebec poet Michèle Lalonde published a poem called "Speak White" that made a strong link between the two causes. "Here, language is the equivalent of the issue of colour for American Blacks," she explained. "The French language is our black colour." The title of the poem hit home with Quebeckers to the extent that now, forty years later, people still quote it, even if few have ever read any of her poetry.

Quebec was not an isolated case among North American francophone communities. The same resentment was simmering in New Brunswick, Ontario, Manitoba and Louisiana. As in the European colonies in Africa, North American francophones had become fully conscious that they were subjects of political domination, and they were determined to do something about it. Their resentment took different forms and led to different results. In Quebec, francophones went as far as threatening secession. Their stance forced other Canadians to reconsider the foundation of their national identity, but also produced a prosperous francophone society within the Commonwealth, where it had been buried for two centuries. On the heels of Quebec, Cajuns, Acadians and French Canadians outside Quebec also organized to fight for their language and identity. Canadian francophones succeeded in reconfiguring the language policy of their entire country. Even in Louisiana, where French had almost disappeared, Cajuns mobilized their community and found a way to inject the French language back into their culture.

The target of the French-Canadian uprising was not simply English. By the 1920s French Canadians in Quebec were starting to feel alienated by the dominant political and religious discourse in their own province. The majority of francophones were living in cities by this time, but the Catholic Church still portrayed urban life as a source of temptation and a threat to the French language. Where language was concerned, the Church was not entirely wrong: Roughly eighty percent of the economy was owned by "the English" (who were in fact English, Scottish and Irish industrialists). As an urban proletariat, francophones had little power to refuse the bosses' language. But with its increasingly out-of-touch idealization of traditional life on the farm, the Church was ignoring an important change: Quebec was quickly transforming itself from a rural to an industrial society. The urban French Canadians, well schooled and up to date, were about to modernize the province and transform it almost entirely over a two-decade period known as the Quiet Revolution.

It began in the 1960s, when a generation of "Young Turks" took power in Quebec with the singular goal of changing the society wholesale. They were led by a former federal civil servant, Jean Lesage. Within a few years Lesage's *"équipe du tonnerre"* (thunder team) had created the French Language Board, the Ministry of Education, Quebec Hydro and the Quebec Pension Plan—institutions that were all necessary for economic development and the survival of French. Lesage's successors made French the language of business and produced strict language laws to protect it (see chapter 18). They also created freestanding diplomatic services for Quebec, which sometimes operated in conflict with Canada's.

In 1967 Montreal hosted the World's Fair, Expo 67, which would turn out to be one of the most widely attended ever, with sixty million visitors, including seventy-five heads of state. One of these visitors, French president Charles de Gaulle, provoked a political earthquake in Canada when he concluded a speech from the balcony of Montreal's city hall by declaring, "*Vive le Québec libre!*" ("Long live a free Quebec!"). De Gaulle's words were a catalyst for the rising Quebec independence movement, and Canada is still feeling their effect today, as tensions persist over the question. The Parti Québécois, a political party created in 1968 with the specific goal of making Quebec an independent country, conducted two controversial referendums on Quebec separation, in 1980 and 1995. The first rejected separation solidly, with a fifty-nine percent majority, but in the second the separatists lost narrowly, by less than one percent of the popular vote.

Political activism was only one part of the picture. Quebec was also in a period of radical social change and going through a powerful cultural renaissance that would, in turn, create a vibrant, productive, modern society—the province of Quebec alone was the U.S.'s eighth-largest trade partner in 2005. Up until then French Canadians had devoted most of their energy to survival, and their contribution to the arts, industry, culture, technology and science in the French-speaking world had been nowhere near that of Belgium or Switzerland. The 1960s sparked a reversal of a two-hundred-year-old trend of isolation. French Canadians began to contribute to French intellectual and industrial production and even to export their own culture, to the point that, today, cultural exchange between Canada and France is actually a two-way street. Dozens of Quebec artists,

writers, musicians and cultural figures—from Félix Leclerc and
Robert Charlebois to Nelly Arcand—are celebrities in France. In
recent years the French have had so much exposure to Quebec
singers, actors and films that they have begun to think of them
as their own. Quebec has six general-interest TV channels, ten
daily newspapers and eighty radio stations. Quebec multinationals run by francophones are now active in sectors as varied
as aviation, retail, transport, finance, the construction industry
and printing.

The road to this cultural renaissance was a rocky one for all
North American francophones. One of the great paradoxes of
the Quiet Revolution is that, while it boosted Quebec's presence
in Canada and the world, it cut off other French Canadians and
Acadians from Quebec, leaving them isolated inside Canada.
In the 1960s Quebec appropriated all the symbols of French-
Canadian nationalism for itself, from music to cuisine to the
fleur-de-lys flag. French-Canadian culture became "Quebec
culture" practically overnight. About a thousand associations
inside Quebec replaced the "French-Canadian" in their name
with "Quebec"; for example, the Académie canadienne-française
became the Académie des lettres du Québec (Quebec Literary
Academy). French Canadians outside Quebec became cultural
orphans and the "French-Canadian nation" splintered into
Fransaskois in Saskatchewan, *Franco-manitobains* in Manitoba
and *Franco-ontariens* in Ontario.

At the same time, these "other" French Canadians continued to demand their rights in Canada, and more and more
stridently. By the beginning of the 1960s there was no way to
hide from the noise. Canada's prime minister of the time, Lester
Pearson, a former diplomat who had won the Nobel Peace Prize
for his role in defusing the Suez Canal crisis of 1956, was a strong
believer in political compromise. In 1963 he created the Royal

Commission on Bilingualism and Biculturalism to investigate this so-called "French crisis" (a catchphrase used at the time for French Canadians' dissatisfaction). Pierre Elliott Trudeau, the dashing forty-year-old fully bicultural patrician who followed Pearson, made decisive moves to help preserve French in Canada. The most important was the *Official Languages Act*, passed in 1969, which declared Canada officially bilingual and made it mandatory for the Canadian government, its institutions and its agencies to provide services in both French and English. It was a courageous move. A Belgian-style linguistic division of territory (French speakers and Flemish speakers each control half of the country, and minorities within these territories have no linguistic rights) would have been much easier to pull off. Instead, Trudeau applied a bilingual policy to the whole country, setting a national standard and reversing a century of assimilation policies in Canada. The new law stated that designated jobs in the federal civil service would have to be filled by bilingual candidates, and the move lent a distinct advantage to French Canadians, since they have always been more bilingual than English Canadians.

Some Canadian provinces embraced Trudeau's policy willingly, but most refused to apply the changes that their own French-language minorities demanded. In reaction, Franco-Manitobans went as far as challenging the legality of their province's English-only laws. In 1979 Canada's Supreme Court declared all of Manitoba's laws constitutionally invalid, since they were written only in English. On the other hand, Ontario and New Brunswick, the two provinces with the largest francophone minorities, reacted to official bilingualism by opening French schools or greatly improving the ones they already had. Surprisingly, Trudeau's measures were not popular in Quebec. After centuries of assimilation efforts by English Canadians, Quebeckers resented the federal government's

telling them how to protect their English-speaking minority—
who represent a tenth of Quebec's population today—particularly since English Quebeckers had always had constitutional
guarantees protecting education and health services in their
language (and still do). Despite this controversy, Trudeau
enshrined the rights of linguistic minorities when he repatriated
Canada's constitution with the *Constitution Act* of 1982. In 1988
his successor gave some sections of the *Official Languages Act*
precedence over any other government act except the Canadian
Charter of Rights and Freedoms.

Many problems have arisen in the application of official
bilingualism in Canada. Resistance to this policy remains strong
everywhere. The country's capital city, Ottawa, simply refuses to
declare itself a bilingual city. Many government jobs that are
required by law to be reserved for bilingual staff are still given
to unilingual anglophones. And the very large majority of universities of English Canada do not yet require a second language as a condition for graduation and still consider French a
foreign language on a par with German, Spanish or Japanese.

A paradigm shift may be needed in the future to overcome this resistance, but there is no denying that the present
situation is a quantum leap from the situation in the past.
More Canadians speak French than ever, even if the proportion
of native francophones has eroded to twenty-four percent due
to a lower birth rate. Bilingualism laws have pushed most
Canadian provinces to create policies favouring francophones—
like Nova Scotia, which recently declared French mandatory for
provincial services. French teaching is obligatory in most of
Canada's provincial education programs, and though standard
French classes come nowhere near making Canadian children
bilingual, two thousand Canadian schools offer French immersion
programs to some three hundred thousand children every year—
who account for a whopping ten percent of overall enrolment.

In 2005 our twelve-year-old niece, Ceilidh, who has been in French immersion in Ontario since she started school, came to visit us in Paris for ten days. Although she is still a long way from speaking like a francophone, her French is infinitely better than Julie's was after nine years of basic school French, and she was able to understand and participate in conversations within days of arriving in France. The immersion programs are extremely popular among upper-middle-class parents in Canada, who want to make sure their children will be able to get jobs in the federal government (the schools also have good reputations). Today more Canadians speak French as a second language with convincing fluency than there are French Canadians living outside of Quebec. In Ontario alone, 1.3 million people, or about twelve percent of the population, claim to speak French. Only about half a million of those are native French speakers, among whom only seventy-five percent still speak French at home.

Since official bilingualism was put in place, the Canadian government has also invested hundreds of millions of dollars in French-Canadian communities outside of Quebec. Without this legal and financial support, these communities could not have resisted assimilation. In comparison, Quebec has done little if anything for them since the 1970s. To this day Québeckers tend to ignore other French Canadians, or dismiss them as either nearly assimilated or on their deathbed. In the early 1990s the famous Quebec writer Yves Beauchemin called French Canadians outside of Quebec "*des cadavres encore chauds*" ("still-warm corpses"). Other French Canadians also resent the way that Quebeckers tend to dominate communications among French Canadians, especially in radio and television. On the whole they see Quebeckers as condescending and distant—which is the way Quebeckers often speak of the French. In spite of all the problems with the Canadian

Official Languages Act, the commitment of the federal institutions has been remarkable and essential. Our travels have shown us that the presence of Radio-Canada in every province is often the backbone of French cultural life, especially in remote parts of the country. The lack of such an institutional presence is often the main factor that explains the complete erosion of French in the traditonal enclaves of New England and Louisiana.

On the other hand, it was the example of Quebec that inspired French Canadians to exert their own identity and rights so stubbornly. The year we lived in Toronto (2001), the Ontario government raised the Franco-Ontarian flag for the first time, on St. John the Baptist Day (Quebec's national holiday, June 24)—the result of even more lobbying by francophones. This flag has a curious history. Around 1973 a group of young professors and students from Laurentian University in Sudbury designed the green-and-white flag with a trillium, the floral emblem of Ontario, and a fleur-de-lys. The group's leader, history professor Gaétan Gervais, then trademarked the name *drapeau franco-ontarien* (Franco-Ontarian flag). Anxious to get on with business and avoid navel-gazing debates in the community over the flag, he told the Association canadienne-française de l'Ontario (ACFO) that they could take it or leave it. They took the flag, then spent three decades lobbying the provincial government to get it accepted as an official emblem of the province.

In Sudbury the Franco-Ontarian flag is still a hot topic. When we visited the city in the fall of 2004, the Franco-Ontarian lobby was trying to get the municipal government to raise it over city hall, but the administration refused—allegedly out of fear of offending other minorities (Franco-Ontarians make up thirty percent of Sudbury's population). The mayor, Dave Courschesne, dismissed French-speaking militancy as "separatist talk." Along with Ottawa and Toronto, Sudbury is an important cultural centre of French Ontario. It has not only a bilingual university, but also an all-French vocational college, Collège Boréal. Plans are also in the works to open a French-language university in Ontario, and it will probably be located in Sudbury.

As the local representative of the ACFO told us, the main problem in Ontario right now is not schooling, but support services in French. Sudbury has French schools and French immersion programs, but no French bookstores or movie theatres. Newspapers from Quebec arrive by bus a day after publication. Although medical services are available in French, they are insufficient. There is a French school of medicine at the University of Ottawa, but that's far from enough to guarantee service in French. Doctors are often second-language French speakers, so a patient who asks about her *grande opération* (a Canadianism for *hysterectomy*) is likely to be met with a puzzled stare from her physician. Speech therapists who speak French are rare. Paradoxically, though, while their associations remain militant, francophones themselves, especially in Sudbury, are rather self-effacing. This struck us as strange, since anglophones today are more open to French than they ever have been. On the other hand, the period when customers boycotted businesses and vandalized stores that displayed signs in French is not that far in the past. And merchants in Sudbury still hesitate to put simple signs saying *"Bonjour"* on their doors.

Although roughly half a million francophones live in Ontario, they make up only 4.5 percent of the population there. By comparison, the 250,000 Acadians living in New Brunswick make up a third of the population of the province. Because of this strong presence, Acadians have always been in a better position than Franco-Ontarians to get provincial authorities to listen to their demands.

Acadians began organizing and exerting their political power closely on the heels of the Quebeckers. They were even powerful enough to get one of their own, Louis Robichaud, elected as premier of the province in 1960. Robichaud ran New Brunswick competently for ten years and did three things that changed the future of French there forever. In 1962 he created an all-French university in Moncton (Franco-Ontarians, in comparison, have only bilingual universities). Robichaud then abolished the county governments that ran schools and created a ministry of education with a mandate to improve teaching everywhere, especially in poor communities (which most francophone communities were). Then, in 1969, he declared his province officially bilingual, partially to show separatists in Quebec that the rest of Canada could compromise and even be progressive when it came to French. New Brunswick became the first Canadian province—and the first jurisdiction in the world—to translate common law into French. Robichaud's successors went on to create separate administrations to run French and English schools and health care.

But while Lesage's reforms in Quebec corresponded to the wishes of the vast majority of the population, New Brunswick was split over Robichaud's policies—a large segment of the population opposed any measures that would benefit the Acadian minority. To obtain public support for his reforms, Robichaud had to hold elections twice, in 1967 and 1969. His education reform program, called *Égalité des Chances* (Equal Opportunity), was extremely unpopular in conservative circles, where Robichaud was accused of "robbing Peter to give to Pierre," an oblique slander against Acadians. Robichaud managed to sell the policy by convincing reactionaries that his reforms would benefit all the poor, whether French or English.

Although Robichaud played a strong part in the cultural survival of New Brunswick Acadians, he was followed by a generation of young leaders, trained at the University of Moncton, who picked up where he left off. The main sociological difference between Quebeckers and other French Canadians and Acadians is that, by 1960, the vast majority of Acadians led a rural rather than an urban life. Acadian-born Justice Michel Bastarache, who now sits on the Supreme Court of Canada, is famous for having encouraged Acadians to move to Moncton in the 1970s. He warned—rightly—that unless Acadians urbanized and created their own city life, they would miss the boat on modernity and the fundamental transformations of the twenty-first century.

Urbanization had started long before Bastarache. A dynamic insurance company, L'Assomption Vie, created by Acadians working in Massachusetts in 1903, moved to Moncton in 1913. The city later got a French university, attracted a French consulate and opened a French hospital. In the 1990s the New Brunswick government gambled on Moncton's bilingualism to promote call centres, and today most Canadian banks have call centres there. Then, much in the way that Montreal's Expo 67 symbolized Quebec's entry into the modern era, Moncton welcomed the first World Acadian Conference in 1994 and the Francophonie Summit of 1999, which assembled fifty heads of state in the small city. Both events boosted Acadian pride. In 2003 Moncton became Canada's first officially bilingual city—a move that even Ottawa, the capital of an officially bilingual country, has not yet dared to make. Everyone knows that bilingualism works in Moncton's favour: The declaration was made by the English-speaking mayor and city councillors.

Moncton's downtown is modern and tidy, and the city exudes prosperity in a region of Canada that has otherwise seen economic hard times for many decades. If the suburb of Dieppe is included, Moncton today is half francophone. While Moncton's French character was not obvious from the street signs we saw as we strolled through the downtown, every second person we heard was speaking either French or *chiac,* the local slang that mixes French and English. We discovered that Moncton even has a French bookstore outside the university, no small feat compared to Sudbury, which has none.

Despite the wisdom of Bastarache's idea of urbanizing Acadians, we saw the downside when we visited New Brunswick's remote Acadian Peninsula. There is no missing the sense of pride in Caraquet, the heart of traditional Acadian culture, but there is none of Moncton's optimism with respect to the future of French. Caraquet is almost a hundred percent francophone. For Sale signs are written *à vendre,* and the drive-in cinemas present French-language films, mostly from Quebec. The Acadian newspaper, *L'Acadie nouvelle,* is based there. When we visited, the play *L'ode à l'Acadie* was running in a theatre there. Yet we could see that high unemployment and the rural exodus had hit local life pretty hard. Caraquet's French bookstore and cinema had closed recently. Like most of the Canadian Maritime provinces, the area once thrived on the lumber industry and fishing, jobs that mechanization have diminished. The young are fleeing the area to go to work in the city. It is fortunate that these young disenfranchised francophones have a French-speaking city to go to, but it doesn't bode well for rural New Brunswick. Arguably, Bastarache's campaign for the urbanization of Acadian life may not have helped rural Acadians, but urbanization is a worldwide trend and there is no reason Acadians would have avoided it; it may be fortunate that they chose to concentrate in one centre rather than dilute themselves over many.

In Caraquet we met the president of the board of *L'Acadie nouvelle,* Clarence Le Breton, who works at the provincial ministry of fisheries and who deals daily with the other side of the coin of urbanization and modernization. Le

Breton, in his fifties, knows that the key to prosperity is no longer boats and land, but diplomas. Yet he also knows that education threatens the very existence of this part of Acadia. "Isolation saved our culture, but it is hurting us now. The young go to the city to find work, and there they co-exist with English. It will open up huge opportunities, but it will call for great vigilance."

There never was a Jean Lesage, a Pierre Elliott Trudeau or a Louis Robichaud in Louisiana, and it shows. Big Mamou is a sleepy prairie town in western Louisiana. The stores along the town's main artery, Sixth Street, have curiously bilingual names like Ti-Bob's (short for "Petit Bob's") and the town is famous for its Mardi Gras Run, where people race about looking for the ingredients of gumbo, a famous Cajun dish. We were drawn to Big Mamou by another event: the Sunday morning show at Fred's Lounge. The show, where live musicians play Cajun folk songs and zydeco and locals of all ages dance two-steps and waltzes, is a fifty-year-old tradition. We were already late when we showed up at 9:30 a.m. People had been downing beers since eight o'clock and were digging into the *boudin* (a spicy sausage of pork and rice) that was being passed around. The tiny bar was packed. There were even stragglers listening to the show outside on KPVI 92.5 FM. Cajun music and dancing are still alive and kicking in Cajun country, where restaurants and halls host concerts regularly. In fact, Fred's Lounge was just one stop on a circuit of venues throughout western Louisiana that offer Cajun music on Saturdays—the circuit ends in Eunice, at another live broadcast called "Le rendez-vous des Cajuns."

Along with food, music is the heart of Cajun culture, which is arguably one of the liveliest and most original in America today. Yet Cajuns are almost completely cut off from the source of their originality. Although French hasn't disappeared, it is barely discernible in Louisiana. There are still plenty of Ti-Bobs, Ti-Jeans and Ti-Noncs on western Louisiana shop signs, but only fifteen percent of Cajuns still use French, and even fewer among the younger generations. The century after the Civil War was hard on the Cajuns, who faced open policies of assimilation in schools and even in religion (see chapter 10). Many Cajun soldiers learned English fighting in the Second World War; many more went to work in the oil industry, run by Texans who opened wells all over Louisiana in the 1940s. During the same decade the construction of a highway across the Atchafalaya Swamp also hastened assimilation by ending the Cajuns' isolation. The result: It is rare to meet someone under fifty who speaks Louisiana French. Of the 250,000 Cajuns living in Louisiana today, those who speak French are old, and since they have never been schooled in French, most don't know how to read or write it. Basically, though they may still have spoken French, Cajuns educated after about 1930 stopped transmitting French to their children. Some, like the notorious Senator Dud Leblanc, were keenly aware of what was happening and tried everything they could to stop it, but assimilation policies had been so successful by the 1960s that most Cajuns didn't have a clear idea of their origins. Many even forgot they were Acadians.

Quebeckers refer to assimilation as *la louisianisation* (Louisianization), and much of the activism of French Canadians and Acadians in the 1960s was driven by their fear of ending up like Cajuns. But Cajuns also became politically active during this period—in fact, just when their culture was about to disappear. The 1960s were full of contradictions. Author Shane K. Bernard pointed out in his book *The Cajuns: Americanization of a People* that one driving force of the Cajun renaissance in the early 1960s was not a Cajun but a British-born Canadian historian, Raymond Spencer Rodgers. Like many intellectuals of his generation, Rodgers embraced the struggle of all ethnic minorities, whether black, Indian, French Canadian, Acadian or Cajun. He moved to Louisiana to teach at the University of Southwestern Louisiana in 1966, and within weeks went public to denounce Cajuns' lack of concern over the disappearance of their culture. Rodgers shook people up at the Lafayette Chamber of Commerce, particularly one Cajun lawyer and former representative to Congress, James Domengeaux.

Domengeaux spoke French but couldn't read or write it. He was sixty-one at the time and already planning his retirement when he suddenly took up the cause of French in Louisiana with the fury of the newly converted. He and the chamber of commerce successfully petitioned the state Senate and House of Representatives to pass a series of regulations stipulating that French would be taught for five years in high schools and that universities would train French teachers. In 1968 Louisiana created the Council for the Development of French in Louisiana (CODOFIL) to coordinate initiatives to promote and teach French. When non-Cajun (and often anti-French) representatives opposed its creation, Domengeaux argued that French would boost tourism in Louisiana and improve the state's image—and he was right.

Contrary to what most people believe and what Louisiana's tourist brochures now suggest, French never became an official language in Louisiana. However, the state did give CODOFIL broad powers to develop a language policy. With his characteristic energy, Domengeaux managed to bring about two hundred foreign teachers to Louisiana from France, Belgium and Canada. He met French president Georges Pompidou in 1969 and reportedly told him, in his Louisiana French, *"Monsieur le Président, si tu m'aides pas, le français, il est foutu en Louisiane"* ("Mr. President, unless you help me, French has had it in Louisiana").

CODOFIL did have some serious self-imposed limits, though. The most obvious was political. Being, as a Southerner, attuned to the legacy of the Civil War experience, Domengeaux was allergic to radical Quebec-style nationalism. In fact, he blackballed the most vociferous French-language activists who sprang up in Louisiana in the 1970s, starting with singer Zachary Richard. Richard, who would become one of Louisiana's best-known musicians, went on to a bilingual international career and was more popular abroad than in Louisiana. Early in his career he travelled to France and Quebec and discovered radical francophone activism. He also discovered that, outside Louisiana, language was a political issue. Back in Louisiana Richard tried to push his compatriots to become politically radical, but Domengeaux suppressed him, essentially pushing him out of Louisiana by refusing to invite him to events and concerts. For Domengeaux language was an issue of culture and education, but no more. He refused to give it a political dimension as Quebeckers and Acadians had.

The Cajun French dialect is very distinct from Parisian French or even Quebec French. The influence of English is strong, not only in vocabulary, but in calques such as *laisser les bons temps rouler* (let the good times roll). In the same spirit, Cajuns call rednecks *cous rouges*. But aside from anglicisms, Cajun French has many peculiarities that make it beautiful. Cajuns preserved different archaisms than those found in Canadian French. They say *nic* for *nid* (nest), *amarrer* for *attacher* (to tie up), *avenant* for *gentil* (friendly), and gave their own spin to many other expressions. For *oncle* (uncle), French Canadians say *mononcle* (a construction similar to monsieur), but Cajuns trim it to *nonc* or *ti-nonc*. They also developed lively expressions of their own, including *lâche pas la patate* (literally, don't drop the potato, meaning don't give up). Cajuns call thier non-Cajun compatriots *les Améritchains*.

However, the power of the French *norme* is such that Domengeaux, though far from being a brilliant literary figure, still looked down on the Cajun dialect and everything associated with it, including Cajun music. That's why he imported teachers from France, Quebec and Belgium instead of trying to hire locally. The foreign teachers, who often had little teaching experience and even less knowledge of the local culture, openly criticized the Cajun dialect. This obviously sparked resentment among the grassroots Cajuns. After a century of oppression they needed support from other francophones, not criticism, and the situation actually increased their feeling of alienation.

According to the thesis developed by Shane K. Bernard, which our own interviews with CODOFIL support, things began to change in the early 1980s. After a number of studies showed that CODOFIL had achieved little in improving the situation of French, Domengeaux had an epiphany and realized that Cajun French was legitimate French. CODOFIL began hiring more local teachers. At about the same time, Domengeaux and other representatives of CODOFIL visited French immersion schools in Montreal, where they saw how children could be taught all subjects *in French*. Within a couple of months CODOFIL started testing immersion programs in Louisiana, and today there are roughly three thousand children in the program. The heading on CODOFIL's press documents now reads "*Quoi c'est le Codofil?*" ("What's Codofil?" in Cajun French; in standard French it would be "*Qu'est-ce que le Codofil?*"). It's a strong statement of how Cajuns are cultivating their local variety of French.

Yet the results of CODOFIL's work are still controversial. CODOFIL made French teaching a government priority. It played an active role in defending Cajun rights and promoting the region as a tourist destination. It also developed strong ties with France, Belgium and Quebec–CODOFIL was given the right to sign agreements with foreign governments on its own initiative. But through its early efforts to push standard French, CODOFIL actually built an identity crisis back into Cajun culture. When we met the poet David Cheramie, now the acting director of CODOFIL, he gave us a perfect illustration of this conflict. Cheramie's parents were Cajuns, but Cheramie was raised in English and learned French as a second language, thanks to CODOFIL. He is now married to a Frenchwoman. "My neighbour has a boat and spends every minute of his spare time in the swamps hunting deer, squirrels and ducks and catching *barbues* [catfish]. He dances, and he knows everything about Cajun food. But he doesn't speak a word of French. And then there's me, who does none of this, who never hunts or fishes, but who speaks French. Who's the real Cajun?"

Thanks to CODOFIL's turnaround in the 1980s, most francophones of Louisiana are now convinced that music, grassroots and language are all linked. But linguistic identity remains an issue among them. They now draw a distinction between Cajuns who speak French, whom they call Cadiens, and those who don't, called Cajun. Yet many Cajuns believe it's too late to inject French back into the Cajun identity. Between 1990 and 2000 the number of Cajuns who declared themselves French-speaking fell from 250,000 to 200,000. Still, according to recent data, these numbers have stopped falling. So the future of French in Louisiana may be complicated, but it may not be as bleak as people believe. As the famous Cajun folklorist, poet and teacher Barry Ancelet put it, "Every time we've tried to close the coffin on the Cajuns, the body's sprung up and called for a beer!"

Chapter 16 ~

THE FRANCOPHONIE

JEAN-BENOÎT VISITED MONACO in April 1999, to attend a conference of the finance ministers of French-speaking countries. Between interviews he decided to slip in a visit to the Museum of Oceanography, so he hailed a cab. The driver, as it turned out, was one of the rare true-blue Monegasques. Monaco, a tiny principality of 1.5 square kilometres on the Mediterranean coast, has only five thousand natives. The other twenty-four thousand residents are foreigners who live comfortably off one Monaco's three main industries: casinos, money laundering and tax shelters. As he chatted with the driver, Jean-Benoît failed to notice that his notepad had slipped out of his pocket, so when he returned to his hotel, he was surprised to see the concierge produce it. "*Vous êtes Québécois?*" asked the concierge. The taxi driver had brought the pad back to the hotel and simply told the concierge it belonged to a Quebecker. Jean-Benoît realized that with an accent like his, he hardly needed a passport.

There was a reason—aside from the beaches and the weather—why the French-speaking finance ministers had decided to meet in this glitzy fiscal paradise. Monaco is the smallest member of the Francophonie, a kind of French commonwealth of fifty-three countries. We have often used the word *francophonie* (small f) in this book in reference to those who speak French, regardless of their nationality. The other Francophonie (capital F) is an institution that brings together the various organizations, associations and media outlets that promote French and the development of French-speaking countries. Much as the U.N. is the flagship among the thousands of organizations that make up the system of international law, the Organisation internationale de la Francophonie (International Organization of the Francophonie) serves the same purpose for the organizations of the French-speaking world.

The Francophonie is often compared to the British Commonwealth, which started out in 1931 as a sort of informal club designed to maintain links between Britain and its former dominions of Canada, Australia, New Zealand and South Africa. In 1949 the Commonwealth expanded to include the newly independent India (India refused to accept the name "British Commonwealth of Nations" so the British Parliament shortened the appellation). By 1957 the Commonwealth had been thoroughly restructured, with a permanent office and a budget, and it was ready to welcome former British colonies as they gained independence in the following years. It now has fifty-four member countries.

The Francophonie was slower getting off the ground than the Commonwealth, and didn't take shape until late in the second half of the twentieth century. The original idea came from a Quebec journalist, Jean-Marc Léger, who in the early 1950s had played a key role in creating the Union internationale des journalistes de la presse de langue française (International Union of Journalists from the French-Language Press). At a meeting with the French minister of foreign affairs in 1953, Léger proposed creating a consortium of French-speaking states whose representatives would meet to network, exchange knowledge and develop policies together. Initially Léger's proposal went nowhere, but he refused to give up. In 1954 he founded the short-lived Union culturelle française (French Cultural Union). In 1961 he created a network of francophone universities that still exists today: the Agence universitaire de la Francophone (AUF). Meanwhile, in

1960 Léger's idea started to take root and the education ministers of fifteen French-speaking countries decided to establish their own permanent assembly—the first of its kind in the French-speaking world.

At the time the word *francophonie* was not even in use. The French geographer Onésime Reclus had invented the term in 1887, in his book *France, Algérie, et les colonies,* to describe everyone who spoke French, irrespective of nationality. The idea of separating nationality and language was revolutionary at a time when geographers divided the world by race, ethnic type or religion. But the term was forgotten until 1962, when the intellectual journal *Esprit* published a special issue, "Français langue vivante" ("French, a living language"). A number of high-profile intellectuals—including Léopold Sédar Senghor—who contributed to the issue used the word. In fact, they called for the creation of a "francophone" organization exactly like the one Léger had proposed a decade earlier.

By 1965 many French-speaking African countries were keen to organize themselves as a group on the basis of shared language. They received strong support from the government of Quebec, which was just as anxious to start playing a role in international forums with other francophone "nations." In 1966 the President of Niger, Hamani Diori, laid down in front of President de Gaulle the blueprint for a multilateral organization for the cooperation of French-speaking states.

While the British had been the driving force behind the Commonwealth, at the time the French showed no enthusiasm for a francophone organization. The wars of liberation in Indochina and Algeria had traumatized French diplomats, and they wanted to avoid getting involved in anything that sounded even remotely neocolonial. Jean-Marc Léger, now retired and living in Montreal, thought that France's position at the time was wise—and still does. "They weren't recreating the empire under another name. So it had to be very clear that other countries not only wanted it, but demanded it." French diplomats were also not interested in multilateralism. Like any major power, France preferred dealing with other countries, especially weaker ones, on a one-to-one basis (an approach known in political jargon as "bilateral relations"). A multilateral agency that put everyone on an equal footing would reduce the power of its biggest members. Multilateralism was much more to the liking of a country like Canada, which had never aspired to be a great power.

Despite France's early reticence, formal talks to create the organization began in Niamey, the capital of Niger, in 1969. The early negotiations were far more complex that those for the Commonwealth; about two dozen countries were involved, each with its own agenda. Canada and Quebec struggled over who would represent French Canadians (Quebec had its own diplomatic service by this time, even though it did not represent a country), a problem they wouldn't resolve for nearly twenty years.

The word *francophonie,* although it was used informally at this time, did not appear in official documents of the Francophonie until 1996, partly because the French never liked the term. They associated it with colonialism, and so did the North African countries. De Gaulle himself rarely pronounced the word, and never in public.

Still, by the time of the Niamey conferences in 1969 and 1970, France was more willing to get involved in the creation of a French-speaking commonwealth. The main thing complicating negotiations at this point was the ongoing quarrel between the governments of Quebec and Canada. From the start Quebec had been very enthusiastic about the idea of a franco-phone organization, but the Canadian government still considered foreign affairs its exclusive turf and refused to let

Quebec participate on its own. French diplomats were stuck: They believed there could not be a francophonie organization without Quebec, but they needed both Quebec's and Canada's presence to prove that the scheme was not a neocolonial ploy. In the end France proposed including Quebec as a *gouvernement participant* (participating government). The softened terminology appeased Canada, and the federal government invited New Brunswick as well, to mitigate Quebec's influence and to avoid appearing to put it on equal footing with Canada.

In 1970 delegates from twenty-one French-speaking countries and governments gathered in Niamey and created the Agence de coopération culturelle et technique (Agency for Cultural and Technical Cooperation, or ACCT) and appointed Jean-Marc Léger as director general. However, the word *francophonie* was conspicuously absent from the new agency's name. In fact, Léger himself was hostile to it. "The Agency was originally supposed to be focused on international development and foreign aid. The original idea was to create an organization of countries united *by* language, not *for* language," he told us.

The polemic about the Agency's name would last for the next thirty years, but the real problem was defining its purpose. The ACCT was meant to be a stepping stone to a Commonwealth-style summit of heads of French-speaking states, but there was no summit for the next fifteen years. The main problem was, again, the ongoing *guerre de drapeaux* (flag war) between Canada and Quebec. Things got even worse when Quebec elected a separatist government in 1976. This new government saw the ACCT as an ideal way of projecting the image of Quebec as an independent country, a position the Canadian government naturally resisted. The problem wasn't resolved until 1984–85, when new governments in both Ottawa and Quebec were able to reach a compromise. Paris hosted the first Sommet des pays ayant le français en paratage (a clumsy title, and even more so in translation: Summit of Countries That Have French in Common) in 1986. Once again the term *francophonie* was curiously absent, despite the fact that, informally, everyone referred to the meeting as the francophonie summit.

Throughout its development, the Francophonie was plagued by two problems. The first was how to define its membership criteria. Some very obvious francophone countries such as Algeria have never joined (for reasons we explain in Chapter 14). Zaire was also wary of the colonial connotations of the organization, and only joined because Canada was a member and Belgium was not one yet (the French were right on that point). Other countries, including Cambodia and Laos, had reservations but eventually joined. On the other hand, Egypt was admitted in 1983, and even at the time its membership seemed odd, since only a small segment of the society spoke French and Egypt was never a colony of France (the case is all the more interesting because Egypt refused to be part of the Commonwealth but demanded to be part of the Francophonie). Boutros Boutros-Ghali, Egypt's minister of state for foreign affairs at the time, argued that Egypt had always had strong ties with France, including a legal system based on French laws. Even if French is taught considerably less now than it was forty years ago, thousands of children from the Egyptian bourgeoisie are schooled in French in Jesuit colleges and speak French with their families at home. Still, Egypt's membership was a stretch compared to that of Romania and Moldova, who joined in the early 1990s. In both countries the French language is very much alive, even after seventy-two years of communism.

During the 1990s the Francophonie started accepting candidate countries that had only a veneer of French, such as

Albania, Macedonia and Bulgaria, all of whom have fewer francophones than tiny Monaco. Such choices were all the more surprising given that because some very francophone countries—for instance, Israel, which is over ten percent French-speaking—are not members (Israel would have joined long ago, but Lebanon has always rejected its candidacy). Switzerland joined surprisingly late, in 1995, but then the militantly neutral Swiss are particular about joining international organizations: They did not even join the U.N. until 2002, despite the fact that the organization's European office is located in Geneva!

The Francophonie continued to have difficulty defining its purpose, its major stumbling block. It hesitated between being an organization of nonaligned states, a French U.N., a French UNESCO, or a sort of academy of things-French-and-not-English. Until the middle of the 1990s Francophonie summits were mostly spent deciding on the date of the next summit. But gradually members came to agree that the meetings had to produce some concrete results. In 1987 the leaders of Quebec and Ivory Coast convinced their peers to create an Institut francophone pour l'énergie et l'environnement, based in Quebec (this institute has gone on to help poorer members to develop energy policies and energy-production techniques adapted to local conditions and resources). Members also decided to put under its authority some existing francophone bodies such as the TV5 channel and the Agence universitaire francophone, or rather, to put them under the authority of the "summit of heads of state and government." In 1993, at the summit in Mauritius, member countries adopted their first common position on a matter relating to international trade, when they developed the policy of *exception culturelle*. The Anglo-American press has often mistaken this for a French policy, although Quebec was heavily involved in its formulation. The policy stated that cultural goods and services could not be regarded solely as merchandise, and was meant to influence the outcome of negotiations of the World Trade Organization. This resolution, as we will see, contained much of the ferment for the Francophonie's future political actions.

As early as 1987, member countries began inviting guests to the summits: governments, jurisdictions or international organizations that were not members but were considered sympathetic to the cause of French, including representatives of Louisiana, New England, Algeria and the United Nations. One of the guests invited in 1995 was Boutros Boutros-Ghali, who, like most of the Alexandrian bourgeoisie, had been schooled in a French *lycée*. During those years, France, Belgium and the sub-Saharan countries lobbied hard to get the organization to assume its true vocation and to adopt an easy, catchy official name: La Francophonie. In 1995 the ACCT became the Agence internationale de la Francophonie. At the 1997 summit in Hanoi, Vietnam, the Francophonie chose Boutros Boutros-Ghali as its first secretary-general. The Francophonie was split into two bodies: a political head office, the Organisation internationale de la Francophonie, and the Agence internationale de la Francophonie, which managed subsidies and budgets. In 2005 these two entities were finally merged into a single Organisation internationale de la Francophonie.

Strangely, it took Jean-Benoît six years to understand exactly what the francophone finance ministers were doing in Monaco in 1999. They were supposed to discuss joint economic policies at the meeting, but Jean walked away feeling as if it had been just three days of pointless articulations of lofty principles—in short, so much diplomatic hot air. As with many commentators (including francophones), his view of the Francophonie was heavily influenced by his inexperience in covering high-level diplomacy, but also by the organization's legendary difficulties, lack of purpose and tendency to let anyone join. In Monaco he concluded that the Francophonie was scattered, at best. He could see that the French themselves were ambivalent about it, and left with the conviction that the organization was doing nothing more than fighting an ineffectual, perhaps futile, battle against English. He even wrote a report wondering if the Francophonie shouldn't be called the "Franco-phoney." His impression of this conference was partly well-founded; the conference of ministers of economy was a foreign body and the graft never took. Yet the Francophonie has had a lot more success with conferences that gathered ministers of foreign affairs, culture or education.

Since 1999 a lot has changed, including our own understanding of what the Francophonie does. In fact, as we would learn, the Francophonie does a lot more than it has been given credit for. But its reputation suffers from its early incoherence. Under the tenures of Boutros Boutros-Ghali and his successor, former Senegalese president Abdou Diouf, the Francophonie became an international organization with scope and ambition to match the Commonwealth's, and a clearer sense of purpose.

Much of the Francophonie's efforts go towards improving economic and democratic development in member countries, particularly in Africa and Southeast Asia. This is not just humanitarian goodwill; half of the poorest countries in the world are members of the Francophonie (which, on the other hand, also includes two G8 countries—Canada and France—in addition to Belgium and Switzerland, which are not exactly poor either). The Francophonie runs projects ranging from Internet development in Africa to conferences on education in Africa and the Indian Ocean region. It runs some fifty rural radio stations and fifty-three Internet access stations. It also supplies technical training and briefs civil servants to prepare them to participate in international trade talks and forums such as the World Trade Organization. The Francophonie was particularly effective in what it called the Cotton Initiative, a program designed to help Mali, Burkina Faso, Benin and Chad convince the World Trade Organization to deal fairly with subsidies in the American cotton industry. The Francophonie supports the Université Senghor in Alexandria, where top civil servants from African countries receive PhD-level training in specialized fields such as project management and management of financial institutions and cultural programs. It also monitors electoral processes in member countries and sanctions countries where the democratic process is not respected. In 2004 and 2005 it went as far as temporarily suspending a member, Togo, and imposing sanctions on Ivory Coast.

In Senegal we saw the development goals of the Francophonie at work. Jean-Benoît took the rickety train from Dakar to the nearby city of Thiès, seventy kilometres east, to meet Horace DaCosta, local director of the CLAC program. CLAC is a catchy abbreviation for Centre de lecture et d'animation communautaire (Centre for Reading and Community Activity). It is just one of dozens of projects run by the Francophonie in Senegal. This program was the brainchild of an inspired librarian, Philippe Sauvageau, head of Quebec's National Assembly Library, who wanted to support community life in rural areas. His idea was to develop small libraries—of about 2,500 books—that would offer other types of services, including Internet access, games, movie-screening facilities and sound systems for shows. Since the program was inaugurated in 1985, 213 CLACs have been opened in seventeen countries from Lebanon to Haiti, at the extremely moderate cost of forty thousand euros each.

With Horace DaCosta, Jean-Benoît toured three CLACs, each quite different in its approach. In Joal, a coastal city of about forty thousand people that is relatively well equipped, the CLAC serves as a library with seven thousand books and offers musical performances. In Ndiaganiao, a rural community of about twenty-five hamlets that can be reached only by a broken road in the middle of baobab country, the CLAC is a community centre, and the hub of the community's social life. Ndiaganiao's CLAC developed its own daycare centre and offers public health programs—an initiative it started after twenty children and twelve women in the community died suddenly because of poor sanitation. A study done in Burkina Faso has shown that the rate of success in national exams is three to four times higher in communities with a CLAC than those without. Organizations from Portuguese- and English-speaking countries have approached the Francophonie to start their own versions of CLACs.

Because of its minuscule budget of eighty-four million euros, the Francophonie tries to concentrate on original programs, such as the CLACs, that other international agencies don't take on—starting with the promotion of French, but not limited to that. Until the mid-1990s the Francophonie ran the École internationale in Bordeaux, which essentially trained African civil servants to manage Francophonie programs. But since that school became redundant after the opening of the Université Senghor in Alexandria in 1990, Bordeaux switched its mandate to developing the Internet in francophone countries. The Francophonie was also behind the creation of a trade show, the MASA—Marché des arts du spectacle africain (African Entertainment Market). The MASA, which takes place in Abidjan, Ivory Coast, has allowed African artists to escape the folklore ghetto and develop original forms of contemporary art.

At the Beirut summit in 2002, the Francophonie defined stricter rules of membership in order to create more internal coherence. The move was long overdue; after Albania and

Macedonia applied for membership in 1999, a dozen more countries asked to be admitted, including Greece, Austria, Croatia, Hungary, Poland, Slovenia, Slovakia and the Czech Republic. Until then, countries were admitted as so-called observers and then became full members almost automatically. But in Beirut new criteria were established: The status that applicants would be granted depended on the number of French speakers in the country and on its efforts to promote and develop French in the media and in education. So Greece, which has always been a strong defender of French in international forums and teaches the language widely, became an associate member right at the start. But Austria and Croatia will probably remain "observers" indefinitely. Ukraine was simply turned down. Ten states now have observer status, in addition to the forty-nine full members and four associate states.

The reason that non-francophone countries want to join the Francophonie is that its activities, though primarily focused on defending French, now go beyond language. As Abdou Diouf said when we met him at his office in March 2004, "The number of applicants proves that other countries recognize themselves in what we stand for." In fact, both Boutros-Ghali and Diouf succeeded in getting the member countries to operate as a bloc in international forums, where they adopt common positions. At the 2002 Beirut summit, which took place just weeks before the U.N. Security Council met to hammer out a resolution on Iraq, the three heads of state and government agreed to express confidence in the power of institutions such as the U.N.

The Francophonie took a long time to elaborate a coherent policy on language that would satisfy member states. Opposing English seems like an uphill battle, and all the more so since member countries like Canada, Mauritius and Cameroon hold both French and English as official languages. As to the notion

of promoting French, this was also a contentious issue with
the former colonies of France and Belgium, where French co-
exists and often competes with other national languages. At
the Dakar summit of 1989, the Francophonie came up with the
notion promoting French and *langues partenaires* (partner languages) that was politically sustainable to all.

It is from this basis that the Francophonie was capable of
building a very effective stance on plurilingualism. While its positions on democracy, education, development and cooperation
are pretty much the same as those of other international organizations, the support for plurilingualism is what distinguishes it.
The basic idea behind plurilingualism is that a single language (in
this case, English) is not sufficient for international relations.
English-speaking media often ridicule the Francophonie for
waging a rearguard, losing battle against English. There may be
some truth to that, but the Francophonie has very shrewdly
adapted its pro-French stance by pushing the more universal
principle of plurilingualism, which has become its main battle
cry in international organizations and the reason for the
Francophonie's renewed effectiveness in the last few years.

Plurilingualism is different from multilingualism.
Institutions can be said to be multilingual because they have
many official languages, whether people there use them or not.
Plurilingualism refers to the state of actively promoting the use
of different languages in international institutions—ultimately,
to the actual efforts individuals within those organizations
make to practise more than one language. In 1998, at a sympo-
sium on plurilingualism in Geneva, Boutros Boutros-Ghali
made a strong case as to why plurilingualism was necessary:

> [The first reason is] the respect for equality
> between states. We all know that forcing inter-
> national civil servants, diplomats or ministers

to express themselves in a language that is not theirs amounts to putting them in a situation of inferiority. It deprives them of the capacity for nuance and refinement, which amounts to making concessions to those who speak that language as a mother tongue. . . . Also, we all know that concepts that look similar often differ from one civilization to the next. For instance, the word *democracy* in English doesn't refer to the same concept as the word *démocratie* in French. There are many more similar examples. . . . Words express a culture, a way of thinking and a world view. For all these reasons, I think that much in the way democracy within a state is based on pluralism, democracy between states must be based on plurilingualism.

This position explains why countries such as Greece and Austria want to join the Francophonie; even though they don't have French-speaking populations, the organization could give them leverage to protect their own languages on the international stage.

English-speaking countries make regular appeals for the use of English (and the elimination of other languages) in international organizations for the sake of "simplicity" or "efficiency." But Diouf and the Francophonie have shifted the frame of the argument from one of efficiency to one of democratic principles. In their view, language is a political issue in that the use of English puts all non-English speakers at a disadvantage. While not directly attacking English, plurilingualism attaches the issue of language diversity to a political value—democracy—that is very difficult to contest. The defence of plurilingualism has allowed the Francophonie to rally speakers of Arabic, Spanish, Russian, German and more to its cause. Ingo Kolboom, a professor at the University of Dresden and one of the very few specialists on the Francophonie outside the French-speaking world, claims, "Francophonie is an attempt, maybe the only one, to balance the discourse on the American-style global village."

Of course, the Francophonie's purpose is still to protect and promote French. At the moment it is especially preoccupied with the declining use of French in international institutions (the 2002 Beirut summit even called for "urgent action" on this). French and English are both working languages of the Secretariat General of the U.N., but English has been encroaching on French since the 1970s. The Francophonie has permanent representatives in the U.N.'s New York and Geneva offices, as well as in Addis Ababa, at the head office of the African Union, and has created groups of informal ambassadors in various institutions to monitor the use of French in those institutions. It created one for the European Union in 2003, and another for Washington in 2004. "We have taken a lot of flak from people who consider us a nuisance, but there's no turning back. We can't give up," said Ridha Bouabid, a former ambassador who represents the Francophonie at the U.N. in New York. As we explained in chapter 13, the Francophonie's campaign is not driven by hurt pride. The issue at stake is, Who will have the advantage of using their mother tongue in the incredibly finicky and subtle (in fact, politely brutal) discussions that are the mainstay of international institutions?

It is very unlikely that the Francophonie alone will bring French back on a par with English, particularly at the U.N. (more on this in chapter 19). As part of its effort to defend French, the Francophonie has actually been documenting the decline of French in international institutions. Studies made by Francophonie members, most notably France, have measured this decline by watching how often French is chosen for correspondence and public speeches, and how many translations are made into French. The Francophonie has fifty-three members, but at the U.N. only thirty-nine countries request their correspondence to be in French. In the European Union, French and English were still on a par in 1997 as the primary language for written documents, with about forty-two percent each. But by 2003 English had risen to seventy-two percent while French had fallen to eighteen percent. Overall statistics show that English is progressing everywhere to the detriment of all other languages, including French, although French is still faring better than the others. The case of the U.N. office in Geneva has shown that even a francophone environment outside the office door does not stop the progression of English. Putting European institutions in francophone cities such as Brussels, Luxembourg and Strasbourg will not be enough to stop English either. Actions have to be taken, and the Francophonie knows it.

The Francophonie is more hopeful about reversing the trend towards English at the European Union, partly because the decline of French there was caught much earlier. Stéphane Lopez, a sociolinguist, was appointed in May 2003 to run the Francophonie's ten-year program to boost French in the European Union. Lopez has targeted three groups: the ambassadors and negotiators at the EU, the national civil servants who deal directly with the EU and its ministers, cabinet directors and heads of states, and the journalists who cover the EU. The number of national civil servants who take French classes has risen from 1,300 in 2002 to 7,400 in 2005. As for senior EU executives, the number who take French classes has risen from forty to seven hundred. For the politicians Lopez has created a special program in which they are invited for three weeks of immersion in Spa or Avignon, with a private instructor (who

could resist?). Lopez is also working on eight national academies that train diplomats. "Our line with them is that, though
English is necessary, it is not enough," he said, admitting that
it will probably take ten years just to evaluate the program's
results. He added, "But the increase in enrolment shows that
there is a demand for French at the top level everywhere."

Only time will tell if the Francophonie's efforts to boost
the use of French will bear fruit. "Europe is the main battle
ground," says Roger Dehaybe, who was chief executive officer
of the Agence internationale de la Francophonie until 2006. "If
French disappears from European institutions, entire countries
will start to consider it less important for science and diplomacy." To its credit, the Francophonie has recognized that the
sorry situation of French at the U.N. and the European Union
is only partly a result of the attractiveness of English. The
Francophonie and its individual members sat on their hands for
years over the issue. Francophone countries did not take a unified public stance on plurilingualism at the U.N. until 1995, and
did not make it effective before 2002. In the 1990s neither France
nor Belgium nor the Francophonie voiced a complaint when
the European Commission required that Eastern European
countries apply in English (many are part of the Francophonie).
Of course, British and American diplomats did not sit idly by
the whole while (as we saw in chapter 13); the Commonwealth
played a strong role by frequently forming unified blocs over
the issue in international institutions. But the fact that francophone countries took forty years to get the Francophonie up
and rolling cannot be blamed on others.

It is fair to say today that Francophone countries have
learned from their mistakes. They are looking to elbow their
way into the international political arena in a way that will
give them clout to match that of the Commonwealth. In 2005
Abdou Diouf convinced the member states of the Francophonie

to place its subsidy arm, the Agence internationale de la Francophonie (the former ACCT), under the authority of its political arm to create the single Organisation internationale de la Francophonie. This should allow more rapid action. And the Francophonie's decision to demand more militancy of its members comes at a good moment, as Europe recently created a commissioner for multiculturalism. With eleven of the twenty-five European countries also being members of the Francophonie—and soon thirteen out of twenty-seven, when Hungary and Romania are integrated in 2007—many European civil servants and politicians will be hearing about plurilingualism in the coming years.

Even if the position of French has been eroding in the European Union, the language remains well entrenched in related organizations like the European Court of Justice, where proceedings are done in French, the European Tribunal of First Instance, the European Court of Auditors in Luxembourg and the Press Room of the European Commission in Brussels. This is a good institutional base.

The Francophonie's program is to start using its combined weight to act as a unified bloc within important international organizations. In the case of the African Union, twenty-five of the fifty-three member countries are also members of the Francophonie, excluding Algeria and Comoros, which are both de facto francophone countries. In the case of the Arab League, six out of twenty-two member countries are in the Francophonie—again, excluding Algeria and Comoros. In the case of the Organization for Economic Co-operation and Development (OECD), eleven of the thirty member states are part of the Francophonie, as are three of the ten members of the Association of South-East Asian Nations (ASEAN). Even among the thirty members of the South Pacific Commission, five are members of the Francophonie.

After decades of hesitation, the Francophonie has turned itself into an increasingly effective organization, but it still has its defects—the main one being financial. The Francophonie's overall budget is a little over eighty million euros, which compares well to the Commonwealth's thirty-eight million pounds but remains insufficient for everything it's trying to do. All international organizations are facing the same problem—the U.N. can hardly afford to be the U.N. anymore. But in the 1990s the Francophonie's budget did not increase to keep pace with the number of new member countries being admitted. The Africans and Asians lobbied hard to make sure the Francophonie's resources would be shared as little as possible with countries in Eastern Europe.

There's certainly money out there. The French are often criticized for being lukewarm francophones. But France contributes a hefty fifty-five percent of the Francophonie's budget (compared to thirty percent of the Commonwealth's budget from the U.K.). The other rich members—Canada, Belgium and Switzerland—could probably afford to give more than their combined twenty-five million euros, or about forty-five percent of the budget (Canada contributes twenty-two percent of the Commonwealth's budget alone). The rest of the francophone countries have a symbolic contribution of below five percent of the budget. The most surprising figure remains the small contribution of Quebec, which has little excuse for contributing a mere 2.5 million euros or 4.1 percent of the budget. After all, Quebec has an advanced economy and is over eighty percent French-speaking. Yet it contributes less in proportion and in number than Switzerland and Belgium, which have fewer francophones than Quebec, but chip in to the level of 6.6 and 8.6 percent of the budget respectively. "It remains a great mystery," says Jean-Louis Roy, who ran the ACCT from 1989 to 1998. "If Quebec wants to raise its profile internationally, what other official channel does it have? I just don't get it." In fact, neither do we.

If the Francophonie (capital F) were the only organization acting on behalf of French speakers, the francophonie (small F) would be in bad shape, but luckily that's not the case. Much in the way that French survived in North America because French Canadians, Acadians and Franco-Americans organized themselves, francophones of the world started taking care of themselves long before the official Francophonie was created. In the nineteenth century the clerics and intellectuals who created the Alliance française and the Alliance israélite universelle got France's cultural diplomacy rolling. Many francophone associations have done the same thing for the francophonie. The existence of an institutional Francophonie is largely the product of these private efforts.

Throughout the twentieth century, dozens of activists created their own francophone associations for dentists, lawyers, mayors, members of Parliament, composers, union leaders, sociologists, economists, school directors and even deans of medical faculties. The oldest, the Association of French-Speaking Pediatricians, was founded in Paris in 1899. One of the largest, the Fédération internationale des professeurs de français (International Federation of Teachers of French), includes some seventy thousand teachers of French from 180 associations in 120 countries. All of these organizations are international forums where people exchange ideas and get exposed to new ideas and ways of doing things. Many, like the Réseau Poincaré pour le français langue de science (Poincaré Network for French as a Language of Science) and the Centre de coopération interuniverstaire franco-québécoise (the Quebec-France Centre for Inter-university Cooperation), are dedicated to the promotion of French in scientific circles. There are in fact so many French-language organizations that another association was created in 1975 to network the networks: the Association francophone d'amité et de liaison (Francophone Association for Friendship and Liaison); it now has more than 132 francophone associations as members.

The two bright lights in this nebula of francophone organizations are TV5 and the Agence universitaire francophone. Though both now operate under the authority of the Francophonie summit, they were created independently and stand as sister rather than children organizations of the OIF. And both have had impressive results in promoting French. The oldest star among francophone organizations is the Agence universitaire francophone. Founded in 1961 by Jean-Marc Léger to link thirty-three universities in Canada and France, the AUF has mushroomed into a network of 525 universities from sixty countries, twenty of which are not even part of the official Francophonie. Part of the AUF's success dates back to the 1960s, when the rector of the University of Morocco, Mohammed El Fasi, proposed that the AUF extend membership to universities that operated only partially in French. It now networks an additional 350 faculties of French worldwide. In all, some seven thousand researchers work together in some eighteen sectors ranging from engineering to linguistics, demography, agronomy and genetics. The AUF grants about two thousand bursaries a year, as well as awards to researchers such as Van Ga Bui of the University of Dasang in Vietnam, an engineer who designed a new computer model to measure pollution from diesel motors, which he then applied to redesign moped motors in his country.

While in Dakar, we made an impromptu visit to the AUF's virtual campus at the Université Cheikh Anta Diop. Opened in 2000, it is certainly among Dakar's most well-kept buildings, with state-of-the-art electronic equipment and the country's only three video-conference rooms. The campus offers training and tools for technicians working in network management, professors in online program development, students doing research, entrepreneurs looking for a good start-up environment, and archivists who need large-scale capacity to scan documents. When we visited the campus, a marketing professor there had just begun a class on website creation. Frantz Fangong, who is in charge of project development, proudly told us that the University of Saint-Louis, north of Dakar, had created a full curriculum for teaching the brand new field of cyberspace law. "It took them a year to develop it. This is incredibly specialized, and it is stunning to think that it could come from here and not a university in Quebec or France or Belgium."

The AUF's achievement has been to stimulate research in French and even raise the demand for French at some university campuses, notably in Southeast Asia and Eastern Europe. French is still strong among the intellectual elite of Hungary, largely because of the AUF's work. In Southeast Asia the number of Vietnamese, Cambodian and Laotian university students who learn French or learn in French had risen to forty thousand in 2003, and the increase was due largely to the work of the AUF, which runs the Technology Institute of Cambodia, among other things. Such links are also being built elsewhere: Through the AUF, the biology department of the University of Havana is linked with the Pasteur Institute in Paris, and has developed a French-language option in the department. "We do all this with a forty-one-million-euro budget," Michèle Gendreau-Massaloux, the rector of AUF, told us when we met her at her Paris office. "French is still a language of science. And not just for French-speaking countries."

When you visit Beijing, Tokyo or London, your hotel TV will likely receive a French channel. And chances are it will be TV5, the world's most successful French cable channel, to which 160 million households and three million hotel rooms subscribe worldwide. TV5 was created in 1984, when five TV channels (three French, one Belgian and one Swiss) decided to pool their programs into a sort of international TV digest—a collage of their best shows. TV5 did not have auspicious beginnings. It had trouble sticking to a schedule, and the programming choices were not as good as people expected. But the shows got progressively better as other TV channels joined in, most notably Radio-Canada, Canada's National French-language network. In the mid-1990s TV5 acquired a strong private-sector management team and built an international distribution network of six thousand cable companies and fifty-five satellite operators. The channel invested heavily in subtitles in English, German, Spanish, Portuguese, Arabic, Dutch and Swedish to reach audiences outside the French-speaking world. Today, among international channels TV5 ranks third behind MTV and CNN, and ahead of BBC World, Aljazeera and Deutsche Welle. In Europe ninety million homes receive the French-language channel. In Algeria alone, two million people watch TV5.

TV5 also has an educational wing that produces a full range of services for French teachers abroad. Every month some forty thousand French teachers tap into TV5's documentaries and series by consulting eight hundred thousand videos online, and thirty-two thousand teachers are registered in TV5's "Teach and Learn" program. The website TV5.org offers tips on using the French language, an interactive French dictionary and dictation exercises by the popular literary critic and French-language guru Bernard Pivot. In Africa, where infrastructure is always a problem, TV5 is shown in ten *télé-cafés* called the Maisons TV5. These were created in Burkina Faso in 2001 and later spread to Benin and Senegal. TV5 is considering expanding the initiative to all developing countries.

In 2005, for the publication of our previous book, Jean-Benoît spent a couple of hours at TV5's head office in Paris in the company of the channel's assistant news director and star interviewer, Xavier Lambrecht. At a glance, the cramped office had more in common with a regional TV studio than an important international TV channel. As Lambrecht explained, "TV5 used to broadcast the national newscast of national channels. Now the staff rewrites every news item with the world in mind. We found ways of doing this with very little staff." Specifically, TV5 has its own newsroom staffed with forty journalists who tap into fourteen affiliated networks, including Radio-Canada. By the time of the World Trade Center attacks in 2001, TV5 was in a position to deliver real-time reporting on location. During the Iraqi war it produced ten newscasts a day. It has managed to do all this with a shoestring budget of eighty-five million euros, twelve million of which go to the newsroom alone, a pittance compared to the thirty million dollars CNN spent covering the first month of the Iraqi war.

TV5's mission has always been to break the quasi-monopoly of Anglo-American news images and content. Part of its success in doing so has come from the way it has positioned itself as an alternative media source between American news and Aljazeera. This approach is paying off: TV5's biggest viewer gains in 2003 were in English-speaking countries such as the U.S., the U.K. and South Africa. In the latter two the public was attracted by the alternative news perspective. Since then TV5 has become a fixture at the U.N. headquarters in New York, a market from which it was totally absent before 2003.

Since 2005 TV5 has gone even further by relabelling itself TV5-Monde (TV5 World). The late Serge Adda, head of TV5 until his death in 2005 and the main brain behind the channel's renewal, had been adamant about what he called the *décloisement* (decompartmentalization) of cultures. "I didn't want an African film just to be for Africans. African cinema must be seen in Hanoi, Tokyo, Rio, Dakar, Cairo, and conversely."

TV5's motto, taken from seventeenth-century French philosopher Blaise Pascal, is "*Le centre du monde est partout*" ("The centre of the world is everywhere"). It could be the motto of the Francophonie as a whole, and in a way it is a good summary of the next chapters in the story of French.

Part Four ~

CHANGE

Chapter 17 ~

THE STRUGGLE FOR STANDARDS

WHILE WE WERE VISITING Paris in the fall of 2005, the
Catholic newspaper *La Croix* published a special issue exploring
why kids from well-off areas were mimicking the speech of
the *cités,* the low-income suburban housing developments,
particularly around Paris. These suburbs, largely populated by
African and North African immigrants, are well-known for
producing vibrant forms of Arabic-influenced argot. But as the
journalists from *La Croix* noted, middle-class French teenagers
had also started to *bousculer* (upset, shake up) French, using the
language of the *cités.* To illustrate the phenomenon, one journalist quoted an SMS (short message service) text message
passed from one French teenager to another on a cell phone:
"Kestufé? Tnaz? Je VO6né. A2M'1." It was a phonetic transcription, mixing letters and numbers, of *"Qu'est-ce tu fais? T'es naze?
Je vais au ciné. À demain"* ("What are you doing? Are you out of
it? I'm going to see a movie. See you tomorrow").

It was hardly a coincidence that *La Croix* was exploring
the question of argot at this particular time. Several weeks
earlier, two youths in the Paris suburb of Clichy-sous-Bois
had been electrocuted when they hid from the police inside
a transformer. Violence had been brewing for decades in
France's *cités,* but the intensity of the reaction to these deaths
stunned the French. Uprisings started around Paris and quickly
spread to poor suburbs throughout France, where they went
on for four weeks. Every night residents gathered to protest,
while disaffected youth throughout France took to burning

cars at the rate of a thousand a day. French newspapers, TV and radio examined the situation, first from the angle of immigration policies, then of France's failure to integrate immigrants and the role of Islam in the suburbs, before finally looking at it through the lens of language.

Using examples like that of the SMS message, *La Croix* journalists reported that, more and more, French writing was imitating speech rather than speech imitating writing (still considered the ideal in French). They noted that young people were using bad grammar (the *qu'est-ce tu fais* rendered into *kestufé* is incorrect; the correct form would be *qu'est-ce QUE tu fais*); acknowledged the generalization of slang (the expression *naze* originated in argot); and pointed out how teenagers were using phonetic rather than proper spellings, and even numbers.

While the *La Croix* journalists presented their observations as groundbreaking, there was nothing really new about what they wrote. During the two years we spent researching this book, almost all the teachers and commentators we met bemoaned the "declining" state of French in exactly the same terms as those used by the *La Croix* journalists.

Is French really in decline? In the debates over what constitutes ideal versus real French, there is a lot of speculation about where French is going. What is clear is that French is changing. Linguists and sociolinguists have assessed the nature of these changes, or supposed changes, in phonetics, grammar and vocabulary, particularly since 1945. Some of their observations are surprising; at the very least, they prove that change has been going on for centuries and that, contrary to purist ideology, the French language is not fixed, but in constant evolution. But studies also suggest that change is not happening the way most francophones assume it is. Most of this discussion will concentrate on France, with examples from other francophone locations, a choice we made for two reasons. First, we have already established that there are great linguistic variations among francophone countries. And second, France remains to this day the focal point of "standard French"—whether true or imagined—whether linquists call it "central French", "standard French," "Parisian French" or "French from France."

Linguists agree that the most impressive changes in standard French since 1945 have been not in vocabulary, but in pronunciation. Prior to the phonograph, there was no way to record the way people spoke, and before the 1920s, recording quality was so bad that only the clearest, cleanest French could be understood. Linguists had to speculate on pronunciation from rhyming in songs and poetry and other less than scientific sources. But even what they found back then should have shaken the certainty of francophones on the supposed *fixité* (fixedness) of their language. Molière, in the first act of his famous play *The Misanthrope*, makes *je trouve* (I find) rhyme with *veuve* (widow). The very colloquial term *mec* (guy) was a nineteenth-century truncation of *maquereau* (pimp), which people then pronounced *mèquereau*.

New technologies have, of course, made it possible to study phonetics more thoroughly. At the end of the 1990s, for the twenty-sixth volume of the *Histoire de la langue française 1945–2000*, linguist Fernand Carton put together an extensive description of French pronunciation at the turn of the millennium. Some of Carton's findings were surprising—notably, the fact that the accentuation (that is, stress or emphasis) in standard French has been shifting since the Second World War. Among the world's languages, French has traditionally been famous for its lack of accentuation. If there was any, the stress in words fell on the last syllable and, in sentences, on the last word—known as oxytonism. According to Carton that's now changing. French accentuation today is moving towards the penultimate (second-last) syllable in about half its words. One hears it in the lyrics of popular French music, especially in rap and rock. The change is so profound that French speakers not only pronounce final E's that should be silent, they frequently pronounce an E at the end of words where there is none, to mark the displacement of the tonal accent. For example, they say *DONC-e* (so), *bonJOUR-e* and *au reVOIR-e*. In Carton's opinion, Central French is moving back to the tonal system it had in the Middle Ages, which was similar to that of German, English and Italian today, and resembles the French spoken in southern France.

At the same time, some E sounds are disappearing. The French E is a ubiquitous vowel that often works as filler in a language that has few groupings of consonants (the kind one sees in *swim* or *sprout* in English, or in *bleibst* or *abschneiden* in German). But now the French are beginning to group consonants in their sentences, at least through pronunciation, by dropping the vowels between consonants, especially the E's. Sentences like *"Je me le demande"* ("I am wondering") are now pronounced *j'm'le d'mand* or *je me l'demand*.

The consonant system of French has changed very little. However, the pronunciation of vowels, known as vocalization, has changed considerably, and is continuing to do so. Diphthongs disappeared in Paris long ago. Other changes that started centuries ago are now reaching completion, such as the disappearance of long vowels. Around Paris today, words like *mettre* (to put) and *maître* (master) are pronounced exactly the same way (with a sharp *è* sound; the *ai* used to be a long vowel in the latter). The two pronunciations of the short A have also been blurred: *pâte* (dough) used to sound like *pawt* but now sounds like *patte* (leg). Finally, nasal vowels such as *in, an, on* and *un* have almost been merged into a single vowel (a cross between *an* and *on*). As a result, in France a phrase like "*un bon pain brun*" ("a good brown bread") now tends to sound like *ahn bahn pahn brahn* (the vowels still have distinct sounds in other places, notably Quebec). This change in pronunciation explains why French children write A2M'1 (literally, *à deux m'un*) for *à demain*. *Un* used to be pronounced *uhn* but it is now pronounced so it rhymes with *demain*. A similar process of merging is happening with two pronunciations of the vowel E. The È (*eh*) is moving towards É (*ay*), which is why *La Croix*'s sample SMS message read *Je V* for *je vais*–such a shorthand could not have occurred three generations ago, when *vais* was pronounced *veh*.

Of course, these changes in pronunciation apply mainly to Paris, and are not happening in other parts of France or in the francophonie at the same pace, if at all. A Quebec teen not already familiar with the expression would probably have to make a real effort to decode a French teen's "*Je VO6né. A2M'1*" (although the codes are crossing the Atlantic). And the process is advancing quickly in France. A recent cover of the French magazine *Historia*'s language special edition said "*1539: f1 du Lat1*" (*f'un du Lat'un*, or *fin du Latin:* the end of Latin).

In addition to pronunciation, some considerable shifts in French grammar are taking place. The way to ask questions, for example, has changed. In 1900 the acceptable way of asking "What is a cormorant?" was "*Qu'est un cormoran?*" Today, there are five ways to ask the question: "*Qu'est-ce qu'un cormoran?*"; "*Qu'est-ce que c'est qu'un cormoran?*"; "*Qu'est-ce que c'est, un cormoran?*"; "*Un cormoran, c'est quoi?*"; and "*C'est quoi un cormoran?*" Finally, in France and throughout the francophonie, speakers are tending more and more to substitute *on* (one) for *nous* (we) and drop the *ne* in the negative in *ne . . . pas*.

But the most considerable change in grammar has been the almost total extinction of an entire verb tense, the *passé simple* (simple past). This is true throughout the francophonie. Nobody says *je marchai* (I walked). They say *j'ai marché* (literally "I have walked," but understood as "I walked"). The *passé simple* is now restricted to some genres of literature and used only in the first or third person singular. In everyday speech it has been replaced by the *passé composé* (equivalent of the present perfect) or the *présent historique* (the present tense used to convey the past).

This shift is not happening because francophones are losing their capacity to conjugate verbs, or their grasp on time. It is happening because verb conjugation in the *passé simple* is clumsy, so speakers decided to find a way around it. French verbs are divided into three groups: the first group, those ending in *-er* (*marcher, manger, chanter*); the second group, regular verbs ending in *-ir* (*finir, salir, rôtir*); and the third group, irregular verbs ending in *-ir, -oir, -aindre, -endre* (*sortir, voir, craindre, rendre*). The endings for most tenses follow pretty much the same pattern for all three groups. For instance, the *imparfait* (imperfect, equivalent of the past continuous) for *marcher* is *je marchais*; for *courir* it's *je courais*; and for *voir* it's *je voyais*. But in the *passé simple,* endings vary according to the verb group, making these verbs *je marchai, je courus, je vis.* In the plural it gets even more complicated: *vous marchâtes, vous courrûtes, vous vîtes.*

Before universal schooling in France, when only a few *lettrés* spoke the language, the *passé simple* stood the test of common usage. But after the Second World War, when millions of people were speaking French in their day-to-day lives, people found the *passé simple* just too complicated. To avoid engaging in linguistic gymnastics every time they opened their mouths, they started using the *passé composé* instead, where the past is marked by a standard auxiliary (*être* or *avoir*) combined with the past participle. Any speaker would need to know the past participle to conjugate a verb in other past tenses anyway. By the same logic, another verb tense, the *subjonctif imparfait* (past subjunctive), has been completely assimilated to the present subjunctive, or even the regular present tense, because of its clumsiness.

French speakers might not have abandoned the *passé simple* had French grammarians been more attuned to their needs. In Spanish, the Real Academia systematized conjugations, and the simple past is still used. But since no one ever simplified it in French, francophones just voted with their feet and walked away from it. It's not the first time francophones have taken grammatical problems into their own hands, and it won't be the last. Linguist Louis-Jean Calvet has noticed that all the new verbs created since the 1950s have the regular *-er* ending, as in *solutionner*, which is more convenient than the grammatically clumsy *résoudre* (find solutions). In other words, francophones have developed a way of simplifying the verb system on their own, without waiting for academicians to move on the matter. Like many linguists, Calvet believes that it's popular French—not grammarians or the French Academy—that is doing the work of standardizing French today.

The jury is still out, however, on some extreme grammatical oddities of French such as *accord* (agreement in gender and number) of the participles of *verbes pronominaux* (reflexive verbs such as *se parler,* to talk to oneself) and the even more common *accord du participe passé avec avoir* (agreement of participles of verbs whose auxiliary is the verb "to have," as in *j'ai voulu,* I wanted). Normally, French verbs agree with the subject's number—a single person *veut* (wants), but three people *veulent.* And in the participle form, verbs also agree with gender: *elles sont alleés.* However, in the cases of the participle of pronominal verbs and those of verbs that have *avoir* as an auxiliary, things have never been easy. Here, the verb should agree with the object, not the subject, if it is a direct object and the object is placed before the verb. A good example is *je les ai voulus* (I wanted those, or them), where the past participle is put in the plural form even though the subject is singular, because *those* or *them* (the plural direct object) is placed before the verb. As if that's not complicated enough, the rule has plenty of exceptions. Ninety-nine percent of francophones never fully master the exceptions to the rule and require a dictionary, a grammar or a spell checker to get it right. Most francophones who claim to have mastered the rule have actually just learned to avoid the exceptions.

Strangely, nobody has dared to challenge the *accord* rule in order to simply make all participles agree with the subject. This is all the more surprising since the problem of agreement of participles pops up in regular use much more than the complicated *passé simple* does—and francophones did away with that. The reason no one has challenged the *accord* rule is probably that most participles in agreement, even if they are written differently, are pronounced the same way in conversation. That makes it easy for francophones to hide their ignorance. "*Je les ai voulues*" and "*Je les ai voulu*" sound exactly the same. But it's a different matter in writing. Why have so few writers dared challenge the existing rule? They are probably afraid of looking ignorant or illiterate.

We are toying with the idea of doing away with the agreement-of-participle nonsense in the French edition of this book. We will probably have to negotiate this as part of our publishing contract and include an explicit warning to our readers about the change. Even then, we may not overcome resistance from our editors.)

Though French has undergone—and is still undergoing—some significant changes in pronunciation and grammar, neither of these topics attracts nearly as much commentary as the appearance of new words does. New vocabulary and new definitions of existing words are the most visible and spectacular evidence that French is changing. Even foreigners with very little command of French comment on them.

But in a way, new words are the least significant of the changes happening in the language. Vocabulary and definitions shift all the time. A 1976 study of words in the authoritative *Larousse* dictionary showed that, between 1949 and 1960, French dictionaries modified one entry in seven, by changing definitions or by replacing words with others. There is no reason to believe that this process has either slowed down or accelerated in recent years. Dictionaries simply have a limited number of pages, and editors are forced to shed obsolete words in order to make room for new ones. One difference is that while borrowings among international languages used to come from varied sources, now most come from English. That makes them more noticeable, but not necessarily more numerous, nor a bigger threat.

For that matter, words that disappear aren't necessarily gone forever. Before the 1960s the word *obsolète* was itself regarded as obsolete. It reappeared in French most likely because the same term was being used in English. Sometimes the source of the "re-entry" words is documented; for instance, Charles de Gaulle, a very well-read statesman, was notorious for dragging archaic terms such as *quarteron* (small band) out of obscurity for his speeches. In many cases, however, the source remains obscure. One of the great curiosities of French slang in the 1990s was the reappearance of the world *maille* (dough, in the sense of money, a meaning that dates back to the Middle Ages).

The language used in *les cités* is an important source of new vocabulary. The main form of jargon is a word-crunching system called *verlan*, whose origins date back to the seventeenth century. *Verlan* has been popular in France's suburbs since the 1970s. It consists of reversing syllables and writing them phonetically; the term itself is *verlan* for *à l'envers* (in reverse). It has produced one of the most interesting expressions of the political landscape in France: *les beurs, verlan* for *rab*, the Arabic term for Arabs, referring to French of North African descent.

The jargon of the *cités* is evolving constantly and regularly entering mainstream usage, often through publicity. Suburban kids don't speak of *français* but rather *céfran*. The *beurs* who make it to the middle class are now called *les beurgeois*. A *femme* (woman) is *meuf*, a *flic* (cop) is *keuf*, *mère* (mother) is *reum*, *père* (father) is *reup* and a *prof* (teacher) is a *frop*. *Verlan* goes as far as reverlanizing its terms, so that Arabs, first *beurs*, have become *rebeus*, and *femmes*, first *meufs*, have become *feums*. *Comme ça* (like that) was first verlanized as *comme aç*, then as *askeum*, and then as *asmeuk*.

Verlan is closely associated with another popular form of argot called *tchatche*, which is strongly influenced by Arabic. The word *tchatcher* comes from Algerian argot and means *to chat*— itself a derivation of the Spanish *chacharear*. Some *tchatche* terms, including the word *tchatche* itself, have made it into mainstream French. A famous example is *niquer*, derived from Algerian slang for *fuck*. Although the words that make it into mainstream French are mostly of Arabic origin, Wolof, the principal language of Senegal, has contributed words such as *gorette* (woman), while Malian contributed *intourie* (you're crazy).

The use of French slang (whether argot, *tchatche* or *verlan*) is, of course, controversial in a language culture that is strongly normative. Purists consider it linguistic garbage, while linguists and artists tend to see it as a great source of creativity. Linguist Henriette Walter argues that rather than being a sign of the degeneration of French, the wordplay inherent in these slangs demonstrates a highly developed taste in vocabulary and great mastery of expression in its users. Some of the terms used in contemporary argot are truly stunning. Around 2000 a new term for a cop appeared: *kisdé*, an abbreviation of *celui qui s'déguise* (the guy in disguise). One of the most comical, picked up by linguist Jean-Pierre Goudaillier, was the expression *barre-toi* (get out of here), which was verlanized into *barre-oit* and then transformed into . . . Barry White!

Language commentators may not like argot terms like these, but they certainly can't hail them as evidence that the vocabulary of the French is becoming impoverished. On the contrary, young people use more words, not fewer. They speak in two registers: mainstream French (at school) and *verlan* or other argots on their own. In one situation they might say "*J'aime beaucoup son rap*" ("I like his rap") and in another, "*J'kiffe grave son rap.*"

Argot is not going to show up in the Academy's diction-ary any time soon, but commercial dictionaries such as *Le Robert* and *Larousse* include terms that have entered the Parisian mainstream. For example, more than forty words are being used in French for money, including *fric, pognon, grisby* and *thune*. Things don't just *brûlent* (burn) anymore, they *crament*. And when it's cold, *ça caille*. "*C'est la galère*" ("It's a grind"—from the word *galley*, or slave ship) has produced the verb *galérer* (to struggle), which in turn produced the noun *galérien* (unem-ployed). This expression has even been verlanized into *lèrega*. Someone learning French at the Alliance française in New York City is unlikely to learn such terms, but that doesn't make them any less a part of mainstream French. Many of these words and expressions have even been in use for three or four generations.

Not surprisingly, artists, musicians, writers and poets have always been more open and attuned to new words and expressions than have the general population or even teachers. In the 1970s, popular singer Renaud made history by releasing the first record with a *verlan* title, *Laisse béton*, *verlan* for *laisse-tomber* (drop it). Some authors, including Louis-Ferdinand Céline and Raymond Queneau, have based much of their literary creativity on this popular linguistic register. Queneau famously opened his novel *Zazie dans le métro* with the line "*Doukipudonctan?*," a phonetic rendition of "*D'où qu'i' pue donc tant?*" or "Where does he stink that much from?" This example, which dates from 1959, shows that text-only phonetic jargon is nothing new and that today's language commentators are a bit hasty to pin the responsibility for it on teenagers. One of the craziest wordsmiths of the French language was author Frédéric Dart, better known under the name of his main character and narrator, San Antonio, whose language was completely loose, mixing argot and regional forms of all kinds with his own inventions. Dart, who sold two hundred million copies of his novels over his lifetime, is believed to have created no fewer than ten thousand French words and expressions.

Today French teenagers may speak of a girl's *balcon* (balcony) or her *châssis* (chassis). The terms may not be in the best of taste, but they get the idea across. Of course, expressions like these offend schoolteachers, parents and purists of all kinds, who often don't understand them. But that should be no surprise. Such variations are specifically designed to be subversive, if not seditious; teenagers don't want teachers and parents to understand them. To some extent, this kind of rebelliousness is predictable when a group of conservative purists pretend to "control" French. But not all linguists buy the purist line. Gérald Antoine, editor of the twenty-sixth volume of the *Histoire de la langue française,* for one, claims that the French language "has never had this many poets!"

Borrowings from English are, of course, another important source of new vocabulary in French. The phenomenon was quite minor until the 1920s, but since then, thousands of

English words have entered French usage. Anglophones who visit Paris (or Montreal for that matter) are often surprised—some pleased, some disappointed—to see how very present English words and expressions are, especially in publicity. But while English words provoke strong reactions from everyone, they probably don't pose as grave a threat to French as most people assume they do, especially in France. A study showed that in a newspaper such as *Le Monde* only one word in 166 was actually a borrowing. Linguists have demonstrated that less than one percent of French speech is composed of such borrowings.

The main reason that English words are not a threat is that most are either fully integrated into French or swiftly abandoned. According to linguist Françoise Gadet, most borrowings from English are either Frenchified within a decade or fall into disuse. In 1964 French linguist René Étiemble wrote a scathing pamphlet called *Parlez-vous franglais?* (*Do You Speak Frenglish?*), meant to warn his compatriots against the growing number of English words seeping into their language. Twenty years later, hundreds of the English words he used as examples had already gone out of style and were no longer being used (he subsequently argued that this was the effect of his book).

The few linguists who do cross-linguistic comparison point out that French is never affected by anglicisms as much as German or Italian is. When French speakers like an English concept, they tend to make it their own very quickly. In some cases a French alternative is proposed, such as *informatique* for computer science or *baladeur* for Walkman. A computer bug became *un bogue,* which produced a series of derivatives: *boguer, déboguer* and *débogage.* From football, *Le Monde* journalists have produced *le foot,* but also *footeux* (football amateur), *footophile* (a fan), *footocratie* and even *footballistoïde* (footballistic-ish). In Quebec the drug universe borrowed *faire un trip,* which has since spawned the variations *triper* (trip), *tripant* (cool) and *tripatif* (exciting). But these terms are now so fully French that they must be retranslated using unrelated English terms. Many English borrowings are not of vocabulary but of meaning—people speak of *réaliser* in the sense of *to understand* when it used to mean *to make*. *Compétition* in the English sense has been added to the French sense of contest. *Opportunité*, which used to mean strictly *timeliness*, has been extended to include the notion of *occasion* (as in having the occasion, or opportunity, to meet someone). But even when new meanings are added to previous ones, they don't erase the old ones.

Science, invention, industry, fashion, other technical fields and trends are bringing English words into French at a rapid pace. French has appropriated *scan* and transformed it into the forms *scanneur* and *scannage*. The popular appeal or "cool factor" of English (which we discuss in chapter 19) has been so powerful in France since the Second World War that people have even created faux English terms such as *footing* (walking), *lifting* (facelift) and *pressing* (drycleaning), words that have no relation to their real meaning in English (the way that *déjà-vu* and *potpourri* don't mean the same thing in French as in English; *double entendre* doesn't even exist in French). In other words, even though they sound English, they are French.

Bernard Cerquiglini, former director of the Délégation générale de la langue française et des langues de France (DGLFLF), who now teaches at Louisiana State University Baton Rouge, thinks that the threat of English words to French is overdramatized. "Many English expressions enter French because they are fashionable and fall out of use when they are no longer fashionable. French speakers used to use the expression 'smart' to refer to someone who was well-dressed, but now they don't use it any more than English speakers do." Ironically, to the extent that the French *are* adopting English words, Cerquiglini thinks language purism is to blame. "When you force students to write the old-fashioned *auparavant* (before) instead of the more popular *avant,* or when you forbid them to speak of their computers *qui se plantent* (crash), they end up turning to English. We have to get rid of this conservatism. Why should English have the privilege of describing modernity?"

Cerquiglini is certainly accurate when speaking about a conservative force that is working against changes in French. But non–French speakers are mistaken in thinking that purism is limited to a single identifiable group. The fact is, almost all francophones have a quasi-superstitious belief in the existence of a perfect normative French—mainly, but not only, in writing. Francophones' fierce attachment to the *norme* shows up in their sustained fascination with grammar and spelling contests. Although the famous literary journalist Bernard Pivot ended his televised Dico D'Or dictation contest in 2005, French publisher Albin Michel sells collections of Pivot's best dictations. In 2000, academician Erik Orsenna sold no fewer than a million copies of two books titled *La grammaire est une chanson douce* (*Grammar Is a Sweet Song*) and *Les chevaliers du subjonctif* (*The Knights of the Subjunctive*).

Although purism is, to some extent, a religion or an ideology that unites French speakers, like any religion it has its fundamentalists and its moderates; hence the appearance of various "camps." Non-purists are in fact better described as realists. They believe in the *norme,* but they acknowledge that French is changing, and even embrace that change.

The strange thing is, though the hardcore purists represent only a minute proportion of francophones, they have always set the terms of the debate over French. The basis of their position is the claim that, for centuries now, the French language has been "fixed," and therefore it can't change. By idealizing this fixed French, purists identify any evidence of change as a decline in standards. Almost all francophones buy into this slightly circular reasoning about French's fixedness, at least to a degree. The result has been the creation of a huge class of amateur linguists—journalists, public figures and other commentators—who may not be real purists but who perpetuate the agenda of the purists, sometimes with stunningly contradictory proclamations. For instance, journalists will pin the blame for new words and novelties in French on "youth," claiming they do not know how to write anymore. Meanwhile, other writers and self-proclaimed language experts will blame the journalists themselves for setting a bad example by using casual language in their writing.

The basis for the fundamentalists' claim that French is declining is rather hard to substantiate, to say the least. If the general population of francophones are making more *fautes* than they used to—and this has not really been proven—it's because that population is larger than ever before. As for those who used to write well, the well-educated and the *lettrés*, there is no reason to believe that they write any worse today than they did in the past. Reliable data on long-term changes is hard to find, but the few studies on the topic suggest that the number of mistakes people make today is pretty comparable to the number they made in 1900. In 1987 the linguists André Chervel and Danièle Manesse gave dictation to a group of schoolchildren. The text of the dictation was one found in the archives of the City of Paris that was given to three thousand schoolchildren of comparable age, gender and social class between 1873 and 1877. The old copies had been kept in the records, so the linguists could make a thorough comparison based on hard evidence. They found that not much had changed.

The real question is: How do the purists keep their sway over the masses of French speakers, even outside France? The answer is that almost all francophones today believe in a sort of golden age of French, a time when everyone who spoke French knew how to conjugate the *passé simple* and could spontaneously coin French rhymes (while nibbling pastries at the Marquise's salon . . . .) They imagine that time to be the era of Louis XIV, the second half of the seventeenth century. Perhaps they have been watching too many period films. At any rate, it's pure fiction.

In the supposed golden age of French, the time of Louis XIV, three-quarters of French people could not speak French fluently, if at all. Among those who did, only a fraction spoke "pure" French. The rest undoubtedly spoke with great variation and approximations. French literary icons such as Rabelais, Corneille, Descartes, Racine, Montaigne and Molière wrote French with the undefined spellings of their century and in the spirit of their time—that is, very casually, with plenty of what would be considered *fautes* only a century later. In fact, a careful examination of various editions of the French Academy's dictionary shows that half of French words have changed spelling at least once—sometimes two or three times—since 1694. As we showed in chapter 8, publishers updated the classics to nineteenth-century standards during the great wave of purism that followed the introduction of universal schooling in France. As we said in chapter 8, the result of this gigantic revisionist enterprise was that most francophones today—even the best-read—swear that the geniuses of the past wrote in the standard modern French they themselves learned at school in the twentieth century. This belief, in turn, perpetuates the purist stance that French is fixed and should never change.

In a way, it's surprising these beliefs survived the nineteenth century at all, not to mention the twentieth. While French was spreading rapidly throughout France in the nineteenth century, the French were also in the process of transforming their predominantly agrarian society into a modern consumer and industrial society, open to the world. More people were using French in everyday business, so the language was no longer the exclusive property of an educated elite. As French spread into new segments of society, it needed new words to describe new realities. This called for the development of a modern vocabulary, a process that should have challenged the idea that language was fixed. But it didn't. By 1945 France could finally be considered fully French, but since the school system continued to teach that French was immutable, the myth has remained as strong as ever. Throughout this process France's *élites bien-parlantes* (well-spoken elites) never stopped complaining about the low quality of the French being spoken in France.

The other phenomenon that should have shaken purist dogma was a great shift in sources of standards, resulting from the change and expansion of the traditional language elite. The introduction of universal schooling in France broadened the traditional elite to include a new class of teachers and educated French. When they started to gain influence, it was they, not the French Academy, who decided what was French and what was not. Since the Second World War the mass media (newspapers, radio and TV, the Internet) have in turn competed against this elite (schools, teachers, the *lettrés*) in setting the standards of French. Since then, dictionaries have also multiplied, each with a different approach to the language. *Le Robert* and *Le Multi* (from Quebec) challenge the old certainties of *Larousse* and *Le Littré*. The result is that today, teachers, especially in France, still teach a very purist *norme,* but they must justify their position vis-à-vis the competing models provided by dictionaries and the media—which did not exist fifty years ago.

The other change has, of course, been in numbers. French has become the mother tongue of most French citizens, compared to a mere third at the time of the French Revolution. Since 1945 the population of France has increased by half, and the total number of native francophones, school-francophones or partial francophones in the world has grown to at least three times the population of France. The number of French-speaking countries has multiplied eightfold, each with its own sense of nationhood, which is often tied to language. By 2000 French was spoken by 175 million people in over fifty countries.

So the sources of standards for French have become even more diffuse. Every year new editions of dictionaries land on bookstore shelves in France, and French newspapers report on the new words and definitions at great length. The big surprise in 2006 was the entry in the *Larousse* dictionary of Quebec terms such as *trâlée* (a bunch) and *outarde* (Canada goose), and the addition of Quebec meanings for existing French terms such as *calotte* (in France, a skullcap or ice cap; in Quebec, a baseball cap) and *jambette* (in France, a small furniture leg; in Quebec, tripping someone). When Jean-Benoît went to school in the 1970s, the only dictionaries available were from France, with France-oriented references and examples. Today Quebec schoolchildren, teachers and parents have a choice between those dictionaries and half a dozen local dictionaries.

Yet despite all these new—and broadly accepted—sources of standards for French, and even though linguists and language historians have shown that belief in the *fixité* of the French language is pure superstition, the stance of conservative purists hasn't changed. They still invoke the principle of *fixité* to reject new words and expressions, arguing that they don't conform to the language used in the French classics. No institution has openly challenged them on this, which is strange, since French speakers everywhere use their language in a multitude of ways in everyday life and with a casualness that would make many academicians roll over in their graves.

But francophones still believe in the *norme,* so instead of challenging purists, they have developed a kind of doublespeak about their language. Everyone knows that in real life variations occur and that people in different places use French differently, but they still pretend these variations don't exist or dismiss them as illegitimate (since they don't conform to the *norme*), at least in public.

While showdowns between the purists and the realists are ongoing, there is nothing black and white about the struggle over standards and who sets them. The lines between conservative purists and language realists shift constantly. The French Academy itself has played both sides. While to some extent the Academy operates as the head office of language purism, purism was once a progressive force (as we discuss in Chapter 8). But even in recent history the Academy has, from time to time, acted as a progressive force. For example, in 1901–5, the Academy proposed a significant spelling and grammar reform to the French government. The new elite of teachers and *lettrés* that was gaining influence at the time rejected the reform. When the Academy released its dictionary thirty years later, it didn't include the very changes it had recommended earlier, again because of opposition from this group.

Nearly a century later, another group of language reformers took up the cause again and the Academy sided with them. In the late 1980s a group of linguists who were part of the Conseil supérieur de la langue française (High Council of the French Language) proposed a quite progressive spelling reform that would eliminate the circumflex accent in most words and rationalize the plurals of hyphenated words and anomalies in spelling and grammar. In all, it proposed modifying the spellings of some two thousand words, or about five percent of the Academy's dictionary. The French government accepted the recommendations and promoted them as the new standard for government publications and exams. In 1990 the French Academy–some of whose members had been working with the Conseil and the government on the reforms–officially accepted the changes. Once again the Academy had been on the side of reform.

And once again public outrage killed the reform–outrage from the press, intellectuals and authors, but also opinionated members of the public, the amateur linguists we referred to earlier. Some journalists argued that the reform would make the classics unreadable (forgetting that the classics had been completely overhauled in the nineteenth century). One famous literary critic, who had actually been on the Academy's reform committee, opposed the removal of the circumflex accent on the grounds that it would change the aesthetics of the language. But most of the protest boiled down to the fact that people were afraid that if they used the new spellings they would look as though they didn't know how to write. In a culture where the spelling of *nénuphar* (water lily) with a *ph* had been driven into the heads of millions, who would dare be the first to spell it with an F?

In the end, the reform was implemented by some, not by others. *Le Robert* dictionary accepted it, but not *Le Larousse*. It was adopted in France, but never widely taught. (A similar reform of German spelling and grammar took place at about the same time and was sunk after a very similar controversy.) In all fairness, some of the opposition came from the fact that the reform was too timid–a *réformette*, really–and should have instead attacked some of the major stumbling blocks in French grammar. Nevertheless, the Academy had been at the forefront of reform, challenging the reactionary purists.

However, seven years later, in a more typical gesture of conservatism, the Academy refused a proposal from politicians to officially feminize all job titles. Since French has no neutral gender and the role of neutrality falls to the masculine gender without exception, women ministers, judges, professors and captains are not called *la ministre, la juge, la professeure* or *la capitaine*. These titles are reserved for the *wives* of ministers, judges, professors or captains. A female minister in France is *Madame LE ministre*. As part of the women's movement, Quebeckers began feminizing all titles in the late 1970s. So today in Quebec, people use *auteure, écrivaine, ingénieure, professeure* and *avocate* for female authors, writers, engineers, professors and lawyers.

In 1986 a French political commission studied the feminization of some five thousand job titles and made proposals along the lines of those adopted in Quebec. But they ran into a brick wall at the Academy, whose members categorically rejected the idea on grounds that the reform would "attack the neutrality of the functions." (Actually, they didn't mind if trades like butchers took a feminine form, but feminizing functions like "minister" was another matter.) The issue resurfaced in 1997 when a new socialist government appointed a number of female ministers who took the title *la ministre*. Once again the French Academy rose to the defence of *le bon français* and officially opposed the new titles, even though they were widely used.

The Academy has not budged on the issue since 2000, despite the fact that the new permanent secretary is a woman. As we mentioned in chapter 3, Hélène Carrère d'Encausse refuses to be called *Madame la secrétaire perpétuelle* and adamantly maintains that she is *le secrétaire perpétuel*. When we heard her explain her position to French teachers during the conference in Atlanta, we saw many heads shaking in disagreement. Yet most French teachers are under the sway of purism, and we suspect that many of them would actually have rejected the spelling reform Carrère d'Encausse's predecessor had pushed for in 1990.

At the end of her speech we asked Carrère d'Encausse to explain her rationale for opposing feminization of titles. She told us that the Academy's job was to "consecrate usage" and that the feminization of titles was not in usage. In reality, the French Academy and the French administration stand as the last bastions of resistance to this change, because most French media (not to mention most French people) already feminize titles in everyday speech and use *la ministre* and *la juge* when referring to the women who hold these titles (they are not talking about the minister's or the judge's wife). Following the Quebec practice, more and more francophones everywhere feminize titles spontaneously. Switzerland even made it an official practice in 2002.

What francophones don't seem to understand is how discourse on the decadence of French is used to camouflage the real motives of the most extreme purists. In the opinion of famous linguist Claude Hagège, this insistence on the decadence of French is, more than anything, the expression of a class struggle over who gets to set the standard. Most purists' rants about declining French are simply cleverly disguised criticisms of what they regard as bad taste or unacceptable styles of speech. In Atlanta, Hélène Carrère d'Encausse railed against declining French by citing examples of contemporary creation such as *je positive*, literally, "I positivate." The use of the word *positive* as a verb may be offensive to good taste, but it is more a style of speech than an example of the corruption of the French language. Carrère d'Encausse was, in fact, using a common rhetorical tactic among language purists: She packaged her own personal distaste for certain expressions (rather dramatically) as an objective observation of the corruption of the French language.

In fact, many purists are amateur linguists and have no real leg to stand on when it comes to making claims about the decline of French. Permanent secretary and self-proclaimed guardian of the French language though she is, Hélène Carrère d'Encausse is a Russia expert of note, not a linguist, so her judgement on such matters is questionable. For that matter, in the past 130 years only two members of the French Academy, Emile Littré and Gaston Paris, have been trained linguists, and they died in 1881 and 1903 respectively.

Will French speakers someday overthrow the reign of purism and block out the cacophony of amateur linguists? Having had the doctrine driven into their heads for over a century, the idea that there are *many ways of writing French* is not an easy one for French speakers to accept, at least openly. At the same time, modern forms of French show that *speakers* are using the language more casually than they have since the Renaissance. Like French writers prior to the seventeenth century, many modern speakers are fearless about exploring the potential of the language. And more and more, they just don't care about the judgement calls of the purists.

Shocking as this may be to purists, there is not much they can really do to stem the change. Their influence is, in reality, limited to the sphere of beliefs. Of course, francophones still believe in the *norme.* But as they demonstrated with the *passé simple,* if the language doesn't suit them, they won't wait for anyone's permission to change the rules. And as the sources for standards in French continue to multiply, purists will have a harder and harder time maintaining order in their own ranks, let alone pretending to dictate the rules.

Chapter 18

PROTECTING THE FUTURE

WHY HAS FRENCH REMAINED influential even though it has slipped to ninth or twelfth place among the world's languages in number of speakers? One reason, without a doubt, is that francophones have been effective in devising and applying measures to protect their language and culture. But there are many myths and misconceptions about language protection, especially where it concerns French. In fact, few people actually understand the point of language protection, let alone how it works.

The first, and perhaps biggest, myth is that francophones are the only people in the world trying to protect their language. Jacques Leclerc, a professor of linguistics at the Université Laval in Quebec City, has created a gigantic and authoritative website entitled *Aménagement linguistique dans le monde* (Language Planning throughout the World), which studies the policies of more than 150 countries and thousands of sub-jurisdictions. Whether the policies come from the top or the bottom, are implicit or explicit, targeted or general, most countries have them in some form. Most are indirect. Japan, for instance, requires all subsidized studies to be published in Japanese. The United States has no official federal policy, but states have countless indirect policies to reinforce English; no fewer than thirty-five American states have declared English their only official language, as protection against Spanish. If such measures are necessary when English is the world's dominant language, it should come as no surprise that French speakers do the same. The big difference is that francophones are more explicit about it.

The second myth is that language protection is the job of the French Academy. The Academy is typically (and not incorrectly) considered an archaic institution that is trying to ward off modernity by shielding French from the world around it and retreating into a comfort zone of linguistic certainty. But the Academy's role in language protection is greatly exaggerated. Its job—like that of all language academies—is to define the language, not to protect it. In some cases protection and definition go hand in hand, but even where the two objectives overlap, the French Academy plays a nominal role at best in language protection—though this doesn't reduce its symbolic role in francophone culture, which is enormous.

In France, language protection is the job of a set of terminology commissions and the Délégation générale à la langue française et aux langues de France (General Delegation to the French Language and the Languages of France), part of France's ministry of culture. The commissions' mandate is to monitor the use of foreign—mostly English—terminology in French industry and institutions and to propose French equivalents. Then the Delegation sends the commissions' recommendations to the Academy, which more or less rubber-stamps them. But the recommendations are not law; only civil servants are required to follow them, and only in relation to their jobs.

Most of the world's languages have an academy, institute, committee, council or commission that serves as the ultimate authority on standards—English, which has no such body, is the exception. One of the purposes of our field trip to Israel was to visit the Hebrew Language Academy in Jerusalem, which provides the most impressive case of language engineering (along with Turkey). Hebrew had been a dead language until 1878, when Eliezer Ben Yehuda decided to resuscitate it. In 1881 Ben Yehuda moved to Palestine and founded the Hebrew Language Council, which gained official status after the creation of the state of Israel in 1948 and was renamed the Hebrew Language Academy in 1953.

The function of the Hebrew Language Academy makes it a hybrid between the French Academy and France's terminology commissions. It works on standards of grammar and spelling, but it also seeks to replace foreign terms with Hebrew equivalents. As terminologist Barak Dan explained to us in his office on the campus of Hebrew University, the HLA has no more power than the French government does to impose Hebrew equivalents by force. Sometimes a word can take decades to come into use. In the 1960s, for instance, the HLA came up with a word for *cassette.* No one used it until the 1990s, when the media picked it up, after which it became so common that few people remember that it was an invention of the HLA. "But then, most Israelis don't realize that they speak a language that was entirely created." So, up to a point, language engineering works. The challenge to policy makers lies in finding under what conditions it will work.

Which leads to the next myth, that, for better or for worse, the French have the most aggressive language protection measures among francophones, if not in the world. In terms of cultural protection, that might be argued. But where actual language protection measures are concerned, Quebec has been leading the parade for at least half a century. Not only has Quebec become a model and inspiration throughout the francophonie, it is considered a model in France.

Why Quebec? As Jacques Leclerc explained to us, "The countries where language planning policies have succeeded best are those that deal with a specific problem with clear objectives." In other words, language protection measures are strongest where the threat of assimilation is greatest. Few societies have managed to preserve their language against high odds of assimilation; Quebec, Catalonia and Israel are among the rare examples. The case of Quebec stands out for one reason: It was the first society to go head to head with English—and succeed. That's one reason why francophones, including the French, follow Quebec's lead.

Which leads to the biggest misconception of all: that language protection is essentially defensive, motivated by nostalgia, and aimed at blocking out change. Language protection has a bad reputation, perhaps because the Anglo-American press associates it with defensiveness and insecurity (especially when these measures are directed against English). Francophone measures to protect French are often held up as a sign of weakness, proof that, since French can't survive without the help of laws, it is becoming irrelevant. However, Quebec's language protection measures—and, increasingly, France's—were designed not to shield French but to empower it and to make sure it could name, describe and participate in the modern world so that its speakers wouldn't need to constantly turn to English. Better than anyone, Quebeckers know that if they don't keep their language relevant, English will be waiting at the door. That's why Quebec became a world leader in language protection.

Quebec's leap into modernity and its language protection policies were parts of the same process.

During the first half of the twentieth century, all French Canadians came to understand how vulnerable their culture was to assimilation. In North America, all the aspects of modernity—machines, industry, science and technical expertise of all kinds—were expressed in English. After two centuries of isolation from France, French Canadians had no words for the new realities they were encountering, and were quickly becoming a mental colony of English-speaking North American society. One vestige of this period is Quebeckers' habit of pronouncing foreign and specialized terms with an English accent, even if they are perfectly acceptable in French. That is changing, but Jean-Benoît remembers a time when his own father pronounced *à l'anglaise* words such as *cigar* and *guitare*. After the Second World War Quebeckers realized they needed to act decisively. The process began in 1959, when André Laurendeau, editor-in-chief of the Montreal daily *Le Devoir*, argued that Quebec needed more than newspaper columns on French to retain its language. Laurendeau called for the creation of an official institute of linguistics to improve the general quality of French in Quebec.

But it was one of Laurendeau's readers, a modest cleric named Jean-Paul Desbiens, who picked up the idea and really forced the issue to the forefront of public consciousness. Writing under the pseudonym "Frère Untel" (Brother Anonymous), Desbiens published a dozen resounding letters in *Le Devoir* urging French Canadians to take control of their language. His first letter called for the creation of a provincial office of linguistics. "Language is public property," he wrote, "and it is up to the State to protect it. The State protects the moose, the partridge and the trout. . . . Language is also a common good and the State should protect it just as strictly. An expression is well worth a moose, a word is worth a trout."

Laurendeau's and Desbiens's ideas about language protection snowballed. In 1961 the newly elected Liberal government created the Régie de la langue française (French Language Commission). At first the Commission's goal was almost pedagogical: to convince Quebeckers that they could live modern urban lives in French, a revolutionary idea at the time. The Commission sent linguists to France to research vocabulary there and bring back words to describe railways, planes, cars, textiles and power plants. Over the next fifteen years the Commission produced a number of lexicons of terminology for the automobile industry, the energy sector and sports.

The Commission published dozens of specialized booklets describing the proper French terms for different sectors and creating new French words where none existed. Some of its proposals, such as *hambourgeois* (hamburger), *gaminet* (T-shirt) and *oiselet* (birdie), never took root, but a golf green did become a *vert,* a hockey puck a *rondelle* or a *disque,* and a baseball pitcher a *lanceur.* Most Quebeckers don't think twice about using these terms today, and Quebec constantly updates its vocabulary to keep up with the times. In Quebec some car mechanics still talk about *le muffleur* and *le wipeur,* but most mechanics are now trained in schools that use French vocabulary: *pare-chocs* and *essuie-glace.*

The reform movement in Quebec in the 1960s was powerful, and Quebeckers quickly realized that to save French in North America they needed powerful tools, not just new words. During the 1960s some highly publicized studies opened French Canadians' eyes to the social and economic roots of assimilation. They realized that they were at the bottom of the wage ladder everywhere in Canada. Even in Quebec, francophones were better paid when they spoke English. In Canada linguistic assimilation was a one-way street, and Quebeckers knew they needed political tools to get the traffic rolling in both directions—or even just to hang on to their language.

At the same time, Quebeckers realized that immigration was threatening their language. Quebec's view of immigration as a potential cultural threat has always been controversial in officially multicultural Canada, but its stance is not surprising. In the decades after the Second World War, more than seventy-five percent of immigrants to Quebec chose to school their children in English, even though more than eighty percent of Quebec's population was French. By the 1960s it was plain that Quebec women were no longer willing to produce ten or twelve children as they once had, so allowing immigrants to continue assimilating to English threatened to definitively shift Quebec's linguistic balance. In 1969 the Quebec government made a first timid attempt to pass a language law that would force immigrants to learn French and that promoted its use in the workplace. In 1974 the government passed another law: Law 22, *Loi sur la langue officielle,* a framework for a full-fledged language policy that used both carrots and sticks.

In 1976 the separatist Parti Québécois took power and the following year passed Law 101, *Charte de la langue française* (Charter of the French Language). French was made the official language of the province and declared the language of commerce, business, government and education. The law converted André Laurendeau's Régie de la langue française into the Office québécois de la langue française and gave it a much broader mandate than simply keeping an eye on terminology. It included measures to *franciser* (Frenchify) business, and others that applied to the ministries that dealt with education, immigrants, and professionals such as doctors, lawyers and engineers. According to the new law, business signs in Quebec had to be in French and businesses with more than fifty employees had to obtain a certificate of *Frenchification* to prove that they were using French in daily communication. The law stipulated who could keep and who would lose the privilege of schooling their children in English-language public schools: Children already in the English system could continue, but all new immigrants had to send their children to French-language schools (unless they chose unsubsidized private schools, in which case the law did not apply). The government did allow

English-speaking children to be schooled in English if their parents had been schooled in English in Quebec, and the privilege was later extended to the children of parents who had been schooled in English anywhere in Canada.

The law was not well accepted by Quebec's English community, to put it mildly (some of them still refer to it as Bill 101, as if it had never become law), or by the federal government. The issue made waves across the country from the beginning, and the controversy lasted well into the 1990s. Many Canadians disagreed with the very principle of such a law, on the basis that language should be a matter of individual choice—ignoring the fact that late-nineteenth-century assimilation policies in Canada and the U.S. had been designed to protect English *against* French. Almost all the law's articles were challenged in the courts. But most of the acrimony the charter caused in Quebec came not from the law itself, but from the way it was applied. The main bone of contention was the so-called Commission of Protection, whose agents were dubbed the "tongue troopers." English-speaking Quebeckers considered their nitpicking over lettering on signs (the French letters were supposed to be three times larger than any English), or even business cards, as harassment—in some cases, with reason. Although the tongue troopers became notorious, their activity was only sporadic. The Liberal government abolished them in 1993; the Parti Québécois reinstated them in 1997, and then reabolished them in 2002. "At the moment, complaints against companies are dealt with by the advisor in charge of *Frenchification*," Guy Dumas, deputy minister of the Secrétariat à la langue française, told us. Dumas oversees the application of the language policies in the various ministries. "This approach is much better accepted because we try to help businesses rather than sanction them."

Law 101 provoked a lot of Quebec-bashing in both the Canadian and American media. American journalists thought that anglophone Quebeckers had lost their rights to an English-speaking lawyer and trials in English, and even to education and health services in English. The ideas were alarming, but mostly false. At the time of the law's twentieth anniversary, in 1997, the government of Quebec wanted to respond to these misconceptions, so Guy Dumas organized four focus groups in Washington, New York City, Chicago and Atlanta. "We gave a questionnaire to a group of opinion makers and collected the answers, then used the opportunity to give them the right answers," remembers Dumas, who is himself married to an Australian-born, Toronto-raised epidemiologist. "They believed that there were no English public schools in Quebec and that people had no right to speak in English at trials. Some even believed the basic principle of our law was that people were guilty until proven innocent!" Now, nearly thirty years later, the controversy in Canada over the law has waned. It still has its sharp critics, but the general principle is largely accepted. The Supreme Court of Canada is often called upon to rule on specific points of the law's application, but it no longer demands "proof" of the need to protect the French language, a strong indication that the Supreme Court adheres to the basic principle and necessity of language protection in Quebec. At the same time, individual plaintiffs regularly challenge the validity of the law in the courts, and this keeps the Quebec government on its toes.

More important, time has shown that the language law is not only balanced, but also effective. French is now the predominant language of the province. Even in Montreal, where most of the anglophone community and most immigrants live, the situation is best described as one of linguistic peace. And while English remains a force to contend with, language assimilation is no longer a one-way street. Quebec's anglophone community has in fact become much more bilingual than the francophone majority. Immigrants still resist the idea of learning French, but most have accepted the situation and are progressively assimilating to the francophone majority. The face of Montreal, which was English only forty years ago, is now predominantly French. The law does not affect trade-marks, but many companies have chosen to modify their name in order to appeal to local customers. In Quebec, Kentucky Fried Chicken is known not as KFC, but as PFK (Poulet Frit Kentucky), even though in France it remains KFC. And software companies are managing to translate for the Quebec market.

At the turn of the millennium the Office québécois de la langue française refined its approach to its two basic missions of Frenchifying business and creating French terminology. A com-pany seeking its certificate of francisation is evaluated on dozens of criteria, including how the company communicates with its employees and the public. Companies with more than a hundred employees must create a *comité de francisation* (Frenchification committee) composed of equal numbers of representatives of employees and executives. Eighty percent of Quebec companies with more than fifty employees are certified.

Contrary to a popular Canadian myth, the Quebec gov-ernment doesn't have much power to change signs that aren't in French or to actually force Frenchification on large companies. The Office doesn't try to convert businesses to French; it just makes sure that the employees' right to work in French and the public's right to communicate in French are respected. Another popular myth has it that the tongue troopers issue fines. In reality, companies that refuse to comply are taken to court. "Ninety percent of them seek an out-of-court settlement," says Dumas. The government doesn't have the power either to close companies or to remove products from shelves. "But those who refuse to comply with the law cannot get subsidies or do busi-ness with the government," says Dumas.

On the other hand, as Guy Dumas explained to us, the Office realized over time that it could not let its guard down. "At the beginning we thought that the certificate of Frenchification was enough, but then we saw that, to make the measure effective, we had to ask companies to report every three years on their linguistic situation [another condition for obtaining the certificate]." Indeed, changes in ownership or even in personnel mean that the idea of using French has to be driven home again and again. Chrysler now produces manuals in French, but Chrysler's latest Model 300 came out with a computer that displayed extremely faulty French, including *"Bas Fluide de Rondelle"* for "Low Washer Fluid" instead of *"Bas Niveau de Lave-glace."*

The Office typically has other problems with smaller businesses. Although businesses with fewer than fifty employees aren't required to have certificates of Frenchification, their signs must give precedence to French. Out of rebelliousness, or mere practicality, some Montreal merchants push the limits of acceptable French on their signs. We walk regularly in Montreal's Mount Royal Park, and on our way there we pass a garage that was once called George General Auto Repair. To respect the language law, George just added a few letters to his sign by hand; it now reads, in less than passable French, "George Général d'Auto Réparation."

Terminology is the field in which the Office québécois de la langue française really excels; even the French use it as a reference. There are many reasons for Quebec's strong performance. One is size: the Office québécois de la langue française has 215 employees, sixty of whom are terminologists, whereas France's equivalent, the DGLFLF, has about thirty employees and seven terminologists and depends largely on volunteers to report on terms in the workplace. More important, Quebec's terminologists act quickly. Quebec decided long ago that concepts and inventions with English names had to be translated right away, and that catchy French substitutes had to be created before English terms caught on. Quebec's Office monitors new technologies very carefully. This was how they created the famous *courriel* for e-mail, a combination of *courrier* (mail) and *logiciel* (software). The same thinking was applied to junk mail, producing *pourriel*, which combines *pourri* (rotten) and *logiciel*. Another example is *clavardage* (Internet chat), which combined *clavier* (keyboard) with *bavardage* (chat). The latest example of creativity involved the Internet term *phishing*, which they adapted as *hameçonnage* (from *hameçon*, hook). Quebec's language commission doesn't always come up with such great terms as *courriel, pourriel, clavardage or hameçonner*, but in the absence of a good alternative it rapidly Frenchifies English spellings, for example, turning *blog* into *blogue*. The suggestions don't always fly, but many of their terms do take root.

Despite fears and accusations that the language law would isolate Quebec, the province has never been more open to outside influence and ideas than since it applied protective measures. Protection measures have never prevented ideas from circulating, but they circulate in French, and that was the point. "People will speak French if it is modern, if it is up to date," says Dumas. Every year, the OQLF's *Grand dictionnaire terminologique* (*Large Dictionary of Terminology*) receives fifty million requests to translate or verify words, half of which come from Europe. The French Academy's website, in comparison, receives two million requests per year. Over the years Quebec's terminologists have been so effective that they now export their know-how. Quebec was the inspiration and model for the language policy of the Catalan government in Barcelona. And the Brazilian language commission is beginning its work by examining the new ideas from Quebec, which it adapts to Portuguese when it sees fit.

We were surprised to discover that even the French look up to Quebeckers on the issue of terminology creation. This is all the more surprising because it was the French who first confronted the onslaught of English vocabulary, in the 1920s, in reaction to quickly developing and globalizing American industry and technology. In 1937 the French created the Office de la langue française, whose sole purpose was to create French terms to substitute for the English ones creeping into the language. This responsibility was not given to the French Academy, which, of course, is not known for keeping up with the times. Since then France has founded, renamed and refounded a dozen similar offices, commissions, councils, committees and agencies.

In the 1990s it finally settled for Délégation générale à la langue française, later updated with the addition of "*et aux langues de France*" (DGLFLF). Julie visited their office on Rue des Pyramides in Paris. The modern building is no match for the ornate Institut de France, which houses the French Academy, but the DGLFLF plays a far more important role in regulating modern French in France. It coordinates the work of about twenty terminology commissions in eighteen government ministries. The committees comprise professionals in specific fields—engineers or experts in trades, rarely linguists—who work on a volunteer basis to collect terminology being used from foreign languages. Language experts at the DGLFLF then draw up lists of alternatives and send them to the Commission générale de terminologie et néologismes, part of the prime minister's office, for approval. The approved terms are published in the *Journal Officiel*. They are obligatory only for civil servants working in the specific fields to which they apply. According to Bénédicte Madinier, head of language development at the DGLFLF, they are adopted in about seventy percent of cases. The French Academy also views the lists and makes its own recommendations. As the head of the DGLFLF told us, "They only give their opinion at the end of the process." But Bénédicte Madinier told Julie that she was on the phone literally every day with colleagues in Quebec, looking for ideas for French terms to substitute for English professional vocabulary. "In France we don't put nearly as much energy into translating as Quebec does," said Madinier.

Although the French began setting up barriers against English much earlier than Quebeckers did, they have never been as effective at it, mostly because they were never as convinced of its necessity. Unlike Quebeckers, the French don't see English as a real threat to their language—France is not surrounded by a continent of English speakers, as Quebec is. When the French do become alarmed about the influence of English, it is often an echo of foreign policy concerns. French literary critic René Étiemble published *Parlez-vous franglais?* in the early 1960s, when de Gaulle was pushing his program to re-establish France's international status. Similar episodes occurred in the 1970s and the 1990s, for pretty much the same reasons, although it would be false to pretend that such criticisms are purposefully coordinated. Anti-English declarations usually have more to do with diplomatic strategy than language per se.

Institutional responses to the growing use of English terms in France have been mixed. In 1975 and 1994 the French tried to create Quebec-style language laws. The press and, in particular, the French left did not like the law, and ridiculed Jacques Toubon, the minister who sponsored it, by nicknaming him Jacques "All-Good" (a literal translation of his surname). France's Constitutional Council overruled its provision that documents had to be written in French alone, on the grounds that it violated freedom of expression.

Toubon's law is, theoretically, as global as Quebec's French language charter, but it has serious practical limitations. The government forces public institutions and civil servants to use French, but refused to mandate the use of French on signs, although it does require signs to include French translations. Whereas the DGLFLF is in charge of terminology, inspection and policing are carried out by another government service, the Délégation générale de la concurrence, de la consommation et de la répression des fraudes (General Directorate of Competition, Consumer Issues and Suppression of Fraud), which has more important things to deal with. To complicate matters more, the general public cannot file a complaint on language issues directly but must go through one of four recognized associations for the protection of language, which then may or may not take the issue to the courts. This bureaucracy is not totally ineffective, but the system of recourse is so convoluted that it discourages action and reaction on the part of the public.

Why are the French so lax about language protection? Mainly because, unlike Quebeckers, who have to deal directly with the strong presence of English speakers in North America, the French really only have to deal with the growing influence of the English language. That doesn't mean English is not making inroads in France. The French love using English. They think that speckling conversations with English terms makes them seem modern, efficient and fashionable—in short, cool (we return to the problem of this "cool factor" in chapter 19). Over the past few years, French scientists, artists, business people and publicists have taken to communicating in English inside their company laboratories, and even with the public—not for reasons of practicality, but because it lends them a kind of panache (or, as an English speaker would say, a certain *je ne sais quoi*).

The fact is, the French don't really see English as a threat. French is spoken by almost a hundred percent of the population (while there are immigrant ghettos in France, unlike the situation in some other European countries, immigrants in France do not really question the principle of learning the national language). The French Frenchify borrowings from English quickly and spontaneously, usually without any help from language commissions or the French Academy. An older example of this process is the French word for computer, *ordinateur*. It was a creation of IBM France, which in 1954 found it had a problem with the word *computer* in French. Said with a French accent, the syllables of *computer* sound like a combination of the two worst possible insults in the French language: *con* (cunt) and *pute* (whore). A professor of Latin at the Sorbonne, Jacques Perret, proposed the term *ordinateur*, a religious term referring to God as the one who imposed order on the universe. IBM trademarked it, but the word caught on and became a generic term.

However, although France looks to Quebec for terminology suggestions, Quebec's terms don't always go over well with the French. In the late 1990s the French Academy refused the term *courriel* for about five years, on the grounds that it was just a regionalism. It preferred the homegrown *mél* (a contraction of *message électronique*), even though the French terminology commissions had proposed *mél* only as a written short form for business cards, like *Tél* for phone number. The Academy finally endorsed *courriel* in 2004, but is still holding out against *pourriel* and *clavardage*.

Why do French institutions balk at Quebec expressions? There is more to it than plain old snobbery. For one thing, the French have a serious hang-up about neologisms (which we discuss in chapters 8 and 17). They will accept a neologism only if they are certain that there isn't an existing word that will do. Beyond that, this obsession is hard to explain. The French have a special category of words they call *les mots mal faits* (poorly made words), which basically describes anything they don't like. With this circular, and circuitous, reasoning, they accepted *bogue* (computer bug) but not *blogue* (blog), for which they prefer *bloc-notes* (notepad). This latter choice was made despite the fact that the term *bloc-note* means something entirely different and is difficult to turn into verbs and nouns, unlike *blogue*, which has already produced *bloguer* (to blog) and *blogueur* (blogger).

Still, Quebec remains influential in the field of terminology in France and throughout the francophone world. Most francophone countries look to Quebec as an inspiration, including Belgian and Swiss francophones, even though these original domains of French have little to boast of when it comes to defending French against English. Language planning in Belgium and Switzerland is primarily designed to protect French from other national languages, and vice versa. Francophones in Africa and elsewhere also look up to Quebec and tend to be hard on the French for lacking a coherent response to English. Yet they too have little to show in terms of language policies. Of course, this is more understandable in the case of developing countries. For nations whose native languages are in competition with French and whose school systems are failing, the issue of defending French against English is secondary, as indeed it should be.

Though the French might be considered soft on language protection, they do set the standards in terms of cultural policy among francophones and, arguably, in the world. And this has obvious benefits for the French language. Again, though, francophone societies are not the only ones with cultural policies. Because the entertainment industry can translate into billions of dollars everywhere, most advanced countries have clear cultural policies—clearer, in fact, than their language policies—partly because it's easier to put a price tag on culture and entertainment than on language. Even the United States, the only developed nation without a ministry of culture, applies cultural policies. The National Endowment for the Arts spends tens of billions of dollars every year subsidizing museums, artists and other creative people. Many states have their own film policies, and support for the arts is generally ensured by generous tax credits.

Yet France, followed by Canada and Quebec, is regarded as extremely innovative in the cultural policy field. Since François I the French government has been a very active player in the development of culture, as both patron and promoter of the arts. Its policies became more protectionist with the development of the mass media, starting with cinema. In France, the first modern cultural policy was developed to protect national film production in the wake of the First World War, when the war effort had nearly destroyed France's lively film industry, along with most of Europe's. The American film industry had reacted by flooding Europe with cheap silent movies such as Charlie Chaplin comedies. Europeans reacted in turn by slapping quotas on American film productions. The French cinema industry benefited greatly and produced many original filmmakers. Even while France was occupied during the Second World War, its film industry enjoyed a second golden age.

But the Americans didn't give up. After the Second World War, major American producers organized into a powerful lobby, the Motion Picture Association of America, and lobbied the American government to wipe out the quotas. The opportunity popped up when the French asked the U.S. for financial aid for postwar reconstruction. American diplomats responded by demanding what amounted to a reverse quota: At least thirty percent of screen time had to be allotted to American films. With their backs to the wall, the French, like every other country in Europe, had no choice but to accept.

They immediately regretted their decision and spent the next decade developing other means to encourage national film production. In 1947, with the creation of GATT (General Agreement on Tariffs and Trade), Europe managed to get the film industry excluded from trade talks. Over the years they managed to do the same thing with the TV industry.

From then on the French got more creative at finding ways to protect their national film industry. One of their best measures is an eleven percent tax applied to all movie tickets; the money is redistributed only to national producers. Other European countries maintained a laissez-faire approach to the question. The result is that France's film production amounts to twenty-five to fifty percent of overall screen time in France (depending on the year), while national cinema in Britain, Germany and even Italy has virtually vanished. (So it is no wonder that half of the non-English films seen in the United States are French. In all, foreign films amount to only two percent of the U.S. market. Quality or lack of interest from the public is often an issue, but the fact that Hollywood controls distribution is not unrelated to these difficulties.)

In 1994 the French introduced quotas for francophone content on radio, following the same logic they had applied for films. By and large this was the work of a French senator, Michel Pelchat, whom we met at the restaurant of the French Senate, in the Luxembourg Palace in Paris. As Pelchat told us, "In the early nineties, French broadcasters saw French music as corny. The new radio stations had names like Skyrock and FUN." In 1994 he proposed forcing French radio stations to play fifty percent francophone content. The senator received strong endorsement from creative artists and from the head of Virgin France and the former president of Warner France—unlikely allies. As it turned out, the French branches of major U.S. music companies wanted to do more than make millions by selling American pop music; they could make millions *and* develop francophone talent. Even though broadcasters and the Anglo-American press vociferously opposed the measures, Pelchat's bill was adopted by unanimous votes of the Senate and the National Assembly, with a minor modification: The quota of francophone music would be forty percent rather than fifty percent.

In the end, the radio quotas worked to everyone's advantage. The broadcasters' fear of losing their audience proved to be unfounded. The law was also a great boost to the careers of some (now) famous Quebec singers. Céline Dion, for example, was making her re-entry into the French market that very year with a new French repertoire. With her powerful American singing style she was perceived as a welcome change from the usual treacle-voiced French pop singers and (sometimes) corny old-fashioned *chansonniers*. Senegalese rapper MC Solaar's career began to take off around the same time. Today about sixty percent of record sales in France are of francophone musicians. And the top-selling exports of the French music industry are now francophone, not just French, musicians. Aside from English, no other European language has matched the success of francophone music on the French market and abroad. When the law was reviewed in 1999, even more French branches of international music companies gave it their support.

Canada and Quebec didn't figure out that cultural policy should not be left to the private sector until the 1960s, although since then they have become innovative policy makers and outspoken defenders of the principle along with France. The Canadian market is small, but both governments learned that to have their own homegrown cultural products, they needed a toolkit of subsidies, quotas and special laws for the production of magazines, books, music, TV and film.

In Quebec the government worked actively to resurrect its music industry, starting in the early 1980s. In those years Quebec singers could not find a record company because the international record companies had all closed their Quebec offices in a wave of consolidation. The government reacted by creating venture capital funds and special subsidies to develop home-grown music labels. They even created their own music award, the Félix—named after poet Félix Leclerc. In the 1990s Quebec began developing export programs, so when the French radio market opened up in the middle of the decade, Quebeckers were ready to deliver. Since then Quebec has adopted that approach for the book industry, film production and dubbing.

Although Quebec cultural policy is often aimed at defending local turf against American entertainment, the United States is not the only threat. Quebec's policies are directed just as much towards France. Quebec's tax credits for dubbing are aimed specifically at encouraging American film producers to dub their films in Quebec rather than in France. In 1981 the Quebec government developed a policy that forced Quebec libraries to buy books through Quebec booksellers. (The French may welcome Quebec singers with open arms, but the French public trusts only French publishers. In 2004 Quebec sold more books at the Guadalajara Book Fair than at the Salon du livre de Paris.)

In Canada, since the early 1970s, francophone radio and TV have been subject to French content quotas of sixty-five percent and fifty percent respectively. Pelchat's law in France was strongly influenced by Canadian practices and by the active Quebec record industry lobby, which saw a market opportunity. In all, Canada spends no less than three billion dollars a year on culture, and Quebec another six hundred million. These efforts have paid off. The Quebec music industry controls twenty-five percent of its home market, and the book industry forty percent. In film, Canada's performance—five percent of the home market—has more than doubled because Quebec expanded its homegrown film industry from about two percent of the market, ten years ago, to nearly twenty percent in 2005.

To everyone's surprise, Quebec is the only province that is now a net *exporter* of cultural products, with a surplus of 345 million dollars in 2003. (Ontario, Canada's most populous province, is a net importer of culture, to the tune of two billion dollars a year.) Quebec's success in exporting is the result of systematic efforts to build a solid local base. In the past five years, local film productions have even begun to regularly outsell Hollywood blockbusters at the box office. One reason is that Quebec films are getting better. The other is that the Quebec government has got smarter at distributing subsidies to the film industry. Its motivation is still basically the same: Quebec knows that if it doesn't make its own cultural products, someone else will, and they will inevitably be imports.

In the rest of the francophonie, Quebec is seen more and more as a model for cultural policy as well as for language protection. As Pierre Ansay, consul for the Communauté française de Belgique (Francophone Community of Belgium) in Montreal, said, "Quebeckers have managed to create their own star system, not just in TV but in literature. In Quebec, authors don't necessarily have to win Paris awards like the Goncourt, the Femina or the Renaudot to be considered great." By comparison, Belgian authors do have to win one of the six big literary prizes in Paris to be considered great, and they are eligible only if they are published by a Paris publisher. The Belgians, who have to live in the shadow of France, have oriented much of their cultural production towards niche sectors that the French don't cover well, such as documentary film-making, detective literature and comic books, where they excel.

The cultural policies of Quebec, Canada and France are in turn inspiring non-francophone countries to develop cultural policies. Turkey, for instance, applies France's ticket tax system at the box office. France inspired South Korea to reserve forty percent of cinema scheduling for local films. The level of national production jumped from thirteen percent to fifty-one percent of the market in just fifteen years, and South Korea now sends films to the prestigious Cannes Film Festival. Ministers and heads of state often visit the offices of Quebec's Société de développement des entreprises culturelles (Society for the Development of Cultural Enterprises, or SODEC). As SODEC's in-house economist, Marc Ménard, explains, "There is money in culture. Many Third World countries used to think that they could not afford a ministry of culture. Now they realize that they cannot afford *not* to have one. Culture might be their best chance for homegrown development."

France and Canada, with the strong support of Quebec, Belgium and the Francophonie, are now taking cultural protection to the next level and attempting to translate it into international law. Since the beginning of the 1990s trade law has become so important that the rights of states to develop cultural protection policies have been challenged more and more. The American government and the World Trade Organization regard cultural protection measures as policies that obstruct market forces and prevent the free flow of goods and entertainment products.

To counter this position, French-speaking countries managed to get UNESCO to adopt the oddly named Convention on Cultural Diversity in October 2005. For most of the 1990s cultural diversity was referred to as *l'exception culturelle* (cultural exception), a concept that the French conceived in the final stretch of negotiations at the Uruguay Round of GATT talks in 1993.

The Francophonie had given its support to the concept during the Mauritius summit of heads of state the same year. The idea of *l'exception culturelle* quickly gained currency in francophone circles, but very little notice outside of them at first. Even Canadian diplomats regarded it as nothing more than a whim of the Francophonie that didn't apply to them—a country that was mostly English-speaking, a member of the Commonwealth and a close friend of the United States. Canadians thought that the few clauses referring to culture in the WTO and NAFTA treaties were sufficient to protect Canada's cultural policy. Their perspective shifted overnight in 1996, when the United States attacked Canada's measures to protect its magazine industry against American publications. Canada took the issue to the WTO, and the WTO ruled in favour of the United States. English-speaking Canadian diplomats woke up and realized that *l'exception culturelle* was not just a francophone contraption, and France gained its biggest ally in defence of the principle. The Canadians even convinced the French to drop the term *exception culturelle* (which generally irks free traders) and use the more inclusive "cultural diversity" instead.

In the coded world of trade diplomacy, cultural diversity does not refer to multiculturalism or freedom of religion. It relates to the right of nations to support their own culture industry with quotas, subsidies and special laws. The logic of this stance is as follows: Films, books and music cannot be regarded as mere merchandise because their cultural content and symbolic values are central to the identity of nations. So societies must have a right to create regulations that guarantee a place for national production in their home markets. This issue has come up because of the particular economics of culture: Once the production costs of a TV show, a film or a book have been recovered, it can easily be exported at near dumping prices, making sales very profitable. Sounds only fair, but in fact this practice skews the market in favour of countries with the biggest domestic markets, and those whose cultural production is in a major international language. So American TV programs and French books may be sold in Quebec at a fraction of what it costs to produce a local TV program or book.

In 1997 Canada's minister of heritage, Sheila Copps, united a group of culture ministers from sixty different countries who were in favour of cultural diversity. In 2000, Canadian creative artists' associations established the Canadian Coalition for Cultural Diversity, which became the main lobby group on the issue. "We knew we could not just be on the defensive and try to justify our policies every time they were challenged at the World Trade Organization," says Robert Pilon, the executive director. "What we needed was an international accord that took the necessity for cultural policy as a given, not as something for which we should say, 'Sorry, but. . . .' The accord had to be on an equal footing with the WTO, and not subject to its rulings."

Through patient and methodical work, Canada, France and other allies, including Belgium and Senegal, lobbied UNESCO to act on this issue. In 2002 UNESCO decided to create an international Convention on Cultural Diversity that would be binding for signing members—a sort of Kyoto Accord, but for culture rather than the environment. UNESCO got very strong support from the Francophonie, since the concept of cultural diversity was a natural fit with its doctrine of plurilingualism (discussed in chapter 16).

The Convention produced one of the most resounding battles in trade diplomacy in the first decade of this century. The American government, which had quit UNESCO in 1984, rejoined the organization in 2003 to try to water down the accord. But in the end, France and Canada, with the help of Quebec and the Francophonie, managed to convince 161 of the 162 voting countries to sign the Convention—the only opposition came from the United States. The battle is not over, though. The Convention will not become effective until thirty countries ratify it, and its efficiency will depend on the way it is put into practice in the coming years, all the more so since it contradicts some of the basic tenets of the World Trade Organization, according to which any form of goods or service is merchandise, and any form of subsidy obstructs market forces.

Much of this diplomatic success is owed to the work of the Canadian Coalition for Cultural Diversity, which led a very active campaign at home and abroad, rallying national coalitions for cultural diversity in more than twenty-three countries, and acting as their secretariat. Robert Pilon lobbied heads of state and ministers for the better part of five years. Pilon understood the perspective of the American government better than most. Films, he explained, are costlier than ever, and the American economy, as well as the film industry, depends more than ever on exports. This is increasingly true for TV, books and also music. In all, entertainment exports make the biggest contribution to the U.S. balance of trade. "In my opinion, the American government's attitude is not motivated by the will to dominate. Hollywood controls eighty-eight percent of the Australian film market and they have ninety-five percent of Canada, but they *need* ninety-six percent, or ninety-seven percent. They won't stop because they don't have a choice. But then, neither do we!" Pilon did not single out the Americans for opposing the Convention because he knew that the Convention was also designed to protect Quebec from France, and Latin American culture from Spain's.

Why can't culture and language be left entirely to the free market? Over the two years we spent researching this book, we gave careful thought to this question, which is more difficult to answer than it seems. One great myth about the French language, which is entertained by the Anglo-American press in particular, is that France and Quebec are the only societies that have raised language and cultural barriers against the influence of English or against American entertainment (implying that everyone else welcomes them with open arms). This is somehow interpreted as proof that French is on the decline. Yet Canada, Great Britain and Australia all have measures in place to protect their cultural industries against the onslaught of American production—and their cultural production is in English. If such measures are justifiable for culture, it's hard to understand how they wouldn't be justified when they concern another language, which is, after all, the main source and vehicle of culture.

In a way, it is easier to explain why French-speaking countries have been at the forefront of language and cultural protection than to explain why protection measures are necessary at all. When it comes to culture and language, there are good practical reasons for countering the laws of the market. The first reason for supporting cultural diversity is that protecting language and culture allows societies to modernize in their own language, without becoming a mental colony of another, more powerful country. Ivan Bernier, a professor of international trade law at Laval University in Quebec, was trained at the London School of Economics and is one of the world's rare experts on how culture and trade accords are linked. Bernier wrote much of the first draft of the UNESCO Convention. As he told us, "The stakes of cultural diversity are not just a matter of money: They have to do with identity, that is, with the capacity of a Quebecker or a Frenchman to see and interpret the issues of the world in his own terms rather than those of others."

The second, more practical reason is that strong domestic markets are a great boost to trade. As Robert Pilon explained,

> The Convention on Cultural Diversity is not *against* trade. Rather, it sets the stage for more trade—but both ways. At the moment, entertainment is very much a one-way street. But if Quebec exports its music to France, it's because it is good music, and because we have developed our own domestic base; we cannot export without this. And this domestic base was developed thanks to measures of cultural protection. The Convention will bring a more balanced trade in culture by allowing Quebec, or countries like Burkina Faso or Senegal, to develop their own domestic markets as much as they see fit, and then make their own exports.

And this, as it turns out, is exactly what is improving the global perspective of French.

Chapter 19

GLOBAL HESITATIONS

WHILE WE WERE ATTENDING the UNESCO conference on plurilingualism in Tlemcen, Algeria, we were invited for dinner by Abdelkader Tebbal, the most important farmer in the *wilaya* (prefecture) of Tlemcen. Contrary to what we expected, Tebbal and his family didn't live in a farmhouse in the countryside, but in a lovely house in the lower town. We ate hors d'oeuvres in a living room encircled by cushioned benches, and after dinner drank mint tea in a superb courtyard filled with banana trees and grapevines. Like all Algerian families, the Tebbals talked at great length about the civil war. A former fighter in Algeria's war of independence and mayor and deputy of Tlemcen in the 1980s and 1990s, Abdelkader was dismayed to see his country then being torn apart by religious fundamentalism. The Tebbals had their share of horrible stories, but they also spoke of their hope. As proof that things were improving, these avowed francophiles happily informed us that Tlemcen's French Cultural Centre was finally being re-opened after ten years of inactivity.

During dessert Jean-Benoît was surprised to see three copies of a Quebec farming magazine, *Le Québec Agricole,* sitting on the buffet next to the dining table. It turned out that Abdelkader's son, Mohammed, was a veterinarian who specialized in artificial insemination. The Quebec town of Saint-Hyacinthe is a world-renowned centre in the field, so in some ways it was natural that Mohammed would subscribe to Quebec's main agricultural magazine. He and Jean-Benoît were soon joking about a Saint-Hyacinthe celebrity, Starbuck, a bull who had fathered more than a quarter of a million cows during his lifetime and whose sperm was so valuable it outlived him for ten years (he fathered another quarter-million cows post mortem). Mohammed dreamed of visiting the Quebec centre one day and seeing their state-of-the-art techniques for himself.

It was certainly odd to find ourselves in a courtyard in Africa surrounded by banana trees talking with an Algerian veterinarian about the fertility of a bull from Saint-Hyacinthe. Yet there we were. The conversation was all the stranger because it couldn't have happened even a generation ago. But French has globalized tremendously in the past decades. Like English speakers half a century ago, French speakers who live thousands of kilometres apart are busily building networks beyond borders and creating a world of ideas that is spreading across the planet.

It is simply ridiculous to deduce that the world is passing francophones by because they are clinging to their language. English speakers, particularly the British and Americans, have been so effective at building an empire of the intellect that they have branded "global" and "international" as exclusively English-language concepts and virtually synonymous with English: If it's in English, it is therefore global and international, and if it's not, it's local. Since French has a strong reputation as the language of high culture and luxury, people tend to overlook the fact that it is widely used not only in business, but also in research, technology and higher education. The circulation of ideas between different parts of the francophonie today is immense; ideas and concepts travel from Montreal to Casablanca and from Dakar to Brussels—and often skip Paris entirely.

At present the biggest obstacle to francophone globalization is not English, but the French themselves. The French are typically hands-off when it comes to the francophonie. To start with, they don't consider themselves francophones. Some even consider it insulting to be labelled a francophone. To them, *francophone* is a term that applies to speakers of French who are not French. In addition, the term has colonial undertones to many. As a consequence, the French do not feel as strong a bond of solidarity with other societies that speak their language as one might expect them to.

We have already explained (in chapter 18) that the French don't see English as a particular threat to their language the way, say, Quebeckers do. Yet paradoxically they do see English as a threat to French's status as an international language. Actually, many French and francophones alike believe the battle is already over. They claim very seriously that French is finished as an international language and that nobody wants to learn it anymore. Much of the French elite has, at least psychologically, thrown in the towel on French. The Institut Pasteur replaced its famous journal *Les Annales* with an English journal called *Research in Microbiology*. The lure of English is so powerful that Jean-Claude Trichet, president of the European Central Bank, issues communiqués and makes speeches to European deputies in English, even though the only English-speaking country in the euro zone is Ireland.

The consequence of this defeatism and of their luke-warm feelings towards the rest of the francophone world is that, in some ways, the French are really letting the world pass them by. But contrary to what the Anglo-American media tend to argue, the world the French are missing out on is a French-speaking one.

The French language began globalizing, in the modern sense of the term, as soon as France's and Belgium's colonial empires started crumbling. In order to survive and progress on the international stage, newly independent countries turned to other francophone societies in the world. This sparked a movement to create links between francophones. Quebec journalist Jean-Marc Léger was an early pioneer of the movement when he created the International Union of Journalists from the French-language Press in 1951 (discussed in chapter 16). But many others contributed to the circulation of ideas among francophones as well. One of the early advisors of King Sihanouk of Cambodia was an Acadian diplomat named Alexandre Boudreau. In Quebec, Father Georges-Henri Lévesque opened the first school of social science in the 1930s. He trained most of the up-and-coming generation of reformers who would modernize the Québécois and Acadian societies in the 1960s. Then, in 1963, seeing that his ideas were progressing on their own in Canada, Lévesque accepted an invitation to Rwanda, where he opened the Université nationale in Kigali. He ran it until 1972, and even had the honour—rare for a white man—of being named a *père de la patrie* (father of the country) of Rwanda in 1968.

The earliest and most intense networking among francophones took place in the university world. This new phase in the story of French started when francophone scholars created the Agence universitaire francophone in 1961 (see chapter 16). The results are obvious in the world-wide exchange of technologies and expertise today. For instance, Senegal, a rice-eating nation heavily dependent on imported rice, recently hired a hundred Vietnamese agronomists to carry out a multi-year project to develop a homegrown supply of rice—in French.

In 1999, when we lived in France, Jean-Benoît was surprised to see his hometown, Sherbrooke, in the pages of the French daily *Libération*. The newspaper was reporting on a trend among North African students and postgraduates from France of leaving for Canada to pursue their studies, a phenomenon that evidently incensed the journalist. Actually, this was old news in Sherbrooke, home of the first university to develop an MBA program in French, in 1985, and the first to set up an MBA program in Morocco through a partnership with local scholars. The University of Sherbrooke's department of medicine now trains doctors in seventy cities across the francophonie: in Belgium, Switzerland and Morocco but also Brazil, Colombia and Chile—including twenty in France. Among Canadian universities it earns the most from its patents, the most famous of which is the voice compression technology that is vital to the cellular phone industry everywhere in the world. As a result, the city of Sherbrooke, population 125,000, is gradually turning into a lively cultural zone where old-stock Catholic French Canadians rub shoulders with Arab and African graduate students, professors and department heads.

In fact, the Agence universitaire francophone is only the official face of a multi-pronged international network of two hundred thousand francophone scholars and at least as many researchers. Over the past few decades different French-speaking countries have solidified their relationships through this networking, again often completely bypassing France. The Canadian government funded the school of journalism at the University of Dakar, and for about fifteen years all Senegalese students in journalism—and many from other western African countries—went to Montreal, Quebec City or Jonquière for training periods of months, or even years. One of these graduates, Senegal's star political reporter Abdou Latif Coulibayi (whom we discuss in chapter 14), started West Africa's first private school of journalism, where he now trains 172 students from a dozen African countries.

While these intellectual networks were growing, francophone artists from different countries also started increasing their interactions. Now that Quebec performers, Arab singers,

African writers and Belgian filmmakers have large audiences in other francophone societies and beyond, francophone festivals have multiplied in all fields—cinema, music, humour, visual arts and more—showcasing big acts and fostering new ones. These festivals play an important role in francophone culture: In a world dominated by the Anglo-American media and American entertainment, events such as the Festival of Francophone Film in Namur, Belgium; the Francofolies of La Rochelle, France; and the Panafrican Festival of Cinema in Ouagadougou, Burkina Faso, are powerful avenues for the promotion and development of entertainment in French. In TV, francophone programming used to be strictly national, with very little international exchange, but since the middle of the 1990s, French, Belgian and Quebec TV companies and channels have been buying each others' concepts, a totally new phenomenon.

Though it is in many ways a world of its own, French literature is, in fact, a global literature. During our trip to Senegal we had the opportunity to sit in on a French class in a private Catholic school in downtown Dakar: the Institut Notre Dame. The school was a yellow stone open-air pavilion with an inner court shaded by baobab trees. When we arrived, the class of tenth-graders, mostly Muslim, were engrossed in analyzing an excerpt from Flaubert's *Éducation sentimentale,* which is set in the turbulent decade of 1840s France. Just as we were about to deplore the fact that these African students were studying European literature, we noticed that the textbook the students were using was actually an anthology of francophone literature that included selections of poetry and prose, not only from African authors such as Léopold Sédar Senghor and Aimé Césaire, but also from French-Canadian novelist Gabrielle Roy, among others. Evidently the latter has given many students a taste for snow. The teacher told us that his students now dream of going to university in Canada. Their other choice is Belgium. For students who aspire to leave Senegal, France is no longer the only, or the mandatory, first choice.

While cultural exchange is growing among the francophonie, so is business. Francophones are not preceded by their reputation in business, and even in France people have tended to think of French capitalism as an oxymoron. But that's a mistake. Four of the richest members of the Francophonie are advanced industrial countries that play leading roles in critical industrial sectors, including the automobile industry, agribusiness and the energy sector. Stephen Jarislowski, a German-born financier who manages billions of dollars of pension funds from his Montreal office, is known in his field for his no-nonsense stance on everything from the new economy to corporate governance. When Jarislowski published his autobiography, he claimed, "The Francophonie is one of the most surprising things that happened."

Business ideas do circulate in the French-speaking world, and again not necessarily just between France and its former colonies. In the late 1970s Franco-Ontarian businessman Paul Desmarais, who had built his fortune in transportation, began looking for a way to expand his empire into Europe. His search for a partner didn't land him in Paris, but rather in the Belgian town of Charleroi, where he struck up a partnership with Belgian business tycoon Albert Frère. Desmarais's New World savvy was evidently a good fit with Frère's Old World wisdom. The two formed a holding company, Pargesa, which went on to buy substantial shares in the German multimedia empire Bertelsmann, which is active in fifty-eight countries, as well as in Total and Suez, respectively water and construction multinationals.

Business is business and francophone companies, always seeking ways to cut costs in a global environment, often look to other francophone countries for opportunities. Outsourcing call centres is an oft-quoted example of globalization, and a prime example of how globalization is happening in French. For several years now, following an American trend, French businesses have been outsourcing their call centres to francophone countries where labour is fluently francophone but less costly than in France. Their countries of choice: Tunisia, Morocco, Senegal and even Israel.

In some ways the French have been partly oblivious to this activity. Why? There are two reasons. First, the French relationship with the francophonie is paradoxical. On one hand, the French have grown remarkably tolerant of foreign accents, particularly in the seven years between when we went to France to study the French in 1999 and when we published this book in 2006. Back in 1999 we saw a documentary about Céline Dion on French TV in which her family and entourage were being interviewed. To our amazement her Québécois friends and family were subtitled (in French), because it was assumed that French viewers could not understand people speaking with a Quebec accent. Six years later, this is no longer considered necessary, nor is it required. Thanks mostly to the increasing distribution of Quebec music and films, the French have become familiar with the Quebec accent, not to mention various African accents. In the past fifteen years the development of African literature in France has also been remarkable.

At the same time, while the French are not ignorant of the francophonie, they are uneducated about it. Journalists rarely bother to make distinctions between the Francophonie (institutional) and the francophonie (linguistic and sociological). Articles on the topic in the French press are almost unintelligible because reporters, journalists and editors regularly confuse the two. In a country where journalists can nitpick for days about the exact significance of a word in their president's speech, such lack of subtlety regarding the francophonie shows how far behind the French are in integrating the idea. The president of the Agence universitaire de la francophonie, Michèle Gendreau-Massouloux, describes France as the "Wild West" of the francophonie—in other words, uncharted territory.

In defence of the French, some of their misgivings about the francophonie owes to the fact that (non-French) franco-phones play on language solidarity to gain entry to France as immigrants. During our travels to Africa many people com-mented bitterly that France was not as welcoming to immi-grants as it used to be. In 1999, at the Monaco conference of ministers of the economy of the Francophonie, the question was raised with the French minister of economy and finance, Dominique Strauss-Khan, and his response was categorical: "Francophonie will not be about France admitting foreigners who speak French." It's hard to feel sympathetic to the French attitude, but the fact remains: Francophone countries' attempts to use language to further their particular ends have not endeared the francophonie to the French public. This only rein-forces the prejudice in France that the Francophonie is a front for post-colonialism.

There is another reason that France seems to be missing out on the activities of the francophonie. A sizeable portion of the French intelligentsia not only believe their language is losing its international role, but seem to believe that the fight was over before it even started. The result is that, in some ways, they are willingly turning themselves into a mental colony of the English-speaking world. There are signs of this defeatism everywhere. In Parisian legal circles, the new fad for 2005 was *les class actions*. The French press presented this as an "Anglo-Saxon concept," ignoring the fact that Quebeckers have been pursuing *recours collectifs* in French for thirty years. In fact, Quebec long ago coined the vocabulary necessary to launch class-action suits in French in a civil code environment like France's. Laurent Personne, cabinet director of the French Academy's *secrétaire perpétuel,* told us that it was silly to speak of baseball terms in French, since this was obviously an American sport. It's only silly if you don't know that Quebeckers have been playing baseball in French for fifty years.

But French CEOs, entrepreneurs, scholars, researchers and diplomats often echo the belief that French is losing ground and that it has no future. Even when they don't say a word, the actions of the French elite speak volumes. One of the most eloquent examples comes from a famous book series titled *Que sais-je? (What Do I Know?),* published by the Presses universitaires de France (University Presses of France). Created in 1941, this collection of about four thousand short handbooks provides the fundamentals on subjects ranging from mushrooms to thermodynamics. They have been translated into forty-three languages. In 2004 the publisher came out with a new book, titled *Investments.* The entire book was written in English, even though there is a perfectly good word in French for the same thing: *investissements.* In a communiqué the publisher explained: "The field is taught mostly in English today. We took the initiative because it answers a need and makes the collection more modern." In a way the move was not surprising. Parisians who follow the stock market speak of *les traders* instead of *les courtiers.* France Telecom, France's national telephone company, named its Internet service Wanadoo ("wanna do"). Other prime examples of this Paris pidgin are businesses with meaningless but distinctly English-flavoured company names such as Speed Rabbit Pizza and Leader Price (no one has yet been able to explain to us exactly what a speed rabbit is).

But the reasons for French defeatism go much deeper than a failure to plug into francophone culture beyond their borders.

It would be an exaggeration to say that the French are the only French speakers who feel that their language is disappearing from the world, or the only ones who are contributing to the trend. We have identified about half a dozen reasons that may explain the lack of confidence in French among francophones from all countries.

The most obvious is simply that francophones have absorbed the idea that English is *the* language of science, business and diplomacy. In scientific circles, those who defend French are familiar with what is called the *dilemme des congrès* (conference dilemma): Delegates can either speak French and address a small group, or deliver in English and fill a big room. Given the options, many ambitious people choose English; the decision is justified on the grounds of "realism." A second factor, which applies mostly to the French, is the dilution of nationalist sentiment. Given the wars it has caused, nationalism has bad press in Europe. In France only the far right indulges in the kind of flag-waving that would be considered a normal expression of patriotism in the U.S. Since language is an important feature of nation building, a fair chunk of the French elite has distanced itself from French as a political topic, even though, paradoxically, members of the elite tend to be language purists. In other words, for the French, speaking English in international forums and declining to defend French have to some extent become ways of showing that they are not succumbing to the sirens of nationalism and Gaullism.

A third cause that also applies mostly to the French is anglomania. The French are very down on France at present—they themselves call this a period of general *morosité* (gloom). They went through a similar phase in the eighteenth and nineteenth centuries, when they perceived all sorts of defects in their society and were seeking ways to remedy them. When this happens they look elsewhere for solutions, and right now

they are looking to English-speaking societies. Record numbers
of French people are going to Great Britain to work, and the
ambient influence of English caused by this migration is probably one reason the French create so many faux-English terms.
This anglomania is particularly strong in French business sectors. Even an emblematic company such as France Telecom
produced a 2006–8 business plan with the title "Next." In the
document, written in French to its French clients, it announced
a series of new services and products with English names,
including Family Talk, LiveCom, Business Talk, LivePhone,
LiveMusic, LiveZoom, Mobile & Connected, and Homezone.

To combat such abuses, in 1999 a group of four French
associations for the defence of the French language created the
Académie de la carpette anglaise (literally, the English Rug
Academy, but the term *carpette* also means *doormat*). The academy
gives an annual "award of civic indignity" to representatives
of the French elite or institutions who distinguish themselves
for their unremitting servility to English. Predictably, France
Telecom won the 2005 award. Past laureates include the CEOs
of Renault and Vivendi, a minister of national defence, the
editor-in-chief of *Le Monde* and the head of France's most prestigious business school, HEC. In all fairness, not all members
of the French elite share this anglomania. The Chamber of
Commerce and Industry made a first survey on the issue in
2002 to try to measure the phenomenon. In 2005 Jean-Noël
Vianney, president of France's national library, proposed a
European plan for a digital library to compete with Google.
And since 2002, France has required the CIA to use French as
the working language for the new liaison office, named
Alliance base, it shares in Paris with the Délégation générale
de la sécurité extérieure (the French version of the CIA).

Of course, the castrating influence of conservative language purism doesn't help. This is particularly strong in France,

but in the back of the mind of most francophones is an academician who slaps their wrists for uttering new words or allowing
new definitions for already existing words. English speakers
are free of this hang-up. Many French speakers are attracted
to the relaxed aspect of English and to the no-fuss way in which
that language adapts to modernity. As we have seen, francophones are capable of dealing with modernity when they remain
casual about their language and push aside the purist voices in
their heads. But for many, it's clearly easier to use English. In a
way it feels like less of a betrayal of French.

A fifth cause for the disenchantment of some of the francophone elites is psychological; we call it *l'amour trahi* (betrayed
love, in the sense of a spurned lover). Francophones, and particularly the French, have grown up believing in their language's potential to be "universal," to be used by everyone on
the planet. As English makes further inroads (though it's far
from being truly universal), the French have become more
disillusioned than ever about the failure of their language to
deliver on its promise. The result is that many French speakers
feel like jilted lovers: They resent the object of their pain as if
it were the cause. With no small measure of extremism, many
conclude that if French can't be everything, then it can't be
anything. Francophones from outside of France tend to see the
situation differently; as minorities constantly dealing with the
presence of competing languages, they have never harboured
illusions about the universality of French and have a more self-
reliant approach to the language. In other words, they accept
the idea that if French is to flourish, it's up to them to act.
They know no one else will do it for them, especially not the
betrayed lovers in France.

In a closely related point, the French intellectual class
seems to lack ambition. Until the Second World War, the francophone elites' conviction that they wrote for the world drove

the *rayonnement* of French culture. As we saw in chapter 5, there was a time when the French were so imbued with the ethic of their language's clarity and purity that they were full of ambition to communicate to the whole world. Since the Second World War, it seems that in some ways they have turned inwards and become satisfied with writing and thinking only for themselves.

We could write an essay about this point, but two examples stand out. In the world of literary non-fiction and journalism, which we know well, French editorial practices often work against the goal of clarity. The French publish articles without indented paragraphs and books without indexes; they often write in long, windy sentences, to the point where great thinkers such as Michel Foucault are more readable in their English translation than in the French original. And what can explain the universal absence of indexes? Perhaps it's either cost-cutting or an assumption that readers don't need them. But researchers *do* need them. When faced with little time and a lot of material to cover, they will pitch the French books out the window and concentrate on the more accessible and user-friendly English ones. A comparison of the *Encyclopedia Britannica* with the *Encyclopédie universalis* speaks volumes on these different approaches (we used both in researching this book). It is true that *Universalis* articles are often geared to more specialized readers, but the writers make little effort to use plain language (this is all the more curious since, as we discuss in chapter 5, the original goal of encyclopedias was to make knowledge accessible to everyone!). Too often recently, intellectual productions in France have been imbued with a hermetic spirit. French intellectuals have evidently delegated the job of making sense of the world to other languages, and English has been waiting at the door, ready to work.

Another aspect of this lack of ambition is the complacency

of the French university and post-secondary systems. French universities provide good instruction, but they do not capitalize on half the intellectual resources they have at their disposal. Their libraries are notoriously mediocre; faculties have no tolerance for hybrid specialities; universities are continually short of resources and fail to give students access to the most advanced research, because top research in France is done outside of universities in specialized centres. In all fairness, there are fields in which French research is cutting-edge, including mathematics, civil nuclear energy, oceanography, demography, the humanities and history. In those fields foreigners do read French journals—in French. But the competition is fierce and the French need to improve their universities in order to keep their competitive advantage. They have every right to leave their universities the way they are, but as education globalizes, France's schools are not growing as fast as they could. Small may be beautiful, but it is also—well, small.

The debate over the relevance of French is normal. The same debate is taking place among speakers of the other international languages—with the exception of English. In our view the issue is less about reality than about perception. As we saw over the course of researching this book, the root of French's problem is not that there is nothing going on in the language. The problem is one of spirit and attitude. The original domain of French seems to have lost its stamina, its fortitude, its spunk.

Francophone societies outside France also find France's reluctance to defend and modernize the language insulting and alienating. Many North Africans now go to Quebec to pursue their studies, precisely because Quebec has no qualms about providing access to modernity in French. Furthermore, because their language is that of a minority where they live, francophones from Quebec, Belgium, Algeria and Senegal are accustomed to fighting for it. Listening to French defeatism simply appalls them. In the end, the global future of French depends on whether francophones, but particularly the French, decide that it matters, or not. And if the French won't defend the place of French in French journals, who will?

If the French continue along the road they are on, they could miss a fantastic opportunity, the same way they did in America. The continent was up for grabs and they chose the slave islands instead of Canada and Greater Louisiana. The choice was not irrational at the time, but it lacked foresight, to put it mildly.

Basically the future of French boils down to a question of choice. Pro-English propaganda is *de bonne guerre* (fair enough) in a world where language has become an issue of power. But for francophones, believing that propaganda may amount to collective linguistic suicide. It is surprising to hear French people rationalize the success of English by arguing that English is more efficient than any other language for expressing certain concepts. It's fair game for the anglophone media to make such a claim, but nobody is obliged to believe it. The French should know better, since they used the very same argument in the eighteenth century, when they claimed "what was not clear was not French." No language is intrinsically more or less efficient or complicated than another. English is an extremely difficult language to master, primarily because there are so few rules and so many exceptions. Only a fool (or someone who speaks it poorly) would think it's easy. But most of all, the French seem to forget that any language is the most efficient one for expressing its own ideas. Many words in French can be explained in English only through long definitions and clumsy paraphrases—*revendiquer, vie associative, nuire, abandon* and *rayonnement,* to name a few. The frequent and continual borrowings of French terms by English testifies to that. So why are the French so ready to sacrifice their mental universe?

This point was driven home to us by Stéphane Lopez, who runs the Francophonie's program for promotion of French in the European Union. Part of Lopez's job is to wrestle with people who argue that a single language (by which they mean English) is more efficient and less costly for translation. A single language is efficient only for those who master it. English has made remarkable progress in the European Union in the past ten years because non-anglophone diplomats accepted it. However, Lopez discovered that some European agencies have begun to reserve jobs for native English speakers only, on the grounds that they are more fluent in the extremely subtle word game of international diplomacy. "French, German or Italian diplomats have made concessions to English on the basis of courtesy, and also as a cheap means to further their career, but by doing so they have condemned their successors and their children to play second fiddle."

Meanwhile, CEOs of French multinationals pride themselves on posting their communiqués in English, when they could at least post them in two versions. By the same token, it is remarkable that French scientists are not required to publish their studies in French as well as in English, as the Japanese are, as a condition of public funding. As one famous example has shown, it might even be to French scientists' advantage. It took more than a decade for Pasteur Institute professor Luc Montaignier to prove that he had first identified the AIDS virus in 1983 and that the American scientist Robert Gallo had plagiarized his work, falsely claiming to have discovered the virus himself. Gallo had done the peer review for the English journal to which Montaignier had submitted his original findings. Had he published in French, Gallo would not have been able to claim paternity of Montaignier's discovery. In fact, Gallo might even have had to learn French to stay up to date on research in the field. But as Professor Bernard Lecherbonnier puts it in his authoritative book *Pourquoi veulent-ils tuer le français?* (*Why Do They Want to Kill French?*), many French scientists have concluded that it is safer to join U.S. teams of scientists than try to make their name in the field in French.

It is useful to remember that the fundamental reason why English is where it is today is that the British and the Americans never lost their pride, even when they spoke a small language that nobody wanted to learn. As we saw in chapter 5, in the eighteenth century, when no one questioned the supremacy of French, the British recognized its usefulness and took what they needed from it, but never bought into arguments about its inherent value. In the end, it all boils down to choice.

Too much emphasis on how some francophones are surrendering to English might cast a shadow on the reasons for hope. As we mentioned at the beginning of this chapter, not all francophones have thrown in the towel on French. Some actions now being taken to defend French even suggest that the momentum against French is reversible. In diplomacy, the Francophonie countries scored a major victory with the UNESCO Convention on Cultural Diversity. At the European Union, the stellar rise in attendance for the French-language programs is promising. So far, few people are conscious of the fact that eleven of the twenty-five members of the European Union (soon to be thirteen out of twenty-seven, when Hungary and Romania join) are also members of the Francophonie. But if these countries play their cards skilfully on the issue of plurilingualism, the balance could tip in favour of the French geocultural sphere.

After years of pussyfooting and refusing to change their ways, French academic circles have begun merging universities and *grandes écoles* to make larger and more competitive institutions. This started when the first international ranking of universities produced by the University of Shanghai ranked only four French universities in the top hundred; some of the most prestigious *écoles*, such as the engineering Polytechnique, didn't even place in the top two hundred! While a slap in the face to the French, the survey sent shock waves through the system and wiped out long-standing resistance to the idea of merging certain institutions. Since 2003 French institutions of higher learning have been undergoing a gigantic reorganization process. The *grandes écoles* have realized they are not so grand after all, and have accepted the idea of merging with universities.

And French literature is changing. Even if French authors are not as widely read as they used to be, France is finding ways to remain an important literary centre. In particular, French publishers are becoming more and more open to authors from languages other than French and English (the opposite trend is happening in the United States). In fact, many authors enter the international book trade when they are discovered by French publishers. Some have gone on to build considerable careers in French. Milan Kundera fled Czechoslovakia for Paris in 1975, wrote in Czech until 1989 and then switched to French. Canadian novelist Nancy Huston, originally from Calgary, learned French as a teenager in New Hampshire and then studied French literature at Harvard. She moved to Paris in the seventies, where she became part of a circle of left-wing intel-lectuals and began publishing in French. Spanish author Jorge Semprun fled Franco's regime and moved to Paris in the 1940s. He began publishing in French in 1963 and published his first novel in Spanish only in 2003. Award-winning author André Makine left his native Russia and moved to France in 1987, where he began writing in French. And François Cheng, who studied French in China, became a naturalized French citizen in 1971 (that's when he chose the name François). He was the first Asian to enter the French Academy, in 2002. And there are dozens of similar examples, not only in France, but also in Belgium and Quebec, not to mention the many francophone African authors who are now being studied in U.S. universities.

While French business people and CEOs may show a marked preference for English, they are still French, with the clout that carries. At the turn of the millennium 160 French companies opened shop in Slovenia. Overnight, registration for language classes doubled at the country's French cultural centre. Evidently a number of ambitious Slovenians thought learning French would further their careers. The same thing happens wherever French companies and multinationals are active, whether it is Greenville, South Carolina, or Porto Alegre, Brazil.

Like the job market, the picture of any language is a dynamic one, which means that French makes progress in some areas and slips backward in others all the time. French is definitely losing steam in Egypt, but it's holding its own in Israel and progressing in Hungary. It is regressing in Togo, a result of the recent arrival of U.S. oil companies, but progressing in Nigeria, where it recently became an official second language. In South Africa the Alliance française has launched a successful publicity campaign with the slogan *"L'autre langue d'Afrique"* ("Africa's other language"); a third of the staff of the South African foreign affairs department is slated to learn French in the next three years. The largest chapter of the International Federation of Teachers of French is in the U.S., with ten thousand members; the second-largest is, surprisingly, in Brazil, with six thousand teachers. Though French is being taught in fewer places in Brazil, it remains strong where it matters, around Rio de Janeiro and São Paulo and near the border of French Guiana. "The new map for the demand of French doesn't correspond at all to the old colonial map," says Xavier North, who ran the French foreign affairs ministry's department of cultural development and is now executive director of the Délégation générale à la langue française et aux langues de France. "French is an alternative for those seeking a different world view."

From all the numbers we crunched on this issue, two certainties emerge: French, like English, is the only language present in every education system around the world. And, in countries where two second languages are mandatory, particularly in Europe, French is growing beyond expectations. Where education systems are not flourishing, France's cultural diplomacy machine has been efficiently picking up some of the slack. Alain Marquer, who heads international development at the Alliance française, explained to us that the Alliance's traditional adult clientele is changing. Because of cuts to language programs in schools, more and more parents are now sending their kids to the Alliance to learn French, especially in developing countries. Parents evidently still think French is important enough to merit paying for lessons out of their own pockets. And overall, explains Marquer, the number of adult clients doesn't diminish.

The case of the United States is odd. Because of their domination of the media, American perceptions shape many of the world's perceptions. Yet even there the state of French is not bad, if not brilliant. The 2000 U.S. census has shown that the number of Americans who speak French at home, 1.6 million, makes French the number-four national language of the United States, after English, Spanish and Chinese, but well before Italian or German. This number has been stable for years. Yet the identity of these French speakers has changed. The traditional enclaves of New England and Louisiana have been shrinking, and the number of speakers of French has risen steadily in New York, California, Florida and Texas. In education too, statistics show that French is in a class of its own. Of the 1.4 million Americans who study language in institutions of higher learning, 53 percent have turned to Spanish and 15 percent to French—although the proportion has been declining, the number has been stable for 30 years. And the number of people who study French still exceeds the total studying the next three languages. All statistics concur on this point. (See Table 4 in the Appendix.)

According to Robert Peckham, professor of French at the University of Tennessee, the strong preference for Spanish in the United States is curious, because French is still a more practical foreign language to learn. Peckham, whose chutzpah has earned him the nickname "Tennessee Bob" in French-teaching circles, is a veritable French-language learning activist. He is known for pushing French with the formula "We need weapons of mass instruction." His websites, *Tennessee Needs French* and *New York Needs French,* are gold mines of information. Peckham points out that Quebec alone is nearly as big a U.S. trade partner as Mexico, and gives examples of what Americans can learn from the French in agribusiness, nuclear power and aviation.

In fact, if French diplomats, scientists and CEOs read Tennessee Bob's material, that alone might change their gloomy perspective about the future of French in the world.

Chapter 20 ~

THE UNWRITTEN CHAPTERS

THE REMAINING CHAPTERS IN the story of French are not ours to write. We can see some emerging themes—the subjects of the last four chapters—but others are barely discernible. In Jerusalem, Tlemcen, Dakar, Lafayette, Caraquet, Paris, Sudbury, Monaco, Geneva, Brussels and Atlanta—in fact, everywhere we travelled for this book—we met francophones and non-francophones who had widely different views on the future of French. Some argued it has no future. Others said they couldn't imagine the world without it. But between the extremes of optimism and fatalism, a few things remain clear. French is still a language of diplomacy, of science and of business. And most of all, it is still a global language that many people study and even more want to learn.

Who can foresee the tectonic shifts in geopolitics, knowledge, culture or technology that affect a language's status? For that matter, who ever foresaw the ones that have already affected French? Who would have imagined that the forays of the Alliance israélite universelle in the 1860s would spawn a cultural diplomacy movement that would become the backbone of French public diplomacy, and remain so to this day? Who saw the French Revolution coming, or thought the French Academy would outlive the French monarchy? Who imagined that Haiti would become the world's third republic, save French at the U.N. and give Canada a Governor General? It's impossible to predict the future of any language. However, there are some clear forces, both linguistic and geocultural, that are changing French now.

Two centuries ago French was regarded as the universal language of Europe, even though it was confined to elite circles, and even though seventy-five percent of the French people did not yet speak it. Today twenty times more people speak French and the world's elites are still learning it, sometimes for reasons quite similar to those that motivated them two centuries ago, sometimes for new ones. Not as many people are learning French as English, but there are still many more than are studying German, Arabic or Spanish (outside of the U.S.). More than ever, ideas, inventions, modernity, people and decisions are circulating freely among the various centres of French. Considering the fact that France and Belgium were the only hubs of French four decades ago, this new development is great testimony to its vitality.

But the French of the future will certainly be different from that of today. New linguistic trends have announced important shifts to come. Montaigne and Rabelais are difficult to read in the original text, and today's Amin Maalouf or Michel Houellebecq will be equally difficult for francophones four centuries down the road.

The multiplication of French speakers will also provoke changes in the central ideology of French speakers: their purism. More than three centuries after the founding of the French Academy, the French obsession with defining language is still strong. But the multiplication of francophones—in France and around the world—has made it harder for purists to impose a rigid *norme*, both in France and in francophone countries.

Even in France the purists have always had trouble controlling the grassroots, even when there were only a couple of million speakers of French. Now that there are sixty million of them, the language is evolving even faster. While the French continue to profess faith in the *norme*, every day they generate new expressions, new pronunciations and new twists of syntax that are shaking the pillars of the *norme*. The French of 2006 is spoken and written with a casualness that would have shocked people fifty years ago–though it would have been music to the ears of Rabelais. Anglophone commentators usually notice the influence of English on French, but French has been undergoing changes in phonetics and semantics that have nothing to do with English. New words, foreign borrowings and lively inventions from other parts of the francophonie are finding their way into the mainstream faster than ever, through artistic creation, the media and particularly advertising. This constant quest for novelty on the part of so many speakers is what drives much of the creativity of the language, and what propels it away from the dictates of the ayatollahs of purism.

Are we seeing the end of the *norme?* Much the way that French, Italian, Spanish, Portuguese and Romanian are derivatives of Latin, French, like all international languages, will be a victim of its own success; it will become "corrupted" and it will change. Linguists are closely monitoring the language's evolution in Ivory Coast and the Democratic Republic of Congo, where variations are veering towards a Creole of French. But so far, these two examples are more the exception than the rule. Outside of France, French competes directly with Wolof in Senegal, with Arabic in Lebanon and with English in North America. Yet the French *norme* plays a strong unifying role throughout the francophonie, and has given French a degree of cohesion that is unique among international languages. None of us will probably see the appearance of a new Creole of French in Africa during our lifetime, but perhaps our children and grandchildren will.

In addition to demography and linguistics, geopolitical developments will influence how the language spreads in France, Europe, America, Africa and beyond. France is both the greatest strength and the worst weakness of French, its backbone and its Achilles' heel. What the French do, how they understand the world and how the world understands them, will continue to weigh heavily on the future of the French language.

The current anglomania among France's diplomatic, scientific and business elites is often viewed with pessimism. In our opinion it may well be just a phase; French elites have gone through periodic phases of anglomania since the eighteenth century. In general it happens when the French think there is something deeply wrong with their society. They seek a diagnosis and a remedy, often turning to foreign languages as tools of exploration that will give them access to foreign concepts. The French elite did this with Italian in the sixteenth century, with English in the eighteenth century, and with German in the nineteenth century. The current phase of anglomania may lead to another cultural rebound in French science, technology, business and governance.

Of course, the French world view is sometimes at odds with reality, especially when it concerns their language. Everyone agrees that the francophonie will play a crucial role in the future of French, but the French people are oddly oblivious to it. For instance, most histories of the French language produced by the French cover the linguistic peculiarities of French in Ivory Coast, Algeria and Quebec, but they rarely see these developments as part of French's global progress. This sort of cultural myopia is dangerous; France could miss out on the francophonie the way it missed out on America four centuries ago. In 1763 Voltaire wrote, "France could live without Quebec." French could also live without Dakar, Beirut, Brussels, Geneva, Abidjan and Kinshasa, but it is up to the French to decide whether they want to speak an international, or merely a national, language.

And then there is the question of how the French are perceived in the world. Neither the French nor anglophones are conscious that the French language owes some of its current prestige to the influence of English—both because of the way French and France embody values contrary to those of Anglo-American civilization, and because of the way English speakers continue to revere (and romanticize) both French and France. The visceral love/hate relationship that the Anglo-American elites have with France and French is a sociological curiosity. Fortunately their francophobia has been balanced by a healthy dose of francophilia. But much of the potential of this appeal depends on how the French tap into it at home, in the francophonie and in the world.

In our travels we met dozens of people from non-francophone countries who were learning French simply because it was the language of France. Because it represents something bigger than itself, France continues to attract millions of foreigners to its language. Even within the francophonie, the spread of the language is rooted in ideas about France. At least fifty times more Irish than French migrated to the New World—one million, compared to at most fifty thousand—yet many more North Americans speak French today than Irish—at least eight million, compared to estimates of twenty thousand Gaelic speakers (there are allegedly a million speakers in Ireland). The francophones of America derived much of their cultural fortitude from speaking the language of France. And nowadays, what drives the interest in French is not just France, but the fact that French is truly a global language in every sense of the word. The only ones who don't seem to pay attention to it are the French, and this particular myopia could be the undoing of France.

In Europe, much of the future of French depends on whether the Francophonie, Belgium and France manage to impose true plurilingualism on European institutions. It is a tall order, but the Belgians and French have won a surprising number of allies. Judging from statistics on second-language training in Europe, French is still in a category of its own—not anywhere near

English, but far better off than German, Spanish or Italian. Outside of France, Romania and Moldova are proving to be lively centres of the language—Romania will be hosting the Francophonie summit of 2006. Romania is as francophone as Switzerland and almost as much as Belgium; its entry into the European Union in 2007 is bound to make waves in debates over the status of French in Europe. The biggest question mark is the status of Belgium, where the Flemish separatist movement is gaining strength day by day. It is possible that the country could split in the first decade of this century. If Flanders forces the partition of Belgium, what will become of Brussels and the Walloons?

In America, French owes its survival to the complicated geopolitics of the second half of the eighteenth century and, now, to the cultural fortitude of Quebec and Acadia. What will happen if the proportion of francophone Canadians slips to twenty percent? And what if Quebec separates from Canada? What will happen to francophones in other parts of Canada? They may indeed assimilate quickly, like the Franco-Americans and the Cajuns of yesterday. On the other hand, other French-speaking communities on the continent may bolster them. French is now an official language in New Brunswick, and who could have predicted that the number of native French speakers would be rising in California and in Florida, a state that is attracting both Haitians and Quebec "snowbirds"—many of whom are counted in census statistics?

Africa forms the biggest pool of French speakers and has the most potential for growth in the francophonie. If birth rate alone is considered, the number of francophones could potentially double in twenty-five years. In North Africa, French is doing well everywhere, but much depends on whether the sub-Saharan countries can improve their education systems and economies. As a French teacher from Togo told us, "*Le français ne fait plus vivre son homme*" ("French no longer provides a living"). Only

twenty-five percent of Africans are fully schooled, and this proportion is dropping every year, but—a promising change—the
proportion of women among those who are fully schooled is
rising rapidly. This could reinforce French in African households and eventually make it a mother tongue rather than a
learned language. In Mauritius an unexpected turn of events is
shaking up the anglophone elite: Most of the Creole population is now schooling itself in French universities in Réunion,
and eighty percent of the newspapers are now in French. This
rising class of francophones nurtures the ambition of making
Mauritus the Hong Kong of the Indian Ocean.

Although much of the future of French depends on what
happens in Africa, the language is vulnerable to the vagaries of
France's foreign policy there. Any move by the French has the
potential to attract or alienate people. One Senegalese author,
Boubacar Boris Diop, stopped writing in French and turned to
his Wolof mother tongue as a result of France's shady actions
in Rwanda. The gesture, though symbolic, is an isolated one
for the moment, but it could catch on. More seriously, French
made progress in post-colonial Africa because it was perceived
as the language of development; as the continent continues to
stagnate and even regress, will French still be considered useful?
It's hard to predict.

The fringes of the French-speaking world are equally
interesting. More French is spoken in Israel than in Louisiana
(in both percentage and number of speakers), and Israel could
well join the Francophonie if it manages to bury the hatchet
with Lebanon (which opposes Israel's candidacy). French is
spoken more in the United States and in Mexico than it is in
some member countries of the official Francophonie, namely
Bulgaria or Albania. Who knows where that will lead?
Enrolment in programs of the Alliances françaises and French
collèges and *lycées* is increasing. And the inroads made by the

Agence universitaire francophone in Vietnam, Laos and Cambodia show there is still interest in the language there.

In the end, the future of French will depend on a simple question: How useful will French be to its native speakers, partial speakers and francophiles? Very few people ever learn a language just because it is beautiful. People will continue to learn and maintain French only if it provides them with access to things that are useful, productive, challenging or beautiful. That is why this book has focused on the decisions and policies, creations and inventions, achievements and failures that have shaped the destiny of French, as opposed to strictly linguistics.

Statistics show that the use of French in international organizations puts it on a second tier all of its own, well below English, but well above all other international languages in terms of use and learning. Fatalists view this placement not as a tier but as the first step towards free fall. But global statistics on the teaching of French as a second language indicate that French remains solidly established as the *other* global language.

The future of French also depends on individual efforts and initiatives in research, in business, in arts and culture. Business, science and diplomacy have to be carried out in French if it is to remain a language of science, business and diplomacy. At the moment, the elites of many countries are still turning to French because it is the best way to access knowledge, science and business. In some areas of excellence French remains not only useful but necessary, namely mathematics, biology, biomedical research, oceanography and nuclear research. The threat to French right now is not so much English as the mediocrity of the French university system and of the French press in general (French dailies have very low circulation). However, these things are due more to policy decisions than to lack of cultural dynamism, and are reversible.

In diplomacy, the Francophonie's push for plurilingualism and cultural diversity may reap very big rewards. These policies may well be what francophone countries need in order to create a vast economy of culture, but also to become a model themselves. In the Renaissance, people learned Italian because Italian cities were centres of cultural and scientific renewal, not because they were powerful. In the twenty-first century, many people could turn to French because the Francophonie represents the most articulate and progressive alternative to the global American village.

For all we know, French could outlast English. Pop historians of the English language never fail to draw parallels between the triumphant destiny of English and that of Latin during the Roman Empire. But they rarely point out that Roman patricians spoke Latin with a Greek accent, primarily because the Romans looked to the Greeks for culture, knowledge and education; their children were schooled by Greek instructors. And as the western Roman Empire collapsed, only the eastern, Greek-speaking side remained, and Byzantium outlived the Roman Empire by another eight centuries.

The question that motivated this book was why French has maintained its influence in spite of the domination of English. But many linguists point out that the position of English is not as solid as it appears. According to linguist David Graddol, who did two studies of English for the British Council, English may well be the world's lingua franca, but native anglophones may end up being victims of their language's success. As more of the world speaks English, monolingual English speakers may lose their competitive edge to English speakers who also master other languages, particularly since, as Graddol argues, the more people speak English, the less relevant the norms and standards of the language will become. The belief that English is the language of business, science and diplomacy has been beneficial for English to a point, but it has come at a price: that of making

Anglo-American scientists, businessmen and diplomats oblivious to the fact that good science, business and diplomacy are also being conducted in other languages. It can be lonely at the top, and ivory towers are brittle. Linguist Jean Michel Eloy jokes that the best language for business is the language of the client, and this may not do English any favours in the future. Who remembers that nobody at the U.S. embassy in Iran in 1979 spoke Farsi—at the very moment of the Iranian revolution? The language of the client. . . .

The story of French has been, and will continue to be, one of living dangerously. Spoken on many continents by relatively few people, the language is spread much thinner than Spanish, Arabic or Portuguese, but distributed more widely. Outside of France, only minorities speak French. More often than not, only the elite master the language, and the bulk of the population is only partly French-speaking at best. This can be viewed as a sign of decadence or as a starting point. Outside of France, Belgium, Switzerland and North America, French is learned as a second language rather than a mother tongue, and most of the French-speaking elites are in fact bilingual, if not multilingual. Because of this precarious situation, French could be wiped out within several generations. But it also could mean that French is in a better position to reach out and spread its influence almost everywhere on the planet.

This linguistic archipelago, this Polynesia of French, is a return to the situation of French five centuries ago, when only fringe groups of urbanites and *lettrés* spoke the language. The pessimistic see this as a sign of decline. But it could as easily be a condition for French's renewal, a second youth. Much will depend on whether francophones—including the people of France—are able to capitalize on their situation and summon up some ambition.

All of which is to say, the most fascinating chapters of the story of French have yet to be told.

Appendices

Note: All figures are estimates because the definitions of what constitutes a speaker or category of speaker (native, second language, foreign language, true speaker, partial speaker, etc.) vary from study to study.

Table 1: TOP 15 LANGUAGES BY NUMBER OF SPEAKERS

RANK	LANGUAGE	NUMBER (millions)
1	Mandarin	1070
2	English	508
3	Hindi and Urdu	602
4	Spanish	392
5	Russian	277
6	Arabic	246
7	Bengali	211
8	Portuguese	191
9	French	175*
10	Indonesian Malay	159
11	German	128
12	Japanese	126
13	Punjabi	94
14	Korean	78
15	Telugu (India)	76

Source: Quid 2005 *and Organisation internationale de la Francophonie.*
*In some studies, the number of native French speakers is considered as low as 72 million, but the number of secondary speakers and learners can make the figure as high as 260 million. We opted for the OIF's statistic of 175 million speakers, which includes 115 million francophones and 60 million partial speakers (this is a conservative estimate).

Table 2:   TOP ELEVEN INTERNATIONAL LANGUAGES
           (WITH OFFICIAL STATUS)

RANK	LANGUAGE	NUMBER OF COUNTRIES
1	English	45*
2	French	33*
3	Arabic	21
4	Spanish	20
5	Portuguese	7
6	German	5
7	Swahili	5
8	Dutch	4
9	Malayan	4
10	Italian	4
11	Chinese	3

Source: Quid 2005

*These two numbers vary greatly; they can reach 61 for English and 53 for French if overseas territories, such as Guadeloupe and the Falkland Islands, or inferior jurisdictions, such as Quebec and Puerto Rico, are included. When the category is expanded to "countries where it is a language of culture," the number of English countries rises to 105, French doubles from 33 to 66, German increases from 5 to 9, and Russian rises to 16.

Table 3: THE WORLD'S TEN MOST INFLUENTIAL LANGUAGES

RANK	LANGUAGE	POINTS
1	English	37
2	French	23
3	Spanish	20
4	Russian	16
5	Arabic	14
6	Chinese	13
7	German	12
8	Japanese	10
9	Portuguese	10
10	Hindi/Urdu	9

Source: George Weber, "The World's Ten Most Influential Languages," Language Today 2 (December 1997).

Note: George Weber's point system ranks a language's influence according to performance in six categories: number of speakers; number of secondary speakers; number of countries where the language is used; number of major areas of human activity where the language is used (e.g., science, business); economic power of countries where the language is used; and socio-literary prestige of these countries.

Table 4: TOP TEN FOREIGN-LANGUAGE ENROLMENTS IN U.S.
          INSTITUTIONS OF HIGHER EDUCATION (2002)

RANK	LANGUAGE	NUMBER
1	Spanish	746,000
2	French	202,000
3	German	92,000
4	Italian	64,000
5	Sign language	61,000
6	Japanese	52,000
7	Chinese	34,000
8	Latin	30,000
9	Russian	24,000
10	Ancient Greek	20,000

Source: Association of Departments of Foreign Languages (2004).

Table 5:   POPULATION OF FRANCOPHONIE MEMBERS WITH
PROPORTION OF FRANCOPHONES

COUNTRY OR REGION	TOTAL POPULATION	FRANCOPHONES (full or partial, %)
Africa and Indian Ocean		
Benin	6,600,000	25.5
Burkina Faso	12,600,000	5.0
Burundi	6,600,000	8.0
Cameroon	15,700,000	44.8
Cape Verde	500,000	20.0
Central African Republic	3,800,000	5.0
Chad	8,300,000	15.0
Comoros	700,000	17.0
Congo	3,600,000	60.0
Congo, Democratic Republic of	51,200,000	10.0
Djibouti	140,000	20.0
Gabon	1,300,000	80.0
Guinea	8,400,000	15.1
Guinea, Equatorial	500,000	19.0
Guinea-Bissau	1,400,000	1.0
Ivory Coast	16,400,000	70.0
Madagascar	16,900,000	20.4
Mali	12,600,000	16.4

COUNTRY OR REGION	TOTAL POPULATION	FRANCOPHONES (full or partial, %)
Mauritania	2,800,000	10.4
Mauritius	1,200,000	72.7
Mayotte	165,000	57.6
Morocco	30,100,000	33.3
Niger	11,500,000	9.0
Réunion*	710,000	94.5
Rwanda	8,300,000	9.0
São Tomé and Principe	200,000	10.0
Senegal	9,900,000	31.0
Seychelles	100,000	60.0
Togo	4,800,000	30.0
Tunisia	9,700,000	50.0
The Americas		
Canada	31,300,000	35.8
New Brunswick	730,000	76.0
Quebec	7,200,000	83.1
Dominica	100,000	2.0
French Guiana*	158,000	92.7
Guadeloupe*	424,000	95.0

COUNTRY OR REGION	TOTAL POPULATION	FRANCOPHONES (full or partial, %)
Haiti	8,200,000	15.5
Martinique	382,000	95.0
St. Lucia	100,000	1.7
The Middle East, Asia and Oceania		
Cambodia	13,800,000	0.3
Egypt	70,500,000	3.2
French Polynesia*	230,000	90.0
Laos	5,500,000	0.2
Lebanon	3,600,000	43.0
New Caledonia*	208,000	90.0
Vanuatu	200,000	45.0
Vietnam	80,300,000	0.5
Wallis and Futuna Islands*	15,000	92.8
Europe		
Albania	3,100,000	10.0
Armenia**	3,800,000	N/A
Austria**	8,100,000	N/A
Belgium	10,300,000	61.1

COUNTRY OR REGION	TOTAL POPULATION	FRANCOPHONES (full or partial, %)
Bulgaria	8,000,000	10.0
Croatia**	4,400,000	N/A
Czech Republic**	10,200,000	N/A
France (continental)	59,800,000	99.8
Georgia**	5,300,000	N/A
Greece	10,600,000	N/A
Hungary**	10,000,000	N/A
Lithuania**	3,500,000	6.0
Luxembourg	400,000	90.0
Macedonia	2,000,000	10.0
Moldova	4,300,000	25.0
Monaco	32,000	78.1
Poland**	38,600,000	3.0
Romania	22,400,000	28.0
Slovakia**	5,400,000	3.0
Slovenia**	2,000,000	4.0
Switzerland	7,200,000	20.4

Total: 175 million francophones

Source: Organisation internationale de la Francophonie.
* *Overseas French territory, not counted in continental France.*
** *Observer status in the Organisation internationale de la Francophonie.*

Table 6: MAIN CONCENTRATIONS OF FRENCH SPEAKERS

OUTSIDE THE FRANCOPHONIE

COUNTRY	POPULATION	FRANCOPHONES (full or partial)	LEARNERS
Algeria	30,400,000	15,000,000	6,000,000
Australia	19,200,000	65,000	155,000
Brazil	170,400,000	30,000	203,000
Chile	15,200,000	10,000	155,000
Costa Rica	3,800,000	——*	180,000
Dominican Republic	8,400,000	——*	682,000
Germany	82,200,000	200,000	1,700,000
Ghana	19,300,000	——*	286,000
India	1,000,015,000	——*	461,000
Ireland	3,800,000	——*	236,000
Israel	6,200,000	700,000	44,000
Italy	57,700,000	60,000	1,470,000
Japan	126,900,000	——*	210,000
Mexico	98,000,000	——*	420,000
Portugal	10,000,000	——*	434,000
Russia	145,600,000	——*	957,000
Spain	39,500,000	——*	930,000

COUNTRY	POPULATION	FRANCOPHONES (full or partial)	LEARNERS
Syria	16,200,000	—*	294,000
Ukraine	49,500,000	—*	472,000
United Kingdom	59,700,000	—*	357,000
United States	282,000,000	3,600,000**	2,030,000

*These numbers are missing because they are insignificant or unknown.

**According to the 2000 census, 1.6 million Americans speak French at home. But the number of Americans who can be regarded as partial francophones is anywhere between two and five million. We chose the conservative estimate, which is probably underestimated.

Sources: Christian Valantin, La francophonie dans le monde, 2002–2003 (Paris: Larousse, 2003); Quid 2005 (Paris: Éditions Robert Laffont, 2005); and 2000 U.S. Census

Selected Bibliography

This list does not include classics of literature or political thought, original historical sources or other works by Jean-Benoît Nadeau and Julie Barlow.

THE FRENCH LANGUAGE

Antoine, Gérald, and Bernard Cerquiglini. *Histoire de la langue française de 1945–2000.* Paris: Éditions CNRS, 2000.

Biu, Hélène. "Faire-part de naissance." *Historia,* July 2005.

Boucheron, Patrick. "Quand le latin a supplanté le français." *L'Histoire,* September 2005.

Brunot, Ferdinand. *Histoire de la langue française des origines à nos jours.* Paris: Armand Colin, 1905–37.

Cerquiglini, Bernard. *La naissance du français. Que sais-je?* Series. Paris: Presses universitaires de France, 1991.

Cerquiglini, Bernard, Jean-Claude Corbeil, Jean-Marie Klinkenberg and Benoît Peeters. *Le français dans tous ses états.* Paris: Flammarion, 2004.

Certeau, Michel de, Dominique Julia and Jacques Revel. *Une politique de la langue.* Paris: Gallimard, 2002.

Chaurand, Jacques. *Nouvelle histoire de la langue française.* Paris: Seuil, 1999.

Chevalier, Jean-Claude. *Histoire de la grammaire française. Que sais-je?* Series. Paris: Presses universitaires de France, 1994.

Chevé, Joëlle. "Du bon usage des mots." *Historia,* July 2005.

Cornette, Joël. "L'age d'or des dictionnaires." *L'Histoire,* November 2000.

Cornette, Joël. "Et François 1er imposa une langue officielle. . . ." *L'Histoire,* November 2000.

Gaillard, Jean-Michel. "Les bâtisseurs de l'école républicaine." *L'Histoire,* September 1996.

Gaillard, Jean-Michel. "Jules Ferry: La laïcité comme combat." *L'Histoire,* September 1996.

Gaillard, Jean-Michel. "Les victoires de Jules Ferry." *Les collections de l'Histoire* 6 (1999).

Gauvin, Lise. *La fabrique de la langue: De François Rabelais à Réjean Ducharme.* Paris: Seuil, 2004.

Giolitto, Pierre. "Le bon français entre à l'école." *Historia,* July 2005.

Goulemot, Jean-Marie. "Quand toute l'Europe parlait français." *L'Histoire,* November 2000.

Hagège, Claude. *Le français et les siècles.* Paris: Éditions Odile Jacob, 1987.

Hagège, Claude. *Le français, histoire d'un combat.* Paris: Éditions Michel Hagège, 1996.

L'Histoire. "L'aventure du français." November 2000.

Historia. "Du latin au texto: Les grandes dates de la langue française." Special issue, July 2005.

Huchon, Mireille. *Histoire de la langue française.* Paris: Librairie générale française, 2002.

Lodge, R. Anthony. *French: From Dialect to Standard.* New York: Routledge, 1993.

Louis, Patrice. *Toutes les suédoises s'appellent Ingrid: Les étrangers et leurs mots dans la langue française.* Paris: Arléa, 2004.

Picoche, Jacqueline, and Christiane Marchello-Nizia. *Histoire de la langue française.* Paris: Éditions Nathan, 1994.

Vissère, Laurent. "Lecture pour tous." *Historia,* July 2005.

Walch, Agnès. "La langue de Molière devient internationale." *Historia,* July 2005.

Walter, Henriette. *L'aventure des mots français venus d'ailleurs.* Paris: Éditions Robert Lafont, 1997.

Walter, Henriette. "Exit le latin." *Historia,* July 2005.

Walter, Henriette. *Le français dans tous les sens.* Paris: Éditions Robert Laffont, 1988.

Walter, Henriette. *Le français d'ici, de là, de là-bas.* Paris: Éditions Jean-Claude Lattès, 1998.

Walter, Henriette. *Honni soit qui mal y pense: L'incroyable histoire d'amour entre le français et l'anglais.* Paris: Éditions Robert Laffont, 2001.

LINGUISTICS AND OTHER LANGUAGES

Abley, Mark. *Spoken Here: Travels among Threatened Languages.* New York: Houghton Mifflin, 2003.

Bougy, Catherine. "La langue anglaise: Des milliers de mots français." Special issue, *Historia,* May–June 1999.

Bryson, Bill. *The Mother Tongue: English and How It Got That Way.* New York: Perennial, 1990.

Calvet, Louis-Jean. *La guerre des langues et les politiques linguistiques.* Paris: Hachette Littératures, 1999.

Calvet, Louis-Jean. *Le marché aux langues: Les effets linguistiques de la mondialisation.* Paris: Plon, 2002.

Jèrriais Phrasebook. St. Sauveur: Le Don Baleine, 2003.

Malherbe, Michel. *Les langages de l'humanité: Une encyclopédie des 3000 langues parlées dans le monde.* Paris: Éditions Seguers, 1983; Éditions Robert Laffont, 1995.

McCrum, Robert, Robert MacNeil and William Cran. *The Story of English.* London: BBC Books, 2002.

Walter, Henriette. *L'aventure des langues en Occident: Leur origine, leur histoire, leur géographie.* Paris: Éditions Robert Laffont, 1994.

Warren, Tony Scott. *Lé neu c'mîn.* Jersey: Le Don Baleine, n.d.

Weber, George. "The World's Ten Most Influential Languages." *Language Today* 2 (December 1997).

THE FRANCOPHONIE AND OTHER INSTITUTIONS

Barrat, Jacques, and Claudia Moisei. *Géopolitique de la francophonie: Un nouveau souffle?* Paris: La Documentation française, 2004.

Bruézière, Maurice. *L'Alliance française 1883–1983: Histoire d'une institution.* Paris: Librairie Hachette, 1983.

Chouraqui, André. *L'alliance israélite universelle et la renaissance juive contemporaine: Cent ans d'histoire.* Paris: Presses universitaires de France, 1965.

Dauge, Yves. *Rapport d'information sur les centres culturels à l'étranger.* Paris: Commission des affaires étrangères, 2001.

Deniau, Xavier. *La francophonie. Que sais-je?* Series. Paris: Presses universitaires de France, 1983.

Gerbet, Pierre. *Le rêve d'un ordre mondial, de la SDN à l'ONU.* Paris: Imprimerie nationale, 1996.

Gilder, Alfred, and Albert Salon. *Alerte francophone: Plaidoyer et moyens d'actions pour les générations futures.* Paris: Éditions Arnaud Fardel, 2004.

Grant, Peter S., and Chris Wood. *Blockbusters and Trade Wars: Popular Culture in a Globalized World.* Vancouver: Douglas & McIntyre, 2004.

Grimal, Henri. *Le Commonwealth. Que sais-je?* Series. Paris: Presses universitaires de France, 1995.

"Francophonie et mondialisation." *Hermès* 40. Paris: CNRS Editions, 2004

Ménard, Marc. *Éléments pour une économie des industries culturelles.* Montreal: SODEC, 2004.

Robitaille, Louis-Bernard. *Le salon des immortels: Une académie très française.* Paris: Éditions Denoël, 2002.

Sada, Hugo. *Rapport du secrétaire général de la Francophonie: De Beyrouth à Ouagadougou (2002–2004).* Paris: Organisation internationale de la Francophonie, 2004.

Tétu, Michel. *L'année francophone internationale, 2004.* Quebec: CIDEF-AFI, 2004.

Tétu, Michel. *L'année francophone internationale, 2005.* Quebec: CIDEF-AFI, 2005.

Tétu, Michel. *Qu'est-ce que la francophonie?* Paris: Hachette-EDICEF, 1997.

Traisnel, Christophe. *Le français en partage.* Boulogne: Timée-Éditions, 2004.

Valantin, Christian. *La francophonie dans le monde, 2002–2003.* Paris: Larousse, 2003.

Valantin, Christian. *La francophonie dans le monde, 2004–2005.* Paris: Larousse, 2005.

FRENCH IN FRANCE AND EUROPE

Bédaridas, François, François Crouzet and Douglas Johnson. *De Guillaume le conquérant au marché commun: Dix siècles d'histoire franco-britannique.* Paris: Albin Michel, 1979.

Conte, Arthur. *Les bâtisseurs de la France: De l'an 1000 à l'an 2000.* Paris: Plon, 2004.

Floch, Jacques. *Rapport d'information sur la présence et l'influence de la France dans les institutions européennes.* Paris: Délégation de l'Assemblée nationale pour l'Union Européenne, 2004.

Fumaroli, Marc. *Quand l'Europe parlait français.* Paris: Éditions du Fallois, 2001.

Fumaroli, Marc. *Trois institutions littéraires.* Paris: Gallimard, 1994.

Lecherbonnier, Bernard. *Pourquoi veulent-ils tuer le français?* Paris: Albin Michel, 2005.

Le Roy Ladurie, Emmanuel. "Quand Paris était capitale du monde." *Le Nouvel Observateur,* August 2001.

Levenstein, Harvey. *Seductive Journey: American Tourists in France from Jefferson to the Jazz Age.* Chicago: University of Chicago Press, 1998.

MacMillan, Margaret. *Paris 1919: Six Months That Changed the World.* New York: Random House, 2002.

Pavy, Didier. *Les Belges.* Paris: Éditions Grasset & Fasquelle, 1999.

Les politiques des langues en Europe. Paris: Délégation générale à la langue française et aux langues de France & Ministère des affaires étrangères, n.d.

Rapport au Parlement sur l'emploi de la langue française. Paris: Délégation générale à la langue française et aux langues de France, 2004.

Revaz, Gilles. *La Suisse et la Francophonie.* Quebec: CIDEF-AFI, 2003.

Saint Pulgent, Maryvonne de. *Le gouvernement de la culture.* Paris: Gallimard, 1999.

FRENCH IN AMERICA

Allaire, Gratien. *La francophonie canadienne: Portraits.* Quebec: CIDEF-AFI, 2001.

Arseaneault, Bona. *Histoire des Acadiens: Nouvelle édition neuve et augmentée.* Montreal: Éditions Fides, 2004.

Bernard, Shane K. *The Cajuns: Americanization of a People.* Jackson: University Press of Mississippi, 2003.

Blumberg, Rhoda. *What's the Deal? Jefferson, Napoleon and the Louisiana Purchase.* Washington, DC: National Geographic Society, 1998.

Bouchard, Chantal. *La langue et le nombril: Une histoire sociolinguistique du Québec.* Montreal: Éditions Fides, 2002.

Conlogue, Ray. *Impossible Nation: The Longing for Homeland in Canada and Quebec.* Toronto: Mercury Press, 2002.

Conrad, Glenn. R., ed. *The Cajuns: Essays on Their History and Culture.* Lafayette: Center for Louisiana Studies, 1983.

Cormier, Michel. *Louis J. Robichaud: Une révolution si peu tranquille.* Moncton, NB: Éditions de la Francophonie, 2004.

Daigle, Jean, ed. *L'Acadie des Maritimes: Études thématiques des débuts à nos jours.* Moncton, NB: Université de Moncton, 1993.

Duby, Georges, ed. *Histoire de la France: Des origines à nos jours.* Paris: Larousse Bordas, 1997.

Germain, Georges-Hébert. *Les coureurs des bois: la saga des Indiens blancs.* Montreal : Libre-Expression, 2003.

Gervais, Gaétan. *Des gens de résolution: Le passage du «Canada Français» à l'«Ontario français».* Sudbury, ON: Institut franco-ontarien / Prise de Parole, 2003.

Grescoe, Taras. *Sacré blues: Un portrait iconoclaste du Québec.* Montreal: VLB Éditeur, 2002.

Havard, Gilles, and Cécile Vidal. *Histoire de l'Amérique française.* Paris: Flammarion, 2003.

Hétu, Richard. *La route de l'ouest.* Montreal: VLB Éditeur, 2002.

Johnson, Paul. *A History of the American People.* New York: Harper Perennial, 1999.

Leckie, Robert. *A Few Acres of Snow: The Saga of the French and Indian Wars.* New York: John Wiley & Sons, 1999.

"L'esclavage: Un tabou français enfin levé." Special issue, *L'Histoire,* November–December, 2002.

"La liberté et la terreur: La révolution française." Special issue, *L'Histoire,* October–December, 2004.

Nye, Joseph S., Jr. *Soft Power: The Means to Success in World Politics.* Cambridge: Perseus Books, 2004.

Plourde, Michel, Hélène Duval and Pierre Georgeault. *Le français au Québec: 400 ans d'histoire et de vie.* Montreal: Fides, 2003.

Rioux, Marcel. *Les québécois.* Paris: Éditions du Seuil, 1974.

Serfaty, Simon. *La France vue par les États-Unis: Réflexions sur la francophobie à Washington.* Paris: Institut français de relations internationales, 2002.

De Tocqueville, Alexis. *Regards sur le Bas-Canada.* Montreal: Éditions Typo, 2003.

Vaugeois, Denis, and Jacques Lacoursière. *Canada-Québec: Synthèse historique.* Montreal: Éditions du renouveau pédagogique, 1978.

FRENCH IN AFRICA, ASIA AND THE MIDDLE EAST

Ainval, Christiane d'. *Les belles heures de l'Indochine française.* Paris: Perrin, 2001.

Barthélémy, Pascale. *Un africain sur sept va à l'école. L'Histoire,* October 2005.

Brocheux, Pierre, and Daniel Hémery. *Indochine: La colonisation ambiguë 1858–1954.* Paris: Éditions La Découverte, 1994.

Calvet, Louis-Jean. *Linguistique et colonialisme.* Paris: Petite Bibliothèque Payot, 2002.

Edgerton, Robert B. *The Troubled Heart of Africa: A History of the Congo.* New York: St. Martin's Press, 2002.

Ferro, Marc. *Le livre noir du colonialisme, XVIe–XXIe siècle: De l'extermination à la repentance.* Paris: Éditions Robert Laffont, 2003.

Glaser, Antoine, and Stephen Smith. *Comment la France a perdu l'Afrique?* Paris: Calmann-Lévy, 2005.

Hochschild, Adam. *King Leopold's Ghost: The Story of Greed, Terror and Heroism in Colonial Africa.* New York: Houghton Mifflin, 1999.

Messmer, Pierre. *Les blancs s'en vont: Récits de décolonisation.* Paris: Albin Michel, 1998.

Sorel, Jacqueline. *Léopold Sédar Senghor: L'émotion et la raison.* Saint-Maur-des Fossés: Éditions Sépia, 1995.

Stamm, Anne. *L'Afrique de la colonisation à l'indépendance.* Paris: Presses universitaires françaises, 1998.

Stora, Benjamin. *Histoire de l'Algérie coloniale (1830–1954).* Paris: Éditions La Découverte, 2001.

Wesseling, Henri. *Le partage de l'Afrique 1880–1914.* Paris: Éditions Denoël, 1996.

DICTIONARIES AND GENERAL REFERENCE

The Canadian Encyclopedia. Toronto: McClelland & Stewart, 2000.

Dictionnaire historique de la langue française. Paris: Dictionnaires Le Robert, 1992.

Le Petit Robert des noms propres. Paris: Dictionnaires Le Robert, 2004.

Quid 2005. Paris: Éditions Robert Laffont, 2005.

Shorter Oxford English Dictionary on Historical Principles, 5th ed. New York: Oxford University Press, 2002.

Index

Partners in life and in writing, Canadian journalist-authors JEAN-BENOÎT NADEAU and JULIE BARLOW are award-winning contributors to Quebec's national news magazine *L'actualité*. Their writing has appeared in many publications, including the *Christian Science Monitor*, the *International Herald Tribune*, and the *Courrier international*. In 2003, Nadeau and Barlow published their critical and popular success, *Sixty Million Frenchmen Can't Be Wrong*. They live in Montreal.